CASE STUDIES IN OBJECT-ORIENTED ANALYSIS AND DESIGN

CASE STUDIES IN OBJECT-ORIENTED ANALYSIS AND DESIGN

Edward Yourdon
and
Carl Argila

Who dares to teach must never cease to learn.
John Cotton Dana

For book and bookstore information

http://www.prenhall.com

YOURDON PRESS
Prentice Hall Building
Upper Saddle River, NJ 07458

Library of Congress Cataloging-in-Publication Data

Yourdon, Edward
      Case studies in object-oriented analysis and design / Ed Yourdon.
Carl Argila.
    p. cm. -- (Yourdon Press computing series)
    Includes bibliographical references and index.
    ISBN 0-13-305137-4 (alk. paper)
    1. Object-oriented programming (Computer science)   2. System
analysis.   3. System design.   I. Argila, Carl.   II. Title.
III. Series.
QA76.64.Y695   1996
005.1′2--dc20
            96-11309
            CIP

Acquisitions editor: Paul W. Becker
Editorial assistant: Maureen Diana
Editorial/production supervision/design: Patti Guerrieri
Art director: Gail Cocker-Bogusz
Manufacturing buyer: Alexis R. Heydt
Cover design director: Jerry Votta
Cover designer: Talar Agayasan

©1996 by Prentice Hall PTR
Prentice-Hall, Inc.
A Simon & Schuster Company
Upper Saddle River, NJ 07458

The publisher offers discounts on this book when ordered in bulk quantities.
For more information, contact: Corporate Sales Department, Prentice Hall PTR,
One Lake Street, Upper Saddle River, NJ 07458, Phone: 800-382-3419, Fax: 201-236-7141,
e-mail: corpsales@prenhall.com

System Architect is a trademark of Popkin Software & Systems. Visual Basic, Microsoft Word,
Windows, and MS-DOS are registered trademarks of Microsoft Corporation. PowerBuilder is a
trademark of the Powersoft Corporation. Delphi is a trademark of Borland International. All
other products are trademarks of their respective companies.

From *Famous Quotes*. Copyright © 1994, Infobases, Inc. Reprinted by permission of
Infobases, Inc., Provo, Utah.

Printed in the United States of America
10 9 8 7 6 5 4 3 2 1

ISBN   0-13-305137-4

Prentice-Hall International (UK) Limited, *London*
Prentice-Hall of Australia Pty. Limited, *Sydney*
Prentice-Hall Canada Inc., *Toronto*
Prentice-Hall Hispanoamericana, *S.A., Mexico*
Prentice-Hall of India Private Limited, *New Delhi*
Prentice-Hall of Japan, Inc., *Tokyo*
Simon & Schuster Asia Pte. Ltd., *Singapore*
Editora Prentice-Hall do Brasil, Ltda., *Rio de Janeiro*

To Toni, without whose love and support none of these book projects would be possible.

Edward Yourdon

To Cecilio,

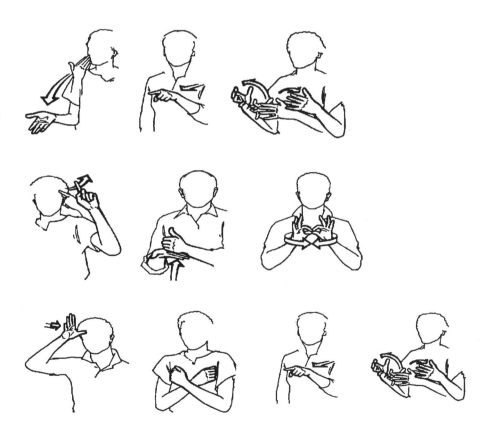

Carl Argila

Contents

Preface

As a graduate student in mathematics, one of the authors was forced to endure the presentation of innumerable mathematical theorems. Each theorem was rigorously proved by a learned professor. Each proof was presented as a finished product—elegant and beautiful. As a student, however, the author found the proofs more obscure and confusing than elegant and beautiful!

On one occasion, while presenting a particularly long proof, the professor became confused and uncertain about the next step. With a somewhat pensive expression, he walked to a side blackboard, picked up a piece of chalk and began drawing a figure. He drew circles, arcs, lines and eventually, a look of recognition flashed across his face. He quickly erased what he had drawn, returned to the front of the classroom, and proceeded with the proof! But, as you might imagine, the students were more interested in what the professor had erased than what he was attempting to prove!

The analysis and design of large, complex software systems are not unlike mathematical proofs; they are usually presented as finished products. They may be documented with reams of paper or presented as finished models. Rarely, however, do software analysts or designers document the *anatomy* of their analysis or design. In the past, a savvy software manager could sneak into the offices of his workers, rummage through their trash cans, and pull out traces of their thinking. With the advent of CASE tools however, that's harder to do! And, few books on software analysis and design go deeply into heuristics.

This situation is particularly egregious in the area of *object-oriented* analysis and design. Although there are numerous books on the subject (and more coming out all the time!), few go beyond presenting the terminology, notation and structure of their own unique models. And, when it comes to the genesis of the process—establishing an initial set of objects—guidance is superficial at best. Yet the wrong choice of objects can have a profound impact on the success of the whole object-oriented development process. As one C++ instructor recently lamented about a class, "These guys are just hacking at the object level! They'll never get any of the object-oriented benefits out of this stuff."

The authors fervently believe that object-oriented analysis and design are *real*, with *real* benefits to be gained. But we also believe, quoting H. L. Mencken, that "for every complex and difficult problem there is a simple solution. And it is always wrong." Analyzing and designing large, complex software systems is difficult. Period. Object-oriented approaches don't make analysis and design easier than earlier methods. They help us build a better product; they help us improve productivity—but they're no panacea.

What's missing from the object-oriented analysis and design practitioner's literature, we feel, is more insight into *how* object-oriented analysis and design are done—for real systems. That's what we've tried to present in this book. Although we present a solution to the case study problems, the nature of the solution is far less important than how we arrived at it. Our principal contribution, we feel, is in presenting insight—not technique. Unfortunately, readers seeking the beauty and elegance of a mathematical proof will have to look elsewhere.

After an introduction to the case study problems, we present a synthesis of OOA and OOD methods to develop an analysis model and design model. Separate chapters are devoted to each of the building blocks of the OOA model (Subject Layer, Object-Class Layer, Structure Layer, Attribute Layer and Service Layer), as well as the various components of the OOD model (Problem Domain Component, Human Interaction Component, Task Management Component and Data Management Component). Additional chapters provide some comments on analysis, design and project management issues.

We have produced object-oriented analysis and design models using the notation of the Coad and Yourdon technique. Our *methodology* however, differs significantly from the Coad and Yourdon approach. Indeed, we have taken advantage of components of other object-oriented methodologies—e.g., Ivar Jacobson's ObectOry approach for the discussion of messages between objects—where they provided useful illuminations. We believe that the principles demonstrated in this book are applicable to object-oriented analysis and design in general.

We also took advantage of older, more classical structured analysis methodologies; the entity-relationship diagram and event-response model of both case studies proved particularly useful for discovering relevant objects, as well as for providing a deeper understanding of the interactions between objects. Indeed, we strayed even further afield than structured analysis. For instance, a purely linguistic analysis of the narrative user specifications of the two case studies provided a very methodical approach for identifying candidate objects for further investigation.

While object-oriented enthusiasts may have a favorite methodology—e.g., Booch, Rumbaugh, Jacobson, Shlaer-Mellor or Coad and Yourdon—we have found that there is general acceptance of the notion that one might be able to borrow ideas and concepts from *all* of them to attack a problem effectively. On the other hand, the notion of using the older, structured methodologies may well offend the purists in the object-oriented camp, who might argue that the same results could have been achieved without any reference whatsoever to textbooks written before the dawn of the object-oriented era. For most veteran software engineers, though, a more pragmatic approach is typically required—especially when faced with a difficult problem that must be solved within the constraints of a tight schedule and budget. From this perspective, it seems foolish to eliminate useful concepts, tools and techniques that have served us well in the past.

Though time, money and space prevented us from tackling a problem the size of "Star Wars," we have, nevertheless, selected two very realistic case studies and applied the principles of object-oriented analysis and design to them. One case study has a predominant reactive view and should be of interest to readers in the real-time, embedded systems area. The other case study has a predominant data view and should be of interest to readers in the MIS community. We decided to present *both* case studies in this book; it is interesting and instructive to see how object-oriented techniques can be applied in such different environments. The reader should be able to make a personal judgment about the relevance and applicability of object-oriented methods to different environments.

Because they are larger than the typical "tic-tac-toe" game exercises one often finds in a software engineering textbook, any serious attempt to analyze and design the case study problems in this book will present some non-trivial difficulties. The authors have used both case studies in numerous seminars and workshops during the past few years; we have been constantly amazed by the degree of intense debate and discussion they create with our students. We believe that the case study designs have been developed to the point where these two systems can be delivered to programmers for implementation. Although we have not discussed implementation issues, we have created Visual Basic™ prototypes for both case studies. However, because of the size of the two case studies, we have not provided fully coded solutions.

Since this is *not* a book that explains object-oriented principles and theory in great detail, we have been forced to make some assumptions about you, the reader. We assume that you are a software engineer with some level of exposure to both structured analysis methodologies and object-oriented analysis/design methodologies. However, we assume that your exposure to OOA and OOD has been limited, at most, to reading one of the popular books in the field, or perhaps to some limited training in a seminar or workshop. A background like this would be sufficient for you to work on a "tiny" problem, but probably not adequate to tackle your first mission-critical object-oriented application at your job. This book is intended to provide the bridge between that first introduction to OOA and OOD and a complex real-world application of the theory.

Finally, the authors encourage readers to tell us how this material is being used, what problems have been encountered and what successes have been achieved! Our e-mail addresses are below. From time to time, we may post revisions to the materials on our WEB sites, also given below.

Ed Yourdon
New York City
e-mail: yourdon@acm.org
WWW: http://www.acm.org/~yourdon

Carl Argila
Las Vegas
e-mail: carl@acm.org
WWW: http://www.acm.org/~aLigra

December, 1995

Notation and Conventions

Classes are all upper case with space delimiters.
Examples:

```
ARTICLE
COMPLIMENTARY SUBSCRIPTION
AUTHOR-ARTICLE TRACK
```

Instances of classes (objects) have initial capitalization with space delimiters.
Examples:

```
Article
Complimentary Subscription
Author-Article Track
```

Object attributes are all lower case with underscore delimiters.
Examples:

```
article_title
complimentary_subscription_id
author-article_date
```

Class attributes are all upper case with underscore delimiters.
Examples:

```
TOTAL_NUMBER_SUBSCRIPTIONS
PAYMENTS_TO_DATE
```

Object services have initial capitalization with underscore delimiters. Services are always two or more words (Verb_Noun).
Examples:

```
Enter_Paid_Subscription
Delete_Complimentary_Subscription
Enter_Article
```

Class services are all upper case with underscore delimiters. Class services are always two or more words (VERB_NOUN).
Examples:

```
CREATE_NEW_SUBSCRIPTION
ENTER_PAYMENT
RECEIVE_ARTICLE
```

Attribute and **service names** may be "fully qualified" by pre-fixing their names with the names of their corresponding class or object.
Examples:

```
Subscription.Enter_Paid_Subscription
SUBSCRIPTION.RECOGNIZE_SUBSCRIPTION_REQUEST
Address.address_details
Subscription Termination.termination_date
```

See Notation and Conventions chart on the inside front cover of this text.

Acknowledgments

The authors must first and foremost extend their deepest appreciation and thanks to Professor Joseph Morrell of the Metropolitan State College of Denver. Dr. Morrell has been truly unselfish (and at times un-sleeping!) in assisting the authors with the completion of this manuscript. As the authors schlepped around the world presenting their seminars and workshops, it was Dr. Morrell's patience and endurance which was most responsible for bringing this manuscript to print. Thanks also to two of Dr. Morrell's colleagues, systems engineers Tamara Gillest and Beth Ross, for their assistance with the Visual Basic case study implementations and the *System Architect*™ case study models.

The initial version of the Visual Basic case studies was created by Tom McFarren—a great job which we very much appreciate.

Special thanks to Paul Becker, our editor at Prentice Hall, whose regular telephone calls asking, "…so how's the book doing…" helped us not to forget that we were writing one!

Thanks also to Ron Sherma and Steve Schroer of Popkin Software and Systems, Inc. for providing the authors with the *System Architect* product for use with this project.

Sir Isaac Newton has been quoted as saying, "If I have been able to see farther than others, it was because I stood on the shoulders of giants." We have had the most unique opportunity to stand on the shoulders of numerous giants—our fantastic workshop students. Over the past two years, they have endured various versions and revisions of this material, they have provided insight, they have been patient, understanding and, most importantly, they have laughed at our jokes (well, most of the time). A partial list of our workshop groups is included in Appendix T. Thank you dear friends!

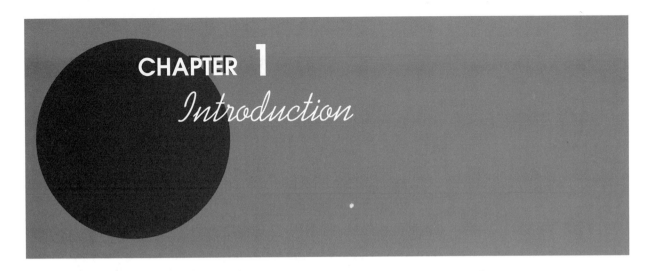

CHAPTER 1
Introduction

There is nothing more difficult to take in hand, more perilous to conduct or more uncertain in its success, than to take the lead in the introduction of a new order of things.

— Niccolo Machiavelli
The Prince, Ch. 6

1.1 Background: The Philosophy of Software Development

"Philosophy" may seem like an unusual word with which to start off a book of case studies on software development. However, the authors, whose combined experience totals well over 1500 fortnights, have witnessed during their careers dramatic changes in the commonly accepted "philosophy" of building software systems. When computing began in the 1950's, programs were created using an ad hoc software development approach; each system was a unique, custom-built intellectual product. There was no concept of reusability, interchangeability of parts, or, for that matter, formal design. Although pioneering, these software systems were difficult to maintain or enhance. And each change to a system produced a system which was even more difficult to maintain or enhance!

In the 1960's, efforts to produce more maintainable software, in a more predictable fashion, resulted in the first major change in software development "philosophy." Ad hoc software development gave way to a more methodical approach. This approach, commonly referred to as the waterfall approach, required that a number of formal phases be completed in the process of creating a software system. Phases such as requirements analysis, high-level design, detailed design, etc. had to be completed before a subsequent phase could begin. The completion of each phase was marked by the delivery of one or more milestone documents. Hence, the waterfall approach to software development was frequently characterized by the production of voluminous documentation. However, despite the more formal approach, large complex software systems were still being delivered over budget, over schedule and not meeting user requirements.

The 1970's saw another major change in software development "philosophy." Tom DeMarco, in his seminal book, *Structured Analysis and System Specification*[1], introduced the concept of *model-based software engineering*. Complex software systems, DeMarco argued, should be built like any large, complex engineering system—by first building working paper models of the system before committing the resources to implement the system. His philosophy was such that users should be able to "visualize living with the system of the future" before actually going out and building the damned thing! In the 1970's, this was a radical departure from simply "hacking out the code" and declaring success if the code gave some illusion of operating correctly. And, if the code didn't work…well, we didn't have to worry about that until after the system was deployed—months, if not years, in the future!

As illustrated in Figure 1.1, this model-based approach is the same as that taken by architects to specify and design large complex systems, i.e., buildings. Architects build scale models of houses so that users can visualize living with the system of the future. These models serve as vehicles for communication and negotiation between users, developers, sponsors, builders, etc.

Virtually all modern software engineering approaches have adopted this model-based "philosophy." What varies greatly from one software engineering method to another is the kinds of models that should be built, how they should be

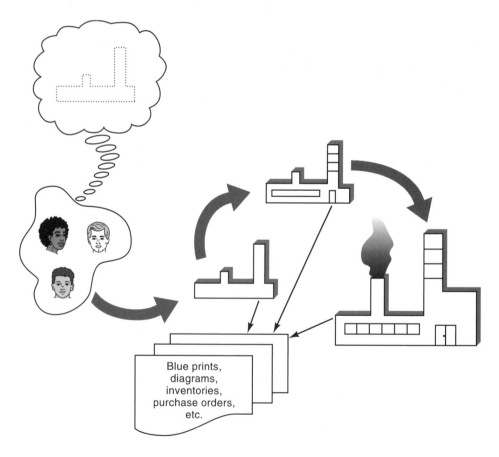

Figure 1.1
Model-based
software development.

built and who should build them. A generic model-based software engineering life cycle is shown in Figure 1.2. We show various models constructed by different communities of users for different purposes. A requirements definition model may be built to capture and negotiate overall system requirements; this model may be built by representatives from a marketing organization, as well as systems and software analysts.

An important heuristic concept reflected in most model-based software engineering methods is the principle of *Separation of Concerns*. This is typically expressed by constructing an analysis model separate from a design model. Analysis models (which are a focus of concern in this book) capture software system requirements which are essential or "logical," as opposed to implementation-based or "physical" requirements. That is, analysis models describe what a system will do, independent of any particular implementation approach or technology. On the other hand, design models (also a focus of this book) specify how a particular system will be built within the context of a given implementation environment (platform, network, operating system, database, user interface, etc.) Analysis models are typically built by those with extensive application domain knowledge; they may serve as vehicles of communication between customers, users and developers. Design models, by contrast, are built by those with extensive implementation environment knowledge; they serve as vehicles of communication between developers, implementers, testers, etc. This principle of *Separation of Concerns* is a fundamental driving force behind the approach taken in this book.

Our approach, therefore, is like other engineering disciplines—it is based heavily on understanding the problem and establishing requirements by building

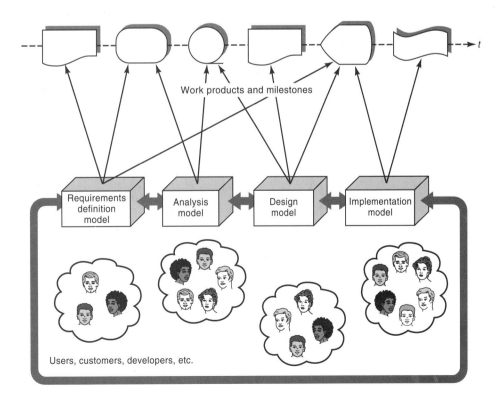

Figure 1.2
A typical software development life cycle.

suitable models of proposed systems. Like other engineering disciplines, we will build one set of models for the purpose of establishing the essential behavior of a proposed system and another set of models as blueprints, which specify how to build the proposed system within a given implementation environment.

1.2 Today's Challenge

It has become humdrum to talk about the software crisis. Any reader who has stumbled upon this book knows full well that there has been a software revolution in our society. Readers know the critical role which software systems play in numerous applications. Readers know that the software component of delivered systems may not be the most expensive component, but is usually in series with the hardware component, i.e., if the software doesn't work, the hardware is useless.

What may be less apparent, is the challenge software developers face in delivering ever larger, ever more complex software systems with a reasonable expectation of being on budget, on schedule and meeting user requirements and expectations. To illustrate how difficult this is, Philippe Kahn, founder of Borland International, presented what he called "Philippe's Law" (see Figure 1.3) in his keynote address at COMDEX (Las Vegas, 1992). As can be seen from the figure, the larger the size of a software development team, the less efficient is each member of the team. This effect is contrary to one of the basic principles of industrialization. That is, when production processes scale up, <u>each</u> member of the production team is supposed to become *more* efficient—not *less* efficient!

At the very same COMDEX conference, Toshiba Corporation announced its newest three-inch disk drive product, which had a capacity of 1.2 gigabytes and could be installed in a laptop or desktop PC. Does any reader doubt that they could easily fill up a 1.2 gigabyte disk drive with applications?!! Yet, if one believes Philippe's Law, creating 1.2 gigabytes of application code, with traditional techniques, would require enormous human resources.

One conclusion from these two observations is that conventional software development techniques, which depend on humans typing away at code, are

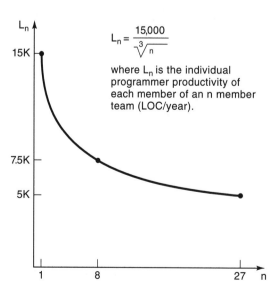

Figure 1.3
Philippe's Law.

inherently flawed. There simply aren't enough people, nor money, to build the large, complex applications of the future with the techniques of today.

Much of this software might eventually be developed in third world countries, where labor costs are low. However, if the U.S. is to remain pre-eminent in this industry, software development techniques must change—and they must change dramatically. The authors believe that object-oriented techniques are part of the solution.

1.3 The Concept of Object-Orientation

It surely must be difficult for today's young software professionals to appreciate the dramatic improvements in computer hardware technology since the 1950's. To make computers do anything seemingly useful in the 1950's and 1960's required extracting every last "bit" of performance out of the available hardware. Words of computer memory and clock cycles were counted, tallied and parsimoniously doled out only when cleverness failed to offer an alternative. Cleverness, however, led to computer programs which were large, monolithic and intractable.

Sometime during the 1960's, about the time when new transistorized computers were replacing the water-cooled, vacuum tube behemoths, a new school of thought began to emerge. These radicals (including the authors) preached that the large, monolithic computer program, though clearly the most efficient solution to a problem, was not the best solution. The better computer program, we sermonized, was the computer program which was *understandable*! Why understandable? So that such a computer program could actually be maintained and enhanced! In some organizations, these were radical thoughts!!! The kinds of arguments we heard were statements like, "Once you've found the best algorithm for computing Bessel's function, why would you want to change it?!!" As computer technology spread beyond just the scientific and engineering areas, these arguments became weaker. For example, the statement that, "Once you've found the best payroll administration program, why would you want to change it?" isn't very convincing today.

We radicals preached that modularized computer programs were, though less efficient, more understandable, extensible and maintainable than large, monolithic computer programs. As the performance of computer hardware advanced, this approach became more widely accepted within the software engineering community.

Once everyone agreed that modularized computer programs were better than monolithic computer programs, software engineers began arguing about how the modules should be created. One school of thought announced that clearly the best way to "chunk" modules was by function. "Every module does one and only one thing. Period." These "functional decompositionists" were challenged head-on by the "dukes of data." This school of thought preached that, "Every module should encapsulate one data structure. Period." People involved in real-time systems development thought that both of the former camps were made up of a bunch of crackpots. Clearly, said the third group, modules should be chunked by events! "Every module should recognize and respond to one and only one event. Period." was this camp's cry.

While these three camps waged war, a fourth school of thought emerged. Clearly, they announced, *God's way* to modularize computer programs is to make,

"Every module correspond to one and only one thing in the real world. Period." Hummm…that's radically different! Rather than structuring computer programs in accordance with some analysis approach, the object-oriented campers were saying that we should structure computer programs in accordance with the problem to be solved. This is fundamentally appealing! Experience suggests that the components of a problem domain are perhaps the most stable components of any software system. (We're told, for example, that the principles of dual-entry bookkeeping haven't changed in the last 300 years, though the implementation technology has moved from quill pens to PCs.) We have seen in our own experience that when software systems are enhanced, they usually are enhanced by problem-domain component. And when systems break, they tend to break by problem-domain component.

An example of this comes to mind. At the nadir of his career, one of the authors was associated with avionics software development for an aircraft project. At one point, the "crisis of the day" was the incorrect wiring of the solenoids which controlled the aircraft flight surfaces. The solenoids were wired in reverse. Hence, when the flight surfaces were commanded to move up, they actually moved down; when commanded to move down, they moved up. Management decided that at this point in the project, too late to re-wire the aircraft, the problem should be fixed in the flight control software—which turned out to be a monumental problem. Had the software been developed using object-oriented techniques, this indeed would have been a trivial fix. The secret of solenoid polarity would have been encapsulated into a single program chunk—an object.

Although the term "object-oriented" is used in a variety of different ways (particularly in marketing literature!), the term should always suggest an association between (abstractions of) things in the real world and computer program chunks, or objects. So what is an object? Informally, an *object* is an independent, asynchronous, concurrent entity which "knows things" (i.e., stores data), "does work" (i.e., encapsulates services) and "collaborates with other objects" (by exchanging messages) to perform the overall functions of the system (being modeled).

It is not our intention to sell object-oriented approaches. However, the reader may well be wondering at this point: "Why bother?" "Why, exactly, should I care about objects?" The answer is simple—reuse. Although we have been reusing *code* since the dawn of computers, object-oriented techniques allow us to reuse far more than code. We can reuse requirements, analysis, design, test plans, user interfaces and architectures. In fact, virtually every component of the software engineering life cycle can be encapsulated as a reusable object.

In the view of the authors, there are some real advantages to be gained by object-orientation. We hope that will become apparent as we demonstrate the application of this approach.

1.4 Object-Oriented Analysis (OOA)

This book illustrates the application of the principles of Object-Oriented Analysis (OOA) and design. We view the process of analysis, within the context of software engineering, to be one of establishing fundamental (i.e., essential) system behavior—behavior which must be maintained independently of how the system will ultimately be built. As discussed above, our approach will be to construct formal models of a proposed software system (similar to an architect's scale model of a building) which capture essential system requirements. Insofar as the mechanics of model building are concerned, we have chosen Coad and Yourdon notation, which has been documented in detail in [2]. Our techniques, however, are general and applicable to other forms of OOA as well.

An OOA model depicts the objects representing a particular application domain together with various structural and communicational relationships. This will be summarized below and elaborated upon in subsequent chapters. The OOA model serves two purposes. First, it serves to formalize the "view" of the real world within which a software system will be built. It establishes the objects which will serve as the principal organizational structures of that software system and the various rules or constraints which the real world imposes upon any software system built within that application domain.

Secondly, the OOA model establishes how a given set of objects collaborates to perform the work of the software system being specified. This collaboration is represented in the model as a collection of message connections which show how each object communicates with other objects.

In our approach, the OOA model is constructed as five layers or views (see Figure 1.4).

These layers allow us to view the OOA model from different perspectives. This structure also allows us to deal effectively with quite large OOA models.

The five layers of the OOA model are:

- Object-Class Layer
- Attribute Layer
- Service Layer
- Structure Layer
- Subject Layer

These layers are discussed briefly below.

The first of these layers, the *Object-Class Layer*, presents the basic building blocks of the proposed system. The objects are abstractions of real world application domain concepts. This layer represents the foundation of the entire OOA model.

Truly the core of any OOA is the process of what we call *information modeling*. In OOA, the difficult part of the problem is establishing what are the "things in the real world," alluded to so casually above. These will establish the basic building blocks from which the system will be constructed.

Information modeling is the procedure by which the fundamental structure of an application domain is abstracted from the real world and captured. This is one of the most elemental and crucial activities of the OOA process. Traditionally, information modeling has been implicit within the software engineering process—some understanding of an application domain has always been required to build any software system. With object-oriented methods, however, more emphasis has been placed on information modeling as a formal procedure within the software engineering process.

This concept is illustrated in Figure 1.5. Alice is a real person in the real world. As seen through the object-oriented looking glass, Alice may be viewed in a very specific, simplistic manner. Within the context of the application domain, which in

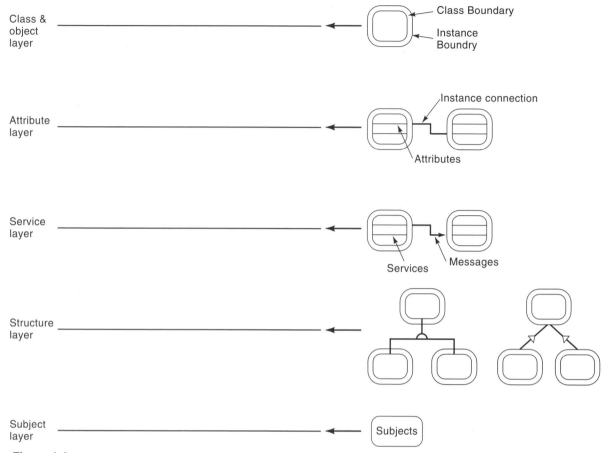

Figure 1.4
Structure of the OOA model.

the figure is *physical anatomy,* she has been abstracted into a fundamental set of concepts. In this application domain, Alice is seen as a collection of body parts. In another application domain, Alice might be viewed as an economic opportunity; her component parts might be a credit history, consumption profile, residence, etc. In yet another application domain, Alice might be seen as, perhaps, the operator of a motor vehicle, with a history of accidents, violations and an insurance rating.

For the remainder of this book, we shall refer to the "things in the real world" (the chunks) as objects, and we shall denote them graphically as shown in Figure 1.6. Since objects are chunks of computer programs, and since computer programs store data and do work, it may be convenient at this point to think of objects simply as agents which store information and/or do some job. Furthermore, objects should be thought of as (an unspecified number of) multiple (or sets of) agents, all of which are similar, but have some distinguishing characteristic. When necessary, we will refer to any one such agent as an *instance* of the associated object; similarly, if it is necessary to refer to the set of multiple similar objects, we will use the term *class*. Unfortunately, confusion in terminology has become a part of the object-oriented discipline.

Figure 1.5
The object-oriented looking glass.

In Figure 1.6, the outer boundary of the icon is referred to as the *instance boundary*; it visually indicates that the object is non-empty. The inner boundary of the icon is called the *class boundary*. This notation is useful in that it allows us to visually distinguish between an entire class (as a whole) or simply members of that class, i.e., objects.

Sometimes it is useful to define objects which will not be implemented as computer program chunks. We refer to these as *template classes* or *abstract classes* (see Figure 1.7). Template classes may provide a convenient way to consolidate higher level aggregations, though such aggregations will never be explicitly implemented.

We refer to those data stored (or encapsulated) by an object as the object's *attributes*; the work it does is referred to as its *services*. In our notation, object attributes and services may be represented graphically as shown in Figure 1.8.

It is frequently the case that pairs of instances of classes may be constrained, that is, forced to adhere to some application domain constraint or business rule. For example, it may be a business rule that when a subscription is deleted, the associated subscriber must also be deleted. These constraints are referred to as *instance connections*. Object attributes, together with instance connections, constitute the *Attribute Layer* of the OOA model. A portion of an Attribute Layer might look like the following (Figure 1.9).

At a glance, we can see that in the application domain of the system being modeled, a SUBSCRIPTION has various attributes or characteristics, such as its

Figure 1.6
Object icon.

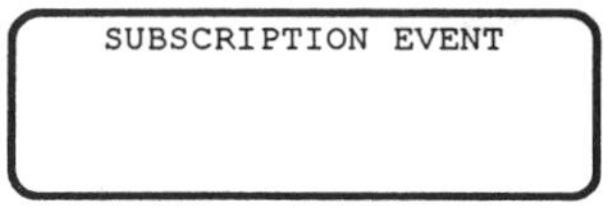

Figure 1.7
Abstract or template
class icon.

status, and various other unspecified details. Also clear at a glance is an application domain constraint or business rule. In this particular application domain, a SUBSCRIPTION must be associated with <u>precisely one</u> SUBSCRIBER no matter how we build the system and no matter the implementation technology or who builds it. A subscription is associated with precisely one subscriber. Period.

Figure 1.8
Object with attributes
and services.

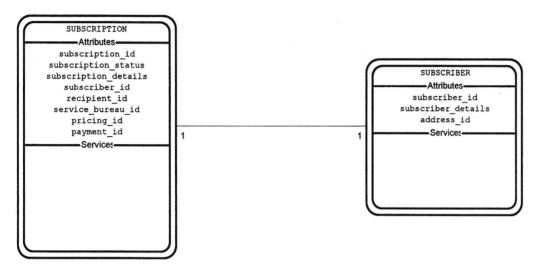

Figure 1.9
Portion of an Attribute Layer.

Object services, together with any message communication between instances of those objects, constitute the *Service Layer* of the OOA model. For example, in Figure 1.10, we observe that both SUBSCRIPTION and SUBSCRIBER perform work or functions. They also communicate between themselves, that is, they collaborate, as shown by the directed arrow.

The *message connection* shown in Figure 1.10 indicates that one of the services of SUBSCRIPTION is communicating with one of the services of SUBSCRIBER.

Another layer of the OOA model is the *Structure Layer*. This layer captures certain application domain structural relationships. One type of Structure Layer is shown in Figure 1.11 (another kind of structure will be considered in Chapter 6).

Although this is a different system, within a different application domain, it is clear at a glance that some kind of relationship exists between an ELEVATOR

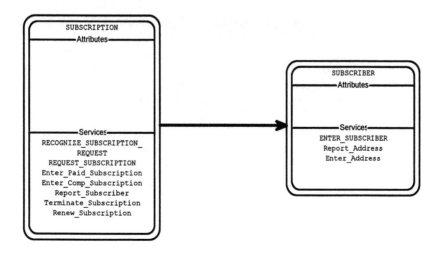

Figure 1.10
Portion of a
Service Layer.

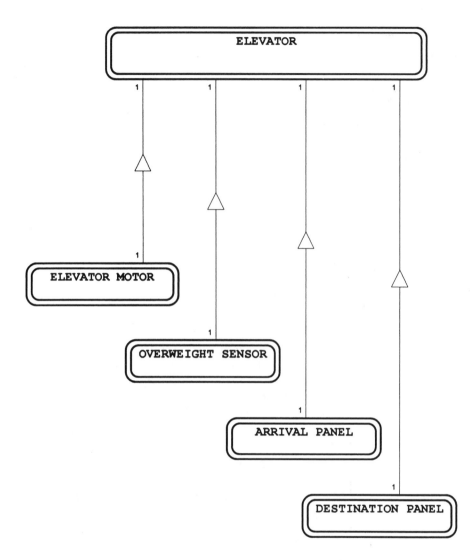

Figure 1.11
Portion of a
Structure Layer
(Whole-Part structure).

MOTOR, OVERWEIGHT SENSOR, ARRIVAL PANEL and DESTINATION PANEL.
The notation in Figure 1.11 portrays what is known as a *Whole-Part* structure. It
says that an ELEVATOR, as a "whole," must consist of an ELEVATOR MOTOR,
OVERWEIGHT SENSOR, ARRIVAL PANEL and DESTINATION PANEL. Again, it
doesn't matter how we build the system, how we apply the implementation technology or who builds it. More so, this simple picture tells us that a single elevator
<u>must</u> contain precisely one motor—no back-up motors in this system—and that a
single motor <u>must</u> be part of an elevator. Perhaps this application domain is a
"control system." In such an application domain, only motors in service would be
of interest to us. If the application domain were changed, perhaps to an elevator
maintenance system, then we might have a situation where one elevator could be
associated with multiple motors and vice versa. Perhaps we could consider the
history of which motors have (at some point in time) been installed in which elevator. In such an application domain, we might have motors which are not a part
of any elevator; such motors might be part of a stock of spare motors.

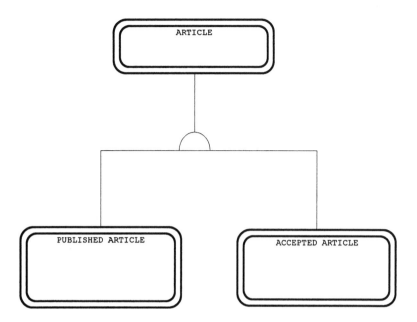

Figure 1.12
Portion of a
Structure Layer
(Gen-Spec structure).

A second type of structure is the *Generalization-Specialization (Gen-Spec)* structure (see Figure 1.12). This type of structure is quite different from the Whole-Part structure shown above. In this case, we have identified PUBLISHED ARTICLE and ACCEPTED ARTICLE as *specializations* of ARTICLE (the *generalization*). The Gen-Spec structure exhibits the property of *inheritance*, that is, attributes or services of the generalization class are shared (i.e., inherited) by the specialization classes.

Since OOA models are large, flat structures, the number of objects may become unwieldy. Objects may be consolidated into subjects; this is accomplished by enclosing related objects within a subject border. Subjects can be thought of as sub-models or even sub-systems. The subjects are contained in the *Subject Layer*. Figure 1.13 shows a single subject within a Subject Layer. The subject, "editorial management," includes only those objects which perform system functions associated with "editorial management."

At this point, the reader may wish to reference Appendices I and J for examples of completed OOA models. For convenience, we have summarized OOA model notation in Figure 1.14.

1.5
Object-Oriented
Design (OOD)

We stated in the previous section that, within the context of software engineering, we view the process of analysis to be one of establishing fundamental (i.e., essential) system behavior. By contrast, we view design as the process of specifying the "blueprints" for construction, that is, the instructions, directions, guidelines, recommendations, stipulations, qualifications, rules, etc. by which a given software system should be implemented within a particular environment.

The Object-Oriented Design (OOD) model is constructed as an extension of the OOA model (see Figure 1.15). Building a design model as an extension of the

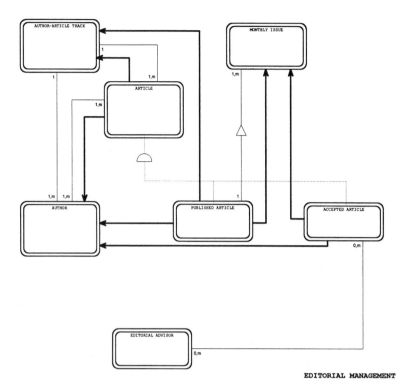

Figure 1.13
Portion of a
Subject Layer.

analysis model facilitates the (sometimes painful) transition from analysis to design. The OOD model contains the same five "layers" and uses the same notation as the OOA model but is extended into four "components." These components are:

- Problem Domain Component
- Human Interaction Component
- Task Management Component
- Data Management Component

These components are discussed briefly below. The first of these components, the *Problem Domain Component*, presents those objects which perform essential application domain functions. The OOA model may become the initial version of the Problem Domain Component; this will be discussed further in Chapter 15. This initial Problem Domain Component is then refined to account for implementation constraints, idiosyncrasies, performance deficiencies, etc.

The *Human Interaction Component* models the interface technology which will be used for a particular implementation of the system. This is another example of how the principle of Separation of Concerns has been incorporated into our approach. The details of interface technology are isolated from the "work" done by the system.

The *Task Management Component* of the OOD model specifies the operating system components which will be established to implement the system.

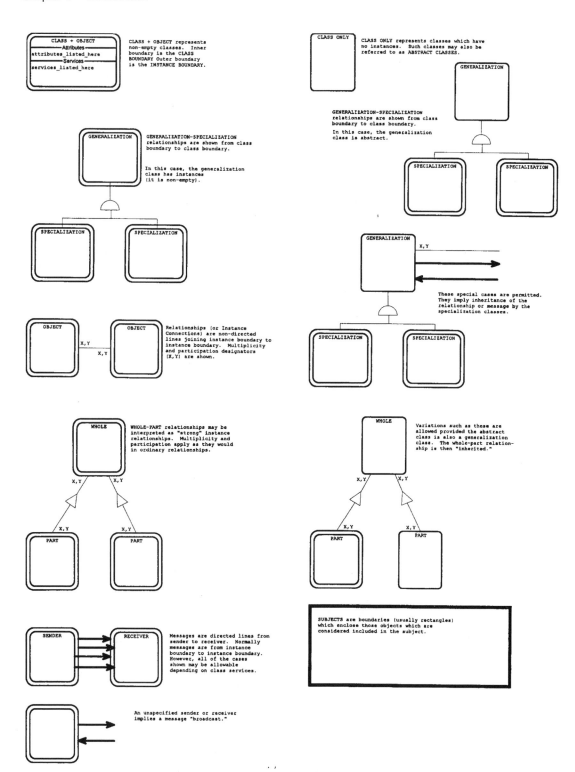

Figure 1.14
OOA model notation.

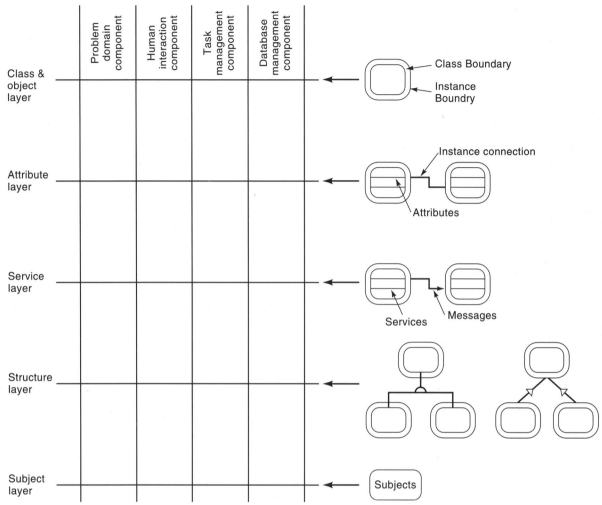

Figure 1.15
Structure of the OOD model.

Finally, the *Data Management Component* defines those objects required to interface to the database technology being used. As with the Human Interaction Component, the Data Management Component is another example of the application of the principle of Separation of Concerns; the details of database technology are isolated from essential system functions.

The rationale for this approach is technology-independence and therefore reusability. For example, when a given application system is upgraded from a GUI interface to, say, a voice-response interface, it should only be necessary to replace the Human Interaction Component—the remainder of the system should not be changed. In fact, the remainder of the system should be oblivious to the change in user interface technology.

1.6
About This Book

Although there are numerous books on the subject of object-oriented analysis and design, few go beyond presenting terminology, notation and the structure of their own unique models. And when it comes to the genesis of the process—establishing an initial set of objects—guidance is superficial at best. Yet, it is at this embryonic stage that the success or failure of an object-oriented project is established—though that success or failure may not become apparent until months or years later.

What's missing from the object-oriented analysis and design practitioner's literature, we feel, is more insight into how object-oriented analysis and design are done—for real systems. That's what we've tried to present in this book. Our principal contribution, we feel, is in presenting insight—not technique.

Charles Dickens once remarked that "I should never have made my success in my life if I had not bestowed upon the least thing I have ever undertaken, the same attention and care that I have bestowed upon the greatest." In presenting these case studies, we have attempted to bestow the greatest attention to even the least of details—just as would be necessary for real projects.

We hope you will profit from our efforts.

**References
for Chapter 1**

1. Tom DeMarco, *Structured Analysis and System Specification* (Englewood Cliffs, NJ: Prentice Hall, 1979).

2. Peter Coad and Edward Yourdon, *Object-Oriented Analysis*, 2nd edition (Englewood Cliffs, NJ: Prentice Hall, 1990).

3. Peter Coad and Edward Yourdon, *Object-Oriented Design* (Englewood Cliffs, NJ: Prentice Hall, 1991).

 *Key Points*

▲ The principle of Separation of Concerns distinguishes between *essential* requirements and *implementation* requirements.

▲ Today's software development techniques can't scale up for the systems of tomorrow.

▲ The concept of object-orientation is very different than the traditional top-down, functional decomposition approach.

▲ Object-oriented techniques are an *enabling* technology for full software life cycle reuse.

▲ An *object* is an independent, asynchronous, concurrent entity which knows things, does work and collaborates with other objects to perform the functions of a system.

▲ The Object-Oriented Analysis model has five layers; we use a specific notation and syntax to represent objects, attributes, services and other object-oriented concepts.

▲ The Object-Oriented Design model has four components. It has the same structure as the OOA model.

The path up and down is one and the same.

— Heraclitus

2.1 Introduction

In this chapter, we present a summarized version of a functional specification for the two case study applications; these will be discussed throughout the remainder of the book. If either of the case studies were "real-world" projects, the written specification might be much longer, and the requirements might be much more detailed. On the other hand, they might not be written at all—especially in the case of the second application, *Small Bytes*—and the systems analyst would have to determine the true user requirements through a combination of questions, discussion and prototypes.

The text of each case study specification will be used as the basis for a series of analysis and design models in subsequent chapters; however, we will also discuss some of the implications and relevant issues of each case study in this chapter.

For the remainder of this book, we shall reference the complete description of each case study that is included in Appendices A and B.

2.2 The Elevator Control System

2.2.1 Specification of the Problem

The general requirement is to design and implement a program to schedule and control four elevators in a building with 40 floors. The elevators will be used to carry people from one floor to another in the conventional way.

Efficiency: The program should schedule the elevators efficiently and reasonably. For example, if someone summons an elevator by pushing the down button on the fourth floor, the next elevator that reaches the fourth floor traveling down should stop at the fourth floor to accept the passenger(s). On the other hand, if an elevator has no passengers (no outstanding destination requests), it should park at the last floor it visited until it is needed again. An elevator should not reverse its direction of travel until its passengers who want to travel in its current direction have reached their destinations. (As we will see below, the program cannot really have information about an elevator's actual passengers; it only knows about destination button presses for a given elevator. For example, if some mischievous or sociopathic passenger boards the elevator at the first floor and then presses the destination buttons for the fourth, fifth, and twentieth floor, the program will cause the elevator to travel to and stop at the fourth, fifth, and twentieth floors. The computer and its program have no information about actual passenger boardings and exits.) An elevator that is filled to capacity should not respond to a new summon request. (There is an overweight sensor for each elevator. The computer and its program can interrogate these sensors.)

Destination button: The interior of each elevator is furnished with a panel containing an array of 40 buttons, one button for each floor, marked with the floor numbers (1 to 40). These destination buttons can be illuminated by signals sent from the computer to the panel. When a passenger presses a destination button not already lit, the circuitry behind the panel sends an interrupt to the computer (there is a separate interrupt for each elevator). When the computer receives one of these (vectored) interrupts, its program can read the appropriate memory mapped eight-bit input registers (there is one for each interrupt, hence one for each elevator) that contains the floor number corresponding to the destination button that caused the interrupt. Of course, the circuitry behind the panel writes the floor number into the appropriate memory-mapped input register when it causes the vectored interrupt. (Since there are 40 floors in this application, only the first six bits of each input register will be used by the implementation; but the hardware would support a building with up to 256 floors.)

Destination button lights: As mentioned earlier, the destination buttons can be illuminated (by bulbs behind the panels). When the interrupt service routine in the program receives a destination button interrupt, it should send a signal to the appropriate panel to illuminate the appropriate button. This signal is sent by the program's loading the number of the button into the appropriate memory-mapped output register (there is one such register for each elevator). The illumination of a button notifies the passenger(s) that the system has taken note of his or her request and also prevents further interrupts caused by additional (impatient?) pressing of the button. When the controller stops an elevator at a floor, it should send a signal to its destination button panel to turn off the destination button for that floor.

Floor sensors: There is a floor sensor switch for each floor for each elevator shaft. When an elevator is within eight inches of a floor, a wheel on the elevator closes the switch for that floor and sends an interrupt to the computer (there is a separate interrupt for the set of switches in each elevator shaft). When the computer receives one of these (vectored) interrupts, its program can read the appropriate memory mapped eight-bit input register (there is one for each interrupt, hence one for each elevator) that contains the floor number corresponding to the floor sensor switch that caused the interrupt.

Arrival lights: The interior of each elevator is furnished with a panel containing one illuminable indicator for each floor number. This panel is located just above the doors. The purpose of this panel is to tell the passengers in the elevator the number of the floor at which the elevator is arriving (and at which it may be stopping). The program should illuminate the indicator for a floor when it arrives at the floor and extinguish the indicator for a floor when it leaves a floor or arrives at a different floor. This signal is sent by the program's loading the number of the floor indicator into the appropriate memory-mapped output register (there is one register for each elevator).

Summons buttons: Each floor of the building is furnished with a panel containing summon button(s). Each floor except the ground floor (floor 1) and the top floor (floor 40) is furnished with a panel containing two summon buttons, one marked UP and one marked DOWN. The ground floor summon panel has only an UP button. The top floor summon panel has only a DOWN button. Thus, there are 78 summon buttons altogether, 39 UP buttons and 39

DOWN buttons. Would-be passengers press these buttons in order to summon an elevator. (Of course, the would-be passenger cannot summon a particular elevator. The scheduler decides which elevator should respond to a summon request.) These summon buttons can be illuminated by signals sent from the computer to the panel. When a passenger presses a summon button not already lit, the circuitry behind the panel sends a vectored interrupt to the computer (there is one interrupt for UP buttons and another for DOWN buttons). When the computer receives one of these two (vectored) interrupts, its program can read the appropriate memory mapped eight-bit input register that contains the floor number corresponding to the summon button that caused the interrupt. Of course, the circuitry behind the panel writes the floor number into the appropriate memory-mapped input register when it causes the vectored interrupt.

Summon button lights: The summon buttons can be illuminated (by bulbs behind the panels). When the summon button interrupt service routine in the program receives an UP or DOWN button vectored interrupt, it should send a signal to the appropriate panel to illuminate the appropriate button. This signal is sent by the program's loading the number of the button in the appropriate memory-mapped output register, one for the UP buttons and one for the DOWN buttons. The illumination of a button notifies the passenger(s) that the system has taken note of his or her request and also prevents further interrupts caused by additional pressing of the button. When the controller stops an elevator at a floor, it should send a signal to the floor's summon button panel to turn off the appropriate (UP or DOWN) button for that floor.

Elevator motor controls (Up, Down, Stop): There is a memory-mapped control word for each elevator motor. Bit 0 of this word commands the elevator to go up, bit 1 commands the elevator to do down, and bit 2 commands the elevator to stop at the floor whose sensor switch is closed. The elevator mechanism will not obey any inappropriate or unsafe command. If no floor sensor switch is closed when the computer issues a stop signal, the elevator mechanism ignores the stop signal until a floor sensor switch is closed. The computer program does not have to worry about controlling an elevator's doors or stopping an elevator exactly at a level (home) position at a floor. The elevator manufacturer uses conventional switches, relays, circuits, and safety interlocks for these purposes so that the manufacturer can certify the safety of the elevators without regard for the computer controller. For example, if the computer issues a stop command for an elevator when it is within eight inches of a floor (so that its floor sensor switch is closed), the conventional, approved mechanism stops and levels the elevator at that floor, opens and holds its doors open appropriately, and then closes its door. If the computer issues an up or down command during this period (while the door is open, for example), the manufacturer's mechanism ignores the command until its conditions for movement are met. (Therefore, it is safe for the computer to issue and up or down command while an elevator's door is still open.) One condition for an elevator's movement is that its stop button not be depressed. Each elevator's destination button panel contains a stop button. This button does not go to the computer. Its sole purpose is to hold an elevator at a floor with its door open when the elevator is currently stopped at a floor. A red emergency stop switch stops and holds the elevator at the very next floor it reaches irrespective of computer scheduling. The red switch may also turn on an audible alarm. The red switch is not connected to the computer.

Target machine: The elevator scheduler and controller may be implemented for any contemporary microcomputer capable of handling this application.

Figure 2.1 illustrates the various components of the elevator control system.

**2.2.2
Discussion
of the Problem**

Although we will be concerned with the analysis and design of this system from an object-oriented perspective, we would expect that the *behavior* of the Elevator Control System (ECS) will be the same no matter what kind of techniques were used in its development—object-oriented, structured, ad hoc or otherwise. In fact,

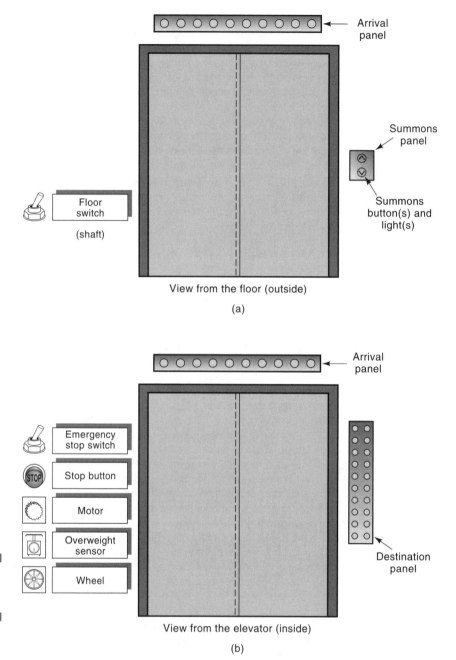

Figure 2.1
(a) A sketch of a typical elevator—view from the floor, outside the elevator.
(b) A sketch of a typical elevator—view from inside the elevator.

as we will see in Chapter 5, some non-object-oriented, traditional structured techniques are quite useful in capturing the required behaviors of the ECS.

Independent of analysis and design techniques, we know, for example, that elevators have to be "scheduled." That is, when summons or destinations are requested, or when an elevator moves past a floor, some decisions have to be made about the control of a particular elevator. As it turns out, there is a related, but different concept, i.e., "dispatching." We use this term to refer to the initiation of activity of a particular elevator. The ECS therefore is *primarily* concerned with the scheduling and dispatching of elevators. Our point is that the *specification* of how we want the ECS to schedule and dispatch elevators is independent of analysis and design techniques and needs to be understood as a discipline unto itself.

Most readers of this book will not be familiar with elevator scheduling algorithms and the like—neither are the authors. In the course of teaching our workshops, however, we have developed some understanding of the behavior of elevators. Aside from the distinction between *scheduling* and *dispatching*, the reader should be aware of several additional concepts.

First, elevators obviously have directions of movement (up, down or none). As it turns out, understanding how elevators behave requires identifying a second kind of direction, "intended direction," or what we call *status direction*. An elevator's status direction may be different from its *actual direction*. For example, when an elevator is stopped at a floor, but has pending upward destinations, its actual direction will be *none*, but its status direction will be *up*.

Another concept which is necessary to understanding the behavior of elevators is that of a *scheduled floor*. A floor may be "scheduled" with respect to a particular elevator, if that elevator must stop at that floor, for whatever reason. This may be the result of pending destinations or an appropriately pending summons request at the given floor. As it turns out, establishing whether or not a given floor is a "scheduled floor" for a given elevator, at the point in time at which the elevator approaches the floor, is the crux of elevator scheduling. And now, the reader must ponder on the following statement: Establishing whether or not a given floor is a "scheduled floor" can be accomplished solely on the basis of destinations pending (for that elevator), summons pending (for that floor), the actual direction of the elevator and the status direction of the elevator.

One final note regarding the behavior of elevators from this generic perspective. The approach taken above is biased; it is biased in the sense that elevator scheduling is done independently, for each elevator, at the moment in time when an elevator reports its approach to a given floor. For lack of a better name, we will refer to this approach for scheduling elevators as "asynchronous, floor-based scheduling."

Clearly, the scheduling of elevators could be accomplished on a different basis, say, every 10 seconds. That is, every 10 seconds the entire system could be re-examined and elevators re-scheduled accordingly. Or, say, every 100 seconds. Or perhaps, based on historical data, elevators could be set on their schedules once every 24 hours (similar to a commuter train). These might all be considered examples of "synchronous scheduling."

In our workshops, students frequently object to this scheduling bias. They accuse us of biasing the analysis in favor of one particular implementation—asynchronous, floor-based scheduling. This is not true. The assumption that elevator scheduling will be asynchronous and floor-based, is simply part of the application domain, or context within which we study the ECS. By analogy, if we were to specify an accounts receivable system, there would probably be no objection to the tacit assumption that we specify the system within the context of commonly accepted accounting principles and practices.

For the remainder of this book, we will focus on the analysis of the ECS assuming asynchronous, floor-based scheduling. Readers interested in learning more about elevator control systems should consult the references at the end of this chapter. As it happens, this problem is of far broader interest than simply for elevators (see "The Pure Theory of Elevators," referenced below).

Now, let's start talking about the ECS from an object-oriented perspective.

While there are obviously a number of items in the problem description that will be identified as objects, and while many of those objects have a number of interesting data-related characteristics, our attention is drawn to the *behavior* of the objects. Our focus is on such issues as: *when* does an elevator have to go up or down? *How* does the summons button communicate with the summons light, and with what other objects must it communicate? Under what circumstances is it legal for the elevator motor control to respond to an up or down command?

Within this context, it is also evident that the elevator problem cries out to be modeled as a number of asynchronous, communicating "things"—whether we call those things objects or entities or poobahs is less important than the fact that we want to stay away from a classical, synchronous structured design model in which a single executive module controls the execution of a number of subordinate modules. By contrast, since the *Small Bytes* problem described below exhibits no real-time characteristics, the issue of asynchronous behavior doesn't arise; a classical transaction-based model would suffice just as well. Note that an IE approach, which deals with entities, is less appealing than an object-oriented approach for the elevator problem. A key characteristic of the application is the *communication* between various components, which the object-oriented approach handles naturally with the concept of messages between objects.

There is one other characteristic of the elevator problem description that must be emphasized: there is a great deal of discussion of *implementation technology.* Unlike the *Small Bytes* problem description below, which is basically technology-independent, the elevator problem description talks about microprocessors, memory-mapped input registers, relays, vectored interrupts, interrupt service routines, sensors, signals and a scheduler. Some of these details may be associated with the electromechanical environment in which our computer system will be placed; other details obviously involve the user's assumption about the hardware and software technology that will be employed to implement the system. An important task for the systems analyst—regardless of whether he or she uses an object-oriented approach or any other methodology—is to eliminate as many of these irrelevant technology details as possible from the analysis model, to provide a "perfect technology model" of the essential user requirements.

2.3
The Small Bytes Subscription System

2.3.1
Specification of the Problem

A small, independent software journal, *Small Bytes*, has asked you to design a new system for managing its subscriptions; they have a jury-rigged system today using various Macintosh-based spreadsheet, word-processing, and flat-file database packages, and it has gotten completely out of hand. While the concept of managing subscriptions is quite straightforward, the details are numerous, as will be seen below.

Small Bytes is published on a monthly basis; a typical monthly issue consists of 5-10 articles, each written by one or more authors in the software engineering field. Though the authors receive no payment for their articles, they do receive a year's free subscription as a token of appreciation for their efforts; if they already have a subscription, then the expiration date is extended for a year. Most authors have written only one article during the journal's five-year history, but a few have written several; management is concerned with keeping track of this information, for it wants to avoid publishing more than one or two articles from any one author in a single year.

Small Bytes also has an editorial board of advisors, some of whom may also be authors from time to time; the editorial board normally serves for a one-year or two-year term, and they too receive a complimentary subscription to the magazine. The editorial board reviews submitted articles, and also makes suggestions to *Small Bytes*'s publisher and managing editor about topics for future issues, and prospective authors who should be contacted to write articles on those topics. As with most magazines, issues are scheduled and planned months in advance; hence, the editor is dealing with several issues and its associated authors simultaneously, as well as receiving numerous unsolicited articles from a variety of past, current, and would-be authors.

Small Bytes is sold on a subscription basis; most subscriptions are for a one-year period, but the publisher accepts subscriptions for periods longer than or shorter than a year by simply pro-rating the annual subscription price. There are only a few thousand subscribers; most are "corporate" subscribers, but some are individuals who have *Small Bytes* sent to their home address in a plain brown wrapper. Most of them are "single-copy" subscribers; however, it is not uncommon for large companies to order multiple copies, all of which are sent to the same person. (However, in some cases, the organization is adamant that a person not be named in the subscription, and that the magazine be sent to a title, such as "Technical Librarian," instead). Multiple-copy subscriptions typically involve a small discount from the single-copy price; in addition, various other discounts have been offered from time to time, though the overwhelming majority of subscriptions are at a standard price. (Note, however, that the "standard" price is different for North American subscriptions and international subscriptions, in order to cover the higher cost of shipping overseas.)

There are a few cases of multiple-copy subscriptions where the subscribing organization asks that the constituent copies be sent to named individuals; of course, it is important to keep track of the "primary" subscriber from whom payment is received, and to whom any correspondence should be addressed. Generally, these issues are sent to multiple people within one "site" (e.g., one division or department, located at a single corporate address); however, there are a few cases where the multiple copies are sent to individuals in different sites within the corporation. In any case, the publisher finds it convenient to identify subscribers within a site, and the various sites associated with an organization.

Most subscriptions are received directly from the subscriber; however, the publication also deals with a number of agencies, or subscription service bureaus, such as EBSCO, Faxon, and Readmore. These agencies receive a small commission for the subscriptions they provide, though this fact is generally kept hidden from the subscriber; it means, though, that the publisher must keep track of the "retail" price that the subscriber is being charged, as well as the commission paid to the agency.

In addition, the magazine is distributed in several foreign countries by distributors who have an quasi-exclusive right to market the magazine in their territory. The distributors receive a somewhat larger discount for a bulk shipment of magazines (in addition to paying for the shipping costs, which can be substantial), which they then distribute to their subscribers. Typically, some "direct" subscriptions from the distributor's country existed prior to the distributor-publisher agreement, and *Small Bytes* continues to supply those subscriptions directly. In addition, the distributor is supposed to supply the names and addresses of his own subscribers (in case the distributor goes out of business) to the publisher; in practice, this has not been done consistently in the past, but the publisher is determined to enforce this provision when the new system is developed.

As noted earlier, contributing authors and members of the editorial board of advisors receive a complimentary one-year subscription to the magazine; in addition, the publisher provides a limited number of additional complimentary subscriptions to respected gurus and in the field, as well as a few friends and relatives. This list of "comps" is reviewed from time to time to see if any should be deleted. Also, the "comp" list is queried periodically in order to confirm that they still wish to receive their complimentary copy of *Small Bytes*.

A large percentage of existing subscribers renew their subscription from one year to the next; the renewal activity is typically the result of renewal notices that the publisher begins sending several months before the actual expiration. On the final month of a subscription, the publisher includes a large note with the magazine that says "THIS IS YOUR LAST COPY." For several months after the subscription has expired, the publisher continues to send renewal notices. (Note also that the subscription service bureaus make their own solicitation efforts to their subscribers, in addition to the publisher's direct letters to those same subscribers.) Renewals sometimes straggle in several months after a subscription has expired, so it is vital to maintain the subscription records on the database indefinitely.

Payments for new subscriptions and renewals are normally received by check; the check may be accompanied with a subscription offer or a renewal notice, but such notices are not considered "invoices" in the normal sense of the word. In some cases, subscribers ask that a formal invoice be generated, with a purchase order number, so that it can be submitted to their accounting department for proper payment. Some subscribers pay by credit card, but the publisher insists(because its bank insists) that credit card payments be accompanied by a signature; this means that the credit card orders and renewals are typically sent by fax or mail.

In addition to full-year subscriptions, the publisher also sells limited numbers of individual copies of *Small Bytes*. In most cases, these are "back-issue" orders; they may be paid, as indicated above, by check, credit card, or invoice. On rare occasions, a customer will order multiple copies of a back issue, in which case a discount is offered. And on even rarer occasions, a customer (typically an author, or a vendor whose product was favorably reviewed in the magazine) will order several thousand copies of an individual article in an issue, and will ask that it be packaged as a "mini-issue" of the magazine; each of these special orders is priced separately, depending on volume, etc.

Although there are only a small number of subscribers, the publisher has a large list of "prospects," which it has accumulated from various sources over the years. Many of these prospects have asked for sample copies of SmallBytes; some have received a "trial" subscription for a few months, but then decided not to "convert" to a paid subscription. Many others have received various promotional mailings from time to time, including unsolicited sample copies and/or trial subscriptions. Obviously, all of this information is useful to the publisher.

2.3.2
Discussion
of the Problem

From the description above, it is evident that the *Small Bytes* system is a classical business data processing application; clearly, it is a very different kind of system than the ECS project described earlier. While the details may seem overwhelming at first, it is clearly not a mega-project requiring hundreds of people; indeed, we would expect that such a system could be implemented by one or two people within a relatively brief period of time.

It is not immediately apparent why such a system *must* be approached from an object-oriented perspective. A structured analysis or information engineering approach, particularly if combined with a CASE tool and/or a 4GL, might do just as well. As will become more and more evident in the next several chapters, this application lends itself to an object-oriented approach, and large productivity gains might be expected if, for example, the publisher decides to add a new journal to its list of publications. And while the description in Section 2.3.1 says nothing about the implementation of the system, we can easily imagine that a graphical user interface will be highly desirable to the user, especially since the publisher and editor have used Macintosh packages to carry out the business activity up to this point. Thus, it may well turn out that the biggest argument for adopting an object-oriented approach is not that it improves the *analysis* phase of the project, but rather that it facilitates a subsequent object-oriented design and implementation activity.

Note also that the most dominant characteristic of this application is its *data*. Clearly, *Small Bytes* is not a real-time system; while it will presumably be implemented as an on-line application, and while much of the activity revolves around a monthly cycle of publication, we don't have to worry about microsecond response times, concurrency, synchronization and all of the other difficult issues of real-time systems. Similarly, the processing or number-crunching component of the system is likely to be fairly trivial; it will involve such things as multiplying the number of copies times the unit price of the magazine to compute the total subscription price charged to a customer. This is hardly the stuff that requires functional decomposition and elaborate structure charts.

On the other hand, the problem description abounds with data descriptions. There are various items in the problem description that immediately cry out to be recognized as objects or classes; veteran information engineering practitioners would recognize the same items as entities. There are clearly relationships between various items, e.g., between subscribers and their subscriptions, and there are numerous attributes associated with each item. All of this will be the primary focus of our analysis activity.

Other applications, such as the elevator problem described above, may have a different dominant theme. As a result, our strategy for discovering objects, which we will discuss in Chapter 4, may be quite different from the strategy we would use on the *Small Bytes* system.

References for Chapter 2

1. "Systematic concurrent object-oriented programming," (A simplified approach to retain distributed and sequential features in object-oriented application development) (one of eight articles on concurrent object-oriented programming; special issue), *Communications of the ACM*, Sept. 1993, v36, n9, p56(25).

2. "An entity-life modeling approach to the design of concurrent software (Computing Practices)," *Communications of the ACM*, March 1989, v32, n3, p330(15).

3. "A comparison of techniques for the specification of external system behavior," *Communications of the ACM*, Sept. 1988, v31, n9, p1098(18).

4. Edward Yourdon, *Modern Structured Analysis* (Prentice Hall, 1988).

5. "Using material handling in the development of integrated manufacturing," *Industrial Engineering*, March 1992, v24, n3, p43(5).

6. "Entity-life modeling and structured analysis in real-time software design - a comparison," *Communications of the ACM*, Dec. 1989, v32, n12, p1458(9).

7. "How Otis Elevator keeps on moving to the top," (Company Profile), *PC Week*, March 31, 1987, v4, n13, p45(2).

8. "Object lessons to be learnt," (Related articles on Petroleum Science and Technology Institute's use of Object Design's Objectstore, object database and

elevator manufacturer Schindler's use of Hitachi's Object IQ object-oriented software), *Computer Weekly,* Jan. 27, 1994, p30(2).

9. "Elevator traffic simulation," (Technical), *Simulation,* Oct. 1993, v61, n4, p257(11).

10. "Intelligent elevator dispatching systems," *AI Expert,* Sept. 1989, v4, n9, p32(6).

11. Knuth, Donald, *The Art of Computer Programming,* v3, "One-Tape Sorting," pp357-360.

12. Wuffle, A., "The Pure Theory of Elevators," *Mathematics Magazine,* Jan. 1982, v5, n1, pp30-37.

 *Key Points*

▲ The "analysis" of a system takes place within an application domain context—this context is not a bias in the usual sense, but rather a constraint to which all analyses must conform.

▲ System requirements may be determined by subjective factors, such as the scope and scale of the system as seen by the user. In other words, system requirements are always established within the context of a user environment.

CHAPTER 3
Finding and Keeping Good Objects

The formulation of a problem is often more essential than its solution, which may be merely a matter of mathematical or experimental skill.

— Einstein and Infeld
The Evolution of Physics (1938)

3.1 Introduction

True story. A small European country with a large European social system installed a new information system. This system replaced an existing legacy system which had become enormously expensive to maintain. The system was massive, tracking and reporting on all of the various government benefits, pensions, programs, etc. The analysts who were responsible for the specification of the new system decided to use an object-oriented approach. Their analysis led them to identify objects with names like *citizen, pension, beneficiary* and various other "appropriate" object names.

It was not until some time after the delivery of the system that the failure of this object-oriented analysis became apparent. As explained by one of the systems developers, most of the maintenance changes involved changes in so-called "legislative rules." Nowhere, however, was there a *legislative rule* object—or anything similar. The secrets of legislative rules were embedded throughout the system. Therefore, whenever one of these legislative rules changed, it usually required that very significant system-wide changes be made.

Object-oriented techniques hold the promise of very significantly improving both the quality and productivity of software development. However, the benefits of object-orientation can be reaped only if the right set of objects are identified. An appropriate set of objects, for a given application domain, assures reusability, promotes extensibility and helps to insure the quality and productivity improvements inherent in the object-oriented paradigm. Without a formal method for establishing what are the objects, software developers risk simply hacking at the object level.

In this chapter we introduce a number of practical techniques to help find and keep good objects. Much of what is presented in this chapter is akin to a chaos effect for software; that is, identifying small things, at the start of a process, which can have a big impact in the future. In this chapter we will illustrate these techniques with snippets from the case studies introduced in Chapter 2. More complete application of these techniques will be given in Chapters 4 and 5.

3.2 Motivation

As software engineering practitioners, we are concerned with making things work. It has been frustrating, therefore, not to find practical, down-to-earth object-finding techniques; techniques which can be readily applied to real-world problems. Although there are numerous books on Object-Oriented Analysis (and more coming out all the time!), few go beyond presenting terminology, notation and the structure of their own unique models. And when it comes to the genesis of the process—establishing an initial set of objects—guidance is superficial at best. Yet the wrong choice of objects can have a profound impact on the success of a project.

In grappling with this problem, two insights have been revealed. First, objects "know things" (i.e., store data) and objects "do work" (i.e., have services). Since virtually all of the traditional tools of systems analysis are concerned with defining data or specifying processes, traditional systems analysis tools should, in some way, be very useful for object-finding.

In particular, we have found three traditional systems analysis tools to be useful: data-flow diagrams (or variants, including context diagrams), entity-relationship diagrams (or variants) and state-transition diagrams (or variants, including event-response models). These tools capture three different, independent system views (process, data and control). We refer to the application of these tools to the software systems analysis process as *3-View Modeling* (3VM).

Our second insight deals with the fundamental nature of objects. Clearly objects are inextricably bound to application domain concepts. To truly find good objects, we must be able to clearly identify and define application domain concepts. Although understanding the application domain has always been the crux of software systems analysis, that process has typically been an informal and subjective one.

In attempting to learn more about the human conceptual process, we have been led from Aristotle to Rand [1]. In software systems analysis, however, humans deal with concepts primarily by means of natural languages, both written and spoken. There is an existing branch of science which deals with the study of language, i.e., linguistics. We investigated, therefore, the use of linguistic tools and techniques for object-finding.

There have been some efforts in the past to apply some linguistic principles to software systems analysis (see, for example [2], [3] and [4]). (One CASE product is based on Nijssen's Information Analysis Model [5].) We refer to the application of linguistic principles to the software systems analysis process as *Linguistic-based Information Analysis* (LIA).

3.3
Approach

Figure 3.1 shows the approach which we have taken in applying both 3VM and LIA to the object-finding process. Both of these techniques will be elaborated below. At this point, it should be noted in Figure 3.1 that 3VM and LIA are activities separate and distinct from Object-Oriented Analysis (OOA). (In fact, both of these techniques are useful for traditional systems analysis.) It should also be noted that, although not shown in Figure 3.1, the application of these techniques is iterative.

Our principal objective in devising this approach has been to reduce, to the maximum extent practical, the subjective nature of object identification.

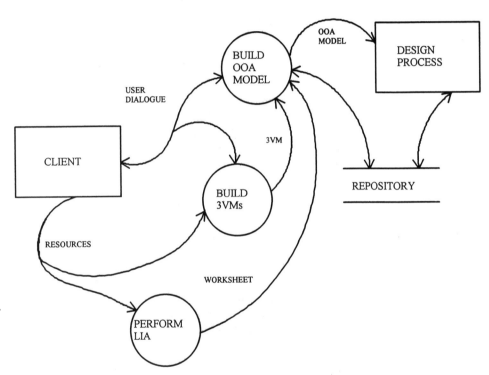

Figure 3.1
Overview of the object-finding techniques presented in this chapter.

3.4
3-View Modeling (3VM)

The use of entity-relationship models, data-flow models and state-transition models is well-known in software systems analysis and will not be discussed in-depth in this book. We have found the construction of the various 3VMs of a proposed system useful for object-finding, as discussed below.

Entity-Relationship Models

It is well-known that Entity-Relationship Diagrams (ERDs) are a useful precursor to OOA. The entities strongly suggest objects, and the attributes of those entities represent data which ultimately must be stored by objects. The relationships between entities may suggest the creation of "associative objects." The so-called "cardinality" and "conditionality" of relationships may suggest services which maintain these relationships.

Although the ERD is a very useful object-finding tool, we have found some inherent problems with its use. First, the identified entities may not be relevant application domain concepts. This is especially true if the analyst has attempted to create entities in third normal form. Also, the ERD is not useful for identifying objects which do not store data; objects which recognize the occurrence of events or which perform a controlling function, for example, frequently fall into this category.

Data-Flow Models

We have found two forms of data-flow models to be useful object-finding tools.

First, the context diagram establishes an overall system boundary which is useful from a systems analysis perspective. The external entities identified on the context diagram represent the ultimate source or destination of the data flows. As such, the external entities are object candidates. The context diagram flows represent the proposed system's inputs and outputs. Any set of objects must therefore account for how these context diagram flows are received, processed and produced.

When appropriate, a leveled set of data-flow diagrams is produced; this model represents a functional decomposition of the proposed system into primitive units. These primitive units are referred to as mini-specifications or Primitive-Process Specifications (PPSs). The PPSs ultimately must correspond to object methods or services.

State-Transition Models

Two forms of state-transition models have been found to be useful object-finding tools.

First, the event-response model (or simply an event list) has proved to be a tremendously useful object-finding tool. This model identifies each happening or occurrence which the proposed system must recognize and to which the proposed system must produce a pre-planned response. The event component of this model helps to identify a set of event-recognizing objects; the response component helps to identify a set of event-producing objects.

In some very specific cases, it has been useful to create one or more state-transition diagrams for a proposed system. (These should not be confused with state-transition diagrams produced at the object level—so called life cycle diagrams.) In addition to identifying event-recognizing and event-producing objects (as transition conditions and actions, respectively), such state-transition diagrams help to identify attributes which maintain state information.

It should be noted that not all 3VM tools are useful for every proposed system. For example, an analyst would want to use different tools to model an elevator control system than an inventory control system.

3VMs for the case study systems are included in Appendices G and H.

3.5 Linguistic-Based Information Analysis

We have found the techniques of 3VM to be quite useful for identifying components of objects; however, they offer no guidance in specifically identifying the right set of objects for a proposed system. Judgment, intuition and insight still rule the object-finding process.

Linguistic-based Information Analysis, on the other hand, offers considerable guidance in the object-finding process. In addition, LIA also helps to identify object components and as such, there is some overlap with 3VM.

The goal of LIA is to identify a universe of application domain concepts and relationships between these concepts. In this chapter we will discuss the two LIA techniques which have worked well for us; these techniques are *Phrase Frequency Analysis* (PFA) and *Matrix Analysis* (MA).

Both of these techniques require the identification of a resource base or resource repository. The resource base includes relevant documents, models, software, people and whatever other resources contain knowledge of the application domain or proposed system. If the application domain has a body of reference materials (text books, practices, procedures, etc.), those materials should be included in the resource base.

Other information in the resource base may included:

- Transcriptions of interviews
- Formal or informal system specifications
- User's manuals of existing or related systems
- Printed forms
- Logs (for example, system change requests or trouble reports)

All of these resources contain a base of text to which the LIA techniques can be applied.

The techniques of LIA are usually applied to some subset of the resource base depending on what view into the application domain or the proposed system the analyst desires. In general, resources which relate to the application domain will yield different results than those which relate specifically to the specification of a proposed system.

Phrase Frequency Analysis involves searching the selected resource text to identify terms which may represent application domain concepts. Figure 3.2 shows a partial listing of the results of such an analysis on the SBSS textual description given in Appendix B. (A complete list is included in Appendices C and D for both case studies.) The creation of a PFA list is primarily an objective process (in fact, it can be significantly automated). As might be appreciated by reviewing Figure 3.2, most of the concepts identified might prove to be irrelevant. We feel that a strong virtue of PFA is the identification of a broad set of application domain concepts, evaluating them and then deciding which of those are irrelevant; this is vastly better than simply overlooking such concepts in the first place.

On the surface, PFA may seem similar to a technique which has been widely used in data modeling. That is, identifying nouns and verbs as candidate entities and attributes. However, phrase frequency analysis is quite different. We have found that noun/verb identification is very subjective. Both in terms of what is a noun or verb (since words in English can frequently be interpreted as both), as well as the fact that the perceptions of the analyst usually determine which nouns

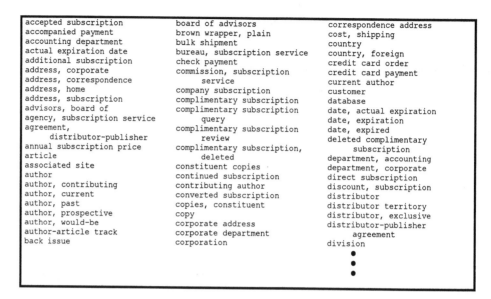

```
accepted subscription       board of advisors            correspondence address
accompanied payment         brown wrapper, plain         cost, shipping
accounting department       bulk shipment                country
actual expiration date      bureau, subscription service country, foreign
additional subscription     check payment                credit card order
address, corporate          commission, subscription     credit card payment
address, correspondence         service                  current author
address, home               company subscription         customer
address, subscription       complimentary subscription   database
advisors, board of          complimentary subscription   date, actual expiration
agency, subscription service    query                    date, expiration
agreement,                  complimentary subscription   date, expired
    distributor-publisher       review                   deleted complimentary
annual subscription price   complimentary subscription,      subscription
article                         deleted                  department, accounting
associated site             constituent copies           department, corporate
author                      continued subscription       direct subscription
author, contributing        contributing author          discount, subscription
author, current             converted subscription       distributor
author, past                copies, constituent          distributor territory
author, prospective         copy                         distributor, exclusive
author, would-be            corporate address            distributor-publisher
author-article track        corporate department             agreement
back issue                  corporation                  division
                                ●                            ●
                                ●                            ●
                                ●                            ●
```

Figure 3.2
Partial list of application domain concepts resulting from Phrase Frequency Analysis.

and verbs are found. PFA, on the other hand, identifies concepts rather than grammatical units. We have found that the creation of a PFA list is not significantly influenced by who prepares the list.

A PFA for any significant application domain resource may result in the production of a long list of concepts. Many (if not most) of these will be identified as irrelevant and ultimately discarded. Others will become components of an OOA model, including objects. We have found it useful to convert the PFA list into an *OOA/OOD worksheet*. Figure 3.3 shows a portion of such a worksheet. (Complete worksheets for both case studies are included in Appendices E and F.) This worksheet has been tailored to our version of OOA; it could be adapted, of course, for any version of OOA.

The OOA/OOD worksheet provides a systematic approach for reviewing a lengthy PFA list and identifying an initial set of OOA components. It is at this point where various OOA criteria are applied to the PFA list.

The second LIA technique which we will discuss is Matrix Analysis (MA). MA is a more sophisticated technique, and is more difficult to perform, than PFA. Also, MA is usually performed only after an initial object identification.

A portion of a two-dimensional MA for the SBSS is shown in Figure 3.4. The rows and columns of this matrix represent application domain concepts, which usually produce an initial set of identified objects. The cells in this matrix represent associations between the corresponding row and column concepts. Although an initial matrix could be mechanically constructed from resources, we have found MA to be most useful as a discussion tool. Analysts review and discuss the matrix, cell-by-cell, identifying application domain relationships (business rules). Analysts may also find new objects; objects which may not have been revealed during the initial PFA.

Clearly, an N-dimensional version of this matrix is possible. In practice, however, we have only found two-dimensional matrices to be feasible.

OOA/OOD WORKSHEET

Small Bytes Subscription System

ITEM	(0)	(1)	(2)	(3)	(4)	(5)	(6)	(7)	(8)	COMMENTS
ACCEPTED SUBSCRIPTION				X						An attribute of SUBSCRIPTION
ACCOMPANIED PAYMENT	X									We do not distinguish between different types of payments.
ACCOUNTING DEPARTMENT	X									Outside the application domain of the SBSS.
ACTUAL EXPIRATION DATE				X						Attribute of SUBSCRIPTION.
ADDITIONAL SUBSCRIPTION			X	X						Possible attribute of SUBSCRIPTION or possibly suggests a sub-type/super-type structure.
ANNUAL SUBSCRIPTION PRICE				X						Attribute of SUBSCRIPTION.
ARTICLE		X								
ASSOCIATED SITE				X						Attribute of SITE.
AUTHOR		X								
AUTHOR-ARTICLE TRACK									X	
BACK ISSUE				X						Attribute of SPECIAL ORDER.
BOARD OF ADVISORS	X									Outside the SBSS application domain.
BULK SHIPMENT				X						Possible attribute of SUBSCRIPTION?
CHECK PAYMENT				X						Attribute of PAYMENT.
COMPANY SUBSCRIPTION				X						Attribute of SUBSCRIPTION.
COMPLIMENTARY SUBSCRIPTION				X						Attribute of SUBSCRIPTION.
COMPLIMENTARY SUBSCRIPTION QUERY									X	One of several types of database queries.
COMPLIMENTARY SUBSCRIPTION REVIEW		X								Possible event-related object-class.
CONSTITUENT COPIES	X									Too general to be useful.
CONTINUED SUBSCRIPTION				X						Attribute of SUBSCRIPTION.
CONTRIBUTING AUTHOR	X									We do not distinguish between different types of authors.

(0) Not applicable. Possibly irrelevant, outside the context of the system being specified, etc.
(1) Possible object-class.
(2) Possibly part of sub-type/super-type structure. Includes Gen-Spec and Whole-Part relationships.
(3) Possibly describes an object-class attribute or instance relationship.
(4) Possibly describes an object service.

(5) Implementation specific. Possible Problem Domain Component item.
(6) Possible Human Interaction Component item.
(7) Possible Task Management Component item.
(8) Possible Data Management Component item.

Figure 3.3
Portion of OOA/OOD worksheet resulting from the application of LIA techniques.

As with PFA, we have found the principal virtue of MA to be its systematic And Methodical Nature.

3.6
Object-Oriented Analysis (OOA)

Referring back to Figure 3.1, both 3VM and LIA are precursors to the OOA process. It is during OOA that the results of 3VM and LIA are consolidated into an OOA model. Using the OOA/OOD worksheet as a guide, the various application domain concepts are examined vis-à-vis the various components identified by 3VM.

As an illustration of the technique, refer to the partial event list given in Figure 3.5. Notice that a number of these events are temporal events; for example, "time to review *comp* list." We turn to the OOA/OOD worksheet for the SBSS (Appendix F) and look for an application domain concept associated with this event. Although there are several possibilities, we select "Complimentary Sub-

	ARTICLE	AUTHOR	BOARD	COMPLIMENTARY SUBSCRIPTION
ARTICLE		monthly issue consists of 5-10 ARTICLEs, each written by one or more AUTHORs in the software engineering field ...management is concerned with keeping track of this information, for it wants to avoid publishing more than one or two ARTICLEs from any one AUTHOR in a single year		
AUTHOR	the AUTHORs receive no payment for their ARTICLEs...			...they do receive a year's free subscription as a token of appreciation for their efforts; if they already have a subscription, then the expiration date is extended for a year.
BOARD	The editorial BOARD reviews submitted ARTICLEs...	...and also makes suggestions to Small Bytes's publisher and managing editor about...prospective AUTHORs who should be contacted... ...editorial BOARD of advisors, some of whom may also be AUTHORs from time to time		the editorial BOARD normally serves for a one-year or two-year term, and they too receive a COMPLIMENTARY SUBSCRIPTION to the magazine

Figure 3.4
Partial matrix of application domain relationships.

scription Review" as most appropriate. We decide that "Complimentary Subscription Review" will be an SBSS object; it is an example of an event recognizer object. That is, it is an object which encapsulates the secret of how the time-to-review event is recognized. It is also an example of an object which is not revealed through entity-relationship modeling because it stores no data.

From this perspective it becomes apparent that <u>every object</u> must be either an *event recognizer* or an *event responder*. If an object does not either recognize the occurrence of some event, nor participate in the production of a response to some event, that object simply does not belong in the system.

It should also be mentioned that this is an iterative process; although 3VM and LIA are enormously useful in creating an initial OOA model, this model must still be validated against user requirements. Refinements of this model may well result in the elimination of existing, or the creation of new, objects.

3.7 Summary

In summary, we have found the combined techniques of 3VM and LIA to be enormously useful as precursors to OOA. We have found that our clients and students readily grasp and apply these tools; equally important, these tools allow analysts to initiate OOA in an objective and systematic fashion.

1. PAID SUBSCRIPTION REQUESTED	A. CREATE NEW SUBSCRIPTION RECORD
	B. CREATE NEW SUBSCRIBER RECORD AS REQUIRED
	   B.1 CREATE OR UPDATE ADDRESS RECORD AS REQUIRED
	C. CREATE NEW RECIPIENT RECORD AS REQUIRED
	   C.1 CREATE OR UPDATE ADDRESS RECORD AS REQUIRED
	D. ESTABLISH SUBSCRIPTION PRICING
	E. POST PAYMENT AS REQUIRED
	   E.1 ISSUE INVOICE AS REQUIRED
	F. NOTIFY SERVICE BUREAU OF SUBSCRIPTION AS REQUIRED
	G. ESTABLISH EXPIRATION DATE FOR SUBSCRIPTION
	H. ESTABLISH EXPIRATION WARNING DATE FOR SUBSCRIPTION

2. COMPLIMENTARY SUBSCRIPTION REQUESTED	A. CREATE NEW SUBSCRIPTION RECORD AS REQUIRED
	B. CREATE NEW SUBSCRIBER RECORD AS REQUIRED
	   B.1 CREATE OR UPDATE ADDRESS RECORD AS REQUIRED
	C. CREATE NEW RECIPIENT RECORD AS REQUIRED
	   C.1 CREATE OR UPDATE ADDRESS RECORD AS REQUIRED

3. PAYMENT RECEIVED	A. POST PAYMENT AS REQUIRED B. ISSUE INVOICE AS REQUIRED
4. TIME TO SEND RENEWAL NOTICE	A. INITIATE NOTIFICATION SEQUENCE
5. SUBSCRIPTION TERMINATES	A. DISCONTINUE SUBSCRIPTION
6. SUBSCRIPTION RENEWED	A. CREATE NEW SUBSCRIPTION RECORD B. UPDATE SUBSCRIBER ADDRESS RECORD AS REQUIRED C. UPDATE RECIPIENT ADDRESS RECORD AS REQUIRED D. ESTABLISH RENEWAL PRICING E. POST PAYMENT AS REQUIRED E.1 ISSUE INVOICE AS REQUIRED F. NOTIFY SERVICE BUREAU OF SUBSCRIPTION AS REQUIRED G. ESTABLISH EXPIRATION DATE FOR SUBSCRIPTION H. ESTABLISH EXPIRATION WARNING DATE FOR SUBSCRIPTION
7. TIME TO REVIEW "COMP" LIST	A. TERMINATE COMPLIMENTARY SUBSCRIPTION AS REQUIRED

8. SPECIAL ORDER RECEIVED	A. CREATE NEW CUSTOMER RECORD AS REQUIRED
	   B.1 CREATE OR UPDATE ADDRESS RECORD AS REQUIRED
	C. ENTER SHIPPING ADDRESS
	D. ESTABLISH SPECIAL ORDER PRICING
	E. POST PAYMENT AS REQUIRED
	   E.1 ISSUE INVOICE AS REQUIRED

9. ARTICLE RECEIVED	A. CREATE NEW ARTICLE RECORD B. CREATE NEW AUTHOR RECORD(S) AS REQUIRED B.1 CREATE NEW ADDRESS RECORD AS REQUIRED C. UPDATE AUTHOR AUTHOR-ARTICLE TRACK
10. ARTICLE ACCEPTED FOR PUBLICATION	A. TENTATIVELY SCHEDULE PUBLICATION ISSUE B. ENTER COMPLIMENTARY SUBSCRIPTION(S) C. UPDATE AUTHOR AUTHOR-ARTICLE TRACK
11. ARTICLE PUBLISHED	A. UPDATE AUTHOR AUTHOR-ARTICLE TRACK
12. PROSPECT IDENTIFIED	B. CREATE NEW PROSPECT RECORD AS REQUIRED B.1 CREATE NEW ADDRESS RECORD AS REQUIRED

Figure 3.5
Partial event list for the *Small Bytes* Subscription System (SBSS).

We will be applying the LIA technique to the two case studies (in Chapter 4). The 3VM technique will be illustrated in Chapter 5.

References for Chapter 3

1. Rand, A., *Introduction to Objectivist Epistemology*, 2nd ed., New American Library, 1990.

2. Nijssen and Halpin, *Conceptual Schema and Relational Database Design* (Prentice Hall, 1989).

3. Bird, C., "Modeling gaining ground...," *Software Magazine*, Jan. 1992, v12, n1, p67.

4. Barbier, F., "Object-oriented analysis of systems through their dynamical aspects," *Journal of Object-Oriented Programming*, May 1992, v5, n2, p45.

5. Taylor, A., "InfoModeler 1.0," *DBMS*, July 1994, v7, n8, p30.

6. Yourdon, E., *Object-Oriented Systems Development: An Integrated Approach* (Prentice Hall, 1994).

 *Key Points*

▲ Finding the right objects is difficult—but crucial—if the objects are to be re-usable.

▲ The combination of Linguistic Information Analysis and 3-View Modeling provides a fairly straight-forward, repeatable process for finding an initial universe of application domain concepts.

▲ The OOA/OOD worksheet provides a mechanism for extracting an initial set of objects from the universe of application domain concepts.

CHAPTER 4
Class and Object Identification

If names are not correct, language will not be in accordance with the truth of things.

— Confucius

4.1 Introduction and Discussion

Our objective in this chapter is to apply the techniques of Chapter 3 to develop a universe of application domain concepts for the case study systems. This effort, as well as the object refinement effort in the next chapter, will lay the foundation for all subsequent analysis and design efforts. The initial set of concepts that we develop in this chapter will be reviewed, discussed, debated and eventually revised. A great deal of thought and consideration needs to go into this process since it forms the basis for software re-use; our investment in this up-front analysis will have dramatic pay-offs when objects are re-used. At the conclusion of this chapter we will have a list of application domain concepts for the case study systems; we will use the LIA techniques of Chapter 3.

You should begin by reviewing the case study descriptions given in Chapter 2; these descriptions constitute the resources discussed in Chapter 3. You may wish to apply PFA as described in Chapter 3. PFA has the advantage of exhaustively revealing all concepts identified from the resources. Many of these concepts may be outside of the application domain or simply irrelevant; we will deal with these concepts later.

A less rigorous technique would be to manually identify, from the text, words and phrases which you feel are application domain concepts. Look for key words and phrases which may suggest candidate objects. Keep in mind the application domain in which you are working. When you identify candidate concepts, are they truly part of the problem domain of elevators and magazine subscriptions, or are they simply part of an implementation aspect of the problem?

We have applied PFA to the case study resource materials (see Appendices A and B). Figures 4.1 and 4.2 present small portions of these PFA lists for the two

```
ACTUAL PASSENGER            ALARM, AUDIBLE              APPROPRIATE BUTTON
APPROPRIATE COMMAND         APPROPRIATE MEMORY MAPPED   APPROPRIATE PANEL
                            EIGHT-BIT ... REGISTER
ARRAY OF BUTTONS            ARRIVAL LIGHT               ARRIVAL, ELEVATOR
AUDIBLE ALARM               BEHIND THE PANEL BULB       BOARDING, PASSENGER
BOTTOM FLOOR                BOTTOM FLOOR SUMMONS PANEL  BUILDING
BULB, BEHIND THE PANEL      BULB, PANEL                 BUTTON
BUTTON DEPRESSION           BUTTON ILLUMINATION         BUTTON INTERRUPT SERVICE ROUTINE,
                                                        SUMMONS
BUTTON INTERRUPT, DESTINATION  BUTTON INTERRUPT, SUMMONS  BUTTON LIGHT, SUMMONS
BUTTON NUMBER               BUTTON PANEL, DESTINATION   BUTTON PANEL, FLOOR SUMMONS
BUTTON PRESS                BUTTON PUSH                 BUTTON VECTORED INTERRUPT, DOWN
BUTTON VECTORED INTERRUPT, UP  BUTTON, APPROPRIATE      BUTTON, ARRAY OF
BUTTON, DESTINATION         BUTTON, DOWN                BUTTON, DOWN SUMMONS
BUTTON, STOP                BUTTON, SUMMONS             BUTTON, UP
BUTTON, UP SUMMONS          BUTTONS, ARRAY OF           CAPACITY, ELEVATOR
CERTIFICATION, MANUFACTURER CIRCUIT, ELEVATOR           CIRCUITRY
CIRCUITS                    CLOSED SENSOR SWITCH        COMMAND
COMMAND, APPROPRIATE        COMMAND, COMPUTER           COMMAND, DOWN
COMMAND, INAPPROPRIATE      COMMAND, STOP               COMMAND, UNSAFE
COMMAND, UP                 COMPUTER COMMAND            COMPUTER CONTROLLER
COMPUTER INTERRUPT          COMPUTER OUTPUT             COMPUTER PROGRAM
COMPUTER SCHEDULING         COMPUTER SIGNAL             CONDITIONS, MOVEMENT
CONTEMPORARY MICROCOMPUTER  CONTROL PROGRAM, ELEVATOR   CONTROL SYSTEM, ELEVATOR
CONTROLLER, COMPUTER        CONTROLLER, ELEVATOR        CONTROLS, ELEVATOR MOTOR
CURRENT DIRECTION           CURRENTLY STOPPED ELEVATOR  DEPRESSION, BUTTON
DESTINATION                 DESTINATION BUTTON          DESTINATION BUTTON INTERRUPT
DESTINATION BUTTON PANEL    DESTINATION REQUEST         DIRECTION OF TRAVEL
DIRECTION, CURRENT          DIRECTION, DOWN             DIRECTION, REVERSE
DIRECTION, UP               DOOR, ELEVATOR              DOOR, OPEN
DOWN BUTTON                 DOWN BUTTON VECTORED INTERRUPT  DOWN COMMAND
DOWN DIRECTION              DOWN SUMMONS BUTTON
```

Figure 4.1
Partial listing of
application domain
concepts for the ECS.

case study systems. (Complete lists are available for reference in Appendices C
and D.) As you review these lists, you will notice a profusion of things which may
turn out to become objects or other components of an object-oriented model
(attributes, services, messages, etc.); or, they may be simply irrelevant.

```
ACCEPTED SUBSCRIPTION       ACCOMPANIED PAYMENT         ACCOUNTING DEPARTMENT
ACTUAL EXPIRATION DATE      ADDITIONAL SUBSCRIPTION     ADDRESS, CORPORATE
ADDRESS, CORRESPONDENCE     ADDRESS, HOME               ADDRESS, SUBSCRIPTION
ADVISORS, BOARD OF          AGENCY, SUBSCRIPTION SERVICE  AGREEMENT, DISTRIBUTOR-PUBLISHER
ANNUAL SUBSCRIPTION PRICE   ARTICLE                     ASSOCIATED SITE
AUTHOR                      AUTHOR, CONTRIBUTING        AUTHOR, CURRENT
AUTHOR, PAST                AUTHOR, PROSPECTIVE         AUTHOR, WOULD-BE
AUTHOR-ARTICLE TRACK        BACK ISSUE                  BOARD OF ADVISORS
BROWN WRAPPER, PLAIN        BULK SHIPMENT               BUREAU, SUBSCRIPTION SERVICE
CHECK PAYMENT               COMMISSION, SUBSCRIPTION SERVICE  COMPANY SUBSCRIPTION
COMPLIMENTARY SUBSCRIPTION  COMPLIMENTARY SUBSCRIPTION QUERY  COMPLIMENTARY SUBSCRIPTION REVIEW
COMPLIMENTARY SUBSCRIPTION, CONSTITUENT COPIES          CONTINUED SUBSCRIPTION
DELETED
CONTRIBUTING AUTHOR         CONVERTED SUBSCRIPTION      COPIES, CONSTITUENT
COPY                        CORPORATE ADDRESS           CORPORATE DEPARTMENT
CORPORATION                 CORRESPONDENCE ADDRESS      COST, SHIPPING
COUNTRY                     COUNTRY, FOREIGN            CREDIT CARD ORDER
CREDIT CARD PAYMENT         CURRENT AUTHOR              CUSTOMER
DATABASE                    DATE, ACTUAL EXPIRATION     DATE, EXPIRATION
DATE, EXPIRED               DELETED COMPLIMENTARY SUBSCRIPTION  DEPARTMENT, ACCOUNTING
DEPARTMENT, CORPORATE       DIRECT SUBSCRIPTION         DISCOUNT, SUBSCRIPTION
DISTRIBUTOR                 DISTRIBUTOR TERRITORY       DISTRIBUTOR, EXCLUSIVE
DISTRIBUTOR-PUBLISHER AGREEMENT  DIVISION               EDITOR
EXCLUSIVE DISTRIBUTOR       EXISTING SUBSCRIPTION       EXPIRATION DATE
EXPIRATION DATE, ACTUAL     EXPIRED DATE                EXTENDED SUBSCRIPTION
FINAL MONTH                 FINAL SUBSCRIPTION MONTH    FOREIGN COUNTRY
GURU, RESPECTED             HOME ADDRESS                INDIVIDUAL SUBSCRIPTION
INTERNATIONAL SUBSCRIPTION  INVOICE                     ISSUE
ISSUE TOPIC                 ISSUE, BACK                 ISSUE, NEXT
ISSUE, SAMPLE
```

Figure 4.2
Partial listing of
application domain
concepts for the SBSS.

4.2
Application Domain Concepts for the Elevator Control System (ECS)

For example, in this application domain, are BUTTON and APPROPRIATE BUTTON the same thing? In the written specification in Chapter 2, the user makes reference to both. Is there a subtle difference between them that we need to know about and that we need to reflect in our analysis model? Better we find out now rather than after implementing the ECS.

Let's look at the list in more detail. For example, consider everything related to *elevator*:

```
ELEVATOR, ELEVATOR (NO PASSENGERS), ELEVATOR ARRIVAL,
ELEVATOR CAPACITY, ELEVATOR CIRCUIT, ELEVATOR CONTROL
PROGRAM, ELEVATOR CONTROL SYSTEM, ELEVATOR CONTROLLER,
ELEVATOR DOOR, ELEVATOR INTERIOR, ELEVATOR INTERLOCK,
ELEVATOR INTERRUPT, ELEVATOR MANUFACTURER, ELEVATOR
MECHANISM, ELEVATOR MOTOR, ELEVATOR MOTOR CONTROLS,
ELEVATOR MOVEMENT, ELEVATOR NUMBER, ELEVATOR PANEL,
ELEVATOR PARK, ELEVATOR POSITION, ELEVATOR SCHEDULE,
ELEVATOR SCHEDULER, ELEVATOR SHAFT, ELEVATOR STOP,
ELEVATOR TRAVEL, ELEVATOR VISIT, ELEVATOR WHEEL,
CURRENTLY STOPPED ELEVATOR, STOP ELEVATOR
```

We can eliminate some of these items immediately because they are clearly related to *how* the ECS will be implemented rather than *what* it does. For example, things like *elevator circuit, elevator interrupt* and *elevator wheel* are not essential aspects of the system we're building. Others in the list are clearly important; they will become objects, attributes, structures or services. For example, *elevator capacity, elevator number* and *elevator position* are probably *really* important—but then again, they might simply be attributes of a particular elevator. (e.g., a freight elevator has a different capacity than the passenger elevator, all elevators have a current position, etc.)

We might want to consider *elevator control system, elevator control program* and *elevator controller*, all of which are mentioned in the case study description. Are they the same? Are they simply implementation details? Or, is there some *essential* object which *must* be a part of our system which provides some controlling and coordination intelligence, separate and distinct from the individual elevators? Or, is this function satisfied by the *elevator scheduler* (also mentioned)?

Let's look at another item on this list. For example, many items refer to *buttons*.

```
APPROPRIATE BUTTON, ARRAY OF BUTTON, BUTTON, BUTTON
DEPRESSION, BUTTON ILLUMINATION, BUTTON NUMBER, BUTTON
PRESS, BUTTON PUSH, DESTINATION BUTTON, DESTINATION
BUTTON PANEL, DOWN BUTTON, DOWN BUTTON VECTORED
INTERRUPT, DOWN SUMMONS BUTTON, FLOOR SUMMONS BUTTON
PANEL, STOP BUTTON, SUMMONS BUTTON, SUMMONS BUTTON
INTERRUPT, SUMMONS BUTTON LIGHT, UP BUTTON, UP BUTTON
VECTORED INTERRUPT, UP SUMMONS BUTTON
```

Are all of these distinctions meaningful in the application domain? Or, was the user just sloppy in the words he/she used to describe the problem to us? (Is a *press* really different than a *push*?) Which of these are solely of implementation interest? Is it possible that there might be an object BUTTON which simply has the attributes of *up* and *down*? Or, here's something to think about: maybe there *isn't even a BUTTON object*! Maybe it will turn out that a BUTTON is an aspect of implementation technology, in which case, it should be part of the design model, not the analysis model.

The remaining issues in the list are interesting too. For example, is there any distinction between *passengers* and *would-be passengers*? Well, there might be. In the ECS of the future, there could be Passive Infrared Detectors (PIRs) located in each of the floor lobbies. These detectors could provide the system with a rough estimate of how many people are waiting for an elevator. The ECS would then know if it should send more than one elevator (or, if it should ignore the request of a single would-be passenger to service the request of a whole crowd!) You may ignore this future enhancement for the time being.

For the moment, we'll ignore such future enhancements; but, in the next chapter, we will consider these issues in more detail to establish a final list of objects. In addition, we'll consider some perspectives on object discovery that were discussed in Chapter 3.

4.3 Application Domain Concepts for the *Small Bytes* Subscription System (SBSS)

As with the ECS, our initial list of words and phrases derived from the *Small Bytes* description contains many more items than will eventually be analysis components. We made this list as thorough as possible so as not to omit any subtle or obscure objects, as well as to establish the semantic level used in this application domain. For example, in this application domain, are SUBSCRIPTION and ACCEPTED SUBSCRIPTION the same? (Would a subscription ever be rejected? Even from Bill Gates?) The user makes reference to both. Is there a subtle difference between them that we need to know about? We'd better find out now rather than after implementing the SBSS.

Let's look at the list in more detail. First of all, the following is a list of everything related to *subscription*:

```
ACCEPTED SUBSCRIPTION, ADDITIONAL SUBSCRIPTION, ANNUAL
SUBSCRIPTION PRICE, COMPANY SUBSCRIPTION, COMPLIMENTARY
SUBSCRIPTION, COMPLIMENTARY SUBSCRIPTION QUERY,
COMPLIMENTARY SUBSCRIPTION REVIEW, CONTINUED
SUBSCRIPTION, CONVERTED SUBSCRIPTION, DELETED
COMPLIMENTARY SUBSCRIPTION, DIRECT SUBSCRIPTION, EXISTING
SUBSCRIPTION, EXTENDED SUBSCRIPTION, FINAL SUBSCRIPTION
MONTH, INDIVIDUAL SUBSCRIPTION, INTERNATIONAL
SUBSCRIPTION, MULTIPLE SUBSCRIPTION, NEW SUBSCRIPTION,
NORTH AMERICAN SUBSCRIPTION, PAID SUBSCRIPTION, RECEIVED
SUBSCRIPTION, STANDARD SUBSCRIPTION PRICE, SUBSCRIPTION,
SUBSCRIPTION ADDRESS, SUBSCRIPTION DISCOUNT, SUBSCRIPTION
NAME, SUBSCRIPTION OFFER, SUBSCRIPTION PERIOD,
SUBSCRIPTION PRICE, SUBSCRIPTION PRICE PRO-RATING,
SUBSCRIPTION RECORD, SUBSCRIPTION RENEWAL, SUBSCRIPTION
SERVICE AGENCY, SUBSCRIPTION SERVICE BUREAU, SUBSCRIPTION
SERVICE COMMISSION, SUBSCRIPTION SHIPPING TITLE,
SUBSCRIPTION TERM, SUBSCRIPTION YEAR, TRIAL SUBSCRIPTION
```

We can eliminate some of these items immediately because they are clearly redundant. For example, things like *subscription service agency* and *subscription service bureau* are no doubt the same … or are they?! Others are clearly important, but will not become objects since they don't satisfy our various criteria. They may, however, suggest object attributes, structures or services. For example, *subscription price, subscription address* and *final subscription month* are probably *really* important—but they might simply be attributes of a subscription.

The user talks about COPY, as well as ISSUE. Is a copy just one *instance* of an issue? Or, are they the same thing? There are COMPANY SUBSCRIPTIONS—but CORPORATE ADDRESSes! Is there a fine distinction here to which we should be sensitive? What makes someone a RESPECTED GURU and why is he/she treated any differently than just a plain SUBSCRIBER?

Consider the remainder of this list. There are some interesting issues which arise. For example, note that there are several items such as AUTHOR-ARTICLE TRACK, RETAIL-PRICE TRACK and PRIMARY-SUBSCRIBER TRACK. How did they arise? What function do they serve? Should they become objects?

4.4 Final Comments

Several points should be apparent at this stage in the development of our OOA model:

1. Initial identification of OOA model components, including classes-objects, can be carried out in an orderly fashion. This assumes that the analyst has access to a reasonably detailed and thorough description of the user's application domain and/or requirements. On the other hand, if the user says, "Ummm…I think I'd like a general-purpose information retrieval system, but I'm not at all sure what I mean by that," it will be very difficult to identify application domain concepts with any confidence. In the absence of *any* concrete information from the user, the analyst may have to begin with a prototype; on the other hand, we don't think it's unreasonable to expect at least as much information about the problem domain as was provided in the case study descriptions in Chapter 2.

2. Identifying all of the application domain concepts—even in a tentative fashion—is a non-trivial process. It's not simply a matter of writing down the first ten nouns that come to mind; it requires careful study and thought. It has been our observation, in fact, that simply writing down the first ten nouns that come to mind is highly biased by who does the writing.

3. A typical user description is likely to be filled with information that is redundant, ambiguous, confusing and/or contradictory. We can attempt to sort things out, using the LIA technique, as discussed in Chapter 3; but inevitably, we will need to confront the user with a number of concepts that appear to be highly similar to confirm our tentative decision to consolidate them into a single object-oriented construct.

4. Even though we may have winnowed our initial list down substantially at this point, we should not expect that we will have a truly refined list of objects. Chapter 5 will discuss some techniques that will allow us to refine the initial candidates to a reasonable subset that can be used as the basis for

subsequent OOA modeling. It is highly likely that analysis components, including objects and classes, will continue to be refined even further into the process as we continue to identify attributes, services and other components of the model.

5. An initial list of application domain concepts provides us with a useful indication of the scope of a project. For example, it is evident from this initial analysis that the *Small Bytes* system does not have the capability for producing payroll checks. Also it is evident that the ECS does not have a requirement (or capability) for recording or logging any aspect of its operational behavior. Documentation specialists often remark, "If it ain't written down, it don't exist." The OOA analyst would paraphrase this by saying, "If a requirement don't have an object, then it ain't a requirement."

 *Key Points*

▲ We expect user requirements to contain redundant, ambiguous, confusing and contradictory information—that's why we do analysis!

▲ We attempt to identify *all* concepts and let the user decide which may or may not be relevant. (It's not the job of the analyst to decide if a "sociopathic passenger" is or is not important for the user's view of an elevator control system.)

▲ The linguistic techniques applied in this chapter provide us with a starting point for finding objects, but further refinement is necessary.

CHAPTER 5
Class and Object Refinement

The whole of science is nothing more than a refinement of every day thinking.

— Albert Einstein

5.1 Introduction and Discussion

In Chapters 3 and 4, we discussed various approaches for identifying an initial list of candidate objects and other constructs for an OOA model. We will now refine that list by creating an initial OOA model Object-Class Layer. The final set of objects will form the basis for all subsequent work in this book.

The PFA lists created in the previous chapter (see Appendices C and D) can be unwieldy; consequently, we have found it useful to convert these lists into *OOA/OOD worksheets* (see Figure 3.3). These worksheets allow each identified application domain concept to be allocated to a particular object-oriented model component. Worksheets for the two case studies are included in Appendices E and F.

The refinement process involves more than simply reviewing identified application domain concepts and allocating them to model components. As discussed in Chapter 3, we will also use *3-View Modeling* (3VM) for finding objects and refining them. It will become apparent, we believe, that creating one or more 3VM components is enormously useful for object-finding.

For example, the event-response view identifies happenings or occurrences to which your system must respond. For each happening or occurrence, which of the candidate objects recognizes the happening or occurrence, and which of the candidate objects produces the systems response? As we pointed out in Chapter 3, every object must be either an *event recognizer* or *event responder*. If an object neither recognizes the occurrence of some event, nor participates in the production of a response to some event, the object simply does not belong in the system.

Similarly, it is quite likely that a conventional entity-relationship diagram (data view) will provide some useful insights. This is particularly valuable for conventional business data processing applications such as *Small Bytes*, but typically less important for real-time systems like the ECS. When the authors examined the two case studies closely, it was the entity-relationship diagram that provided the inspiration for a number of objects that had been overlooked during our initial review.

It is also important to consider the application domain within which you're building your OOA model. If there are a number of (seemingly) unrelated things going on, perhaps the system should be analyzed as multiple sub-systems. It might be helpful to draw one or more context diagrams (process view), and use them to help clarify and consolidate your choice of classes and objects.

As part of the refinement process, we may discover concepts which the user did not identify during the initial analysis; these new concepts may become objects. We may also choose to clarify our analysis by renaming concepts so as to avoid ambiguity or confusion.

For each of your final objects, it's a good idea to write a brief (25 words or less) description. This description should be crafted so as to unambiguously specify class membership. You may choose to specify inclusion criteria, exclusion criteria, object enumeration, etc.

5.2 3-View Models (3VMs)

A context diagram for the ECS is given in Figure 5.1. This diagram was constructed using conventional *structured analysis* techniques (see [3]).

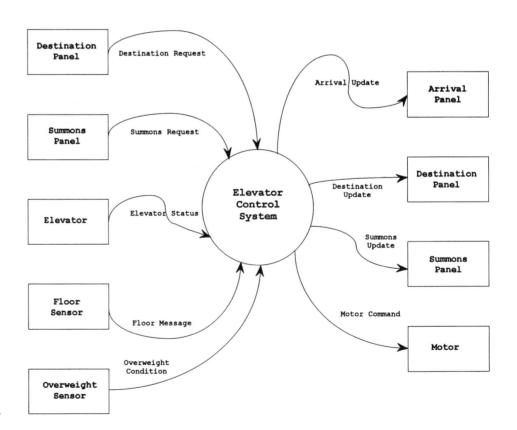

Figure 5.1 Context diagram for the ECS.

The context diagram allows us to establish the scope of the ECS independently of object-oriented considerations. The external entities on the context diagram strongly suggest objects. The flows on the context diagram suggest inter-object communication (i.e., messages).

5.2.1
3-View Models
for the Elevator
Control System (ECS)

When referring to Figure 5.1, many of our students are surprised to find that *passenger* is not an external entity on the context diagram for the ECS. This is related to the concept of the *semantic level* mentioned in Chapter 4. Although *passenger* certainly is in the application domain of *elevator systems*, it is not in the application domain of *elevator control systems*. That is, the elevator control system which we are specifying is oblivious to what the elevator may carry. This refinement of the scope of the proposed system is a direct result of creating the context diagram. Again, we must make the point that basic analysis tools (in this case the context diagram) can be of great value in OOA.

Figure 5.2 presents the data view of the ECS (in the form of an entity-relationship diagram). Not surprisingly, this model is trivial. We would not expect the ECS to store significant or complex data. We observe that the ECS must store information about floor arrivals, pending summons and destination requests. Primarily the ECS is reactive and so we would expect the event-response model to be its most interesting view.

Although we'll discuss this later, it's worth mentioning at this point that FLOOR is usually an issue when building 3VMs. A great deal of debate centers around whether or not FLOOR need to be identified in the data model (Figure 5.2). Clearly, SUMMONS and DESTINATION represent stored data requirements of the ECS; these entities on the entity-relationship diagram are consistent with the external entities SUMMONS PANEL and DESTINATION PANEL, respectively, on the context diagram. However, FLOOR is not an equivalent to FLOOR SENSOR. In fact, is it possible to build an ECS *without* storing FLOOR information? More about this in Section 5.2.

The event-response model for the ECS (see Figure 5.3) identifies all the happenings or occurrences for which the system must have a pre-planned response and which:

- Occur at a specific point in time
- Are perceivable by the system

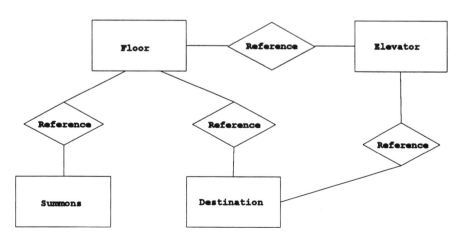

Figure 5.2
Entity-relationship
diagram for the ECS.

1. ELEVATOR SUMMONED	A. Summons panel updated. B. Elevator scheduled in accordance with elevator schedule policy.
2. DESTINATION REQUESTED	A. Destination panel updated. B. Elevator scheduled in accordance with elevator schedule policy.
3. ELEVATOR ARRIVES AT SCHEDULED FLOOR	A. Arrival panel updated. B. Destination panel updated. C. Summons panel updated. D. Elevator stops at floor.
4. ELEVATOR ARRIVES AT NON-SCHEDULED FLOOR	A. Arrival panel updated
5. ELEVATOR BECOMES READY	A. Elevator dispatched in accordance with elevator schedule policy.
6. ELEVATOR BECOMES OVERWEIGHT	A. Elevator dispatching disabled.
7. ELEVATOR BECOMES NOT-OVERWEIGHT	A. Elevator dispatching enabled.

Figure 5.3
Event-response model for the ECS.

As anticipated, we have found the event-response model to be of enormous value in this refinement process. A complete event-response model, in many respects, fully defines the proposed system. If we account for every event and every response—we're done! There are, however, three areas which have proven difficult for our students.

First, to what level of detail should events be specified. Our pat answer to this is that the "level of detail should be consistent with the `semantic level' of the application domain and the user." This rather nebulous statement simply means that when the user is shown a candidate event, he or she should say, "Yup, that makes sense!" Related to this issue is that of the complexity of stated events. We have a useful guideline for this issue. In general, we've found it better to have *non-conditional* responses rather than *unqualified* events. A good example of this are events 3 and 4 in Figure 5.3. The *single* event, "Elevator Arrives at Floor," could be stated. This, however, would necessitate a conditional response (if floor is scheduled, then…else…). We find events with non-conditional responses to be preferable.

The second area of difficulty for our students is the fundamentally subjective nature of the event-response model. The event-response model represents the user's view of the world. Like it or not, different users, different worlds, different event-response models. We like to tease our students with the following question: Would "Earthquake Occurs" be an event for the ECS? The immediate response is always "No! Of course not!" But why not? Verify the three criteria for an event. Does an earthquake occur at a specific point in time? Within the application domain of elevator control systems, we say yes (even though this may be an abstraction). Is the ECS capable of detecting the occurrence of the event? Again, the immediate response is "No." We differ. In fact, if an earthquake occurred, we would expect that all of the 160 floor sensors would trigger simultaneously. That simply is not possible in the usual course of operation of the ECS. We will there-

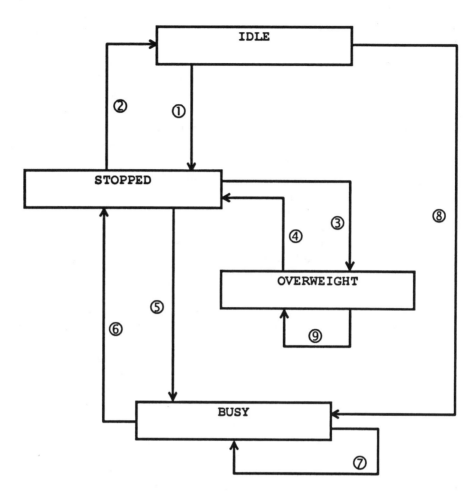

Figure 5.4
State-transition
diagram
for the ECS.

fore consider the simultaneous triggering of all 160 floor sensors to be an earth-quake. (Our assumption is that the ECS will have been disabled prior to any demolition of the building.)

Okay, so why isn't "Earthquake Occurs" an event for the ECS. The reason is that it fails the third criterion. There is not a *pre-planned* system response should the event occur. Clearly, however, a different user might decide that there is a response—and then "Earthquake Occurs" would be included in the event-response model.

The third area of difficulty for our students is applying the principle of *Separation of Concerns* (Chapter 1) to this context. Note that the ECS event-response model makes no reference to buttons or lights. We view these as being within the *implementation technology*. Could we have elevators without buttons and lights? Absolutely! Any number of other technologies could be used to interface with an elevator. So, rather than have an event such as "Summons Button Depressed," we have "Elevator Summoned." Buttons and lights belong on our *OOD model*, which we'll discuss in subsequent chapters.

One final comment about the event-response model. Note event 5 in Figure 5.3, "Elevator Becomes Ready." This event did not appear on the authors' original event-response model. It was not until we had completed the first iteration of our analysis and design that we recognized the need for this event. The user told us that the ECS had no way to manage the doors. In particular, it had no way of knowing that the doors had been secured and the elevator was ready to be moved. On a real project, we would identify this problem and discuss possible solutions with the user. In this case, (we assume that) the user agrees and decides to add an additional interrupt signal—one which informs the ECS that an elevator has become ready. Clearly the virtue of this process is that we identified the problem *before* we built the system!

(We did have one student vociferously insist that the "Elevator becomes ready" event was *really* unnecessary. That all the ECS should do is signal to the elevator motor to start and rely on the elevator mechanisms to assure that the motor did not actually start until the doors were closed. We argued that this approach violated the user's stated concern for safety. This alternative approach also made it more difficult to handle overweight conditions. Nevertheless, the student was unconvinced.)

We have alluded to other forms or representations of 3VMs which may be useful in understanding the behavior of a proposed system. In the above section we used the event-response model to represent a form of the control view. For the ECS, it is useful to also represent the control view with a state-transition diagram, such as the one shown in Figure 5.4. Readers who are familiar with state-transition diagrams may wish to refer to Appendix G for a more detailed description of this diagram. The usefulness of the state-transition diagram will become more obvious as we explore the dynamic behavior of the ECS.

Another form of 3VM is the *decision table*. The decision table is a form of process view. For the ECS, it is useful to represent processing associated with the scheduling and dispatching of elevators in the form of a decision table. Figure 5.5 illustrates a portion of the decision table for the ECS; the complete decision table is discussed in Appendix G.

The 3VMs for the ECS are included in Appendix G.

5.2.2 3-View Models for the *Small Bytes* Subscription System (SBSS)

A key insight in the analysis of the SBSS is that there are three separate and distinct activities described by the user. Clearly the principal activity is subscription management. However, the system also performs editorial management functions. And, the SBSS also performs special orders processing. Viewing the *Small Bytes* system as three sub-systems helps to manage the complexity of the system.

Figure 5.6 shows the context diagram for the SBSS.

One issue which frequently comes up when discussing this context diagram is the monthly issue flow from the SBSS to *Recipient*. Students frequently suggest that the system actually produce a monthly issue mailing list or mailing labels. And that these actually go to a printer or distributor. All this is true. And it's another good example of the principle of *Separation of Concerns* discussed in Chapter 1. At the *analysis* level, we simply don't care *how* issues get to recipients. The *fundamental* (or essential) requirement is that, in fact, issues get to recipients.

Figure 5.7 presents the data view for the SBSS (in the form of an entity-relationship diagram). Not surprisingly, this model is considerably more complex

DPA	DPB	DPC	SPU	SPD	CD	SD	FLR SCHD	USD
T	T	T	T	T	UP	UP	YES	UP
T	T	T	T	T	UP	NO	YES	UP
T	T	T	T	T	DN	DN	YES	DN
T	T	T	T	T	DN	NO	YES	DN
T	T	T	T	F	UP	UP	YES	UP
T	T	T	T	F	UP	NO	YES	UP
T	T	T	T	F	DN	DN	YES	DN
T	T	T	T	F	DN	NO	YES	DN
T	T	T	F	T	UP	UP	YES	UP
T	T	T	F	T	UP	NO	YES	UP
T	T	T	F	T	DN	DN	YES	DN
T	T	T	F	T	DN	NO	YES	DN
T	T	T	F	F	UP	UP	YES	UP
T	T	T	F	F	UP	NO	YES	UP
T	T	T	F	F	DN	DN	YES	DN
T	T	T	F	F	DN	NO	YES	DN
T	T	F	T	T	UP	UP	YES	UP
T	T	F	T	T	UP	NO	YES	UP
T	T	F	T	T	DN	DN	YES	DN

Figure 5.5
Partial decision table
for the ECS.

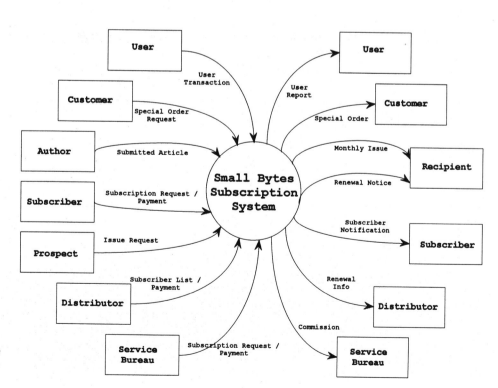

Figure 5.6
Context diagram for the
SBSS.

than the corresponding model for the ECS. We would expect that the SBSS must store significantly more data.

Glancing at Figure 5.7, it would seem that a number of the identified entities would be candidate objects. More about this later.

It is not obvious to many of our students that the event-response model for the SBSS provides useful information. This is probably due to the fact that this tool has been used primarily by real-time analysts and not typically by MIS analysts. In fact, we have found the event-response model to be very useful in the analysis of non-real-time systems.

Figure 5.8 shows the event-response model for the SBSS. A few observations are in order. First, as with the previous 3VMs, this model was constructed independently of any OOA considerations. That is, independent of analysis (or design, or implementation) techniques, *any* SBSS must recognize when subscriptions are requested and produce a number of responses as indicated in this model.

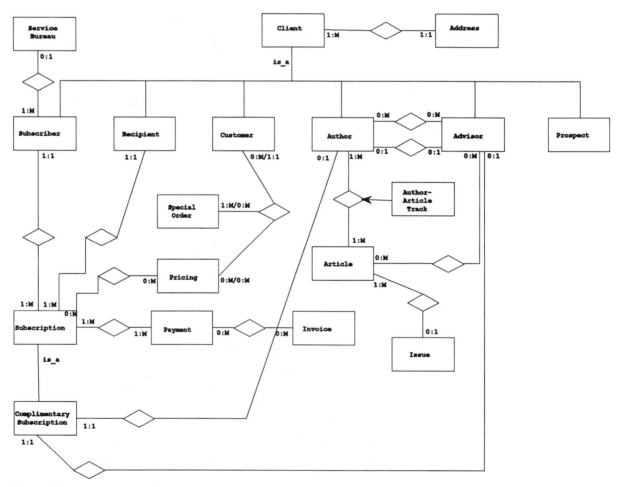

Figure 5.7
Entity-relationship diagram for the SBSS.

Secondly, a number of these events are temporal, i.e., they represent elapses of time (for example, *time to review "comp list"*). These events may suggest objects which are not evident from the other two model views.

Finally, this model could be extended significantly, if we incorporated trivial events. Such events might include things such as address change requests, the creation or deletion of new distributors, etc. We choose to postpone these considerations until the design activity.

1. PAID SUBSCRIPTION REQUESTED	A. CREATE NEW SUBSCRIPTION RECORD.
	B. CREATE NEW SUBSCRIBER RECORD AS REQUIRED.
	  B.1 CREATE OR UPDATE ADDRESS RECORD AS REQUIRED.
	C. CREATE NEW RECIPIENT RECORD AS REQUIRED.
	  C.1 CREATE OR UPDATE ADDRESS RECORD AS REQUIRED.
	D. ESTABLISH SUBSCRIPTION PRICING.
	E. POST PAYMENT AS REQUIRED.
	  E.1 ISSUE INVOICE AS REQUIRED.
	F. NOTIFY SERVICE BUREAU OF SUBSCRIPTION AS REQUIRED.
	G. ESTABLISH EXPIRATION DATE FOR SUBSCRIPTION.
	H. ESTABLISH EXPIRATION WARNING DATE FOR SUBSCRIPTION.

2. COMPLIMENTARY SUBSCRIPTION REQUESTED	A. CREATE NEW SUBSCRIPTION RECORD AS REQUIRED.
	B. CREATE NEW SUBSCRIBER RECORD AS REQUIRED.
	  B.1 CREATE OR UPDATE ADDRESS RECORD AS REQUIRED.
	C. CREATE NEW RECIPIENT RECORD AS REQUIRED.
	  C.1 CREATE OR UPDATE ADDRESS RECORD AS REQUIRED.

3. PAYMENT RECEIVED	A. POST PAYMENT AS REQUIRED. B. ISSUE INVOICE AS REQUIRED.
4. TIME TO SEND RENEWAL NOTICE	A. INITIATE NOTIFICATION SEQUENCE.
5. SUBSCRIPTION TERMINATES	A. DISCONTINUE SUBSCRIPTION.

Figure 5.8
Event-response model for the SBSS.

6. SUBSCRIPTION RENEWED	A. CREATE NEW SUBSCRIPTION RECORD. B. UPDATE SUBSCRIBER ADDRESS RECORD AS REQUIRED. C. UPDATE RECIPIENT ADDRESS RECORD AS REQUIRED. D. ESTABLISH RENEWAL PRICING. E. POST PAYMENT AS REQUIRED. E.1 ISSUE INVOICE AS REQUIRED. F. NOTIFY SERVICE BUREAU OF SUBSCRIPTION AS REQUIRED. G. ESTABLISH EXPIRATION DATE FOR SUBSCRIPTION. H. ESTABLISH EXPIRATION WARNING DATE FOR SUBSCRIPTION.
7. TIME TO REVIEW "COMP" LIST	A. TERMINATE COMPLIMENTARY SUBSCRIPTION AS REQUIRED.

8. SPECIAL ORDER RECEIVED	A. CREATE NEW CUSTOMER RECORD AS REQUIRED.
	   B.1 CREATE OR UPDATE ADDRESS RECORD AS REQUIRED.
	C. ENTER SHIPPING ADDRESS.
	D. ESTABLISH SPECIAL ORDER PRICING.
	E. POST PAYMENT AS REQUIRED.
	   E.1 ISSUE INVOICE AS REQUIRED.

9. ARTICLE RECEIVED	A. CREATE NEW ARTICLE RECORD. B. CREATE NEW AUTHOR RECORD(S) AS REQUIRED. B.1 CREATE NEW ADDRESS RECORD AS REQUIRED. C. UPDATE AUTHOR AUTHOR-ARTICLE TRACK.
10. ARTICLE ACCEPTED FOR PUBLICATION	A. TENTATIVELY SCHEDULE PUBLICATION ISSUE. B. ENTER COMPLIMENTARY SUBSCRIPTION(S). C. UPDATE AUTHOR AUTHOR-ARTICLE TRACK.
11. ARTICLE PUBLISHED	A. UPDATE AUTHOR AUTHOR-ARTICLE TRACK.
12. PROSPECT IDENTIFIED	B. CREATE NEW PROSPECT RECORD AS REQUIRED. B.1 CREATE NEW ADDRESS RECORD AS REQUIRED.

Figure 5.8 *(cont.)*

The 3VMs for the SBSS are included in Appendix H.

5.3 Refinement of Classes and Objects

We will now consolidate the various techniques introduced in thus far as we establish a final selection of objects for the two case study systems.

We will begin with the OOA/OOD worksheets (Appendices E and F); these worksheets serve as a useful guide. At this point, we will concern ourselves only with the identification of objects. The 3VMs (Appendices G and H) identify system requirements which must be met independently of object considerations. So, we now review these models vis-à-vis the worksheets. Entities on the entity-relationship diagram, for example, represent data which are stored by the system. Is there a corresponding item on the worksheet which, if identified as an object, could store those data? If so, we will identify that item as an object. This is an iterative process, so we won't worry about getting it perfect our first time through!

Continuing this process, we examine the event-response model. Are there events which correspond to (or are at least similar to) items on the worksheet. If so, these can become event-recognizer objects. Similarly evaluate the response side of the model.

Note again the external entities on the context diagram. Are they related to items on the worksheet? If so, they may represent objects which serve an external interface role.

We have not constructed data-flow diagrams for the case study systems. If we had, we would look at the primitive processes and consider which items on the worksheet those processes could be identified with.

As an illustration of this process, a portion of the partially completed OOA/OOD worksheets is shown in Figure 5.9.

It's useful to go through the OOA/OOD worksheet one time, evaluating each item vis-à-vis the 3VMs, to identify a first set of objects. We may then apply other criteria to finalize our selection. It's useful at this point to conduct a group meeting.

One activity should be to *challenge* each candidate object. If you're performing this activity as part of a team, you may find it useful to have various members of your group assume the roles of different objects; have them justify their existence as a distinct object (please, no fisticuffs!). Refine the objects identified above; you should be able to come to some consensus on most of the candidate objects. Those which are controversial can be set aside.

For each candidate object ask yourselves these questions: Does each object do work? Do other objects ask this object to do work? Does each object store information? Do other objects ask this object to report on its stored information? Does each object encapsulate a secret? Does each object have a life cycle that describes its birth, its various states during its lifetime and its eventual demise? Finally, if you were to describe this candidate object to an application domain expert, would he/she *immediately* understand its significance? For a given candidate object, not all of these questions need to be answered in the affirmative, but they can't all be answered in the negative.

For a moment, stop thinking objects and start thinking systems. Write down a list of all happenings or occurrences which occur outside the system you are specifying, which your system recognizes and to which your system must respond. (It may be useful to create a *context diagram* for the system you're specifying.) For each happening or occurrence on this list, which of the candidate objects recognizes the happening or occurrence? Which of the candidate objects produces the systems response? Are all of the candidate objects accounted for? Do additional

OOA/OOD WORKSHEET

Elevator Control System

ITEM	(0)	(1)	(2)	(3)	(4)	(5)	(6)	(7)	(8)	COMMENTS
ACTUAL PASSENGER	X									We shall not distinguish between various types of passengers (actual vs. would-be) for this version of the ECS.
APPROPRIATE BUTTON	X									The use of the word "appropriate" is not a technical distinction in this application domain.
APPROPRIATE COMMAND	X									
APPROPRIATE MEMORY MAPPED EIGHT-BIT ... REGISTER	X									
APPROPRIATE PANEL	X									
ARRAY OF BUTTONS	X									Not meaningful by itself. We will only consider buttons as part of a designated "panel."
ARRIVAL LIGHT		X								This will be included in an ARRIVAL PANEL object-class.
AUDIBLE ALARM	X									Outside the scope of the ECS.
BEHIND THE PANEL BULB	X									Ditto.
BOTTOM FLOOR				X						Probably an attribute of FLOOR.
BOTTOM FLOOR SUMMONS PANEL				X						Probably an attribute of SUMMON PANEL.
BUILDING	X									Outside the scope of the ECS.
BUTTON							X			BUTTON is an aspect of how we interface with the ECS.
BUTTON DEPRESSION	X									Too general to be useful.
BUTTON ILLUMINATION							X			Like BUTTON, it is an aspect of how we interface with the ECS.
BUTTON NUMBER	X									Too general to be useful.
BUTTON PRESS	X									Ditto.

(0) Not applicable. Possibly irrelevant, outside the context of the system being specified, etc.
(1) Possible object-class.
(2) Possibly part of sub-type/super-type structure. Includes Gen-Spec and Whole-Part relationships.
(3) Possibly describes an object-class attribute or instance relationship.
(4) Possibly describes an object service.

(5) Implementation specific. Possible Problem Domain Component item.
(6) Possible Human Interaction Component item.
(7) Possible Task Management Component item.
(8) Possible Data Management Component item.

Figure 5.9 (a)
Partial OOA/OOD worksheet for ECS.

objects need to be created? Are there candidate objects which are neither involved with the recognition of happenings or occurrences nor with the producing of system responses? If so, what purpose do they serve?

Again, suspend object think mentality for a moment and revert back to a systems think approach. Does your system interface with other persons or systems? (If not, then save time, trouble and money—don't bother building it!) Have you identified those objects which mediate these interfaces (refer to the context diagram)? Warning: Don't confuse these objects with objects which *implement* the interface (e.g., network objects, GUI objects, etc.)—we'll deal with the latter objects later!

Challenge each candidate object by role-playing. Eliminate the candidate object and ask yourself, "So what?" "What piece of my system goes away, doesn't work, becomes useless, etc. if I throw out this object?" And ultimately ask yourself, "If this object becomes a re-usable chunk of bits in a box, will it in fact get reused? Does it serve sufficiently general purposes now *and in the future* so that it can become a part of the system I'm building today as well as the systems I plan to build in the future?"

OOA/OOD WORKSHEET

Small Bytes Subscription System

ITEM	(0)	(1)	(2)	(3)	(4)	(5)	(6)	(7)	(8)	COMMENTS
ACCEPTED SUBSCRIPTION				X						An attribute of SUBSCRIPTION
ACCOMPANIED PAYMENT	X									We do not distinguish between different types of payments.
ACCOUNTING DEPARTMENT	X									Outside the application domain of the SBSS.
ACTUAL EXPIRATION DATE				X						Attribute of SUBSCRIPTION.
ADDITIONAL SUBSCRIPTION			X	X						Possible attribute of SUBSCRIPTION or possibly suggests a sub-type/super-type structure.
ANNUAL SUBSCRIPTION PRICE				X						Attribute of SUBSCRIPTION.
ARTICLE		X								
ASSOCIATED SITE				X						Attribute of SITE.
AUTHOR		X								
AUTHOR-ARTICLE TRACK								X		
BACK ISSUE				X						Attribute of SPECIAL ORDER.
BOARD OF ADVISORS	X									Outside the SBSS application domain.
BULK SHIPMENT				X						Possible attribute of SUBSCRIPTION?
CHECK PAYMENT				X						Attribute of PAYMENT.
COMPANY SUBSCRIPTION				X						Attribute of SUBSCRIPTION.
COMPLIMENTARY SUBSCRIPTION				X						Attribute of SUBSCRIPTION.
COMPLIMENTARY SUBSCRIPTION QUERY									X	One of several types of database queries.
COMPLIMENTARY SUBSCRIPTION REVIEW		X								Possible event-related object-class.
CONSTITUENT COPIES	X									Too general to be useful.
CONTINUED SUBSCRIPTION				X						Attribute of SUBSCRIPTION.
CONTRIBUTING AUTHOR	X									We do not distinguish between different types of authors.

(0) Not applicable. Possibly irrelevant, outside the context of the system being specified, etc.
(1) Possible object-class.
(2) Possibly part of sub-type/super-type structure. Includes Gen-Spec and Whole-Part relationships.
(3) Possibly describes an object-class attribute or instance relationship.
(4) Possibly describes an object service.

(5) Implementation specific. Possible Problem Domain Component item.
(6) Possible Human Interaction Component item.
(7) Possible Task Management Component item.
(8) Possible Data Management Component item.

Figure 5.9 (b)
Partial OOA/OOD worksheet for SBSS.

Document the results of this activity. You may simply list your initial set of objects (drawing is not required at this time). Each object should be accompanied by a brief (25 words or less) justification. No further documentation is required at this time.

Please note that, as this is an iterative process, we might add to and subtract from this list as new objects become apparent and existing ones are found to be useless. This is almost certain to happen as we begin identifying detailed attributes, services and messages associated with each object. This refined list of object names will usually differ from the list produced in Chapter 4, especially if we have had a chance to clarify the meaning of application-domain-specific names with the user. And, if you have been working on your own, the names you have developed at this point may be different than ours—and perhaps even better! However, we hope you'll be able to accept our list as the basis for the modeling effort that continues in the subsequent chapters of this book.

**5.3.1
Final Selection of
Objects for the ECS**

In this section we present our final set of objects for the ECS.

ARRIVAL EVENT

This object was derived directly from the event-response model. It encapsulates all of the various services which must be performed when an elevator arrives at a floor (whether or not it is a scheduled floor). We chose to establish this as an *event object* rather than encapsulate these various services into a FLOOR object.

ARRIVAL PANEL

This object is a re-naming of our original ARRIVAL LIGHT. We felt that this is a better name since it is technology-independent.

DESTINATION EVENT

Again, this object is derived from the event-response model. It encapsulates the secret of how a destination request is perceived; we also felt that this was a better name.

DESTINATION PANEL

As discussed above, buttons are clearly part of a (implementation-related) person-machine interface technology. In fact, some elevators might be operated by robots (which transmit destination requests), or passive infrared detectors.

Also note that DESTINATION PANEL tells us which *elevator* to send to that destination. (Sending elevator 3 to the 10th floor because destination button 10 was pushed in elevator 2 would create problems.)

ELEVATOR

We choose to regard any type of controller object (e.g., ELEVATOR CONTROLLER or SCHEDULER) as implementation-related—we will incorporate such objects into our OOD model.

This tends to be an area of intense debate with our students. However, since we're writing the book, we get the last word! You *can* have elevator control systems without centralized controllers or schedulers. Therefore, any centralized controller or scheduler is not an *essential* requirement—it is an implementation issue.

The reader should note carefully what we *did not* say. We did not say that you can have an elevator control system without *controlling* or *scheduling*. Clearly you must control and schedule elevators. We simply said that it is not necessary to have *centralized* control or scheduling.

At an analysis level, this object encapsulates data required for the management and control of elevators and it also encapsulates various services which report the current status of the elevators.

ELEVATOR MOTOR

ELEVATOR MOTOR is interesting. Although it encapsulates various control services, one might argue that those services could just as well be encapsulated within the ELEVATOR object. Indeed, introducing an ELEVATOR MOTOR object into the OOA model might seem too implementation-oriented. We decided to make ELEVATOR MOTOR a separate object for two reasons. First of all, our application domain expert assures us that in all present and *future* elevators, we do and *will* have motors (i.e., motors are *essential requirements*). However, the technology of these motors is changing rapidly. Identifying an ELEVATOR MOTOR object gives us a convenient place to encapsulate secrets about motor technology so that our control system is as extensible as possible.

FLOOR

We decided to make the FLOOR responsible for holding the secret of how to dispatch an elevator.

In this approach, where floors dispatch elevators, an important concept is which floor "owns" the elevator, i.e., which floor can control the elevator. A floor is said to "own" an elevator(s) if the elevator(s) is/are currently at or arriving at that floor. Our protocol for controlling elevators dictates that the status direction of any elevator may be updated <u>only</u> by the floor which currently owns that elevator. As elevators move upwards and downwards, their control is passed off from floor to floor in a relay fashion. In object-oriented terms, this implies that an elevator may be controlled only by a single instance of FLOOR. We have attempted to illustrate this scheme in Figure 5.10; an elevator moving down from floor 40, is successively controlled by floors 39, 38, ... until its arrival at floor 34.

Over the years of presenting this material to our students, there has been a good deal of debate concerning FLOOR. (This will probably be the case with some objects on your own projects.) Initially, the authors decided *not* to have FLOOR as an object class; it seemed that the only attribute of a floor is its floor number, which could just as easily have been incorporated into some other object. In that version of the ECS, the secret of how elevators are dispatched was encapsulated within ELEVATOR. In fact, the authors considered themselves clever by *not* having

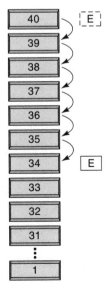

Figure 5.10
Elevator control
scheme.

a FLOOR object. In this version of the ECS, however, elevators negotiate between themselves as to who should respond to summons or destination requests.

A walkthrough of this version of the ECS caught the authors by surprise. Under certain, obscure circumstances, the ECS could exhibit a phenomenon called runaway elevators. That is, an elevator could be dispatched to a summons, for some reason that summons could be addressed by a different elevator, and the original elevator would now be moving upwards or downwards—and would never stop.

Creating a FLOOR object solves the problem of runaway elevators and allows the dispatching of elevators to be handled in what we believe is a more elegant fashion.

One final comment on FLOOR. Had the original specification of the system indicated that some floors were different than other floors, then there would have been no question about having a FLOOR object. For example, if some floors have front and back doors, or if some floors have restricted access, then these attributes would be encapsulated in FLOOR. There would still be the issue, of course, as to where one would encapsulate the secret of elevator dispatching.

OVERWEIGHT SENSOR

The same argument that we applied to ELEVATOR MOTOR applies here too. Rather than simply have the ELEVATOR object encapsulate sensor technology secrets, we choose to establish a separate object.

SUMMONS EVENT

See discussion above for DESTINATION EVENT.

SUMMONS PANEL

See discussion above for DESTINATION PANEL.

Now let's examine some items which did *not* become objects in our model, and why they failed our selection criteria:

Building

It's simply outside the application domain of the ECS as stated by the user. If there were a requirement that the ECS be installed in multiple buildings, perhaps with different floors or different numbers of elevators, BUILDING would be an appropriate place to encapsulate such attributes.

Button (all kinds)

As discussed above, a significant insight into the problem is that buttons are clearly part of a (implementation-related) person-machine interface technology. In fact, some elevators are operated by robots (which transmit destination requests), or passive infrared detectors. BUTTONs belong on our OOD model.

Door

DOORs may be a very important component of the application domain of *elevators*, but our ECS doesn't know, or care about them. DOORs are managed by the mechanical systems of the elevator; the elevator simply reports when it becomes ready.

Elevator Schedule

Although we have decided that an elevator controller would not be an object in our analysis model, it is certainly plausible that an *elevator schedule* should be. Again, however, we argue that an elevator schedule is not an *essential* component of elevator control systems. Rather, it is one (very common) technique for implementing those systems.

Floor Sensor

The `ARRIVAL EVENT` is a non-implementation-specific version of `FLOOR SENSOR`.

Light (all kinds)

As with `BUTTON`s, `LIGHT`s are clearly part of an (implementation-related) person-machine interface technology.

Figure 5.11 shows a diagram of an initial OOA model Object-Class Layer.

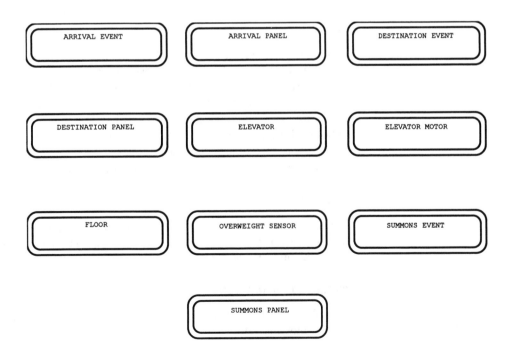

Figure 5.11
Object-Class Layer
for ECS.

5.3.2
Final Selection of Objects for SBSS

The following is a list of the SBSS objects we established on the basis of the foregoing analysis.

ACCEPTED ARTICLE

This object encapsulates recognition of the *article accepted for publication* event. This object also encapsulates relevant article data.

ADDRESS

It is convenient to establish a separate object solely for maintaining addresses because there are so many different kinds of addresses. It also facilitates having one large address database which contains subscribers, customers and recipients.

AUTHOR

This object encapsulates relevant author data.

AUTHOR-ARTICLE TRACK

The user specifically mentions tracking author-article information (our PFA revealed that). The data model interprets this as an *associative entity,* that is a store which maintains related data about both authors and articles. It seems reasonable to create an object which encapsulates those data.

COMPLIMENTARY SUBSCRIPTION

This object encapsulates recognition of the *time to review "comp" list* event, as well as any relevant data. Note that we discovered it *both* from the event list *and* from the event-response diagram.

CUSTOMER

Some insight suggests that the SBSS is dealing with three *different* types of people. *Subscribers* order and pay for subscriptions. However, they don't necessarily *receive* individual issues of the publication. *Recipients* (though frequently the same as subscribers) receive issues of the publication and are a distinct object. Finally, it is possible that someone is neither a subscriber nor a recipient. (For example, a vendor who purchases a large number of copies of one single issue. Such persons constitute a third object: *customers*.)

This object encapsulates relevant information about customers.

EDITORIAL ADVISOR

This object was discovered by reviewing the entity-relationship diagram, primarily because of the relationships it has: an ADVISOR is granted a complimentary subscription to *Small Bytes*.

EXPIRATION WARNING

This object encapsulates recognition of the *time to send renewal notice* event, as well as any relevant data.

INVOICE

This object encapsulates the various secrets associated with the computing and processing of invoices.

MONTHLY ISSUE

This object encapsulates recognition of the *time to release issue* event together with relevant issue data.

PAYMENT

This object encapsulates recognition of the *payment received* event, as well as all relevant payment data.

PRICING

This object encapsulates the various secrets associated with discounts, pricing of domestic subscriptions, international subscriptions, etc.

PROSPECT

This object represents individuals who are not subscribers, authors or recipients, etc.—i.e., these are people to whom the *Small Bytes* marketing department expects to solicit potential subscriptions.

PUBLISHED ARTICLE

This object encapsulates recognition of the *article published* event.

RECIPIENT

(See discussion of CUSTOMER above.)

RENEWAL

This object encapsulates recognition of the *subscription renewed* event.

SERVICE BUREAU

The realization that this object plays a distinct role in the system came from the entity-relationship diagram. The relationships between subscribers, subscriptions and the service bureau made it evident that SERVICE BUREAU needed to be a distinct object-class.

SPECIAL ORDER

Encapsulates recognition of the *special order received* event.

SUBSCRIBER

(See discussion of CUSTOMER above.)

SUBSCRIPTION

This object encapsulates recognition of the *subscription requested* event; it maintains stored data related to subscriptions.

SUBSCRIPTION TERMINATION

Encapsulates recognition of the *subscription expired* event.

Among items which did *not* become object classes were all various distinctions of *subscription*; we felt that those distinctions could be accommodated within the single SUBSCRIPTION object. Whether this was a wise choice remains to be seen. If the only thing distinguishing various categories of subscriptions is the value of a *status* attribute, we will indeed be happy that we chose a single object to represent subscription. But, if it turns out that the various categories of subscriptions exhibit substantially different behavior and also require different kinds of attributes—two different kinds of detail which we can't yet evaluate—then we may need to reconsider.

We also removed DISTRIBUTOR from our list of candidate objects; this insight came from a careful review of the entity-relationship diagram (Figure 5.7). While DISTRIBUTOR is obviously a distinct application domain concept, and implies a unique identity, we concluded that a DISTRIBUTOR has the same characteristics and behavior as any other subscriber who happens to create a multiple-copy subscription. Note the use of the words "characteristics" and "behavior" in the previous sentence: an object has "characteristics" that are defined by its attributes, as well as "behavior" defined by its services and its dynamic interactions with other objects. Thus, our conclusion that a DISTRIBUTOR is just another form of SUBSCRIBER needs to be verified with the user, and may be subject to revision when we have a more detailed understanding of its associated attributes and services.

Finally, Figure 5.12 is our version of the Object-Class Layer for our initial OOA model.

5.4 Final Comments and Discussion

From the objects we have chosen for the two case studies, several interesting comments and observations can be made:

1. The list of objects that we end up with cannot be proven to be absolutely right or wrong—different analysts might come up with slightly different lists. By applying the linguistic analysis technique described in Chapter 3, and by using familiar tools from structured analysis (e.g., 3VMs) we can be reasonably certain that we have not omitted any major objects. And, we can be reasonably certain that the objects that we have included in our model serve a specific purpose. But one of the reasons that we cannot be certain that there is one, and only one, set of "true" objects for a particular application is that fundamentally, objects are derived from application domain concepts. And the identification of application domain concepts is inherently subjective.

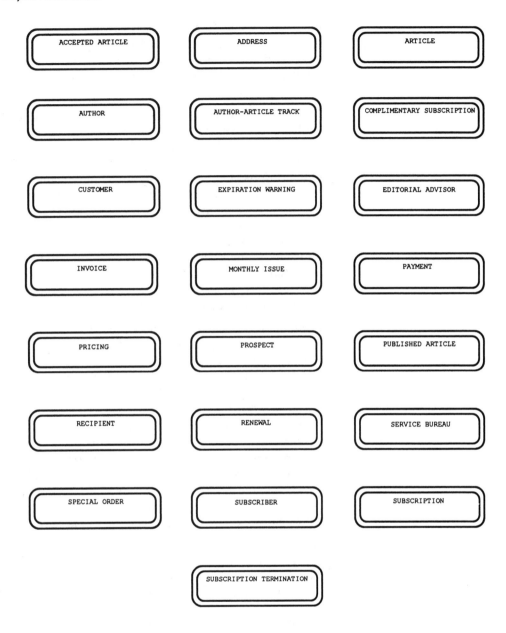

Figure 5.12
Object-Class Layer for
SBSS.

2. The user's preferences have an enormous influence on the final choice of objects in our model. This book is written as a dialogue between analysts, designers and software engineers who are interested in using object-oriented techniques to develop an application. The end-user has been treated as a silent observer, hovering on the sidelines, providing some input from time to time. But as we all know, the user ultimately pays our salaries, and the user determines whether or not the model (including the choice of objects) is acceptable.

Thus, even though the analyst may have decided that an ELEVATOR CONTROLLER is not an appropriate analysis-level object, the user may insist on including it in the model. Users are becoming more and more computer-literate these days, and some of them may insist on including objects that are associated with a specific implementation technology with which they are familiar. We can discourage them from doing so, but we may not be able to impose our wishes upon them.

3. Our choice of final candidates should *not* be regarded as final, and we may continue to make revisions as we extend the analysis model in the next several chapters. The reason for this is very simple: our decisions have been based on a relatively superficial understanding of the behavior and attributes of the various objects. The analyst may have some *a priori* concept of what a SUBSCRIPTION object consists of, and the user may have provided some informal information about the attributes and behavior of some of the objects. However, there is an *enormous* amount of additional detail to be filled in; inevitably, this will cause us to revise the model we have developed thus far. Thus, the modeling process we are describing in this book should definitely be considered an iterative or spiral methodology; it is definitely *not* intended to be a waterfall methodology, where the candidate objects discovered in this chapter are frozen without any possibility of subsequent change.

4. Even though our understanding of the objects is far from complete, it is already evident that some are simple and some are complex. Most of the objects in the ECS, for example, are almost trivial—it appears, at this stage, that most will have only one or two attributes, and perhaps one or two services. Things are not quite as simple in the *Small Bytes* system—and it is clear that some objects, such as CUSTOMER and SUBSCRIPTION, may turn out to be very complex.

   Indeed, it is probably already intuitively obvious to the analyst that there are some abstraction possibilities—e.g., various "sub-classes" of CUSTOMER that can be identified in order to simplify the overall model. And, it may have occurred to the reader that words like "author" and "recipient" and "subscriber" could be regarded as *roles* that can be carried out by a person. We will begin to explore these possibilities in the next chapter.

5. We note that all three perspectives of classical structured analysis—process, data and state-behavior—are valuable in helping discover objects in an OOA model. We run the risk of overlooking potential objects if we restrict our perspective to *only* data, or *only* state-behavior. For example, if we analyzed the *Small Bytes* system from a pure entity-relationship perspective, we probably would not have identified SUBSCRIPTION-EXPIRATION as an object. We have found, in practice, that different tools cross-check one another.

6. We will discuss quality issues in Chapter 11; however, at this point we offer a few comments regarding the mechanics of the Object-Class Layer:

   Object names must be appropriate, describing a class and not simply a function performed by that class or a characteristic of that class. Names must be unique. Names must be meaningful within the application domain and must not represent implementation technology. Names should be in a noun or possibly an adjective-noun form. Names in the noun-verb form should be avoided. The conjunctions "and" or "or" should not appear in a name. Names ending in "er" should be closely scrutinized.

Objects are clearly described and inclusion/exclusion criteria are clearly stated in a non-ambiguous form.

Every object has a clearly stated responsibility. Every object encapsulates at least one secret which is known *only* to that object. Objects with only a single instance should be closely scrutinized.

Objects must be used appropriately. Every object either participates in the recognition of an event or participates in the production of a response (to an event). Every object must be either an event recognizer or event responder.

7. Finally, we mention again that one of the virtues of the techniques we have introduced thus far is in visualizing the system of the future *before* we build the system. It might possibly be devastating for the ECS to have ignored the *Elevator becomes ready* event or the phenomenon of runaway elevators.

References for Chapter 5

1. Peter Coad and Edward Yourdon, *Object-Oriented Analysis*, 2nd edition (Prentice Hall, 1991).

2. Edward Yourdon, *Object-Oriented Systems Development: An Integrated Approach* (Prentice Hall, 1994).

3. Edward Yourdon, *Modern Structured Analysis* (Prentice Hall, 1988).

 *Key Points*

▲ 3-View Models (3VMs) are a set of well-established systems analysis tool that can help to boot-strap into object-oriented analysis.

▲ Data flow diagrams, context diagrams and related tools (including mini-specifications and decision tables) model the process view and are useful for establishing object services and messages.

▲ Entity-relationship diagrams model the data view and are useful for establishing objects and attributes.

▲ Event-response models and state-transition diagrams model the control view and are useful for establishing object services and messages.

▲ OOA/OOD worksheets provide a systematic way to extract an initial set of objects from a potentially large universe of application domain concepts.

▲ The object-finding techniques introduced in this chapter provide an *initial* set of objects; however, this is still an iterative process and we would expect to see modifications to this initial set.

CHAPTER 6
Dealing with Complexity: Identifying Structure

Some problems are so complex that you have to be highly intelligent and well informed just to be undecided about them.

— Laurence J. Peter
Peter's Almanac

6.1 Introduction and Discussion

The Structure Layer identifies relationships between objects which establishes their composition, as well as inheritance relationships. Since inheritance allows us to define something *once*, and then re-use it in different forms, it is important to identify these structures in our OOA model. The Structure Layer is one of the mechanisms we use to deal with complexity in the OOA model.

We identify two types of structures: Generalization-Specialization (Gen-Spec) and Whole-Part. Gen-Spec structures establish inheritance relationships and Whole-Part structures identify relationships of composition.

Gen-Spec relationships are established when the parent, or generalization object in the relationship, possesses attributes or characteristics which are shared by all of its children, or specialization objects. This sharing of attributes between parent and children is referred to as inheritance.

A point which seems to be confusing for most of our students is that inheritance applies to structure, form or definition, not to *value*. For example, the fact that COMPLIMENTARY SUBSCRIPTION is a specialization of SUBSCRIPTION implies that one or more attributes and/or services are shared, say subscription_status. This implies that the *definition* of subscription_status is shared between COMPLIMENTARY SUBSCRIPTION and SUBSCRIPTION. The *value* of a particular subscription_status, however, is not shared between the parent and child objects.

Whole-Part relationships are established when the parent object is in some way composed of a number of child objects. Typically these relationships are established on the basis of physical composition. Other types of composition are possible. Although Whole-Part relationships do not exhibit inheritance, as do

Gen-Spec relationships, they possess the characteristics of *multiplicity* and *participation*. Multiplicity refers to the number of child objects which may compose a parent. (For example, a *car* has four *tires*.) Participation refers to whether or not a parent or child object must participate in a Whole-Part relationship. (A *car* must have four *tires*, however a *tire* is not a necessary part of a *car*.)

Other informal techniques for identifying Whole-Part relationships include looking carefully at the object names; they frequently suggest Whole-Part relationships. This is particularly evident in the ECS. Although we haven't discussed *instance connections* yet, informally consider how the various objects might be related to one another. A number of similar relationships from one object to multiple other objects suggests a Gen-Spec relationship.

To establish the multiplicity and participation of Whole-Part relationships try using the *anchor-point* method. For example, identify a Whole-Part relationship between ELEVATOR and ask yourself, "If I have just one instance of ELEVATOR, how many instances of ELEVATOR MOTOR could I have? Must an instance of ELEVATOR have an instance of ELEVATOR MOTOR?" Remember, when you ask yourself these questions you must answer them *within the context of the application domain* of the system being specified. For example, elevators probably always have motors in the application domain of (operational) elevator control systems but elevators might exist without motors in the application domain of elevator *maintenance* systems! Multiplicity and participation are also established on the basis of *static*, not *dynamic* criteria. For example, can (or must) an ELEVATOR be associated with an ELEVATOR MOTOR, not just at this moment in time, but at all times. Or, if I look at *all* instances of the ELEVATOR MOTOR class, how many will be associated with any single instance of ELEVATOR?

Finally, it should be noted that the identification of structures will almost certainly reveal the existence of additional objects. In the case of Gen-Spec structures, it is frequently convenient to identify a parent which is a class with no instances. Such *generic* classes or *template* classes are simply used to consolidate attributes or services which would otherwise have to be defined multiple times in each of the child components.

The OOA/OOD worksheets of Appendices E and F can be used to identify Whole-Part and Gen-Spec relationships. LIA can be applied in a different way. For example, the existence of a Whole-Part relationship is frequently associated with the English words "has" and "has a". The existence of a Gen-Spec relationship is similarly associated with the English words "is" and "is a". Candidate relationships should pass the "is a" or "has a" test; the case study examples below will illustrate this.

6.2 Structure Layer for the ECS

The complete structure layer for the ECS is shown in Appendix I.

We have identified several Gen-Spec and Whole-Part relationships. The most obvious Whole-Part relationship is that between ELEVATOR and various other objects (see Figure 6.1). The relationship illustrated is between ELEVATOR and its various physical components, namely OVERWEIGHT SENSOR, ELEVATOR MOTOR, ARRIVAL PANEL and DESTINATION PANEL. The multiplicity of each of these relationships is one-to-one. This is true even for ARRIVAL PANEL. The reason for this is that the arrival panel on each floor is the same as the arrival panel inside the associated elevator; this is a good example of the principle of *abstraction*.

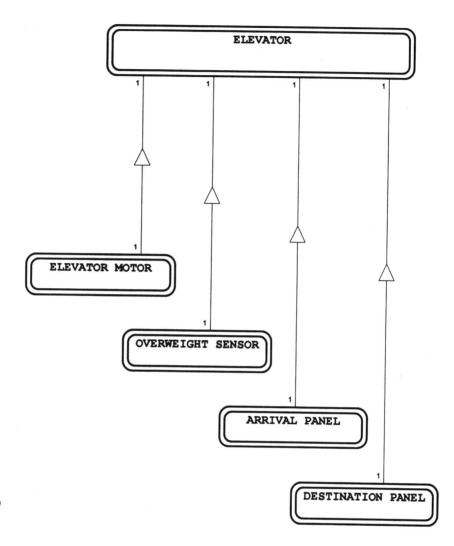

Figure 6.1
Whole-Part relationship
for the ECS.

A second Whole-Part relationship is shown in Figure 6.2. This relationship is different than the one shown in Figure 6.1 in that the relationship is established on the basis of physical association rather than physical containment.

Neither one of the Whole-Part relationships identified above suggests the creation of a new object for the ECS. However, two new generic classes are established on the basis of the Gen-Spec relationships shown in Figure 6.3. In both cases, generic classes were established which consolidate attributes of their children. As a result, we have created a new *generalization* class, ELEVATOR EVENT, recognizing (or perhaps anticipating) some commonality between different categories of events—e.g., they probably all share the attribute floor_number. We suspect that SUMMONS EVENT, ARRIVAL EVENT and DESTINATION EVENT will all share attributes such as event_time and floor. We have also created a new generic class, PANEL, to deal with the commonality of ARRIVAL PANELs and DESTINATION PANELs.

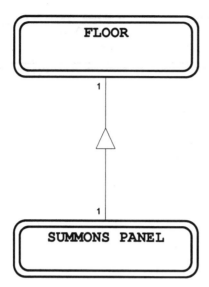

Figure 6.2
Whole-Part relationship
for the ECS.

6.3
Structure Layer
for the SBSS

The complete structure layer for the SBSS is shown in Appendix J.

We have identified several Gen-Spec and Whole-Part relationships. The most obvious Whole-Part relationship is that between MONTHLY ISSUE and PUBLISHED ARTICLE. The relationship is based on conceptual composition rather than physical composition. This relationship is shown in Figure 6.4. It is worth mentioning that a monthly issue in fact has other component parts such as a front cover, rear cover, book review, table of contents, etc.; these are currently outside the scope of the system, but they might become relevant in the future— e.g., if we decide to have invited book reviews, or guest editors who write the introduction to an issue, in addition to another article.

As previously mentioned, a number of Gen-Spec relationships were identified for the SBSS. As shown in Figure 6.5, a new class was created: ARTICLE is a generalization of ACCEPTED ARTICLE and PUBLISHED ARTICLE. We noticed, of course, the similar names but more importantly, we recognized that these two objects share common attributes (for example, *title*) and participate in common relationships (for example, with AUTHOR). We choose not, however, to consolidate ACCEPTED ARTICLE and PUBLISHED ARTICLE. Why? What about articles which are *submitted*, but neither accepted nor published? Note that we allow ARTICLE to have instances; these instances represent such articles. (This also makes it easy to add another specialization of REJECTED ARTICLE, so that we can keep track of articles that we've rejected in the past and don't want to reconsider in the future.)

Figure 6.6 shows a variation of Figure 6.5. In this case, we removed the instance boundary from ARTICLE, making it a generic class. In this example our

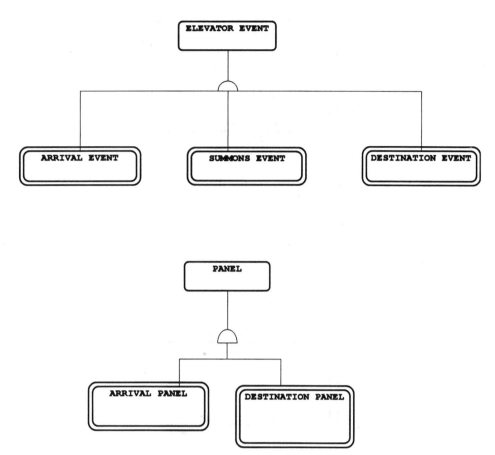

Figure 6.3
Gen-Spec relationships
for the ECS.

system does not know about articles which are neither accepted nor published. We simply don't enter them into the system.

Finally, Figure 6.7 shows the case where PUBLISHED ARTICLE is a specialization of ARTICLE. This variation, however, is not acceptable for our system. An accepted ARTICLE, for example, has a tentative_publication_date attribute, whereas a PUBLISHED ARTICLE has an actual_publication_date attribute. We will allow, however, a relationship such as that shown in Figure 6.8. COMPLIMENTARY SUBSCRIPTION is a valid specialization of SUBSCRIPTION since all of its attributes and services are inherited by COMPLIMENTARY SUBSCRIPTION.

As shown in Figure 6.9, an interesting Gen-Spec relationship exists between CUSTOMER, SUBSCRIBER, RECIPIENT, DISTRIBUTOR, AUTHOR and ADVISOR. Since all of these objects have an ADDRESS (and some may have multiple addresses), it seemed appropriate to create a new generalization class above them. We consulted our thesaurus to find an appropriate name to describe this new generic object, and decided to call it CLIENT. Many of the students in our classes feel an instinctive need to call this object PERSON—but not all of the sub-

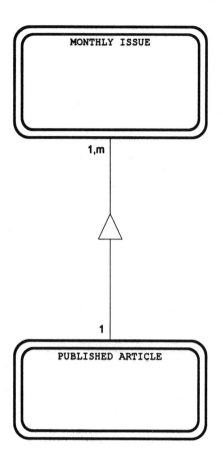

Figure 6.4
Whole-Part relationship
for the SBSS.

classes are necessarily individuals; note, for example, that some subscriptions are sent to a corporation without identifying an individual, and some copies of *Small Bytes* are sent to an anonymous person called Technical Librarian.

A less obvious Gen-Spec relationship was established with the generic class SUBSCRIPTION EVENT (Figure 6.10). Although this structure was initially identified by considering shared attributes, it was also intuitively appealing to consider that a subscription termination, payment, renewal, etc. would constitute a *subscription event*.

6.4
Final Notes
and Discussion

1. Note that in the ECS the ARRIVAL PANEL participates in two different Whole-Part structures: it is part of a FLOOR and also part of an ELEVATOR. Recall our discussion regarding the use of the principle of *abstraction* to consider all *physical* arrival panels as one conceptual object ARRIVAL PANEL. Note how, in this case, we can consider a *single instance* of ARRIVAL PANEL as being a part of two different "wholes," even though it is two different *physical* arrival panels which establish those relationships.

   By the way, the reason we can consider all of the physical arrival panels as a single entity is that we have no need (within our application domain) to

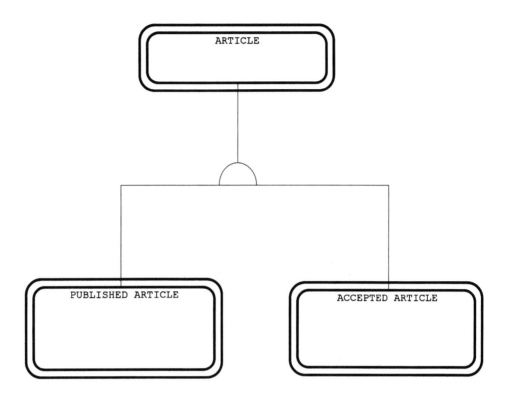

Figure 6.5
Gen-Spec relationship
for the SBSS.

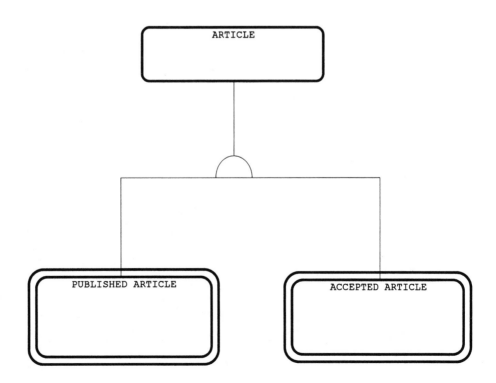

Figure 6.6
An alternative version of
the ARTICLE Gen-Spec
relationship.

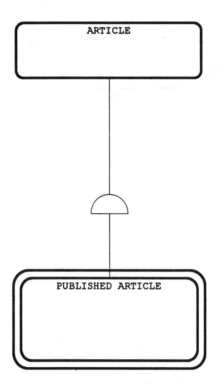

Figure 6.7
Another variation of the
ARTICLE Gen-Spec
relationship.

distinguish between physical panels. If it were necessary to distinguish between the physical arrival panels, say to identify the *current floor* arrival panel as being different from all others, then it would be necessary to make each *physical* arrival panel a distinct instance of ARRIVAL PANEL.

2. In over two years of presenting object-oriented modeling to groups of analysts, we have found that the Whole-Part structure seems to be a difficult concept to grasp. In particular, students frequently confuse Whole-Part structures with *instance connections*, which are discussed in Chapter 9. For novice analysts, we suggest that the Whole-Part structure be used *only* when *physical* composition is implied and is significant within the application domain. Readers may wish to ignore Whole-Part structures altogether (substituting instead instance connections)—at least until they have gained more experience with OOA.

3. We haven't considered issues such as whether someone (a real person) could simultaneously be an AUTHOR, SUBSCRIBER, RECIPIENT, etc. In fact, an actual person in the real world could be associated with instances of each of these various objects. As far as our analysis model is concerned, these entities *are* different. Some analysts would like to see an object identified called ROLE. This is illustrated in Figure 6.11. Although understanding this figure requires a knowledge of instance connections (covered in Chapter 9), the intended heuristic should be clear. A CLIENT could take on the ROLEs of AUTHOR, SUBSCRIBER, etc. We have not done this; it is simply a heuristic which we have not found useful for novice analysts.

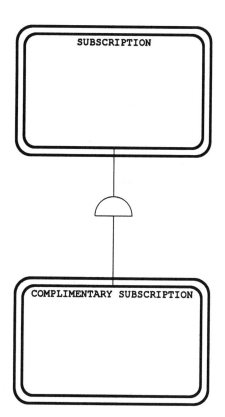

Figure 6.8
A Gen-Spec relationship for SUBSCRIPTION.

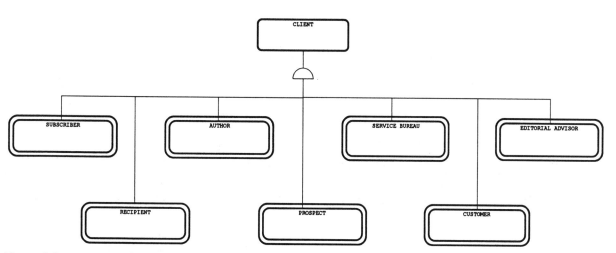

Figure 6.9
A Gen-Spec relationship for CLIENT.

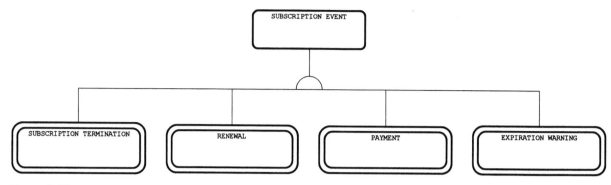

Figure 6.10
A Gen-Spec relationship for SUBSCRIPTION EVENT.

4. As has been pointed out previously, this *is* an iterative process. We expect that our initial identification of structures will reveal new components, which will alter our view of the problem, which will lead to changes in these structures, etc.

5. We will discuss quality issues in Chapter 11, however, at this point a few comments regarding the mechanics of the structure layer are appropriate:

    All structures must be meaningful within the application domain.
    Whole-Part structures join from instance boundary to instance boundary except as noted: In the case where the "whole" participant in a Whole-Part relationship is a generic class, each sub-type of the generic class must participate as the "whole" in the Whole-Part relationship. In the case where the "part" participant in a Whole-Part relationship is a generic class, each sub-

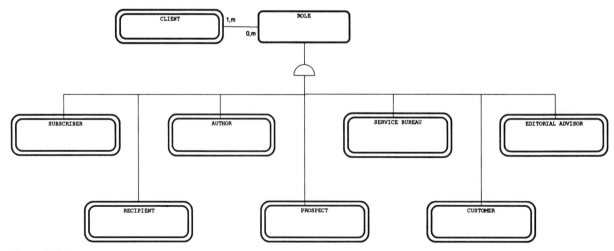

Figure 6.11
Use of a ROLE class.

type of the generic class must participate as the "part" in the Whole-Part relationship.

Every Whole-Part structure must have both multiplicity and participation designated.

Gen-Spec structures must join from class boundary to class boundary except as noted: In the case where the "specialization" participant in a Gen-Spec relationship is itself a generic class, each sub-type of that generic class must participate as the "specialization" in the Gen-Spec relationship. In the case where the "generalization" participant in a Gen-Spec relationship is a specialization of another generic class, each sub-type of the generic class must participate as the "specialization" in the Gen-Spec relationship.

 *Key Points*

▲ Structures allow us to deal with application domain complexity.

▲ Generalization-Specialization (Gen-Spec) structures involve inheritance; inheritance allows us to define an attribute or service *once* and then to re-use it in other (specialization) objects.

▲ Whole-Part structures involve some type of aggregation; they capture an application domain constraint or business rule.

▲ In a Gen-Spec structure, it is the *definition* of attributes or services which are inherited, *not* values.

▲ Whole-Part structures are similar to instance connections (Chapter 9); we use Whole-Part structures *only* when aggregation is involved.

CHAPTER 7
Dealing with Complexity: Identifying Subjects

Grasp the subject, the words will follow.

— Cato

7.1 Introduction and Discussion

One of the characteristics of the structured analysis/design methodology you may have practiced in the past was that of hierarchical decomposition. This technique allowed complex functions, data structures, etc. to be decomposed into manageable chunks. The "7 ± 2 Rule" has been widely used as a guideline for hierarchical decomposition. Unlike structured models, however, most OOA models are relatively flat, unless the application domain lends itself to substantial use of Gen-Spec or Whole-Part structures. The complexity of large models may, instead, be dealt with by establishing a number of subjects. Each subject may be viewed as a sub-model, or perhaps even a sub-system. In this chapter we discuss the *Subject Layer* of the OOA model for both the ECS and SBSS.

Note that the case studies used in this book are sufficiently simple that each could reasonably be considered a single subject. The Subject Layer developed in this chapter is thus more for pedagogical benefit than technical necessity.

The concept of a subject tends to be in the eye of the beholder; some analysts may distinguish subjects on the basis of sub-domains, sub-systems, even organizational (i.e., political) or geographical subjects. Any of these criteria will work if applied consistently. You may find it useful to think of a subject as a Whole-Part relationship on the application domain. Ask yourself the question: "If I decide that *x* should be an application domain, sub-system, or whatever, what are all the things which must compose *x*?"

Gen-Spec structures often *strongly suggest* a subject. However, it is possible that the components of a Gen-Spec structure may be split between different subjects.

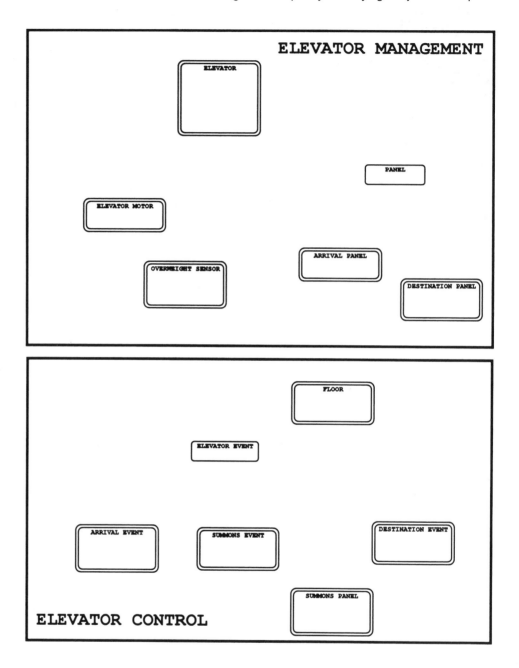

Figure 7.1
Subject Layer
of the ECS.

7.2
Subject Layer
for the ECS

The Subject Layer for the ECS is included in the complete OOA model given in Appendix I. The Subject Layer alone is shown in Figure 7.1.

We think the reader will find these subjects to be trivial, and perhaps even artificial (they were the best we could come up with!). We relied on the existence of the two structures to suggest two subjects. First, an *elevator management* subject was established which deals *primarily* with controlling the hardware. A second subject, *elevator scheduling* is concerned with detecting the occurrence of events and scheduling the elevators accordingly.

Again, we should point out that for a relatively small model, such as the ECS, the use of multiple subjects may not be necessary.

7.3 Subject Layer for the SBSS

The Subject Layer for the SBSS is included in the complete OOA model given in Appendix J. The Subject Layer alone is shown in Figure 7.2.

We think that the reader will find the subjects identified for the SBSS to be considerably more meaningful than those identified for the ECS. As discussed in an earlier chapter, some thinking and insight suggests that there are three distinct types of activities being performed in the SBSS. Obviously, subscription management is the primary function. However, the SBSS also performs editorial management functions. Finally, the SBSS performs special orders processing. These three sub-systems could be the basis to establish three subjects. Gen-Spec relationships do not, in this case, strongly suggest subjects.

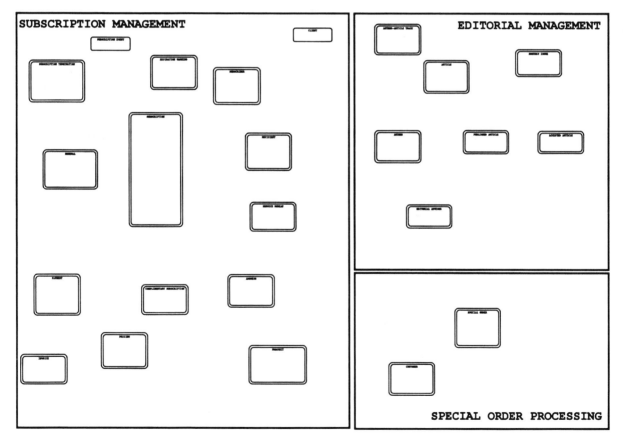

Figure 7.2
Subject Layer for the SBSS.

7.4
Final Notes
and Comments

1. For very large and complex models, we can create multiple levels of subjects. A caution, however: multiple levels of subjects can easily become hierarchical decomposition—that is, data-flow diagrams drawn with object-oriented symbols. One hint that you've lapsed into functional decomposition is in choosing your subject names. Names which express action, i.e., verbs, are red flags. Subject names in the form verb-noun are a dead give-away!

2. Subjects can overlap. For complex models, we would expect to see some objects (e.g., ADDRESS in the SBSS) to reside in multiple subject areas. We have chosen to show such objects in only one subject area for our case studies.

3. Subjects may be discovered in either top-down or bottom-up fashion. We used the former approach for the SBSS. We used the latter approach for the ECS. That is, for the SBSS, we identified three system functions or responsibilities, (subscription management, editorial management and special order processing). We then imposed these on the model as subjects. For the ECS, we *first* examined the model and *then* decided on a reasonable set of subjects for that model.

4. How would you go about creating an OOA model for a rather complex system, say, *Microsoft® Word™*? For such a system, the application domain is large, and the identified system responsibilities are numerous. For a system of this complexity, it's hard to imagine creating an OOA model without first establishing some constraints.

   One way to approach the problem is to divide and conquer. Divide the application domain into smaller application domains—then analyze these as we've done thus far. Thus, each of these sub-domains becomes a subject.

   For *Microsoft Word*, we might consider establishing a collection of subjects such as: text processing, print management, document management, drawing, spell checking, style management, etc. Even with a decomposition such as this, it might be necessary to create additional "nested" subjects. For example, within text processing, we might create sub-subjects such as font management, hyphenation, paragraph management, tabulation management, etc. Note that these subjects may be established even before we have identified any initial objects.

   Clearly in a large model like this, it would be easy to lapse into functional decomposition. We might avoid this, however, by being conscientious and by strictly applying OOA principles at the subject level. In addition, after some number of subjects are created, we would want to perform an affinity analysis between subjects so as to identify common objects.

   Our advice? Don't attempt *Microsoft Word*, or a similar large complex system, as your first OOA project.

5. We will discuss quality issues in Chapter 11, however, at this point a few comments regarding the mechanics of the Subject Layer are appropriate:

   If subjects are used, each object should be included within a subject boundary.

   Subjects must be appropriately named. Names must be meaningful within the application domain and must not represent implementation technology. Names must be unique. Noun-verb subject names should be avoided. The conjunctions "and" and "or" should not appear in a name.

Subjects may overlap. If this convention is adopted, it should be applied consistently. A subject should be independent in the following sense: If a subject is printed on a single sheet of paper, it should be understandable with only minimal reference to other parts of the model. Structures should be included within a single subject. If necessary, a component of a structure may also be included within an overlapping subject.

 *Key Points*

▲ For small OOA models, a Subject Layer may not be necessary.

▲ A model can be partitioned into subjects in a variety of ways—the subjects must simply be meaningful to the user.

▲ Very large OOA models may best be approached by *first* establishing subjects, then component objects.

CHAPTER 8

Things Objects Remember: Identifying Attributes

God and all the attributes of God are eternal.

— Spinoza

8.1 Introduction and Discussion

The *Attribute Layer* of the OOA model incorporates *both* object attributes, as well as relationships between objects (instance connections). The object attributes establish which data are encapsulated in objects; objects can only do work on those data which they encapsulate. The instance connections, which we will focus on in Chapter 9, can be thought of as capturing business rules, or application domain constraints. These connections tell us how an object in one class *must* be related to an object in another class. When these object classes are implemented, these business rules dictate how services (which we will discuss in Chapter 10) must work to be consistent with our established system policies.

Our objective in this chapter is to use the results of the modeling efforts in previous chapters to establish a set of attributes for the objects in the ECS and SBSS.

Our basic strategy is to identify attributes, make modifications to other OOA model layers to accommodate these attributes, revise objects if necessary, and then repeat the process.

There are a number of techniques which can be used to identify attributes. If you've followed our approach and created OOA/OOD worksheets, numerous identified concepts will represent characteristics of things, stored data requirements or have some unique structure (e.g., Social Security number) which cries out to be an encapsulated attribute. Simply put, check-marks in the appropriate column—you can sort through these candidate attributes as you look at the Attribute Layer from other perspectives.

If you've created 3VMs as a pre-analysis activity, the data view (usually an Entity-Relationship Diagram (ERD)) is a good starting point. The attributes of an entity in an ERD represent stored data requirements. These stored data must, somehow, be represented in our OOA model. It may be that an entity corresponds to some object. In that case, the entity attributes may simply become object attributes. It may be that an entity does not correspond to a single object. In that case, the entity attributes must be allocated to various objects in our OOA model. Regardless of how this allocation is done, we *must* be able to account for all attributes identified in the ERD.

Another approach to identifying attributes is to describe each object. In doing so, you should be able to identify a set of criteria or characteristics which allows you to look at anything in the real world and make a yes/no decision—is this thing IN my class or NOT IN my class. What makes objects in a class belong together? They share a common set of characteristics which makes them different from other things which are not in the class, i.e., their attributes. This process may reveal that an object was, initially, poorly identified.

A dead giveaway that you should re-think an object is when its attributes take on the value of "not applicable." All attributes of an object must be applicable to all instance of that class, even if they take on the value of "null." "Not applicable" is not acceptable.

Our favorite example of this is in the application domain of municipal information management. Initially, we might have identified an object of LICENSE since municipalities issue licenses (see Figure 8.1). The attributes of a license may be things like: date of issue, fee paid, expiration date, etc. However, our municipality issues several types of licenses, including marriage licenses, dog licenses and fishing licenses. An attribute of say, *expiration date*, might not be applicable to a marriage license. An attribute such as *name of spouse* might not be applicable to a dog license. An attribute of *date of birth* might not be applicable to a fishing license, etc. Clearly, we should re-think the object LICENSE, perhaps creating a Gen-Spec structure which specializes LICENSE into MARRIAGE LICENSE, FISHING LICENSE and DOG LICENSE. A more refined structure is shown in Figure 8.2.

Figure 8.1
An initial object selection.

```
            LICENSE
        ┌── Attribute ──┐
           license_id
           issue_date
         expiration_date
            fee_paid
         name_of_spouse
          date_of_birth
          type_of_breed
        annual_allotment
```

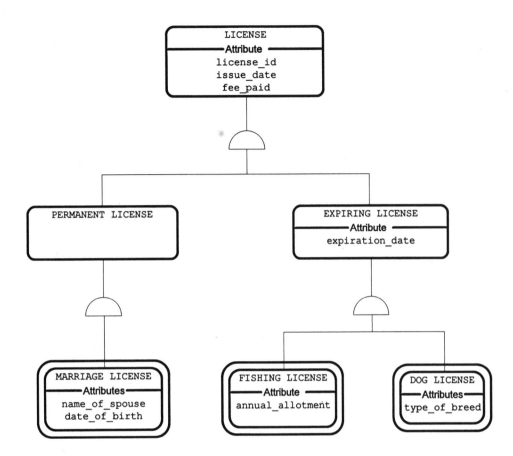

Figure 8.2
An object refinement
based on attribute
considerations.

8.2
Attributes
of the ECS

The Attribute Layer for the ECS is included in the complete OOA model given in Appendix I. We have identified the following object attributes for the ECS.

ARRIVAL EVENT	arrival_id arrival_floor elevator_id
ARRIVAL PANEL	arrival_panel_id
DESTINATION EVENT	destination_id destination_floor elevator_id
DESTINATION PANEL	destination_panel_id destination_pending

ELEVATOR	elevator_id current_direction current_floor current_state status_direction
ELEVATOR EVENT	event_id floor_id
ELEVATOR MOTOR	elevator_motor_id
FLOOR	floor_id elevator_id
OVERWEIGHT SENSOR	overweight_sensor_id overweight_status
PANEL	panel_id elevator_id
SUMMONS EVENT	summons_id summons_type summons_floor
SUMMONS PANEL	summons_panel_id summns_pending_up summons_pending_down

8.3 Attributes of the SBSS

The Attribute Layer for the SBSS is included in the complete OOA model given in Appendix J. We have identified the following object attributes for the SBSS.

ADDRESS	address_id address_details
ACCEPTED ARTICLE	
ARTICLE	article_id article_details
AUTHOR	author_id author_details address_id
AUTHOR-ARTICLE TRACK	author_article_id author_article_details
CLIENT	address_id client_id
COMPLIMENTARY SUBSCRIPTION REVIEW	

CUSTOMER	customer_id customer_details address_id
EDITORIAL ADVISOR	editorial_advisor_id
EXPIRATION WARNING	subscription_id expiration_warning_id expiration_warning_date
INVOICE	invoice_id payment_id invoice_details
MONTHLY ISSUE	monthly_issue_id monthly_details
PAYMENT	payment_id payment_details
PRICING	pricing_id pricing_details
PROSPECT	prospect_id prospect_details address_id
PUBLISHED ARTICLE	
RECIPIENT	recipient_id subscriber_id recipient_details address_id
RENEWAL	renewal_id renewal_date old_subscription_id new_subscription_id
SERVICE BUREAU	service_bureau_id service_bureau_details subscription_id
SPECIAL ORDER	special_order_id customer_id special_order_details payment_id pricing_id
SUBSCRIBER	subscriber_id address_id subscriber_details

SUBSCRIPTION	subscription_id subscriber_id subscription_details subscription_status service_bureau_id recipient_id pricing_id payment_id
SUBSCRIPTION EVENT	subscription_id
SUBSCRIPTION TERMINATION	subscription_termination_id termination_date subscription_id

8.4 Final Comments and Notes

1. For an OOA model, attributes should represent the application domain characteristics of their associated objects. Attributes which are specifically implementation-related should be included in the design model. Examples of implementation-related attributes would include GUI attributes, presentation attributes, such as size and format of fields, etc.

   Note that for the SBSS, we have frequently identified attributes with the suffix "_details" (e.g., address_details, subscription_details, etc.). This simply implies that there will be various details which will be elaborated on in the design model. We have found this a useful technique since at the OOA model level, we are focusing on essential requirements. In other words, we want to understand the basic nature of the system. It is not important at this stage that an address may ultimately have three lines or four lines or an international postal code, etc. If our user demands this level of detail in our OOA model, we will, of course, provide it. It would be best, however, to omit such details at least in the *initial* versions of the OOA model.

2. Note that there is a distinction between an attribute and the value(s) which it may assume. For example, the *attribute* social_security_number may assume the *value* 123-45-6789. Although we are not especially concerned with attribute values when constructing an analysis model (their format, range of valid values, etc. is a design issue), considering values of attributes may suggest a restructuring of the OOA model. For example, if the *value* of an object attribute may be "not valid" or "not defined", that is a sure give-away that we have done a poor job in defining that object. We should consider redefining that object as two or more other objects, possibly associated in a Gen-Spec structure.

3. There is always a good deal of controversy in our workshops concerning the use of a unique instance identifier in each object; these attributes are usually suffixed with "_id." The fact is that each instance of a class must be uniquely identifiable. So, at least some kind of an "ID" attribute (or attributes) is implied. These will certainly be specified in the OOD model. Whether or not you choose to explicitly show them in the OOA model is a convention. Adopt the convention which makes your user happy—then be consistent.

4. Another controversial convention, related to the above, is that of showing the pointer attribute associated with an instance connection on the diagram (such as `address_id` as an attribute of `SUBSCRIBER`). Once again, such attributes are redundant in that an instance connection implies their existence. Again, these will be specified in the OOD model. Whether or not you choose to explicitly show them in the OOA model is a convention.

5. We will discuss quality issues in Chapter 11; however, at this point, a few comments regarding the mechanics of the attribute component of the Attribute Layer are appropriate:

    Attributes must be appropriately named, describing characteristics, qualities or stored data requirements of the associated object. Names must be meaningful within the application domain and must not represent implementation technology. Names must be unique within a given object. Names are usually in the noun or adjective-noun form; verb names should be avoided. The conjunctions "and" and "or" should not appear in a name.

    Each object must have at least one attribute which allows instances of the object to be uniquely identified.

    Classes may have attributes which apply only to the class; such attributes must be used consistently and apply to the class or all instances of the class. Such attributes may not apply to a specific instance of the class.

    Values of attributes must be well-defined; attributes cannot assume values of "not-applicable."

    The objects which participate in Gen-Spec relationships must inherit attributes consistent with the Gen-Spec relationship. Specialization objects cannot inherit attributes which are undefined for that specialization. Inherited attributes must be meaningful within the application domain.

    The definition of an attribute must be unique to that attribute and may not be shared by any other attribute.

    All system-stored data requirements must be accounted for as attributes.

 *Key Points*

▲   Earlier we characterized objects as "independent, asynchronous, concurrent entities which **know things**... Attributes are the mechanism by which objects "know things."

▲   All stored data requirements for a proposed system must appear as object attributes.

▲   Attributes may also be viewed as characteristics of objects.

▲   There is a distinction between *instance attributes* and *class attributes*.

▲   Instance attributes must be applicable and appropriate for each member of a class. (They cannot take on values of "not-applicable.")

▲   A number of techniques may be used to identify attributes; however, the identification of attributes is an iterative process.

CHAPTER 9
Identifying Instance Relationships

Marriage must be a relation either of sympathy or of conquest.

— George Eliot
(nee Marian Evans Cross)

9.1 Introduction and Discussion

The Attribute Layer of the OOA model incorporates *both* object attributes, as well as relationships between objects (instance connections). The instance connections can be thought of as capturing business rules, or application domain constraints. These connections tell us how an object in one class *must* be related to an object in another class. When these object classes are implemented, the business rules dictate how services (which we will discuss in Chapter 10) must work to be consistent with our established system policies.

Our objective in this chapter is to use the results of the modeling efforts in previous chapters to establish a set of instance connections for the classes and objects in the ECS and SBSS. An important part of this activity is to define the multiplicity (1:1, 1:M, M:M) and participation (optional or mandatory) for each instance connection. With the work we did in Chapter 6, we can use the anchor-point technique to establish multiplicity and participation for each instance connection.

After we have identified the instance connections, we may wish to refine the objects. For example, many-to-many relationships *are* permitted in an OOA model—they express a behavior in the application domain. However, we should at least consider the possibility of new objects which might be generated if a many-to-many relationship were eliminated.

Many-to-many instance connections can *always* be decomposed into two one-to-many instance connections with a third object. Sometimes that new (third) object is meaningful in the application domain—in that case, we've just found a new object! In other cases, it is purely artificial and the original many-to-many relationship should be maintained.

In Chapter 3 we introduced two linguistic-based techniques for object identification: Phrase Frequency Analysis (PFA) and Matrix Analysis (MA). Although we applied PFA extensively in Chapter 4, we have not yet used MA. We have found MA to be very useful for identifying *relationships* between concepts—specifically objects. Having identified an initial set of objects we may construct a matrix with all of the identified objects along the column-headers and row-headers. Each entry in this matrix represents a possible constraint (or business rule) between the associated objects. We may then examine the case study descriptions, interview the user, etc., to fill in the matrix.

9.2 Instance Connections for the ECS

The attribute layer for the ECS is included in the complete OOA model given in Appendix I. The instance connections alone are shown in Figure 9.1.

The identified instance connections represent fundamental application domain rules which the ECS must adhere to. Let's examine these in more detail:

1. An instance connection establishes that an ARRIVAL EVENT must be associated with precisely one ELEVATOR and ELEVATOR may be associated with zero to multiple ARRIVAL EVENTS. What does this mean? First, an ARRIVAL EVENT must report the arrival of *one specific* elevator. In our application domain, it would not be helpful for an ARRIVAL EVENT to report the arrival of *any* elevator without specifying *which* elevator has arrived. This instance connection also requires that an ELEVATOR can be associated with zero to multiple ARRIVAL EVENTS. Multiple, because we would expect that a single ELEVATOR can arrive more than once (the alternative would be to reset the ECS after each ELEVATOR arrival); and zero, because we could have an ELEVATOR which has never arrived—for example, when the ECS is first executed.

2. A DESTINATION EVENT must be associated with precisely one DESTINATION PANEL (although DESTINATION PANELs may be associated with zero to multiple DESTINATION EVENTs). As with the first instance connection, in our application domain, it would not be helpful if a DESTINATION EVENT did not report the ELEVATOR reporting the event. Sending ELEVATOR No. 1 to the 5th floor because someone in ELEVATOR No. 2 pressed the 5th floor button, would be unacceptable. As with the first instance connection, a DESTINATION PANEL can be associated with zero to multiple DESTINATION EVENTs.

   There was a tacit assumption in the previous paragraph that a DESTINATION PANEL uniquely identifies a specific ELEVATOR. We cannot just assume that. We do in fact have an instance connection between ELEVATOR and DESTINATION PANEL. That instance connection is in the form of a Whole-Part relationship. One ELEVATOR contains precisely one DESTINATION PANEL. This is a good example of the fact that a Whole-Part relationship is a strong instance connection.

3. Similar to the above instance connection is the instance connection between SUMMONS EVENT and SUMMONS PANEL. Again, in our application domain we *must* be able to associate a SUMMONS EVENT with a *unique* SUMMONS PANEL.

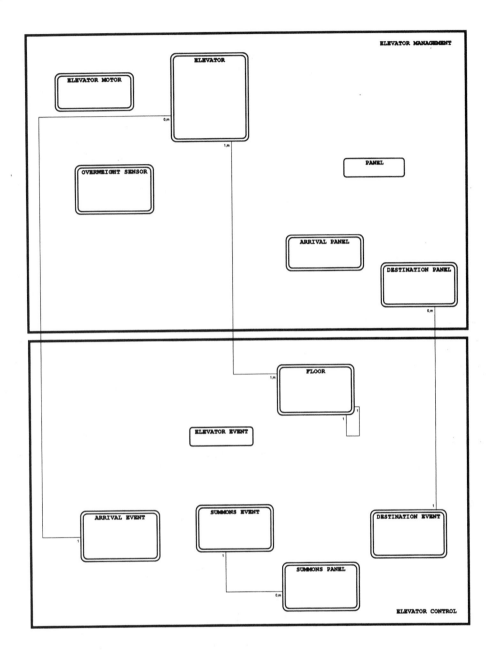

Figure 9.1
Instance connections
for the ECS.

(Otherwise, we might send an elevator to the 5th floor when a first floor summons button was pressed.)

4. Finally, note the many-to-many instance connections between ELEVATOR and FLOOR. That is, all ELEVATORs are associated with all FLOORs. This is not quite as trivial as it seems. It says that, for this application domain, there are no restricted floors. Students frequently misinterpret this relationship as meaning that all ELEVATORs are associated with all FLOORs *at any point in time*. Instance connections are *static*. Time, as in an instant of time, should

never be considered when establishing application domain constraints. The many-to-many instance connection between ELEVATOR and FLOOR simply means that an ELEVATOR can be associated with multiple FLOORs. And that, *over the life* of the application domain, a FLOOR can be associated with multiple ELEVATORs. This application domain constraint is true, it always has been true and it must be true for the entire future of the ECS.

5. What is not considered an instance connection? Many of our students want to have establish an instance connection between SUMMONS EVENT and ELEVATOR. Although a many-to-many relationship could be established (as in 4 above), we have not done so because it is simply irrelevant in the application domain. A more significant instance connection between SUMMONS EVENT and ELEVATOR would be a one-to-many relationship. This relationship, however, is not true in our application domain. It suggests that a SUMMONS EVENT could specify *which* particular ELEVATOR it wanted. That might be useful in some hotels where only one of four elevators goes to the roof-top restaurant. However, it' not relevant in our application domain.

6. We made reference in 5 above that instance connections must be relevant within the application domain. People with creative imaginations can establish relationships between any two things in the Universe. However, the fact that *every* object in our OOA model is related by virtue of them all being in the same model, is irrelevant to our application domain.

7. Somewhat related to the idea of relevance is the idea of *redundant* instance connections. For example, aren't ARRIVAL EVENT and ARRIVAL PANEL related? Yes, indeed they are. And that relationship is *implied* by the fact that ARRIVAL EVENT is associated with ELEVATOR, which in turn is associated with ARRIVAL PANEL (remember, a Whole-Part relationship is a strong instance connection). It is not necessary, therefore, to explicitly show the instance connection on the OOA model. We may choose, however, to explicitly show redundant instance connections when they are especially important, and therefore meaningful, to the user. Or, for that matter, when the user simply wants to see them.

8. Another possibility, of course, is that redundant instance connections exist— and we don't recognize them. This is frequently the case in large, complex models. As shown in Figure 9.2, if we can identify a closed loop (shown with bold lines), we may have a case where one of the instance connections is redundant (it depends on the multiplicity and participation of each instance connection). In this figure we added the (redundant) instance connection between ARRIVAL EVENT and ARRIVAL PANEL (as discussed in 7). We also added one of the Whole-Part relationships (see Figure 6.1).

9.3 Instance Connections for the SBSS

The Attribute Layer for the SBSS is included in the complete OOA model given in Appendix J. The instance connections alone are shown in Figure 9.3. The comments in the previous section for the ECS are also relevant for this system.

A number of important business rules are captured on this Attribute Layer. For example, *all* of the various objects which are related to SUBSCRIPTION can exist *only* if they are associated with a particular subscription (or subscriptions). That

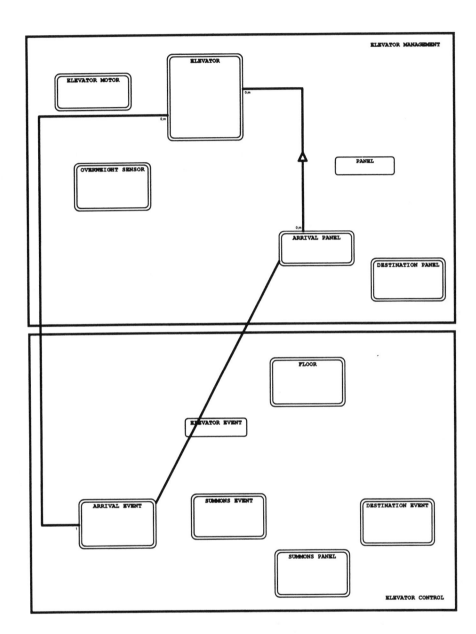

Figure 9.2
Closed loops may identify redundant instance connections.

is, we will *not* allow (in this application domain) a payment to exist *without* an associated subscription. Likewise for SPECIAL ORDERs; they cannot exist without CUSTOMERs. And similarly, a CUSTOMER cannot exist without a SPECIAL ORDER. A SUBSCRIBER cannot exist without a SUBSCRIPTION. However, what about subscribers with *terminated* subscriptions? As we mentioned above, instance connections are *static*. Time, as in an instant of time, should never be considered when establishing application domain constraints. The instance connection between SUBSCRIPTION and SUBSCRIBER simply means that a SUBSCRIBER must be associated with a SUBSCRIPTION *over the life* of the application domain.

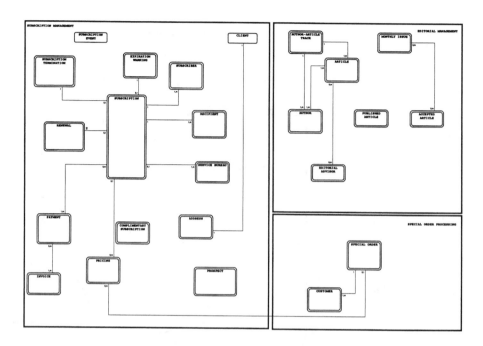

Figure 9.3
Instance connections
for the SBSS.

As you examine the instance connections, you may wish to consider if any new objects might emerge. (Remember, this is an iterative process.) For example, how do we deal with subscriptions which go to multiple recipients and recipients which receive multiple subscriptions? Should we create a new object? Or, should we simply change our business rules? Similar issues arise when considering payments and subscriptions (how about an object class called SUBSCRIPTION PAYMENT), as well as authors and articles.

Consider the inheritance relationship between ARTICLE, ACCEPTED ARTICLE and PUBLISHED ARTICLE. Based on the object attributes, could *multiple inheritance* better reflect this relationship?

9.4
Final Notes
and Comments

1. As mentioned above, many-to-many relationships *are* permitted in an OOA model because they express a relationship in the application domain. Note that the existence of a many-to-many instance connection between AUTHOR and ARTICLE led us to create a new associative entity kind of object called AUTHOR-ARTICLE-TRACK.

2. We have not yet discussed the *Service Layer*. It should be noted, however, that services, or constraints on services, may be suggested by instance relationships. For example, the requirement that a SUBSCRIPTION *always* be associated with a SUBSCRIBER and a RECIPIENT, imposes constraints on the services which manage instances of SUBSCRIPTION, SUBSCRIBER and RECIPIENT.

3. We will discuss quality issues in Chapter 11; however, at this point a few comments regarding the mechanics of the instance connections component of the Attribute Layer are appropriate:

Instance relationships must be consistent with and represent application domain constraints (i.e., business rules). The attributes of objects which participate in instance relationships must be consistent with those relationships. (This is equivalent to foreign key relationships in data models.)

All essential instance relationships must be shown on the OOA model. Only essential instance relationships should be shown on the OOA model. Redundant instance relationships, or so-called "So what?" instance relationships (which do not express a business rule or application domain constraint) should be avoided.

 *Key Points*

▲ Instance connections are part of the Attribute Layer (together with attributes).

▲ Instance connections are shown only if they are meaningful within the application domain and capture an application domain constraint, or business rule.

▲ Redundant instance connections are usually not shown.

▲ Many-to-many instance connections are permitted in the OOA model.

▲ The existence of a many-to-many instance connection may suggest the existence of a new associative object. Such an object, however, must be meaningful within the application domain.

CHAPTER 10
Things Objects Do and Say: Identifying Services and Messages

There never was a bad man that had ability for good service.

— Edmund Burke

10.1 Introduction and Discussion

Thus far, every component of our OOA model has represented some *static* aspect of our application domain, e.g., elevators engage in Whole-Part relationships with their motors, regardless of where the elevators are going or how the motors are moving—they always have, they do now, and they always will; subscribers are related to subscriptions, independent of who (or what) the subscriber or subscription is—they always have, they do now, and they always will; accounts have balances regardless of who owns the account or what is the balance—they always have, they do now, and they always will. However, in this chapter, we will establish *dynamic* relationships between objects. These are expressed as services performed by objects and messages which flow between objects.

These dynamic relationships establish how the various objects we've identified *collaborate* to perform the work of the system. Our deliverable for this chapter will be the *Service Layers* of the OOA models of the ECS and SBSS. We will begin by identifying the set of services which must be encapsulated within each object; these should be verified for consistency, by comparing the services with the object's attributes (and vice versa). If we have already identified the object's attributes (as we did in Chapter 9), then each attribute must be associated with some service—otherwise the attribute is trapped within the object and can never be accessed.

Next, we will draw message communication paths between the objects which are required to orchestrate the behavior of the system. One way to do this is to interview each object. We ask, "Okay, Mr./Ms. Object...how do you get born? And then, what do you do next? And then?..." This life cycle will suggest a number of states which the object passes through from birth to death. Each change of state is associated with the receipt of (and possibly transmission of) a message between objects. This is a bottom up approach—we begin with objects and work up.

Alternatively, we could conduct this interview process using the event-response approach discussed in earlier chapters, whereby each happening or occurrence must be recognized by an object, which must produce messages for other objects, which must (ultimately) produce responses. From this perspective, we can ask what services must be performed to receive, process and generate each message. This is a top-down approach. We begin with system behaviors and work down into objects.

We have found an enormously useful tool for identifying and documenting inter-object communication. That is, the *Event-Response Object-Interaction* (EROI) diagram, based on fence-post diagrams used in tele-communications. Our extension to these diagrams is their integration with the event-response model discussed in Chapter 3. That is, for each event, the EROI diagram shows which object recognizes the occurrence of the event, which messages are produced, which other objects receive those messages and which responses are produced. (EROI diagram notation is given in Appendix K.)

EROI diagrams for the ECS and the SBSS are included in Appendices L and M and will be discussed below.

10.2 Service Layer for the ECS

In earlier chapters of this book, we identified the relevant objects for the ECS; this was based on our tentative conclusions about the characteristics and behavior of the various objects. However, although the attributes and instance connections between the objects are helpful and interesting, the heart of the ECS is reflected in the dynamic behavior between the objects—i.e., by the services and messages.

At first, it seems like a fairly straight-forward task to allocate appropriate services (or methods, or functions) to each object in the model. The final result of that process is presented below, but we want to comment extensively on the thought process that led to that result. Invariably, when we have observed students in our workshops looking at this problem, an argument has broken out about the control aspect of the system: which object is in charge of the overall behavior of the system? Students occasionally come to fisticuffs over the issue of whether or not there *must* exist a centralized controller object. Actually, there are two key questions that confront the analyst:

- Which object(s) "remember" pending summons-requests and pending destination-requests?
- Which object(s) contain the "secret" of the algorithm for dispatching an elevator to a requested floor?

There may be a tendency to bundle these two issues together, for the dispatching of an elevator obviously requires some knowledge of what pending requests exist. However, there is no *a priori* reason why this must be the case. The object responsible for making the dispatching decision could interrogate some other object, via messages, to ascertain the nature of pending requests. Therefore, whether or not there should be a *centralized* controller should not be an issue; the issue is *how* controlling should be accomplished—centralized or not.

We have found that there are four fundamental choices when answering these questions. For example, regarding the question of how the system should remember pending requests:

1. Each instance of a FLOOR can remember whether it has a pending destination request and/or a pending summons request. There is an intuitive argument for this, since all requests made by passengers and would-be passengers are related to a specific floor; also, all of the dispatching decisions are made when a floor is reached. The whole purpose of the elevator is to travel from one floor to another; thus, it makes sense to have the floors remember whether anyone wants them.

2. Each instance of a DESTINATION PANEL (in the elevator) and each instance of a SUMMONS PANEL (on the floor) can remember appropriate requests. Indeed, it could be argued that these two objects *should* remember their associated requests, since they are required (according to the user's specification) to display the status of those requests, on a continuous basis, on the panel lights. Thus, for FLOOR to remember the same information requires some undesirable redundancy; and, even if we want FLOOR to make the dispatching decisions (which we'll discuss below), it would be possible for FLOOR to interrogate the PANEL objects to see if there are pending requests.

   Consider now the issue of object responsibility. It could well be argued that DESTINATION PANEL and SUMMONS PANEL should remember their own requests since this is more consistent with the responsibility of those objects. Clearly this enhances reuse; we could reuse DESTINATION PANEL and SUMMONS PANEL in applications where there may be no floors at all (for example, in a Material Movement System). On the other hand, encapsulating the secret of requests in the same object as the secret of dispatching enhances FLOOR *cohesion* (see Chapter 19), making FLOOR more reusable. These difficult choices are what makes OOA challenging and interesting!

3. Each instance of an ELEVATOR could remember its destination. But, this "elevator-centric" approach is a disaster; if an elevator were initially summoned from, say, floor 1 to floor 40, it might need to stop at intermediate floors along the way to service summons requests that had been entered after it left floor 1.

   It makes sense for an ELEVATOR to at least remember which *direction* it's going. Some object has to remember that fact, and it might as well be the ELEVATOR itself.

4. If a centralized approach is adopted, an elevator scheduler or elevator controller object could remember *all* pending requests. We have no object called ELEVATOR SCHEDULER, but one could be created, if necessary. It is tempting to do so, since the user makes a reference to such a *controller* in the specification. On the other hand, such an object is not *required* to make the elevator system behave in the manner specified by the user, and, it has the disadvantage of concentrating virtually all of the complexity of the system in one object (primarily because the decision to remember all pending requests in a scheduler object usually results in allowing that same object to make all of

the dispatching decisions). In other words, an elevator scheduler or elevator controller is not an *essential requirement*, hence we have decided *not* to follow this approach.

We took the position that destination requests and summons requests should be maintained within the DESTINATION PANEL and SUMMONS PANEL classes, respectively. This turns out (after numerous alternatives were explored) to be no worse than any other alternative.

Similarly, the secret of how to dispatch an elevator could be encapsulated in three obvious places:

1. As mentioned above, an elevator scheduler could be given the task of dispatching all elevators. We decided *not* to use this approach during the analysis phase of the project, though we can still reserve the option of introducing such an object in the design model if we decide it would be the most convenient implementation technology. This is an important philosophical issue: if we put a scheduler object in the requirements model, it is almost inevitable that the designer/programmer will feel compelled to include the same class in the OOD model; by leaving it out of the OOA model, we give the designer the freedom to choose whatever implementation approach he/she judges best.

2. Each ELEVATOR could determine its destiny by polling the various floors to determine which one(s) have outstanding summons and/or destination requests. Note that this would require the elevators to communicate with one another to negotiate the decision as to which elevator would respond to a given request. While this is a perfectly reasonable approach (and one often chosen by our students), we have chosen the alternative below.

3. The FLOOR objects can make the dispatching decision by negotiating among themselves whenever any one of them learns that an elevator has arrived. We chose this approach because, after exploring the various alternatives, allowing floors to control elevators seemed to enhance the reusability of most classes and also provided the most elegant solution.

Note that this discussion has an enormous impact on the question of whether FLOOR deserves to exist as a distinct object. As was discussed in Chapter 5, if FLOOR does no dispatching (e.g., because we have decided to have the elevators dispatch themselves), and if it has no memory of its pending requests (e.g., because we have put that information in other objects, as discussed above), then FLOOR would contain nothing but a "floor-id" attribute which could just as well be incorporated as an attribute in the various other objects that deal with floors. The real justification for the existence of a FLOOR object seems to be our decision to make it encapsulate the dispatching secret.

To illustrate our strategy for scheduling and dispatching elevators, refer to Figure 10.1. In this illustration, elevators 1, 2 and 4 are at the first floor; they are currently not available. Elevator 3 has just arrived at the 37th floor (its direction of arrival is not important). A single summons request, at floor 32, is pending; no other summons requests are pending in the building. The following scenario is

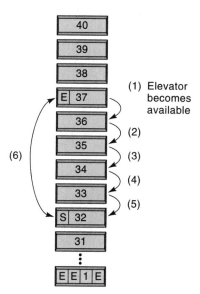

Figure 10.1
Strategy for scheduling
and dispatching
elevators.

initiated at the point in time at which elevator 3 becomes ready (i.e., the doors close and the elevator mechanism reports the "elevator ready" event to the ECS).

(1) Elevator 3 becomes available on floor 37. No summons requests are pending at that floor. No destination requests are pending for elevator 3. Floor 37 reports the availability of an elevator to its neighbor (floor 36). ("I have an elevator available, do you need it?")

(2) Floor 36 checks for summons requests it may have. Since there are none, floor 36 reports the availability of an elevator to its neighbor (floor 35). ("There's an elevator available on 37, do you need it?")

(3), (4) Floors 35 and 34 behave in the same fashion.

(5) Floor 33 also behaves in the same fashion, however when floor 32 receives this report, it has a summons request pending.

(6) Floor 32 sends a message directly back to floor 37 ("I need your elevator!") Floor 37, initiates the dispatch of its elevator (in the direction of floor 32) and reports back to floor 32 that an elevator is on its way. ("OK, you got it!")

In a more general scenario, of course, floor 37 may well have lost its elevator to other floors, and so the reply to floor 32 might be that the elevator is no longer available. ("Sorry!") Also, if there were no summons requests pending in the entire building, eventually the availability message would return to floor 37. (When the availability message gets to floor 1, it is passed on to its neighbor, floor 40.) If the elevator is no longer available, the message is terminated at that time. If the elevator is still available, the message continues to be passed on (again to floor 36, etc.). If the building were vacant and elevators were idle, availability messages would simply circulate continuously around the building until a summons or destination request occurs.

From the discussion above, it is evident that there is more than one solution to the OOA model for the ECS. There are a number of basic questions that one can ask when evaluating the alternative approaches:

- Does it work?
- Is it easy to explain and communicate?
- Does it enhance re-use?
- Will a design based on this analysis be maintainable?
- Is it qualitatively better than alternative approaches?

The question of whether a particular choice of OOA Service Layer works can be answered, fundamentally, by asking whether the model will behave properly in all conceivable scenarios. We will discuss this in detail below for the solution we have chosen, but here is an example of a scenario you might evaluate if you have chosen a different approach for *your* OOA model: how does the elevator system respond if all four elevators are idle, on the ground floor, when a passenger pushes the summons button on the 10th floor?

Whether a particular solution is easy to explain and communicate will depend, to some extent, on the user's ability to understand the metaphor of the solution explained. From an object-oriented perspective, it is common for the analyst to anthropomorphize the solution and describe it as if its constituent objects are living, breathing creatures. An object says, "I am *alive*. I know things about myself, and I can do things. And the manner in which I record my knowledge (state-memory) about myself, and the manner in which I carry out my behavior, are *secrets* that I keep (encapsulate) within myself." So, the question you must ask yourself if you chose our "floor-centric" solution, for example, is whether it makes sense to articulate the following metaphor to the user: "I am a floor. I know about the summons commands that passengers have initiated to bring an elevator to me. I know about the destination requests that passengers within elevators have initiated. I know how to decide whether an available elevator should be dispatched in my direction."

Note that in such discussions, it is important to distinguish between a *class* and one or more *instances* of the class. In the anthropomorphic commentary in the previous paragraph, for example, is it the FLOOR *class* or a Floor *instance* uttering the soliloquy? In our solution, some of the messages involve individual instances of objects—e.g., one instance of ELEVATOR might tell one instance of FLOOR that it has just arrived at that Floor. In other cases, though, it's possible that *all* instances might be involved. When dispatching an elevator, for example, eventually *all* instances of FLOOR might communicate with one another to decide whether the elevator should be commanded to move.

To ensure that the user understands and agrees with the approach we have chosen, it is *extremely* helpful to have a diagram to walk through. When discussing services and messages, we typically examine each event in the environment and trace through a thread of messages to ensure that the system is behaving properly; an alternative is the *use case* approach, in which there may be several interactions (i.e., scenarios) between the system and external environment.

All of this could be accomplished using the object diagrams presented in previous chapters. However, the examination of one scenario or use case typically involves only a few objects, and the presence of other objects on the diagram can be distracting during such a discussion. Thus, it would be extremely convenient to have a CASE tool that would allow us to hide those objects that do *not* participate in a scenario, or are not involved in the response to an event. Even better would be a CASE tool that allows us to animate the model to demonstrate how the system behaves when a specific event occurs. In this book we present the traditional diagrams on paper. For such discussions, we have found EROI diagrams to be extremely useful.

The question of whether one solution is qualitatively better than another is more difficult to evaluate. We will discuss several evaluation criteria in Chapter 19, many of which are based on issues of object inter-connectedness and object complexity. For now, we might ask a simple question: how much of the model would have to change if we added a new elevator to the system (or removed one); what would happen if we added a 41st floor, or if our user wanted the ability to mark certain floors as being temporarily unavailable?

Our solution to the elevator system is described by the Service Layer given in Appendix I and the EROI diagram in Appendix L.

10.2.1
ECS Walkthrough

This section describes system behavior for each ECS event. For each event, the EROI diagram is presented together with a textual description of how the system recognizes the occurrence of that event and how the appropriate responses are produced. A complete set of EROI diagrams for the ECS may be found in Appendix L.

We implore the reader to walk through several of these events in minute detail; the reader will be amazed to discover how insight will evolve.

1. ELEVATOR SUMMONED

    When this event is recognized, the appropriate summons panel is updated. The scheduling of the elevator, however, occurs when an elevator actually becomes "ready." (see Figure 10.2).

    1.1   The class service **SUMMONS EVENT.RECOGNIZE_SUMMONS_REQUEST** detects the occurrence of a summons button depression.

    1.2   This service creates a **Summons Event**. Its attributes are **summons_id** (an arbitrary identifier), **summons_floor** (the floor at which the summons event was generated) and **summons_type** ([UP|DOWN]).

    1.2.1   The service **Summons Event.Report_Summons_Event** sends a unidirectional message to the **Summons Panel** associated with the **summons_floor**. The message is: (**summons_floor, summons_type**,CREATE).

    1.2.1.1   The **Summons Panel.Update_Summons_Panel** receives this message and updates the summons panel associated with **summons_floor** to indicate a summons pending. The appropriate attribute SUMMONS PANEL(**summons_floor**).**summons_pending_up** or SUMMONS PANEL(**summons_floor**).**summons_pending_down** is set to TRUE.

    1.3   This **Summons Event** is terminated.

2. DESTINATION REQUESTED

    When this event is recognized, the appropriate destination panel is updated. The dispatching of the elevator, however, occurs when the elevator becomes "ready." (See Figure 10.3).

    2.1   The **DESTINATION EVENT.RECOGNIZE_DESTINATION_REQUEST** service detects the occurrence of a destination button depression.

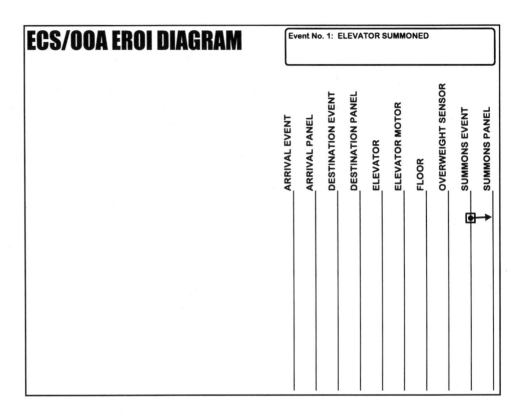

Figure 10.2
ELEVATOR
SUMMONED.

2.2   A **Destination Event** is created. Its attributes are **destination_id** (an arbitrary identifier), *elevator_id* (the elevator in which the event was generated) and **destination_floor** (the requested destination floor).

    2.2.1   The service **Destination Event.Report_Destination_Event** sends a uni-directional message to the **Destination Panel** associated with **elevator_id**. The message is: (**elevator_id,destination_floor**,CREATE).

        2.2.1.1   The **Destination Panel.Update_Destination_Panel** receives this message and updates the destination panel associated with **elevator_id** to indicate the pending destination. The multi-valued attribute DESTINATION PANEL(**elevator_id**).**destinations_pending** (**destination_floor**) is set to TRUE.

2.3   This **Destination Event** is terminated.

3.   ELEVATOR ARRIVES AT SCHEDULED FLOOR

When an elevator arrives at any floor, the appropriate **Floor** must be queried to determine whether or not that floor is a scheduled floor. The **Floor** does this by communicating with the appropriate **Destination Panel**, **Elevator** and **Summons Panels**; these objects encapsulate knowledge of pending destination and summons requests. In this case there is either a destination request or a summons request. The appropriate actions are taken to cause the elevator to stop at the current floor (See Figure 10.4).

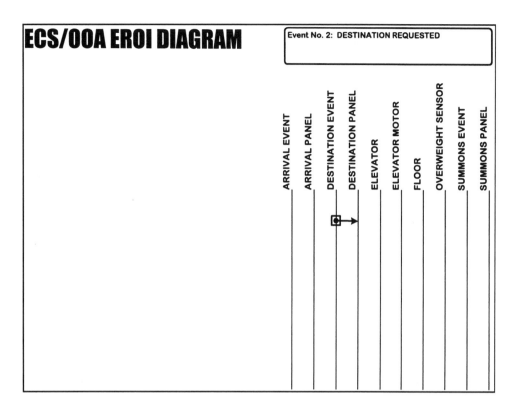

Figure 10.3
DESTINATION
REQUESTED.

3.1   The **ARRIVAL EVENT.RECOGNIZE_ARRIVAL_EVENT** service detects the occurrence of an elevator arrival.

3.2   An **Arrival Event** is created. Its attributes are **arrival_id** (an arbitrary identifier), **elevator_id** (the elevator which generated the arrival event) and **arrival_floor** (the floor at which the event was generated).

    3.2.1   This **Arrival Event.Report_Arrival_Event** sends a unidirectional message to the **Arrival Panel** associated with **elevator_id**. The message is: (**arrival_floor**).

        3.2.1.1   The **Arrival Panel.Update_Arrival_Panel** receives this message and updates the arrival panel appropriately.

    3.2.2   The **Arrival Event.Report_Arrival_Event** service sends a message to the **Floor** associated with **arrival_floor**. The message is: (**arrival_id,report_elevator_id,report_arrival_floor**).

        3.2.2.1   The **Floor.Process_Elevator_Arrival** receives this message. This service may issue a number of messages.

            A bi-directional message is sent to the **Elevator** associated with **report_elevator_id**. This message is: (**report_status_direction?, report_current_direction?**).

            3.2.2.1.1   The **Elevator.Report_Status_Direction** of this instance of Elevator sends a response to this message indicating the value of the attributes **status_direction** and **current_direction**

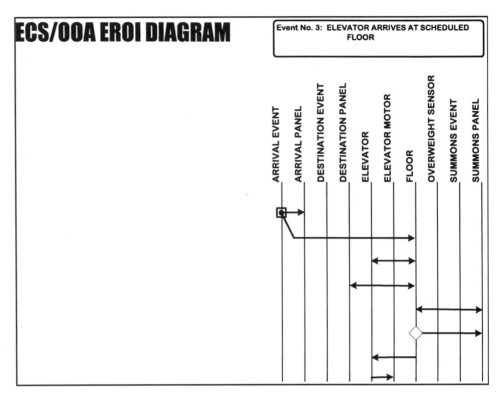

Figure 10.4
ELEVATOR ARRIVES
AT SCHEDULED
FLOOR.

by appropriately updating `report_status_direction` and `report_current_direction`.

3.2.2.2   A bi-directional message is sent to the `Destination Panel` associated with `report_elevator_id`. The message is: (`report_arrival_floor,destination_pending_above?,destination_pending_below?`)

3.2.2.2.1   The service `Report_Destination_Pending` of this instance of **Destination_Panel** sends a response by resolving the validity of `destination_pending_above` as [TRUEIFALSE] and `destination_pending_below` as [TRUEIFALSE] depending on the destination_pending attributes and the value of report_current_floor.

3.2.2.3   A bi-directional message is sent to the `Summons Panel` associated with `arrival_floor`. The message is: (`report_summons_pending_up?,report_summons_pending_down?`)

3.2.2.3.1   The `Summons Panel.Report_Summons_Pending` responds appropriately to this message by updating the parameters with the values of the attributes `summons_pending_up` and `summons_pending_down`.

The service **Process_Elevator_Arrival** includes an algorithm to determine whether the elevator should stop and if a summons is being answered at the arrival floor. The algorithm is based on the reported parameters from the **Elevator**, **Summons_Panel** and **Destination_Panel** instances in response to the messages from the arrival floor. The algorithm determines the values of **Updated_Current_Direction**, **Updated_Summons_Pending_Up**, **Updated_Summons_Pending_Down** and **Updated_Status_Direction**, and honors summons in the committed direction of travel, as well as destinations pending. It will return appropriate STOP commands at floors 1 and 40. The algorithm is included in Appendix U.

3.2.3   For this event, either there is a destination pending for this instance of Floor or there is an appropriate summons. The algorithm updated the instance of **Summons_Panel** appropriately and sent appropriate messages to this instance of Elevator to update the attributes **status_direction** and **current_direction**, and the **current_status**. The elevator received this message and responded by sending a message to the instance of Elevator Motor associated with this Elevator instance. The service **Control_ Elevator_Motor** of this instance of **Elevator_Motor** receives this message and causes the elevator motor to stop. The elevator's mechanical systems then cause the elevator doors to open. See Appendix U for details.

3.3   This **Arrival Event** is terminated.

4.   ELEVATOR ARRIVES AT NON-SCHEDULED FLOOR

When an elevator arrives at any floor, the appropriate **Floor** must be queried to determine whether or not that floor is a scheduled floor. The **Floor** does this by communicating with the appropriate **DESTINATION PANEL** and **Summons Panels**; these objects encapsulate knowledge of pending destination and summons requests. In this case, there are no destination or summons requests for the current floor, so only the appropriate **arrival panel** is updated (see Figure 10.5).

It may be the case that an elevator was dispatched in response to a summons request. And further, that a competing elevator served that request first. An elevator, therefore, may be in motion with no floors scheduled. Such a "runaway elevator" will continue to travel in its current direction until the end of the shaft is encountered, at which point, the elevator will be stopped and subsequently be reported as being "ready."

4.1   The **ARRIVAL EVENT.RECOGNIZE_ARRIVAL_EVENT** service detects the occurrence of an elevator arrival.

4.2   An **Arrival Event** is created. Its attributes are **arrival_id** (an arbitrary identifier), **elevator_id** (the elevator which generated the arrival event) and **arrival_floor** (the floor at which the event was generated).

4.2.1   This **Arrival Event.Report_Arrival_Event** sends a uni-directional message to the **Arrival Panel** associated with **elevator_id**. The message is: (**arrival_floor**).

4.2.1.1   The **Arrival Panel.Update_Arrival_Panel** receives this message and updates the arrival panel appropriately.

4.2.2   The **Arrival Event.Report_Arrival_Event** service sends a message to the **Floor** associated with **arrival_floor**. The message is: (**arrival_id,report_elevator_id,report_ arrival_floor**).

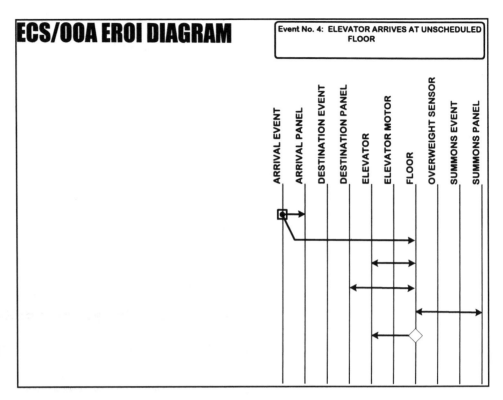

Figure 10.5
ELEVATOR ARRIVES
AT UNSCHEDULED
FLOOR.

4.2.2.1   The **Floor.Process_Elevator_Arrival** receives this
message. This service may issue a number of messages.

A bi-directional message is sent to the **Elevator** associated
with **report_elevator_id**. This message is:
(**report_status_direction?**, **report_current_
direction?**).

4.2.2.1.1   The **Elevator.Report_Status_Direction** of
this instance of Elevator sends a response to this
message indicating the value of the attributes
status_direction and **current_direction**
by appropriate updating **report_status_
direction** and **report_current_
direction**.

4.2.2.2   A bi-directional message is sent to the **Destination Panel**
associated with **report_elevator_id**. The message is:
(**report_arrival_floor,destination_pending_
above?**, **destination_pending_below?**)

4.2.2.2.1   The service **Report_Destination_Pending** of
this instance of Destination_Panel sends a
response by resolving the validity of
destination_pending_above as
[TRUE|FALSE] and **destination_pending_
below** as [TRUE|FALSE], depending on the
destination_pending attributes and the value
of **report_current_floor**.

4.2.2.3   A bi-directional message is sent to the **Summons Panel** associated with **arrival_floor**. The message is: (**report_summons_pending_up?,report_summons_ pending_down?**)

4.2.2.3.1   The **Summons Panel.Report_Summons_ Pending** responds appropriately to this message by updating the parameters with the values of the attributes **summons_pending_up** and **summons_pending down**.

The service **Process_Elevator_Arrival** includes an algorithm to determine whether the elevator should stop and if a summons is being answered at the arrival floor. The algorithm is based on the reported parameters from the **Elevator, Summons_Panel and Destination_Panel** instances in response to the messages from the arrival floor. The algorithm determines the values of **Updated_Current_Direction, Updated_Summons_Pending_Up, Updated_Summons_Pending_Down** and **Updated_Status_Direction**, and honors summons in the committed direction of travel, as well as destinations pending. It will return appropriate STOP commands at floors 1 and 40. The algorithm is included in Appendix U.

4.2.3   For this event, there is neither a destination pending for this instance of **Floor** nor is there an appropriate summons. However, in the event that the committed direction must be updated, a message is sent to this instance of **Elevator** to update the attribute **status_ direction**. For this event, the elevator will not stop. See Appendix U for details.

4.3   This **Arrival Event** is terminated.

5.   ELEVATOR BECOMES READY

When an elevator signals that it is "ready" (i.e,. its doors are secured and the elevator is awaiting a control command), it sends a message to the current **Floor** which checks the appropriate **Destination Panel. Floor** then resolves the appropriate messaging to **Elevator**. If the determination is that no message is sent, the **FLOOR** continuously polls each **Elevator** by checking its neighbor iteratively. Either another floor will need an elevator, the current floor will need an elevator or neither case will apply. In the first case, the **Elevator** will be dispatched. In the second case, the **Elevator** will open its doors. In the third case, the above process will reiterate (See Figure 10.6).

5.1   The **Elevator.Recognize_Elevator_Ready** detects the occurrence of the elevator mechanism becoming ready.

5.1.1   A uni-directional message is sent to the **Floor** associated with **Elevator.current_floor**. The message is: (**report_elevator_id, report_current_floor, report_ status_direction,report_current_direction**) based on the values of the corresponding attributes in this instance of **Elevator**.

The service **Process_Elevator_Ready** of this instance of **Floor** receives this message. This service includes a complex and rigorous algorithm to determine the dispatch of the elevator. This algorithm is included in Appendix V. The algorithm services destinations pending appropriately. In the event that no destinations are pending, it goes through a process of polling neighboring floors to determine if a summons needs to be answered. The algorithm provides for updating the **Elevator** and **Summons_Panel** instances appropriately. In fact, it

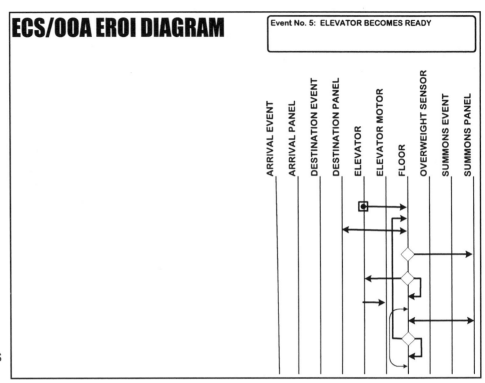

Figure 10.6
ELEVATOR BECOMES
READY.

may set parameters to cause the elevator to open its doors to service a delayed summons. See Appendix V for details.

6. ELEVATOR BECOMES OVERWEIGHT

The processing of this event involves recognizing the event and setting an attribute appropriately (See Figure 10.7).

6.1 An `Overweight Sensor.Recognize_Overweight` service detects the occurrence of an overweight condition.

6.2 The attribute OVERWEIGHT SENSOR(`overweight_sensor_id`).`overweight_status` is set to NOT_OK.

7. ELEVATOR BECOMES NOT-OVERWEIGHT

The processing of this event involves recognizing the event and setting an attribute appropriately (See Figure 10.8).

7.1 An `Overweight Sensor.Recognize_Not_Overweight` service detects the occurrence of overweight condition restored.

7.2 The attribute OVERWEIGHT SENSOR(`overweight_sensor_id`).`overweight_status` is set to OK.

10.3 Service Layer for the SBSS

Though the SBSS has more events and more object classes than the ECS, the interactions are far simpler. Readers with little interest in the ECS may still wish to review the comments given in Section 10.1; those comments may prove relevant and insightful for the SBSS. Our solution to the SBSS is described by the Service Layer given in Appendix J and the EROI diagram in Appendix M.

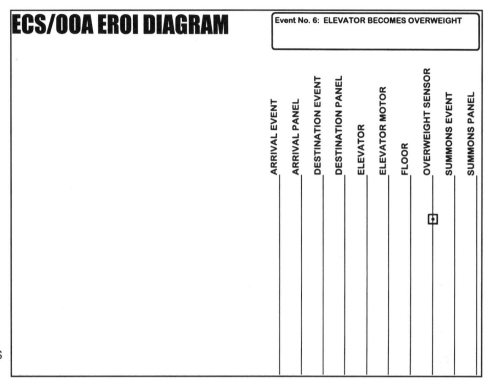

ECS/OOA EROI DIAGRAM

Event No. 6: ELEVATOR BECOMES OVERWEIGHT

ARRIVAL EVENT | ARRIVAL PANEL | DESTINATION EVENT | DESTINATION PANEL | ELEVATOR | ELEVATOR MOTOR | FLOOR | OVERWEIGHT SENSOR | SUMMONS EVENT | SUMMONS PANEL

Figure 10.7
ELEVATOR BECOMES
OVERWEIGHT.

10.3.1
SBSS Walkthrough

This section describes system behavior for each SBSS event. For each event, the EROI diagram is presented together with a textual description of how the system recognizes the occurrence of that event and how the appropriate responses are produced. A complete set of EROI diagrams for the SBSS may be found in Appendix M.

We implore the reader to walk through several of these events in minute detail; the reader will be amazed to discover how insight will evolve.

1. PAID SUBSCRIPTION REQUESTED

    The processing of this event creates or updates records which must be maintained for a paid subscription (see Figure 10.9).

    1.1 **SUBSCRIPTION.RECOGNIZE_SUBSCRIPTION_REQUEST** detects the occurrence of this event and creates a **Subscription** instance.

    1.2 **Subscription.Enter_Paid_Subscription** sends a message to the class service **SUBSCRIPTION TERMINATION.CREATE_SUBSCRIPTION_ EXPIRATION**

        1.2.1 This class service creates the instance **Subscription Termination**. The attributes of **Subscription Termination** identify the associated subscription and its expiration date.

    1.3 **Subscription.Enter_Paid_Subscription** sends a message to **Pricing.Report_Price** of the appropriate **Subscription** instance. This service returns the calculated subscription price.

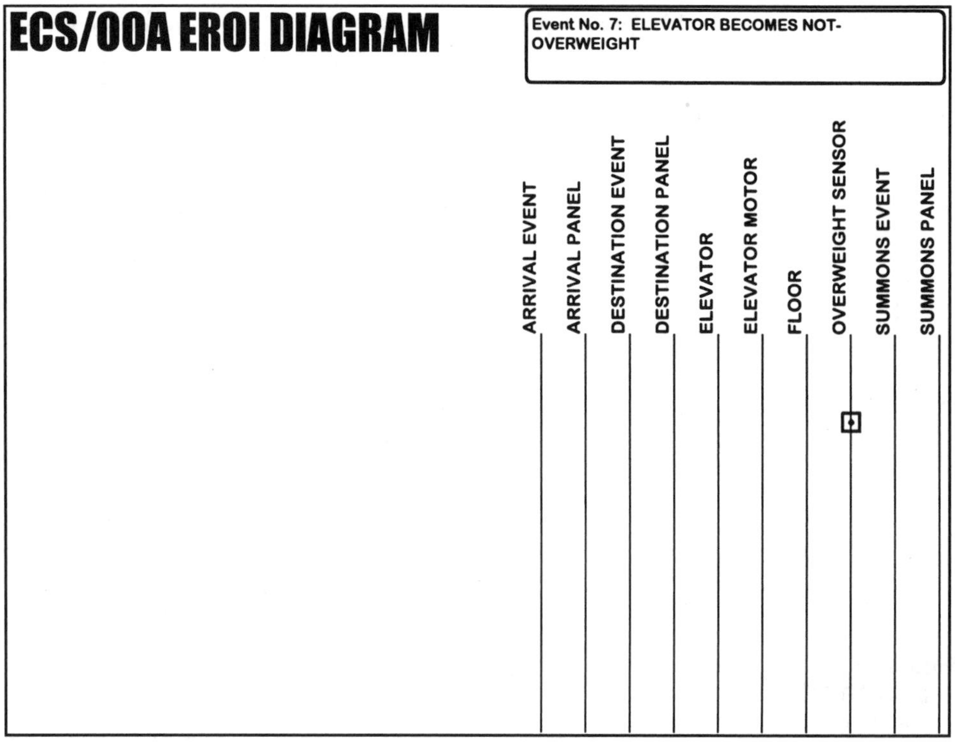

ECS/OOA EROI DIAGRAM

Event No. 7: ELEVATOR BECOMES NOT-OVERWEIGHT

	ARRIVAL EVENT	ARRIVAL PANEL	DESTINATION EVENT	DESTINATION PANEL	ELEVATOR	ELEVATOR MOTOR	FLOOR	OVERWEIGHT SENSOR	SUMMONS EVENT	SUMMONS PANEL
								◻		

Figure 10.8
ELEVATOR
BECOMES
NOT-OVERWEIGHT.

1.3.1   Upon receipt of the subscription price, `Subscription.Enter_Paid_Subscription` sends a message to `PAYMENT.ENTER_PAYMENT.` This class service creates an instance of `Payment`.

    1.3.1.1   If an invoice is requested, `Payment.Issue_Invoice` will send a message to `INVOICE.CREATE_INVOICE.`

        1.3.1.1.1   This class service will create an instance of `Invoice`. The attributes of `Invoice` identify the various invoice details.

1.3.2   Upon receipt of the subscription price, `Subscription.Enter_Paid_Subscription` may send a message to `Service Bureau.Record_Payment`.

1.4   `Subscription.Enter_Paid_Subscription` sends a message to `EXPIRATION WARNING.CREATE_EXPIRATION_WARNING.`

1.4.1   This class service creates the instance `Expiration Warning`. The attributes of `Expiration Warning` identify the associated subscription and its expiration warning date.

1.5   `Subscription.Enter_Paid_Subscription` sends a message to `SUBSCRIBER.ENTER_SUBSCRIBER.`

1.5.1   This class service determines whether or not the given subscriber matches an existing instance `Subscriber`. If there is a match, that instance is associated with the given subscription.

If the given subscriber does not match with any existing instance `Subscriber`, then this class service creates the instance

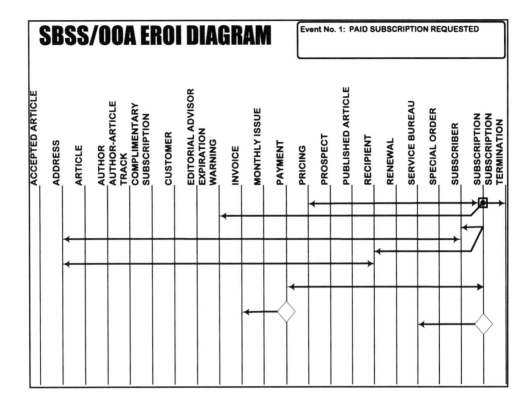

Figure 10.9
PAID
SUBSCRIPTION
REQUESTED.

Subscriber. The attributes of **Subscriber** identify the various subscriber details.

1.5.2 Upon creation of **Subscriber, Subscriber.Enter_Address** sends a message to **ADDRESS.ENTER_ADDRESS**.

1.5.2.1 This class service determines whether or not the given address matches an existing instance **Address**. If there is a match, this class service returns the associated address identification.

If the given address does not match any existing instance **Address**, this class service creates the instance **Address**. The attributes of **Address** identify the various address details. This class service returns the associated address identification.

1.6 **Subscription.Enter_Paid_Subscription** sends a message to **RECIPIENT.ENTER_RECIPIENT**.

1.6.1 This class service determines whether or not the given recipient matches an existing instance of **Recipient**. If there is a match, that instance is associated with the given subscription.

If the given recipient does not match any existing instance **Recipient**, this class service creates the instance **Recipient**. The attributes of **Recipient** identify the various recipient details.

1.6.2 Upon creation of **Recipient, Recipient.Enter_Address** sends a message to **ADDRESS.ENTER_ADDRESS**.

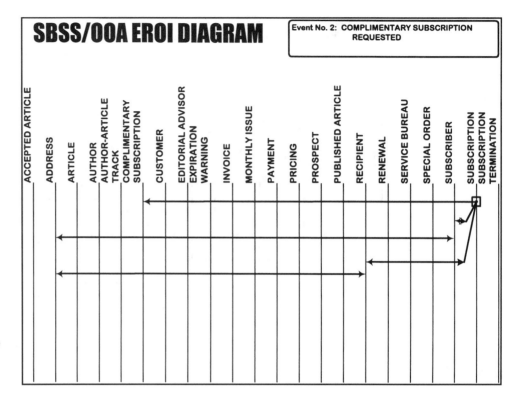

Figure 10.10
COMPLIMENTARY
SUBSCRIPTION
REQUESTED.

1.6.2.1   This class service determines whether or not the given address matches an existing instance of **Address**. If there is a match, this class service returns the associated address identification.

If the given address does not match any existing instance **Address**, this class service creates the instance **Address**. The attributes of **Address** identify the various address details. This class service returns the associated address identification.

2.   COMPLIMENTARY SUBSCRIPTION REQUESTED

The processing of this event creates or updates records which must be maintained for a complimentary subscription (see Figure 10.10).

2.1   **SUBSCRIPTION.RECOGNIZE_SUBSCRIPTION_REQUEST** detects the occurrence of this event and creates a **Subscription** instance.

2.2   **Subscription.Enter_Comp_Subscription** sends a message to **COMPLIMENTARY SUBSCRIPTION.ENTER_COMP_SUBSCRIPTION**.

2.2.1   This class service creates the instance **Complimentary Subscription**. The attributes of **Complimentary Subscription** identify the associated subscription.

2.3   **Subscription.Enter_Comp_Subscription** sends a message to **SUBSCRIBER.ENTER_SUBSCRIBER**.

2.3.1   This class service determines whether or not the given subscriber matches an existing instance **Subscriber**. If there is a match, that instance is associated with the given subscription.

If the given subscriber does not match any existing instance `Subscriber`, this class service creates the instance `Subscriber`. The attributes of `Subscriber` identify the various subscriber details.

2.3.2   Upon creation of `Subscriber, Subscriber.Enter_Address` sends a message to `ADDRESS.ENTER_ADDRESS`.

    2.3.2.1   This class service determines whether or not the given address matches an existing instance `Address`. If there is a match, this class service returns the associated address identification.

        If the given address does not match any existing instance `Address`, then this class service creates the instance `Address`. The attributes of `Address` identify the various address details. This class service returns the associated address identification.

2.4   `Subscription.Enter_Comp_Subscription` sends a message to `RECIPIENT.ENTER_RECIPIENT`.

  2.4.1   This class service determines whether or not the given recipient matches an existing instance `Recipient`. If there is a match, that instance is associated with the given subscription.

    If the given recipient does not match any existing instance `Recipient`, this class service creates the instance `Recipient`. The attributes of `Recipient` identify the various recipient details.

  2.4.2   Upon creation of `Recipient, Recipient.Enter_Address` sends a message to `ADDRESS.ENTER_ADDRESS`.

    2.4.2.1   This class service determines whether or not the given address matches an existing instance `Address`. If there is a match, then this class service returns the associated address identification.

        If the given address does not match with any existing instance `Address`, this class service creates the instance `Address`. The attributes of `Address` identify the various address details. This class service returns the associated address identification.

3.   PAYMENT RECEIVED

The processing of this event updates the appropriate payment record (see Figure 10.11).

  3.1   `PAYMENT.RECOGNIZE_PAYMENT_RECEIVED` detects the occurrence of this event and creates an instance of `Payment`.

    3.1.1   If an invoice is requested, `Payment.Issue_Invoice` will send a message to `INVOICE.CREATE_INVOICE`.

        3.1.1.1   This class service will create an instance `Invoice`. The attributes of `Invoice` identify the various invoice details.

4.   TIME TO SEND RENEWAL NOTICE

The processing of this event recognizes when a renewal notice must be sent for a particular subscription; the appropriate information must be secured to issue a renewal notice (see Figure 10.12).

  4.1   `Expiration Warning.Recognize_Renewal_Due` detects occurrence of this event and sends a message to `Subscription.Report_Subscriber`.

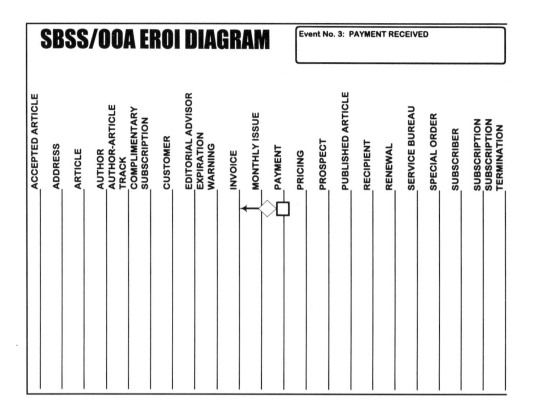

Figure 10.11
PAYMENT
RECEIVED.

4.1.1   Upon receipt of subscriber identification, **Expiration
        Warning.Recognize_Renewal_Due** sends a message to
        Subscriber.Report_Address.

    4.1.1.1   Upon receipt of the message, **Subscriber.Report_
                  Address** sends a message to **Address.Report_
                  Address_Details**.

        4.1.1.1.1   Upon receipt of the address details, **Expiration
                           Warning.Recognize_Renewal_Due** issues
                           the appropriate expiration warning notice.

5.   SUBSCRIPTION TERMINATES

    The processing of this event involves identifying a subscription as "terminated." All
other records (for subscriber, recipient, etc.) are maintained. The termination of a
subscription applies to both paid and complimentary subscriptions (see Figure
10.13).

    5.1   **Subscription Termination.Recognize_Sub_Termination**
        detects occurrence of this event and sends a message to
        Subscription.Terminate_Subscription for the appropriate
        subscription instance.

        5.1.1   Upon receipt of this message, **Subscription.Terminate_
                  Subscription** sets **subscription_status** to indicate the
                  termination of the corresponding subscription.

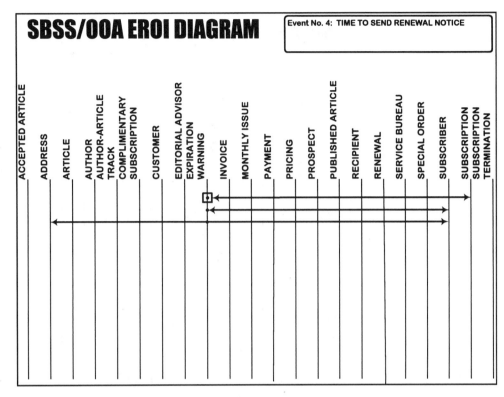

Figure 10.12
TIME TO SEND
RENEWAL NOTICE.

6.   PAID SUBSCRIPTION RENEWED

The processing of this event creates or updates records which must be maintained for
a renewed subscription. A renewed subscription involves the creation of a
subscription instance with a new identifier (see Figure 10.14).

6.1   **RENEWAL.RECOGNIZE_SUBSCRIPTION_RENEWED** detects the occurrence of
this event and sends a message to the appropriate **Subscription** instance.

6.2   **Subscription.Renew_Subscription** sends a message to the class
service **SUBSCRIPTION TERMINATION.CREATE_SUBSCRIPTION_**
EXPIRATION.

6.2.1 This class service creates the instance **Subscription Termination**.
The attributes of **Subscription Termination** identify the
associated subscription and its expiration date.

6.3   **Subscription.Renew_Subscription** sends a message to
Pricing.Report_Price of the appropriate **Subscription** instance.
This service returns the calculated subscription price.

6.3.1   Upon receipt of the subscription price, **Subscription.Renew_**
Subscription sends a message to **PAYMENT.ENTER_PAYMENT.**
This class service creates an instance of **Payment**.

6.3.1.1   If an invoice is requested, **Payment.Issue_Invoice** will
send a message to **INVOICE.CREATE_INVOICE.**

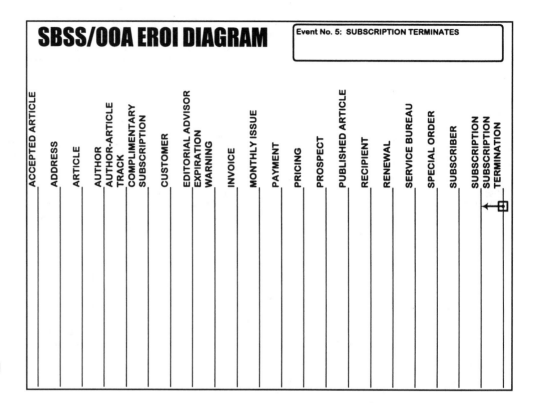

Figure 10.13
SUBSCRIPTION
TERMINATES.

6.3.1.1.1   This class service will create an instance **Invoice**.
The attributes of **Invoice** identify the various
invoice details.

6.3.2   Upon receipt of the subscription price, **Subscription.Renew_
Subscription** may send a message to **Service
Bureau.Record_Payment**.

6.4   **Subscription.Renew_Subscription** sends a message to **EXPIRATION
WARNING.CREATE_EXPIRATION_WARNING**.

6.4.1   This class service creates the instance **Expiration Warning**. The
attributes of **Expiration Warning** identify the associated
subscription and its expiration warning date.

7.   TIME TO REVIEW "COMP LIST"

The processing of this event creates or updates records involved with renewing or
terminating a complimentary subscription (see Figure 10.15).

7.1   **COMPLIMENTARY SUBSCRIPTION.RECOGNIZE_TIME_TO_REVIEW** detects
the occurrence of this event and sends a message to each **Complimentary
Subscription** instance.

7.1.1   The instance service **Complimentary Subscription.Review_
Comp_Subscription** establishes whether or not a complimentary
subscription should be terminated. In the case when a complimentary
subscription should be terminated, this service sends a message to
Subscription.Terminate_Subscription for the appropriate
subscription instance.

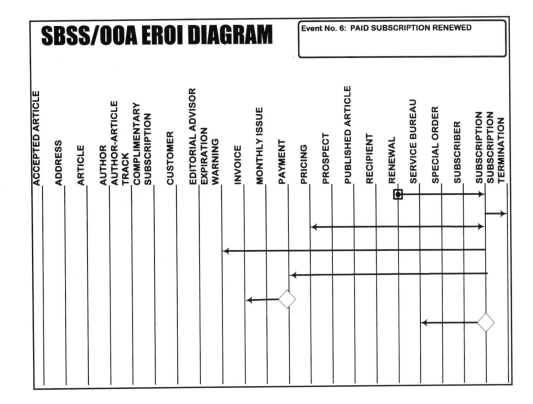

Figure 10.14
PAID
SUBSCRIPTION
RENEWED.

7.1.1.1   Upon receipt of this message, **Subscription.Terminate_ Subscription** sets **subscription_status** to indicate the termination of the corresponding subscription.

8.   SPECIAL ORDER RECEIVED

The processing of this event creates or updates records which must be maintained for a special order (see Figure 10.16).

8.1   **SPECIAL ORDER.RECOGNIZE_SPECIAL_ORDER** detects the occurrence of this event and creates a **Special Order** instance.

8.2   **Special Order.Process_Special_Order** sends a message to **Pricing.Report_Price**. This service returns the calculated special order price.

8.2.1   Upon receipt of the special order price, **Special Order.Process_ Special_Order** sends a message to **PAYMENT.ENTER_PAYMENT**. This class service creates an instance of **Payment**.

8.2.1.1   If an invoice is requested, **Payment.Issue_Invoice** will send a message to **INVOICE.CREATE_INVOICE**.

8.3   **Special Order.Process_Special_Order** sends a message to **CUSTOMER.ENTER_CUSTOMER**.

8.3.1   This class service determines whether or not the given customer matches an existing instance **Customer**. If there is a match, that instance is associated with the given customer.

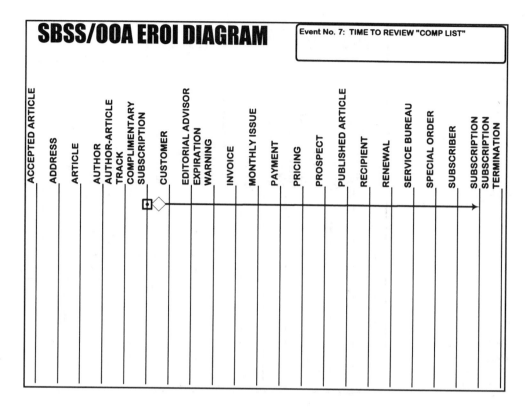

Figure 10.15
TIME TO REVIEW
"COMP LIST".

If the given customer does not match any existing instance **Customer**, this class service creates the instance **Customer**. The attributes of **Customer** identify the various customer details.

8.3.2   Upon creation of **Customer, Customer.Enter_Address** sends a message to **ADDRESS.ENTER_ADDRESS**.

    8.3.2.1   This class service determines whether or not the given address matches an existing instance **Address**. If there is a match, this class service returns the associated address identification.

        If the given address does not match any existing instance **Address**, this class service creates the instance **Address**. The attributes of **Address** identify the various address details. This class service returns the associated address identification.

9.   ARTICLE RECEIVED

The processing of this event creates or updates records which must be maintained for a submitted article (see Figure 10.17).

9.1   **ARTICLE.RECOGNIZE_ARTICLE_RECEIVED** detects the occurrence of this event and creates an **Article** instance.

9.2   **Article.Enter_New_Article** sends a message to **AUTHOR.ENTER_AUTHOR**.

    9.2.1   This class service determines whether or not the given author matches an existing instance **Author**. If there is a match, this class service returns the associated author identification.

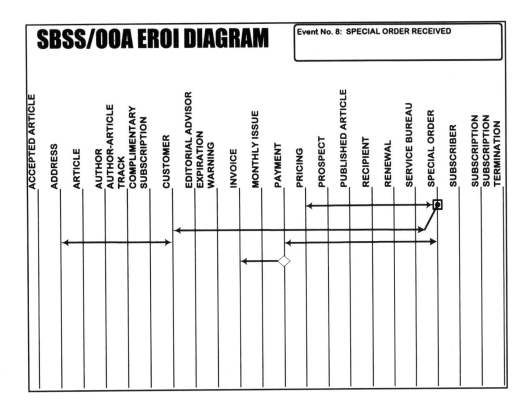

Figure 10.16
SPECIAL ORDER
RECEIVED.

If the given author does not match any existing instance **Author**, this class service creates the instance **Author**. The attributes of **Author** identify the various author details. This class service returns the associated author identification.

9.2.1.1 Upon creation of **Author, Author.Enter_Address** sends a message to **ADDRESS.ENTER_ADDRESS**.

9.2.1.1.1 This class service determines whether or not the given address matches an existing instance **Address**. If there is a match, this class service returns the associated address identification.

If the given address does not match any existing instance **Address**, this class service creates the instance **Address**. The attributes of **Address** identify the various address details. This class service returns the associated address identification.

9.2.2 Upon receipt of **author_id, Article.Enter_New_Article** sends a message to **AUTHOR ARTICLE TRACK**.

9.2.2.1 The service **AUTHOR ARTICLE TRACK.ENTER_AUTHOR_ ARTICLE** creates an instance of **Author Article Track**.

10. ARTICLE ACCEPTED FOR PUBLICATION

The processing of this event creates or updates records which must be maintained for an accepted article. A complimentary subscription is also processed for the author(s) of the accepted article (see Figure 10.18).

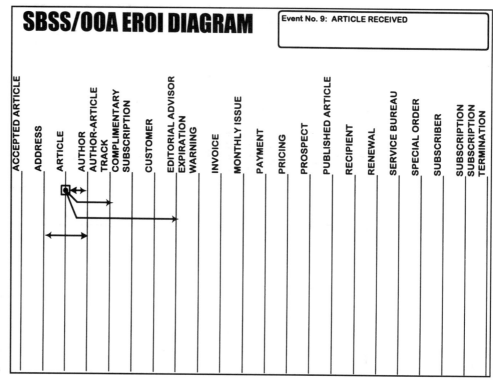

Figure 10.17
ARTICLE RECEIVED.

10.1 **ACCEPTED ARTICLE.RECOGNIZE_ARTICLE_ACCEPTED** detects the occurrence of this event and creates an **Accepted Article** instance. (This operation implies that the corresponding instance of **Article** is terminated.)

10.2 **Accepted Article.Enter_Accepted_Article** sends a message to the corresponding instance of **Author** requesting the associated author_details.

    10.2.1 Upon receipt of author_details, **Accepted Article.Enter_ Accepted_Article**, sends a message to the appropriate instance of **Monthly Issue**.

        10.2.1.1 The service **Monthly Issue.Enter_Article** receives this message and updates the issue details accordingly.

10.3 **Accepted Article.Enter_Accepted_Article** sends a message to **SUBSCRIPTION.REQUEST_SUBSCRIPTION** which then creates a **Subscription** instance.

10.4 **Subscription.Enter_Comp_Subscription** sends a message to **COMPLIMENTARY SUBSCRIPTION.ENTER_COMP_SUBSCRIPTION**

    10.4.1 This class service creates the instance **Complimentary Subscription**. The attributes of **Complimentary Subscription** identify the associated subscription.

10.5 **Subscription.Enter_Comp_Subscription** sends a message to **SUBSCRIBER.ENTER_SUBSCRIBER**.

    10.5.1 This class service determines whether or not the given subscriber matches an existing instance **Subscriber**. If there is a match, that instance is associated with the given subscription.

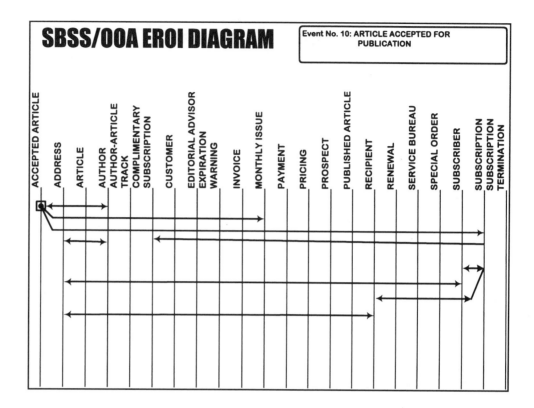

Figure 10.18
ARTICLE
ACCEPTED FOR
PUBLICATION.

If the given subscriber does not match any existing instance **Subscriber**, this class service creates the instance **Subscriber**. The attributes of **Subscriber** identify various subscriber details.

10.5.2 Upon creation of **Subscriber, Subscriber.Enter_Address** sends a message to **ADDRESS.ENTER_ADDRESS**.

10.5.2.1 This class service determines whether or not the given address matches an existing instance **Address**. If there is a match, this class service returns the associated address identification.

If the given address does not match any existing instance **Address**, this class service creates the instance **Address**. The attributes of **Address** identify the various address details. This class service returns the associated address identification.

10.5.3 **Subscription.Enter_Comp_Subscription** sends a message to **RECIPIENT.ENTER_RECIPIENT**

10.5.3.1 This class service determines whether or not the given recipient matches an existing instance **Recipient**. If there is a match, that instance is associated with the given subscription.

If the given recipient does not match any existing instance **Recipient**, this class service creates the instance **Recipient**. The attributes of **Recipient** identify the various recipient details.

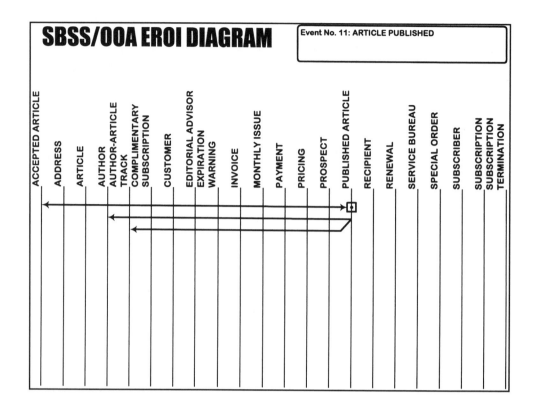

Figure 10.19
ARTICLE
PUBLISHED.

10.5.3.2 Upon creation of **Recipient, Recipient.Enter_Address** sends a message to **ADDRESS.ENTER_ADDRESS**.

10.5.3.2.1 This class service determines whether or not the given address matches an existing instance **Address**. If there is a match, this class service returns the associated address identification.

If the given address does not match any existing instance **Address**, this class service creates the instance **Address**. The attributes of **Address** identify the various address details. This class service returns the associated address identification.

11. ARTICLE PUBLISHED

The processing of this event creates or updates records which must be maintained for a published article (see Figure 10.19).

11.1 **PUBLISHED ARTICLE.RECOGNIZE_ARTICLE_PUBLISHED** detects the occurrence of this event and creates a **Published Article** instance. (This operation implies that the corresponding instance of **Accepted Article** is terminated.)

11.2 **Published Article.Enter_Published_Article** sends a message to the corresponding instance of **Author** requesting the associated author_details.

11.2.1 Upon receipt of author_details, **Published Article.Enter_ Published_Article** sends a message to the appropriate instance of **Author-Article Track**.

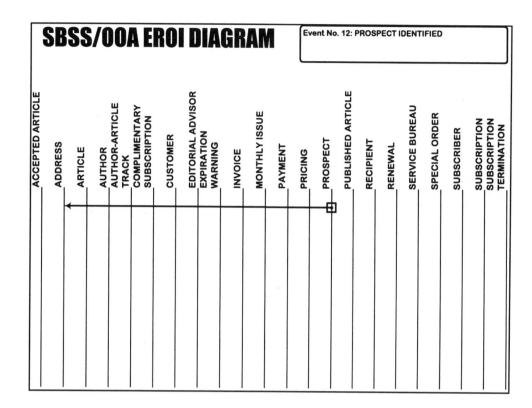

Figure 10.20
PROSPECT
IDENTIFIED.

11.2.1.1 The service **Author-Article Track.Update_Track** receives this message and updates author-article_details accordingly.

11.2.2 Upon receipt of author_details, **Published Article.Enter_ Published_Article** sends a message to the appropriate instance of **Monthly Issue.**

11.2.2.1 The service **Monthly Issue.Enter_Article** receives this message and updates the monthly issue details accordingly.

12. PROSPECT IDENTIFIED

The processing of this event creates or updates records which must be maintained for a prospect (see Figure 10.20).

12.1 The **PROSPECT.RECOGNIZE_PROSPECT_IDENTIFIED** class service determines whether or not the given prospect matches an existing instance **Prospect**. If there is a match, this class service terminates.

12.2 If the given prospect does not match any existing instance **Prospect**, this class service creates the instance **Prospect**. The attributes of **Prospect** identify the various prospect details.

12.2.1. Upon creation of **Prospect, Prospect.Enter_Address** sends a message to **ADDRESS.ENTER_ADDRESS.**

12.2.1.1 This class service determines whether or not the given address matches an existing instance **Address**. If there is a match, this class service returns the associated address identification.

If the given address does not match any existing instance **Address**, this class service creates the instance **Address**. The attributes of **Address** identify the various address details. This class service returns the associated address identification.

10.4 Final Notes and Comments

1. This chapter should pull together the various concepts and techniques introduced thus far. We have now produced OOA models for our case studies. It should be apparent at this point that these models are not simply a bunch of diagrams. As discussed in Chapter 1, we are striving to build working paper models. Users should be able to visualize living with the system of the future before we actually implement that system.

   The fact that we are building working paper models should be very evident from the above walkthroughs. These models have allowed us to visualize the behavior, in considerable detail, of two non-trivial systems, without writing a single line of code.

   With the models we've created so far, we might consider initiating a prototyping activity; prototypes would help us identify and resolve analysis issues before we move on to design. We may, in fact, decide that a prototyping activity should begin (if it hasn't already) simultaneously with a design activity.

2. We will discuss quality issues in Chapter 11; however, at this point a few comments regarding the mechanics of the Service Layer are appropriate:

   Services should be appropriately named, and represent some work, function or process associated with the object. Classes may have services which apply only to the class; such services must be used consistently and apply to the class or all instances of the class. Such services may not apply to a specific instance of the class.

   Names should be unique within an associated object. Names should be meaningful within the application domain and should not represent implementation technology. Names are usually in the verb-noun form; names not in the verb-noun form should be avoided. The conjunctions "and" and "or" should not appear in a name.

   Each object must have at least one class service—the service which allows instances of the object to be manipulated. Each object must have at least one instance service—the service that accesses one or more associated attributes. Services cannot access attributes which are not encapsulated within the encapsulating object.

   Services should be well-defined, that is they should:

   - Have a single entry point
   - Not involve concurrent processing
   - Produce a single or sequential output
   - Be initiated by receipt of a message, or other well-defined event (e.g., time-trigger)
   - Be specified by brief procedural descriptions which are implementation language-independent (e.g., using Structured English [2]).

The objects which participate in Gen-Spec relationships must inherit services consistent with the Gen-Spec relationship. Specialization objects cannot inherit services which are undefined for that specialization.

The services of objects which participate in instance relationships must be consistent with those relationships. Services apply to instances of objects except as noted: In the case where a service participates in an instance relationship with a generic class, then each sub-type of the generic class must be defined for the service.

Messages are always produced by and received by a service. They must be used consistently with their associated services. Messages convey attributes and these attributes must be consistent with the services which produce and receive the message. That is, all of the inputs and outputs for a service are consistent with the specification of that service.

Messages are sent from one instance of an object to another instance of (the same or a different) object except as noted: Services and messages may apply only to classes but must be used consistently. In the case where the participant in a message is a generic class, each sub-type of the generic class must participate in the message.

 *Key Points*

▲ Earlier we characterized objects as "independent, asynchronous, concurrent entities which know things, **do work and collaborate**…" Services and messages are the mechanisms by which objects do work and collaborate, respectively.

▲ The Service Layer provides a dynamic view of the system being modeled.

▲ The EROI diagram is an integration of the event-response and OOA models. It is a useful tool to visualize the dynamic behavior of a system.

▲ With the Service Layer in place, it should be possible to walkthrough the behavior of a proposed system demonstrating that the proposed system will or will not perform in accordance with the user's requirements.

CHAPTER 11

Quality Issues—Completeness/Consistency of the Analysis Model

All men are liable to error; and most men are, in many points, by passion or interest, under temptation to it.

— John Locke

11.1 Introduction and Discussion

Thus far we have not explicitly concerned ourselves with building a *good* OOA model. We have concerned ourselves primarily with modeling the requirements for our two case study systems. In this chapter we will touch upon a few issues related to how we build good models—independent of what those models may model.

The reader should be sensitive to the distinction between building "the right model" and building "the model right." The right model refers to capturing the intended requirements, purposes, spirit, nuances, expectations or *whatever* of the proposed system. If this is achieved, at the completion of the model-building process, the user will exclaim in a loud voice, "By God, you've got it!" This concept is sometimes referred to as the *semantic* correctness of the model.

The semantic correctness of the OOA model can be established only by evaluating the model against stated requirements and user review. Semantic correctness can be assured by exhibiting the desired behavior of the model. This can be accomplished by executing the model and verifying that the events on the event-response model produce the desired responses. As any systems analyst can attest, semantic correctness tends to be subjective; different individuals may well have different opinions as to whether or not a model accurately captures requirements correctly. We will touch upon this further in Chapter 13.

Building "the model right" is quite different than building "the right model." It refers to the completeness and consistency of the OOA model in a mechanical or logical sense. This concept is sometimes referred to as the *syntactic* correctness of the model. In this chapter we will focus only on issues related to syntactic correctness.

135

The various correctness criteria are discussed below within the context of the OOA model; these criteria are applicable however to virtually all OOA methods. Correctness criteria are identified as:

- *Naming conventions*
- *Style conventions*
- *Syntax requirements*

Naming conventions are accepted standards for the form or format of model labels, identifiers, designators, etc. Naming conventions facilitate clear communication and as such can be of enormous value on large object-oriented projects.

Style conventions are also accepted standards for form and format, but apply to structures, procedures, heuristics, etc. Style conventions apply to modeling *techniques*. Again, large object-oriented projects demand clear standards and conventions.

Unlike the conventions noted above, syntax requirements are conditions or behaviors which are required by the modeling techniques used. Every modeling technique should have a collection of syntax requirements which establishes the syntactic correctness of the OOA model built with that technique.

11.2
The Object-class Layer

- Naming Conventions: Object names are appropriate, describe a class and are not simply a function performed by that class or a characteristic of that class. Names are unique. Names are meaningful within the application domain. Names do not represent implementation technology. Names should be in a noun or possibly an adjective-noun form. Names in the noun-verb form should be avoided. The conjunctions "and" and "or" should not appear in a name. Names ending in "er" should be closely scrutinized.
- Syntax Requirement: Objects are clearly described and inclusion/exclusion criteria are clearly stated and not ambiguous.
- Style Convention: Every object has a clearly stated responsibility. Every object encapsulates at least one secret which is known *only* to that object. Objects with only a single instance should be closely scrutinized.
- Syntax Requirement: Objects and generic classes must be used appropriately. Every object either participates in the recognition of an event or participates in the production of a response (to an event). An object must be either an event recognizer or event responder.
- Style Convention: Every event is recognized by precisely one object. Event responses are produced by one or more collaborating objects.

11.3
The Subject Layer

- Naming Conventions: Subjects are appropriately named. Names are meaningful within the application domain. Names are unique. Names do not represent implementation technology. Noun-verb subject names should be avoided. The conjunctions "and" and "or" should not appear in a name.
- Style Conventions: Subjects may overlap. If this convention is adopted, it should be applied consistently. A subject should be independent in the fol-

lowing sense: If a subject is printed on a single sheet of paper, it should be understandable with only minimal need to reference other parts of the model. Structures should be included within a single subject. If necessary, a component of a structure may also be included within an overlapping subject.

If subjects are used, each object should be included within a subject boundary.

11.4 The Structure Layer

- Syntax Requirements: All structures must be meaningful within the application domain.

    Whole-Part structures join from instance boundary to instance boundary except as noted below.

- Style Convention: In the case where the "whole" participant in a Whole-Part relationship is a generic class, each sub-type of the generic class must participate as the "whole" in the Whole-Part relationship.

    In the case where the "part" participant in a Whole-Part relationship is a generic class, each sub-type of the generic class must participate as the "part" in the Whole-Part relationship.

- Syntax Requirements: Whole-Part structures must have designated multiplicity and participation.

    Gen-Spec structures must join from class boundary to class boundary.

- Style Conventions: In the case where the "specialization" participant in a Gen-Spec relationship is itself a generic class, each sub-type of that generic class must participate as the "specialization" in the Gen-Spec relationship.

    In the case where the "generalization" participant in a Gen-Spec relationship is a specialization of another generic class, each sub-type of the generic class must participate as the "specialization" in the Gen-Spec relationship.

- Syntax Requirement: The objects which participate in Gen-Spec relationships must inherit attributes and/or services consistent with the Gen-Spec relationship. Specialization objects cannot inherit attributes or services which are undefined for that specialization.

11.5 The Attribute Layer

- Naming Conventions: Attributes are appropriately named and describe characteristics, qualities or stored data requirements of the associated object. Names are meaningful within the application domain. Names are unique within a given object. Names do not represent implementation technology. Names are usually in the noun or adjective-noun form; verb names should be avoided. The conjunctions "and" and "or" should not appear in a name.

- Syntax Requirements: Each object must have at least one attribute which allows instances of the object to be uniquely identified.

    Values of attributes must be well-defined; they cannot assume values of "not-applicable."

    Attributes must be hierarchically defined to the level of primitive data elements.

The objects which participate in Gen-Spec relationships must inherit attributes consistent with the Gen-Spec relationship. Specialization objects cannot inherit attributes which are undefined for that specialization. Inherited attributes must be meaningful within the application domain.

The definition of an attribute must be unique to that attribute and may not be shared by any other attribute.

All data requirements stored by the system must be accounted for as attributes.

Each attribute must be accessed by at least one service in the encapsulating object; no attribute may be accessed by a service of another object.

Instance relationships must be consistent with and represent application domain constraints (i.e., business rules).

The attributes of objects which participate in instance relationships must be consistent with those relationships. (This is equivalent to foreign key relationships in data models.)

All essential instance relationships must be shown on the OOA model.

- Style Convention: Only essential instance relationships should be shown on the OOA model. Redundant instance relationships, or so-called "So what?" instance relationships (which do not express a business rule or application domain constraint) should be avoided.

- Syntax Requirement: Classes may have attributes which apply only to the class; such attributes must be used consistently and apply to the class or all instances of the class. Such attributes may not apply to a specific instance of the class.

11.6 The Service Layer

- Naming Conventions: Services are appropriately named and represent some work, function or process associated with the object. Names are unique within the associated object. Names are meaningful within the application domain. Names do not represent implementation technology. Names are usually in the verb-noun form; names not in the verb-noun form should be avoided. The conjunctions "and" and "or" should not appear in a name.

- Syntax Requirements: Each object must have at least one class service, that service which allows instances of the object to be manipulated.

  Each object must have at least one instance service, which accesses one or more associated attributes.

  Services must be defined consistently with incoming and outgoing messages, as well as with attributes of the encapsulating object.

  Services cannot access attributes which are not encapsulated within the encapsulating object.

- Style Convention: Services should be well-defined, that is, they should:

  1. Have a single entry point
  2. Not involve concurrent processing
  3. Produce a single or sequential output
  4. Be initiated by the receipt of a message or other well-defined event (e.g., time-trigger)

5. Be specified by brief procedural descriptions which are implementation language-independent (e.g., using Structured English [2])

- Syntax Requirements: The objects which participate in Gen-Spec relationships must inherit services consistent with the Gen-Spec relationship. Specialization objects cannot inherit services which are undefined for that specialization.

    The services of objects which participate in instance relationships must be consistent with those relationships.

    Services apply to instances of objects except in the case where the service participates in an instance relationship with a generic class. In this instance, each sub-type of the generic class must be defined for the service.

    Messages are always produced by and received by a service. They must be used consistently with their associated services.

    Messages convey attributes and these attributes must be consistent with the services which produce and receive the message. That is, all of the inputs and outputs for a service are consistent with the specification of that service.

    Messages are sent from one instance of an object to another instance of (the same or a different) object except as noted below:

    1. Services and messages may apply only to classes, but must be used consistently.
    2. In the case where the participant in a message is a generic class, each sub-type of the generic class must participate in the message.

    Classes may have services which apply only to the class; such services must be used consistently and apply to the class or all instances of the class. Such services may not apply to a specific instance of the class.

11.7
Final Notes
and Comments

Although not discussed in this chapter, an additional form of syntactic correctness can be established at a global level. For example, if a context diagram for a proposed system were created, then all of the context-level data flows would be consistent with the Attribute and Service Layers. That is, all of the data flow components would be represented as attributes and all of the flows would be represented as messages. Similar syntactic correctness requirements can be established for entity-relationship diagrams and state-transition diagrams.

Readers may wish to use the material presented in this chapter as the basis for a style manual for OOA projects. Although we do not discuss Computer Aided Software Engineering (CASE) in this book, the OOA model syntax requirements presented in this chapter should be incorporated into any *good* O-O CASE tool.

 *Key Points*

▲ Syntactic correctness (i.e., did we build the OOA model "right"?) can be established solely on the basis of the model construction rules.

▲ Semantic correctness (i.e., did we build the "right" OOA model?) requires that the OOA model be evaluated against the user's requirements.

▲ The OOA model must be consistent with other analysis work products, for example, the EROI diagrams, 3VMs, etc.

CHAPTER 12
Documenting the Analysis Model

Non multa sed multum.
(It is quality rather than quantity that matters.)

— Lucius Annaeus Seneca
Epistles, 45, 1

12.1 Introduction and Discussion

Tom DeMarco tells an engaging story about "documentation." When presenting the concept of "analysis models," Tom talks about how, in the last century, the British Royal Admiralty office used models of ships as part of the specification process for new ship designs. Any ship builder who proposed a new ship design to the government would have to accompany that proposal with a scale model of the proposed ship. The design would then be reviewed; everyone involved in the operation of the ship, including the captain, boatswain and quartermaster, would huddle around the model, visualizing how they would perform their jobs on this "ship of the future." Tom goes on to say that eventually the French caught on to this idea of modeling. However, the French built their models *after* the ships were built, as "documentation." Tom ends his story with the comment, "Is it any wonder that Britannia ruled the waves?!!"

It is not at all uncommon for the authors to visit consulting clients, ask if they have any analysis models, and be led to a dusty bookshelf holding volumes of, say, data flow diagrams. Usually, we learn that these models were created after-the-fact, as documentation. And worse yet, they are not even consistent with the current design or implementation. Clearly, the entire software development process we introduced in Chapter 1, has been thwarted. The reason for this, of course, is that such documentation is clearly not useful to people, nor is it beneficial to the process. Quite naturally, one would expect such documentation to gather dust. So, when considering documentation, the first question to ask is: Documentation for whom? And for what purpose? In other words, who needs the paper and what will they do with that paper.

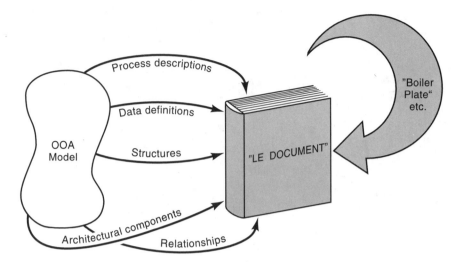

Figure 12.1
Mapping from the OOA
model to a
documentation set.

In the case of the OOA model presented in this book, our target audience for documentation would primarily be our users, sponsors, customers, etc. A secondary audience would be the designers and developers who will create the OOD model and implement the proposed system. The documentation produced will depend on the needs of the audience. If our audience has become comfortable with the notation and methods used to produce the OOA model, our documentation may simply be a CASE tool model. That is, a diskette, which contains the version of the OOA model which we will design and build to.

For customers with specific documentation requirements, it is necessary for us to establish a mapping from the OOA model to the documentation set which the customer specifies. Figure 12.1 illustrates such a mapping.

This figure shows that the OOA model must in a sense be parsed into various components as required by the documentation standard. In addition, various additional information (boiler plate) may be required which is not part of the OOA model. In practice we would expect to see this mapping accomplished by means of scripts which access a CASE tool repository and automatically produce the required documentation format.

There is sufficient detail in the OOA model to produce voluminous documentation. We will end this section by commenting once again that such documentation should be avoided.

12.2 Paper Documentation

This section presents some guidelines for paper documentation when such documentation is required. We stress usefulness and readability; as stated in the previous section, we must clearly understand who needs the paper and what they will do with that paper.

If documentation is being prepared for a customer, user or sponsor, they most likely are concerned with what the proposed system does. That is, they have an inherent bias in favor of function. We have found it useful to begin with a description of a system's purpose. The context diagram, part of 3-view modeling, is useful to illustrate the boundaries of the proposed system, as well as what information will be received and produced by the system.

The above section should be followed by a collection of user scenarios (use cases), or simply an event-response model (again from 3VM). The documentation should allow the reader to walkthrough each scenario or event, verifying step-by-step how an event is recognized and how the associated responses are produced. The EROI diagrams for the associated scenario or event should be included, together with the appropriate components of the five-layer OOA model. It is frequently useful to markup copies of the OOA model with annotations showing the dynamic behavior of the proposed system as the scenario unfolds.

To keep documentation uncluttered, we have found it useful to include detailed descriptions and definitions of attributes and services in alphabetical order or to present hierarchical lists in a document appendix.

The general structure of such user-focused documentation is shown in Figure 12.2.

For the case studies discussed in this book, we would expect that user-focused documentation would be more useful for the SBSS, than for the ECS.

Certainly, a different structure for documentation would be preferable if the target audience were software designers. Designers and implementers would want to see more of the system's structure than the system's behavior. Essentially the entire five-level OOA model would have to be presented on paper. We have found it useful to present the OOA model as a collection of subjects. If subjects can (as they should) be small enough to fit on a single sheet of paper, then a collection of subjects, with underlying details, provides a useful paper form of the OOA model. At the start of such a document, an overview of all subjects is essential. In addition, other documentation, including 3VMs, are useful.

The general structure of such designer-focused documentation is shown in Figure 12.3.

One interesting variation of designer-focused documentation we have seen fully documents *each class* on a single page. That is, each class appears at the center of a page, with all of its connections also appearing on that page. Other connecting classes or components also appear, usually shown on the periphery of the page. Clearly this kind of documentation involves a great deal of duplication. However, for design purposes, a single page reveals the complete specification of a single class.

For the case studies discussed in this book, we would expect that designer-focused documentation would be more useful for the ECS than for the SBSS; our ECS user already knows how an elevator should work!

Appendices I and J contain some examples of paper documentation as produced by a CASE tool.

 **Key Points**

▲ We build the OOA model so that the user can visualize the system of the future—<u>not for documentation purposes!!!</u>

▲ The target audience for the documentation should be identified <u>before</u> deciding what the form, content and structure of the documentation should be.

▲ OOA documentation may be user-focused, or designer-focused.

▲ The best documentation is a CASE tool encyclopedia.

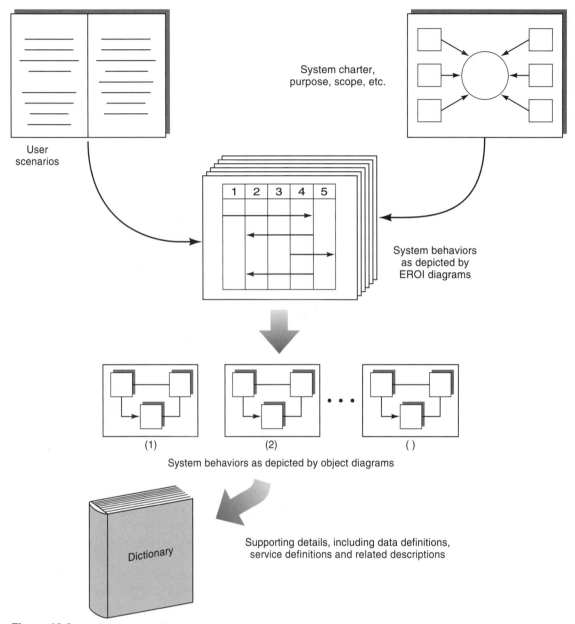

Figure 12.2
General structure of user-focused documentation.

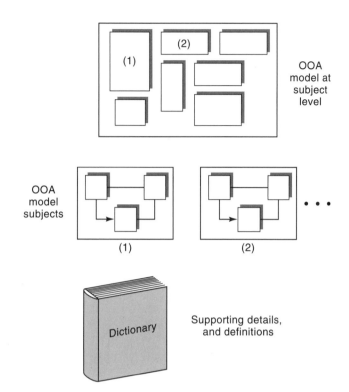

OOA
model at
subject
level

OOA
model
subjects

(1)

(2)

Supporting details,
and definitions

Figure 12.3
General structure of
designer-focused
documentation.

CHAPTER 13
Reviewing and Revising the Analysis Model

One of the greatest creations of the human mind is the art of reviewing books without having read them.

— G. C. Lichtenberg

13.1 Introduction and Discussion

Many of our comments regarding the OOA model review process are similar to comments we made about documentation in the previous chapter. In short, why do we review models? And, what benefit should be derived from this activity?

The purpose of reviewing the OOA model is to assure that we have correctly understood and interpreted the user's requirements *before* we implement the system. Most readers of this book are painfully aware of the fact that frequently we don't become aware of misunderstood or misinterpreted requirements until a system is deployed. The cost of correcting misinterpreted requirements *after* a system is deployed is enormously greater than the cost would be during the analysis phase of a project.

Some readers may be familiar with a formal review process where, say, an OOA model is fully documented, distributed to a number of reviewers and a meeting is convened to review the document. This is akin to what we discussed in Chapter 12 as "documentation for the document's sake." We might consider this a "review for reviewing's sake." The authors have sat in meetings where such reviews consisted of nit-picking at grammar or the quality of illustrations. As with documentation, model reviews need to be substantive. Unlike documentation, the review process should be an informal, on-going process that happens throughout the life of the project.

13.2
An OOA Model
Review Strategy

Based on our discussion in Chapter 11, we have produced a *Reviewer's Check-list* (included at the end of this chapter). This check-list presents a number of review items which will help assure the *syntactic correctness* of the OOA model, that is, did we "build the model right." The reader should consider the Reviewer's Check-list as a starting point; a more elaborate and detailed check-list could be developed for a specific project. To assure a methodical approach for reviewing, each model component could be cross-referenced to such a check-list. Conceptually, this would be equivalent to embedding a check-list into each and every attribute, service, object, etc. Although this is a tedious process, a CASE tool would automate and facilitate this kind of tracking. The benefits of this are obvious. The review process becomes part of the development process. Management reports could be generated which report not only on the progress of the project, but on a level of assurance for each model component.

All of the check-lists in the world, however, cannot assure *semantic correctness*, that is, did we "build the right model." For semantic correctness we have found it useful to adopt a review strategy similar to the strategy we adopted in developing user-focused documentation (see Figure 12.2). That is, validating the *behavior* of our model vis-a-vis user-specified scenarios or use cases. This very definitely needs to be a group activity, although not necessarily conducted in a formal setting.

The event-response model and EROI diagrams provide a natural starting point for checking semantic correctness. Reviewers can walkthrough each scenario or event, verifying step-by-step how an event is recognized and how the associated responses are produced. A CASE tool which allows the OOA model to be animated or even executed makes this an easy process. However, it is useful to simply mark up copies of the OOA model with annotations showing the dynamic behavior of the proposed system.

In actual project reviews, we have found it useful to have two video displays: one showing the OOA model and one showing the EROI diagrams. Events or scenarios are walked through, step-by-step, demonstrating the behavior of the OOA model. For such formal reviews, it is useful to have both a "driver" and a "scribe." The driver controls the computer equipment, navigating the OOA model and the EROI diagrams (it is difficult for the presenter to also drive). The scribe has access to the common CASE tool database; he or she makes interactive modifications to the OOA model, EROI diagrams or other work products. In this way, all changes are seen by the reviewers as they are made.

In this chapter we have offered some fairly high-level concepts and suggestions. On actual projects, we would expect project management to take these ideas and suggestions and transform them into policies and procedures. We know of many system analysts and software engineers who very much enjoy the technical aspects of their jobs; however, many of the same people have a strong aversion to documentation and reviews. This is where good project management is essential. We have found that it takes more than good people and good intentions to produce good systems—it also takes good project management. And good project management is part of an overall project culture which values performance and quality.

A short anecdote might be appropriate as we close this chapter. Both of the authors spend a good deal of time traveling around the world presenting training. One of the authors was setting up for a class in the conference room of a major telecommunications company ("Company A"). As class was about to begin, it was discovered that the over-head projector was not working. While the project manager was checking for burned out bulbs, electrical hook-up problems, etc., one of the project team members came over and casually said, "Oh, that extension cord doesn't work." The project manager tossed the extension cord back into a drawer and went into another conference room to get a working extension cord. On several subsequent visits to that same client, the author noticed the same defective electrical extension cord in the same conference room.

By coincidence, the same author, presenting a class for a small, but growing company ("Company B"), experienced a similar problem with an electrical extension cord. On this occasion, however, one of the non-management members of the class walked to the front of the room, tossed the extension cord into the trash bin, muttering, "This doesn't work, what's it doing here?" This young man then telephoned the person in charge of audio-visual equipment. He simply said, "…Hey, we need an extension cord in the conference room. Can you get one over ASAP?!!"

The differences between Company A and Company B can be summed up in one word. Culture. The project manager at Company A would not have considered throwing out a defective extension cord—after all, that was company property. And, he would probably not have telephoned the audio-visual department— he'd prefer to go through channels. What I found most surprising at Company B, was that the audio-visual person responded to the request for an extension cord, from someone who clearly was neither a supervisor nor even in his same department. At Company B, consciously or unconsciously, employees have been empowered to assure quality.

There is another aspect of Company B's culture which the author found of interest—the Friday afternoon review meeting. All project organizations had a standing meeting on Friday afternoon for reviews. These meetings might be semiformal analysis or design reviews, they might be "lessons learned meetings," they might be "quality circles," etc. Part of Company B's culture was that <u>every</u> Friday afternoon was allocated for review meetings. All work and appointments were scheduled around the meetings. Even the personal lives of employees were scheduled around the meetings.

 *Key Points*

▲ In quality organizations, the technical review process is an informal, on-going activity that occurs throughout the life of a project.

▲ CASE tool reports are typically the only practical way to establish syntactic correctness for large systems.

▲ Semantic corre ctness requires review meetings; the behavior of a system must be validated against user requirements.

OOA MODEL -- REVIEWER'S CHECK-LIST			
OOA MODEL LAYER	**Naming Convention**	**Syntax Requirement**	**Style Convention**
Object-Class	❏ Uniqueness ❏ Application domain ❏ Form	❏ Inclusion criteria ❏ Event recognizer ❏ Event responder	❏ Responsibility ❏ Secret encapsulation ❏ Single event-recognizer
Subject	❏ Uniqueness ❏ Application domain ❏ Form		❏ Overlapping ❏ Independent ❏ Includes all object-classes
Structure	❏ Uniqueness ❏ Application domain ❏ Form	❏ Whole-Part, instance-to-instance ❏ Multiplicity & participation ❏ Gen-Spec, class-to-class ❏ Inheritance consistency, attributes & services	❏ Whole-Part, generic classes ❏ Gen-Spec inheritance
Attribute	❏ Uniqueness ❏ Application domain ❏ Form	❏ Hierarchical attribute specification to the primitive attribute level ❏ Consistent with inclusion criteria ❏ Well-defined ❏ Inheritance consistency ❏ Class attribute consistency ❏ Stored data consistency ❏ Associated with at least one encapsulating service ❏ Instance relationship consistency ❏ Attribute consistency with instance relationship ❏ Attribute-message consistency	❏ At least one attribute ❏ No redundant instance relationships ❏ No "foreign" access
Service	❏ Uniqueness ❏ Application domain ❏ Form	❏ Service specification consistent with in/out messages and attributes ❏ Hierarchical message specification to the primitive parameter level ❏ At least one class service ❏ At least one instance service ❏ Service consistency with encapsulating attributes ❏ Inheritance consistency ❏ Class service consistency ❏ Stored data consistency ❏ Instance relationship consistency ❏ Service message consistency	❏ Each service well-defined ❏ No "foreign" access ❏ Process description notation and style

CHAPTER 14
Transitioning into Design

Life is not a problem to be solved but a reality to be experienced.

— Soren Kierkegaard

14.1 Introduction and Discussion

After spending the last several chapters discussing the OOA requirements model for the ECS and SBSS, we are now ready to move into the world of design. With older methodologies, this was an entirely different world: different notation, different vocabulary, different CASE tools, etc. With object-oriented methodologies, the boundary between analysis and design is blurred and indistinct; this may have been accidental in the early days of object-oriented projects, but now it is a conscious and deliberate feature of the methodology. This is particularly true for prototyping environments, and where the software engineers have a common development environment for *all* of their project activities. If one asks the project team whether they are doing analysis, design, or programming at any particular instant in the project, their answer is likely to be, "Yes."

Ever since the first waterfall methodologies were conceived, software engineers have made a distinction between analysis and design. Analysis is concerned with *what* the system must do; design is concerned with *how* the requirements will be implemented. Analysis, as we have suggested in the previous several chapters, usually takes place with the assumption that "perfect" technology is available; design usually takes place with the conscious or unconscious assumption that the system will be implemented on hardware platform X, under operating system Y, and with programming language Z.

The situation has become further muddled by the fact that issues that were traditionally considered pure design in the 1970's and 1980's have now moved into the area traditionally reserved for analysis. A good example of this is the user-interface component of a system. In olden days, we might show the user a mock-up of

151

report layouts and input screens on a dumb terminal. This approach was pretty simple; the *hard* part was figuring out how to make it work with a telecommunications package like CICS. Now the tables have turned. If one has a GUI-builder package, implementation may be rather straight-forward; the hard part is figuring out, with the user, what the windows and graphical icons should look like.

Even with all these problems, it's crucial to think of design and analysis as distinct activities. They may be overlapped; indeed, they may be taking place at the same time in a typical project. The detailed sub-activities may have changed, as has happened with GUIs. But there is still a fundamental distinction between *what* and *how* that most software engineers recognize. Indeed, the danger of *not* recognizing this distinction is that the analyst or (shudder) the user may begin to incorporate far too many assumptions and constraints about the implementation technology into the statement of requirements. Most readers, for example, would agree that this has been done with the elevator case study discussed in this book.

Another way to think of this is that the OOA model is a "perfect" technology model. We have assumed, for example, that objects have unlimited storage capacity, that objects can communicate with each other as fast as need be, and that the real-world is ideal. We have also neglected to consider how the user will ultimately interact with the system we're specifying, how the system will fit onto a computer platform and other implementation issues. Now it's time to overcome these assumptions. Imagine, for example, that the project manager is writing a cover letter for the OOA model as it is being delivered to the designers. What instructions, constraints, warnings, suggestions, etc. would he/she include in that cover letter?

From this perspective, *Object-Oriented Design* (OOD) consists of three things:

- *Notation*—so we can communicate our ideas about the design to other members of the project team, and to interested outsiders.

- *Strategies*—so we don't always begin each project as if this is the first time the human race has ever considered tackling a problem of this kind, and so that the designs for common domains of problems will begin to fall into familiar patterns of solutions.

- *Goodness criteria*—so we can have an objective way of evaluating a design to see if it should be accepted, rejected or revised.

These are discussed in more detail below.

14.1.1
OOD Notations

Analysis methodologies have been moving toward graphical representations of user requirements for the past decade, but design methodologies have had this characteristic for an even longer period of time. Even before structured design popularized the concept of structure charts in the mid-1970's, software engineers were using HIPO diagrams, flowcharts, and a variety of other diagramming representations. Thus, it should not be a surprise that OOD also uses a graphical modeling notation.

The question is: What kind of representation do we need, and how different must it be from the OOA representation we saw in previous chapters? Since design *is* more concerned with implementation, it should not surprise us to see certain OOD methodologies that have representations for tasks, modules, processors, queues, and other familiar hardware/software components. Nevertheless, most OOD methodologies make a fundamental assumption: OOD notation should be as close as possible to OOA notation.

14.1.2
OOD Strategies

Given a set of requirements, as documented with an OOA model, how does the software engineer go about contriving an object-oriented design? Where does he/she start? What steps does he/she take? What kind of framework, or architecture, should he/she expect to end up with?

A highly creative software engineer might answer, "Who cares? Whatever happens...will happen. *Que sera, sera...*" And many software engineers are rather proud of the fact that their design is intrinsically different than the design that might have been created by another software engineer on the planet. But this is the attitude of the artist, the craftsman who enjoys hand-crafting the solution to every problem. One of the objectives of OOD and all other methodologies is to introduce some consistency and predictability into the software development process. We will probably never reach the point where 100 software engineers, given the same set of requirements, will come up with exactly the same design; but, it would be nice if their efforts fell into three or four predictable patterns.

In the meantime, we may have a more immediate problem. Some software engineers come up with *no* design. They are stymied, and don't know where to begin. One of the objectives of the design strategies discussed in Section 14.2 is to remedy this form of "writer's block."

14.1.3
OOD Goodness
Criteria

While some software engineers may find it impossible to derive any design from an OOA set of requirements, the other extreme is worrisome for many managers: If 100 designers propose 100 different designs, how do we know which one is best? Or, if we can't determine "best-ness," how can we avoid those that are worst? On a more practical basis (assuming that most managers don't have the luxury of a 100-person design competition for every project!), how can we evaluate the *one* design proposed by the lone designer on the project? How do we know if it's any good?

In some organizations, this kind of discussion degenerates into emotional arguments about efficiency, elegance, flexibility, and so forth. But most software engineers will agree that there are some well-known practices (or patterns, to use the term suggested in Section 15.3) that simply don't work. Every time a system exhibits those patterns, testing and maintenance problems ensue.

Older methodologies, such as structured design, have a well-established set of design criteria; among these are such well-known concepts as *coupling* and *cohesion*. We will see in Chapter 19 that there are similar guidelines for OOD—and that some of these guidelines are essentially the same as for older methodologies, while some have a distinctly unique object-oriented flavor.

14.1.4
Other Issues

What else does the software engineer have to worry about, once he or she leaves the warm, fuzzy world of analysis? Obviously, even the design created by an OOD methodology is not the final product of a software project. We must translate the design into some programming language, and then test the resulting code.

This book does not discuss the details of object-oriented programming *per se*; however, it is important to realize that the programming language can have a significant impact on the design process, as well as the mindset of the designer. Indeed, even the methodology can be affected. Several commercial forms of OOD in the marketplace in the early 1990's are evidently influenced by the methodologist's knowledge of, or preference for, such languages as Ada, Eiffel, C++, Smalltalk, etc. These language influences will be discussed briefly in Chapter 21.

14.2 Design Strategies

Once a design has been conceived and documented with appropriate notation—whether on a scrap of paper, or on an elegant CASE tool—what should it look like? What kind of shape should it display?

For many designers, this is a serious problem. They have difficulty conceptualizing *any* design for the problem they have been given. In this sense, the notion of standard architectures is analogous to a cookbook: If you want to bake a chocolate cake, start with these ingredients and follow these steps… A cookbook doesn't guarantee success, for it still relies on the experience, judgment and common sense of the person following the steps (as is evident with such instructions as "stir until well mixed," "season to taste," etc.), but it's better than flailing around in the kitchen with no idea of what to do.

This situation is more common than one might think. When software engineers first make the transition from a function-based structured design methodology to an OOD approach, they have no familiar landmarks to guide them. As noted elsewhere in this book, the old-style designer is likely to look at an object diagram and ask, "Where's the top?" The designer wants to see the control module, so that he/she can trace the architecture by looking for the afferent and efferent legs of the structure chart, etc. In the new world of OOD, what should the designer be looking for? What sort of shape should he/she expect to emerge from his/her design efforts?

14.2.1 An OOD Architecture

Given this need, it is rather surprising that many OOD textbooks pay little attention to this issue of architecture; much of the discussion seems to be focused on issues of packaging objects into modules, etc. But, the Smalltalk community has developed a simple, but elegant, metaphor for such an architecture known as the Model-View-Controller architecture, or MVC. Essentially, it suggests that a typical OOD architecture will have three main components: a group of classes and objects which *model* the underlying application itself; a group of classes and objects which provide a human interface *view* of those model-related classes; and, a group of classes and objects which *control*, or synchronize, the behavior of the others.

Our approach uses a very similar concept, with one additional component; it is shown in Figure 14.1.

The basic idea of this architecture is simple but crucial. It uses the same classes and objects that were documented in the OOA model, and then surrounds them with additional classes and objects to handle the implementation-related activities of task management, data management and human interaction. Unlike classical methodologies, where we basically throw out the analysis model and

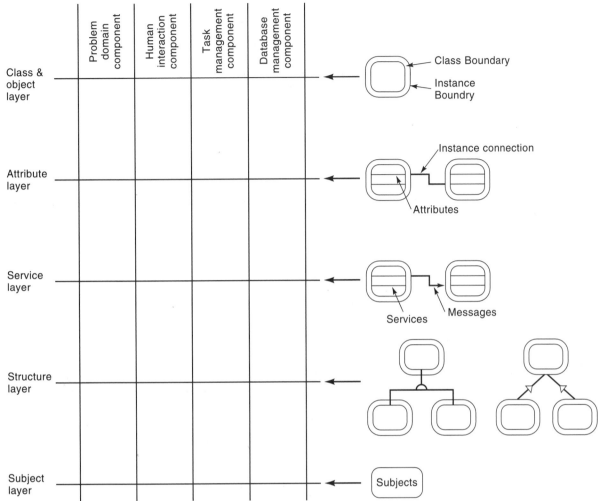

Figure 14.1
The OOD model architecture.

begin afresh with a new design model, this OOD architecture has, as its central theme, making the OOA model the *embryo* of the design model. Obviously, our ability to do this is greatly enhanced if we use the same basic graphical notation for OOA and OOD.

Three of the components in Figure 14.1 are essentially the same as the Small-talk MVC approach: the Human Interaction Component (HIC), Problem Domain Component (PDC) and Task Management Component (TMC). The fourth component deals an ugly reality that most software engineers must accept: No matter how elegant the architecture of the object-oriented software that runs on the CPU, it must interact with legacy data on a database that was designed five, 10, or even 20 years ago. Some of these data may exist in flat-file databases, some may be in a relational form; indeed, there is a tiny possibility that some of them may reside in an object-oriented database management system. Hence, we need a separate architectural component—the Data Management Component (DMC)—to transform objects into database records or tables.

With this explanation, the idea of a separate DMC certainly doesn't sound very radical; similarly, having a separate HIC seems reasonable, because the human interface is a separate and distinct (and, these days, enormously important!) issue. But, there is a crucial consequence of such an approach. It suggests that the central application-oriented classes and objects in the PDC should not be aware of the outside world, and should not have to know how to interact with that world. Without conscious attention to this philosophy, we could end up with an OOD architecture in which each class and object (a) know how to interact with the end-user at his/her PC or terminal, and (b) know how to read and write its permanent data values to and from a disk file. Such an approach would work, and might run a few microseconds faster than a design built around the architecture of Figure 14.1, but it would be quite vulnerable to changes in the human interface or database, and it would complicate the internal structure of the classes and objects which previously only had to be aware of their essential application-oriented details.

We will examine the HIC in Chapter 16, the TMC in Chapter 17 and the DMC in Chapter 18.

14.3 OOD Issues for the ECS

The strategy for designing the architecture of the ECS basically follows the same line of reasoning as that laid out above. However, there are a few areas where we might expect to see some differences between the elevator system and the *Small Bytes* system.

It's important, for example, to eliminate the "perfect" technology assumption of the OOA model. Are there timing and storage requirements which need to be considered? For example, the ECS must be capable of detecting the arrival of an elevator at a floor and determining whether or not the elevator should *stop* at that floor within the last eight inches of elevator travel! What type of performance constraints does this place on the ECS? If we rely solely on the floor sensor detecting the arrival of an elevator, rough calculations suggest that the elevator would have to come to a complete stop in about 66ms. This would result in passengers experiencing several g's of deceleration when the elevator arrives at a floor. Rather than deal with a messy clean-up after each elevator arrival, it might be best to implement a scheduling strategy which allows the ECS to *predict* when an elevator should arrive at a floor.

Also, we've ignored sensor technology in the ECS. Do we have to wait for sensor readings to become stable before we recognize the occurrence of an event? (Remember, we encapsulated sensor technology as secrets in various objects.) A good example is the overweight sensor which is just a piece of nicrome wire bonded to one of the elevator cables. When the cable lengthens and compresses, the electrical resistance of the wire changes very minutely. The process of detecting an overweight condition actually requires monitoring an electrical current; before a determination can be made, the current must have been "damped" to a stable value. Also, the resistance of the wire is *very sensitive* to ambient temperature. If the overweight sensor were calibrated during the summer, it would fail to detect certain overweight conditions in the winter! Should we add a

THERMOMETER object? Or, should we grossly err on the safe side, so that one calibration is good all year long?

An important issue at the design stage of any project is the system's reliability and consistency. The elevator's sensors, for example, are dumb sensors; they could fail without the objects in our OOA model even being aware of it. Perhaps we could incorporate a polling mechanism which periodically interrogates the sensors into each object which encapsulates a sensor? Or, perhaps we should establish some demon objects which monitor the condition of the sensors? Or, we could be even *more* sophisticated and monitor the condition of the sensors over time so as to *predict* failures!

During the design stage of the ECS project, the following question will inevitably arise: How will the system ultimately be implemented? It seems evident that we will require multiple asynchronous, communicating tasks; what kinds of constraints does that place on our implementation, as well as development, environment? What about programming language considerations? What if we have multiple inheritance in our OOA model, but we are programming in a language that only supports single inheritance?

Another design issue involves initialization and termination activities. Our "perfect" technology model assumes that the system has *always* existed in its current (operational) state. In fact, there are both initialization and termination activities which must be performed; these must be specified in the problem domain (and possibly other) components. For example, suppose our user points out to us that the entire building and its component elevators are shut down every night, from midnight to six o'clock in the morning. How does the ECS system start up in the morning? How does it carry out a graceful shut down, without leaving its passengers trapped on the 19th floor all night?

Yet another key design issue involves the DMC. What kind of data are supposed to be managed? From our discussion thus far, there seems to be no need for a database, in the conventional sense of the term, all of the objects in our OOA model are persistent for the duration of the system's operation, which may be 24 hours a day, 7 days a week, until there is a power failure or some human decision to shut the system down is made. But, if the system *is* shut down and then restarted on a normal, controlled basis, it's hard to imagine why it would have to remember its previous state. Indeed, the only plausible argument for saving all of the analysis-based objects onto some form of permanent storage would be the argument of near-instantaneous backup and recovery in the case of unexpected power failures. While this *is* a real issue to think about, we will assume for the remainder of this book that our user is content with the standard mechanical fail-safe systems that accompany all elevators, and does not require us to worry about it in our system.

That leaves the human interface to worry about. How, in fact, *will* we summon elevators and command destinations? Will the technology of that interface impose some special design constraints? Another aspect of this interface is format and protocol. Is there a protocol in communicating commands to the elevator mechanism? Maybe a checksum? And what about help facilities, intelligent assistants and wizards, on-line documentation, etc.? From the user's specification, it appears that the human interface consists entirely of the various lights associated with summons and destination buttons. No mention has been made of an operator's control terminal that would enable a supervisory person to monitor the behavior of the elevators on a multi-color GUI-based PC in the basement of the building. It would be fun to invent such an interface, but if it wasn't mentioned in the requirements document, it isn't appropriate for the designers to add it in.

There is one last design issue we should consider—reuse! Indeed, it may have been the primary argument in favor of using an object-oriented approach in the first place. In addition to thinking about OOA objects that might be implemented by purchasing a commercial class library, a good design also tries to ensure that the objects he/she designs will be potentially useful in future systems—at least, within the domain of elevator control applications.

14.4 OOD Issues for the SBSS

From the discussion in this chapter, our first inclination is to begin creating an OOD architecture base on the one in Figure 14.1 for the *Small Bytes* system. There is obviously no real-time flavor to the system, so we don't need the TMC; but obviously, we *do* need the HIC and PDC components.

As for the DMC component, our designer would have to get a fundamental policy decision from the user such as: Can we build an entirely new database for the subscription system? From the original specification we know that the user currently has a subscription system based on a relatively simple flat-file database. The question is whether that database must be maintained, or whether it can be replaced with something new.

In a situation like this, the most obvious question is: What other systems or applications use that database? If there are several such legacy applications, and if they cannot be changed, we are constrained to continue using the existing database—in which case, the DMC component is necessary. If it turns out, for example, that the other applications are using a relational database package, it would now occur to the designer that the SBSS deals with a number of data stores, yet we have failed to consider normalization issues. Do normalization issues suggest new objects which are meaningful in our application domain?

On the other hand, if it turns out that the subscription system is the only application, or if there are other project teams busily rewriting the other applications in an object-oriented fashion, then it may be possible to replace the flat-file database with an appropriate OODBMS. There is another issue one must consider when looking at the database: How difficult or time-consuming will it be to convert the existing database into a new object-oriented format—i.e., one that directly supports inheritance, as well as encapsulation of data and methods? For the *Small Bytes* system, it's hard to imagine that this would pose a major problem. Assuming that we can write a translation program (or that the OODBMS has a flexible import capability), it should not require more than a few hours to convert even several tens of thousands of records.

And of course, the key assumption here is that a small technical journal is unlikely to have an overwhelming volume of data; the situation would be entirely different, for example, if we were building a subscription system for a national consumer magazine like *Time* or *Newsweek* or *People*. Nevertheless, it's important to ask the user: Just how "small" is *Small Bytes*? How many records do we anticipate we will have to maintain? And what type of response performance does our user expect?

As for the PDC, it's reasonable to assume that little or nothing will have to be changed. It hardly seems appropriate, for example, to bastardize the design of the *Small Bytes* system to save a few microseconds. The OOA model did not rely on multiple inheritance, so we don't have to worry about that kind of change; and, since this is apparently the first object-oriented project the organization has built, it's unlikely that we will find any reusable class hierarchies to take advantage of. Thus, our conclusion (which we should feel free to amend later on) is that the original OOA model can be dropped, intact, into the PDC component of the design architecture.

For the HIC component, we assume that much of the emphasis will be placed on the design of windows and screens to provide a user-friendly GUI; this is discussed further in Chapter 16. But, as mentioned in the elevator discussion above, another aspect of the human interface is format and protocol. What is the format of a new subscription vs. a renewal subscription vs. a complimentary subscription? And, what about a help facility, with intelligent assistants and on-line documentation?

For a real-time system like the ECS, the design issues of reliability and consistency typically involve questions about sensors and physical devices; in a business-oriented application like the SBSS, we might be concerned with consistency issues involving the database. For example, a subscription must always be associated with precisely one recipient (it's one of our business rules). It's appropriate to ask whether such consistency will be assured by the services of the individual objects—or, as an alternative, should we establish new objects whose responsibilities are to assure consistency?

Initialization and termination activities are also relevant for the SBSS, just as they were for the elevator system. It's highly likely that our user will start running the SBSS system at the beginning of a work-day, and shut it down at the end of the day. What kind of initialization and termination activities are required?

Since the SBSS is relatively small, security is probably not an issue. However, in a larger version it might be necessary to identify a particular user and restrict access to certain operations.

Finally, as mentioned in the elevator discussion, we should consider the possibilities of reuse. The issue here is not so much the possibility of using the same objects in a different subscription system (though that might be possible too), but rather the possibility of using some of the objects in other business-oriented applications within the same organization. For example, an ADDRESS object has an obvious possibility of being reused in other environments. What about a SUBSCRIBER? What about a CUSTOMER?

 *Key Points*

▲ Transitioning from OOA to OOD requires that implementation constraints now be placed on the OOA model.

▲ The OOA model must be enhanced with detailed specifications of implementation technology and environment.

▲ The OOD model is akin to construction blueprints. In their most complete form, they completely specify *how* a proposed system is to be built with a particular implementation technology.

▲   We use a common notation for the OOA and OOD models; this facilitates the initial transition from analysis to design and helps maintain the OOA model with the current design and implementation.

▲   The OOD model has the same five-layer structure as the OOA model but is partitioned into four components; these components hide implementation technology from the essential problem domain behavior of the system. This strategy facilitates reuse and upgrading.

CHAPTER 15
Problem Domain Issues

You would be surprised at the number of years it took me to see clearly what some of the problems were which had to be solved…looking back, I think it was more difficult to see what the problems were than to solve them.

— Charles Darwin

15.1 Introduction and Discussion

We begin the construction of the OOD model with the *Problem Domain Component.* However, as was the case with the OOA model, the various OOD components are built iteratively rather than sequentially. The OOA model may be considered a core or nucleus around which *design components* are attached. All of the various assumptions which we made as we created the OOA model must now be overcome. We begin the OOD model by simply copying over the OOA model and calling it the Problem Domain Component of the OOD model—we then modify this component as suggested by the various issues we identified in the previous chapter.

In many cases, the analysis model developed in Chapters 3-13 of this book can be dropped into the PDC components of the OOD architecture with no further changes; indeed, this is one of the most elegant features of the O-O analysis and design methodology. But, there are some circumstances where modifications are appropriate; some of the more noteworthy circumstances are these:

- *Reusable design/programming classes*—When a designer examines the class hierarchies of the OOA model which has initially been placed in the PDC component, he/she may see opportunities to take advantage of existing classes and objects in his/her implementation library. Ideally, this situation would be recognized during the analysis effort; in practice though, it occurs more frequently during design and implementation. In any case, this would involve changing the PDC to treat appropriate OOA classes as subclasses of the pre-existing library classes, and taking full advantage of the ability to inherit pre-existing attributes and methods within those library classes.

161

- *Grouping domain-related classes together to establish a common protocol*—The designer may wish to gather a number of distinct classes together and treat them as sub-classes of a newly created superclass which provides a common protocol for communicating with the DMC, or with other external system components. Such a grouping approach may also turn out to be useful as a library management mechanism.

- *Accommodate available inheritance*—If the OOA model relied on the feature of multiple inheritance, and if the designer knew that the system would eventually be implemented in a programming language that supported only single inheritance, it may have been necessary to change the class hierarchies within the PDC. Typically, this would involve mapping the original multiple inheritance hierarchy into either Whole-Part structures or separate single inheritance hierarchies with instance connections between them. In extreme cases, it would involve flattening the original hierarchy, and suffering redundant duplication of attributes within various classes. However, in most cases, this problem does not occur because (a) analysts and users often regard multiple inheritance as too complicated, and simply avoid it, and (b) at the very outset of a project, everyone typically knows what kind of programming language is going to be used for implementation, and *all* of the project activities are based on that level of inheritance capability.

- *Modify the design to improve performance*—Performance can be a concern if there is a great deal of message communication between objects, if the programming language implements inheritance inefficiently or for various other reasons unique to the O-O approach. The designer may respond to such performance problems by combining two classes (thus permitting intra-object communication, rather than inter-object communication), or by violating the principle of encapsulation through global data areas, etc.

You may wish to consider the implications of implementing classes from a commercially available off-the-shelf domain-specific class library (e.g., the *Smart-A-Vator* Class Library available from Movement Systems and the *Pub-Jects* Class Library available from Periodically Correct Software).

Consider the implications of implementing your system in a programming language/environment that only supports single inheritance. Would this be an issue for your case study? Similarly, you may wish to include speed/performance issues or *perceived* speed/performance improvement (possibly accomplished through caching interim results).

When factoring in acquired classes (whether the classes are from an outside vendor, another project or some shareware classes that you downloaded from a bulletin board system), identify the attributes and services in the OTS (Off-The-Shelf) class(es) that are not needed (you should strive to minimize this). Add a Gen-Spec specialization from the OTS class(es) to the PDC class(es).

When accommodating a single inheritance programming language in OOD, you will need to split objects that have multiple inheritance into multiple hierarchies with mappings between them. You can use Whole-Part or instance connections between the hierarchies. Finally, you could flatten a multiple inheritance hierarchy into a single inheritance hierarchy.

Obviously, any of the modifications described above should be viewed as a trade-off rather than an excuse for unmitigated hacking; efficient performance of the software is important, for example, but it should be balanced against the desire to minimize maintenance and testing costs by keeping the PDC as close as possible to the original OOA model. Before you begin making wholesale changes to the OOA model for the sake of performance improvements, consider these points:

- *Don't create a performance crisis if there isn't one*—Often, the efficiency of the software is irrelevant, especially if it is running on a powerful CPU and interacting with a single user. Most clock time will probably be spent waiting for input from the user.

- *Don't assume that an OOPL like C++ or Smalltalk is necessarily going to be inefficient*—While there may be a few degenerate cases where an OOPL is ten times less efficient than a tightly coded non-OOPL, in most cases, the performance penalty is likely to be more on the order of 10 percent. In any case, as the older generation has learned by now, programmers get tired—compilers don't.

- *It's easier to make a working system efficient than it is to make an efficient system work*—Your first concern should be to build a clean, simple design that can be implemented and debugged with a minimum of fuss and bother; whatever performance improvements are necessary at that point will usually involve a small amount of work. On the other hand, if you *begin* with the objective of building the fastest, smallest, most efficient system the world has ever seen, chances are that it will be so intricate and convoluted that debugging will be a nightmare. In short, efficiency and performance are so important that you should save them for last.

- *80% of the overhead in a typical system is concentrated in 20% of the code*—In some cases, this situation is even more extreme. Rather than destroying an elegant architecture to save overhead *everywhere*, the intelligent thing to do is to find out *where* the overhead is concentrated, by using a performance profiling package, and then optimize only that portion.

- *Software engineers are notoriously poor at anticipating in advance where the software overhead will be concentrated*—The best way to optimize is to use some kind of performance monitoring tools to observe the system as it runs; the nature and location of the overhead usually turns out to be a surprise, particularly when a high level language is involved. This is all the more likely when software engineers use an OOPL for the first time, since its treatment of things like inheritance, dynamic binding, message-passing, etc. may look deceptively simple, but may generate a great deal of overhead. Unfortunately, software engineers tend to think that if a piece of code *looks* complicated, it will probably be inefficient; but, there is no correlation between mental complexity and hardware inefficiency.

- *The greatest performance improvements come from <u>smarter</u> solutions, not by squeezing out microseconds and bytes of memory*—This observation was true long before O-O technology came along, and it remains true in the O-O world too. As one of our colleagues observes, "Microefficiency may destroy macroefficiency."

15.2
PDC
Considerations
for the ECS

The reader should refer to Figure 15.1; the complete PDC for the ECS is given in Appendix N.

First of all, we decided to incorporate a central controller (ELEVATOR CONTROLLER) to control and coordinate all elevator operations. This controller works in conjunction with an ELEVATOR SCHEDULE object (recall our earlier discussion). The elevator performance (not software performance) issues which we discussed in Chapter 14 led us to believe that a centralized controlling class would produce the better design.

We have also added an ELEVATOR MONITOR; we felt that it was best to have a separate object which would perform monitoring functions (performance, safety, etc.) rather than distribute these functions into various other objects. In our specification to the implementers, we would ask that this class be hosted on a separate processor from the main ECS processor. This is a trivial case of a more general problem, so-called *processor allocation*.

Finally, we have enhanced each class with a new service—Self Test. We require that each class encapsulate the secret of proper operation. When invoked, Self Test performs the operations necessary to verify proper functioning and reports these to another class, possibly ELEVATOR MONITOR. It should be noted that a Self Test service is an example of micro-testing, that is, testing at the object level. We would expect, of course, that the ELEVATOR MONITOR also perform macro-testing, that is, testing at the system level.

15.3
PDC
Considerations
for the SBSS

The reader should refer to Figure 15.2; the complete PDC for the SBSS is given in Appendix N.

For the SBSS we made several modifications as we transitioned from the OOA model into the PDC. First, as seen on the diagram, we created an AUDIT object class. We felt that it was important to have some component which could, for example, monitor the integrity of the database, possible attempts to enter subscriptions by unauthorized persons, etc. As with the ELEVATOR MONITOR, we felt that such an entity should be a separate object, rather than distributed to various other objects. Unlike the ECS, however, there is no need for such a class to be hosted on a separate processor.

Recognizing that we will eventually implement the SBSS with a relational database management system, we eliminated many-to-many (M:M) relationships. This resulted in the creation of additional object classes.

Finally, we added a help service to *most* of the SBSS OOD objects; when invoked, that service might give information about how to enter a subscription expiration, how to process a payment or whatever. The implementation of a help facility might take on the form of help windows, cue cards, wizards, tutorials, etc. We decided, in this case, to distribute this facility; we felt that it would be easier to keep such a facility up-to-date if its component pieces were maintained inside the objects to which they belonged.

The issue of adding help services in the PDC always raises a good deal of debate in our classes. The debate centers around whether help is a problem domain issue or a human interaction issue. Our position is that the *content* of a help facility is a problem domain issue, whereas the *presentation* of the help facility is a user interface issue.

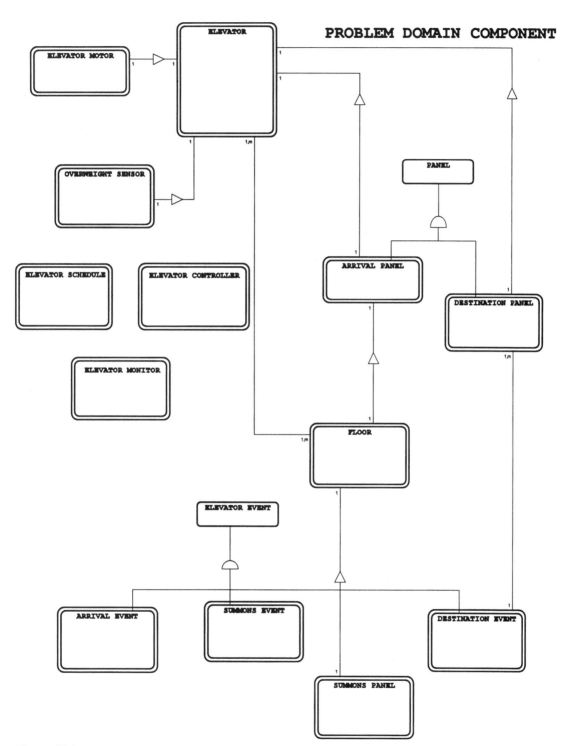

Figure 15.1
The PDC for the ECS.

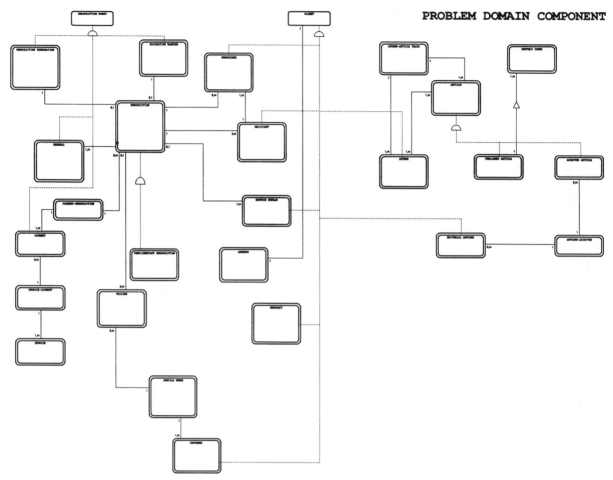

Figure 15.2
The PDC for the SBSS.

And this provides us with a natural segue into the next chapter which discusses the *Human Interaction Component* (HIC).

 *Key Points*

▲ The complete, intact OOA model becomes the initial OOD model's PDC.

▲ We modify the initial PDC to accommodate implementation technology and
   constraints. However, we preserve the *essential system behavior* as captured in
   the OOA model.

▲ Re-usable classes, if used, would be introduced into the PDC.

▲ Other changes may be made to the PDC for reasons of performance, future reuse, programming language constraints, normalization, etc.

CHAPTER 16
Specifying the Human Interface

The most important thing in communication is to hear what isn't being said.

— Peter F. Drucker

16.1 Introduction and Discussion

It's lunch time and one of the authors is standing in a check-out line. Hundreds of office workers, students and tourists crowd one of Hong Kong's busiest supermarkets. The check-out stations are all computerized point-of-sale terminals.

The cashier obviously had never seen the exotic fruits being purchased by one shopper. She furrowed her brow. On her display screen, she scrolled through dozens of product codes. Because there is no alphabetical order for Chinese characters, entries on the screen were ordered by number of strokes in the characters. She frantically scanned the list—first all of the single-stroke characters, then two-stroke characters, then… But by now people standing in line were shouting at her. The author does not speak Cantonese, but clearly the impatient shoppers were not offering her encouragement! She grew more flustered. She finally entered a seemingly random code into the register. The sale was complete and the shoppers muttered their approval.

Yet another example of a poor human interface. A typical North American supermarket check-out station was adapted for the Hong Kong market by simply replacing English menus with Chinese menus. This might work in Hong Kong. But it is highly unlikely that this point-of-sale terminal would sell very well to the millions of markets and shops in mainland China. Now imagine that the point-of-sale terminal displayed images instead of characters. Perhaps images grouped by colors or shapes. We can imagine this cashier thinking, "Let's see…these things are pink, and they're round…" and then spotting a likely picture. Perhaps then she could touch the screen to enter the selection, without needing a numeric code.

Perhaps no other activity is as crucial for the successful implementation of a software system than designing a good user interface. We have learned over the years that no system, no matter how good, can survive a poor user interface.

In this chapter, we will identify OOD human interface issues for the ECS and the SBSS. Our objective is to determine what kind of human interface is appropriate for each system and to identify Human Interaction Component (HIC) objects that will be required to implement that human interface. The HIC in the OOD model includes the actual displays (e.g., screens, reports), and the data needed for human-computer interaction.

When developing our OOA model we specifically avoided implementation-dependent details such as windows and screens. It was our objective to specify the proposed system *independent* of implementation technology. The HIC component now provides a bridge between system behavior and the implementation technology of the user interface. In the case of the SBSS, for example, we know that the user interface will be some kind of GUI. However, suppose that the user decided to create a voice-response version of the system. Our strategy should make that adaptation relatively easy. We should only have to replace the GUI HIC classes with the voice-response HIC classes, and the remainder of the system would remain unchanged and, in fact, ignorant of the change.

You may want to supplement the OOD HIC with additional models which show the relationship between various screens and windows. For example, state transition diagrams are an *excellent* tool for modeling sequences of interactions between the user and system, independent of development methodology.

We will elaborate these techniques as we describe the HICs for the two case study systems.

16.2 The HIC for the ECS

The HIC for the ECS consists of the various elevator buttons, lights and their interfaces; there are no screens, windows, or other so-called "conventional" forms of a user interface for us to design. (See Figure 16.1 and Appendix Q.)

The HIC for the ECS consists of various button and light objects. These encapsulate the secrets of how button presses are received and light displays are activated.

For example, we can partially reveal the secret of how a summons request occurs. In the OOA model, we simply assumed that "when a summons request occurs...," the SUMMONS EVENT object would report that to the SUMMONS PANEL object, etc. In fact, the SUMMONS EVENT object is oblivious to anything until it receives a message from one of the SUMMONS BUTTON objects—this message reports to the SUMMONS EVENT class that a summons event has occurred. This is illustrated in Figure 16.2.

The reader may well wonder how the SUMMONS BUTTON object knows that the button has been pressed—that's *another* secret, still to be revealed!

The same strategy applies to, say, the SUMMONS LIGHT. We assumed that how summons lights were activated or deactivated was a secret encapsulated in the SUMMONS PANEL object. In fact, the SUMMONS PANEL must send a message to the appropriate HIC component class to control the lights. Again, *how* the light is controlled is a *different* secret.

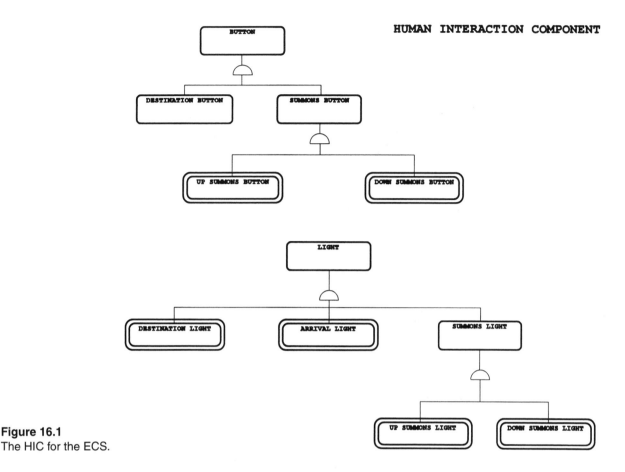

Figure 16.1
The HIC for the ECS.

16.3
The HIC
for the SBSS

The HIC for the SBSS is more interesting. The user interface will be a traditional GUI implemented with, say, Microsoft Windows™. Figure 16.3 shows the HIC. (Refer also to Appendix Q.)

Note that the HIC in Figure 16.3 shows a number of window objects—indeed, there is one for each of the windows that can be presented to the user during his/her interaction with the system. Had we chosen to do so, the window objects could have been further decomposed, using Whole-Part structures, to show the various text fields, selectors, graphic icons, etc. However, we have assumed that the SBSS will be implemented using some kind of GUI-builder package—e.g., a vendor-supplied class library, or a generator of some kind that will create the operational software for displaying windows, etc. on the screen. In that case, all of the text fields, selectors, graphic icons, etc. would normally be provided as input parameters to such a package; hence, we have chosen to show these details as *attributes* within the window objects.

Remember that our purpose is to provide a *blueprint* for the actual implementation of the system. As long as we describe the required windows, the navigation details for those windows and the detailed components of the windows, our programmers should be able to implement them with available technology.

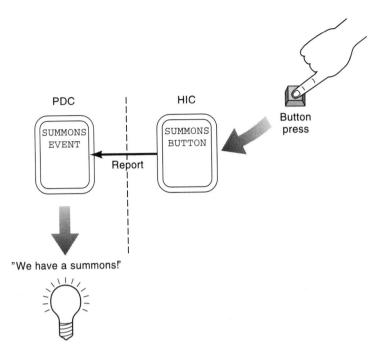

Figure 16.2
Revealing the
"Summons Event"
secret.

The HIC object model can be supplemented with other tools. For example, a *state transition diagram* or a simple menu tree are frequently used to model the topology of a complex system of menus (in this case GUI windows). We have prepared a *single level* of a state transition model for the SBSS, as shown in Figure 16.4. As can be seen, each state becomes a GUI window. Each transition represents the movement between windows. Associated with each transition is a condition/action pair. Conditions represent the user interface selection which causes a transition to occur. The actions represent invocations which occur when transitions occur.

Although the state transition model is useful, we find it cumbersome to use with the SBSS. Instead, a simple menu tree, as shown in Figure 16.5, provides the same useful information with less clutter. The menu tree allows the user to visualize how the interface can be navigated.

Since the simple menu tree represents only the essential structure of the HIC, it is a useful tool for visualizing the global user interface. Understanding, for example, how many different ways an ADDRESS window or form could be accessed. We may strive, for example, for a *mosque* structure for the user interface (see Figure 16.6). That is, at the higher levels of the interface, we would expect to see fan-out greater than fan-in. This represents the fact that the user has a number of selection options at the highest interface level. At the lower levels of the interface, we would expect to see higher "fan-in" than "fan-out." This represents the fact that a single user interface component (e.g., ADDRESS) is used by multiple parent components.

Finally, prototyping, or creating other representations of user screens, is an essential part of designing the HIC. Appendix Q contains a collection of screen prototypes. A sample is shown in Figure 16.7.

16.4
Notes and
Final Comments

When we present the material in this chapter in our workshops, invariably a good deal of discussion centers on *how* to go about designing an HIC for the SBSS, irrespective of a specific technology. Here are some of the things we suggest:

1. Remember that cashier in Hong Kong? Culture! You simply must have a very clear understanding of the user's culture. And we use the word "culture" in a broader sense than simply meaning language, traditions and customs. Every organization has its own culture; every community of users has its own culture. However, the system you build interfaces with a user, and that interface must be consistent with that user's culture.

   Perhaps one of the most exciting adaptations to user culture that we've seen is the so-called visual metaphor. Rather than changing how users do business to adapt to a computer interface, the visual metaphor changes the computer interface to adapt to the user! The usual visual metaphors we see today are standard forms which serve as user interfaces. For example, personal computer programs which use on-screen income tax forms or blank-check forms as the interface medium. One of our clients has developed a very

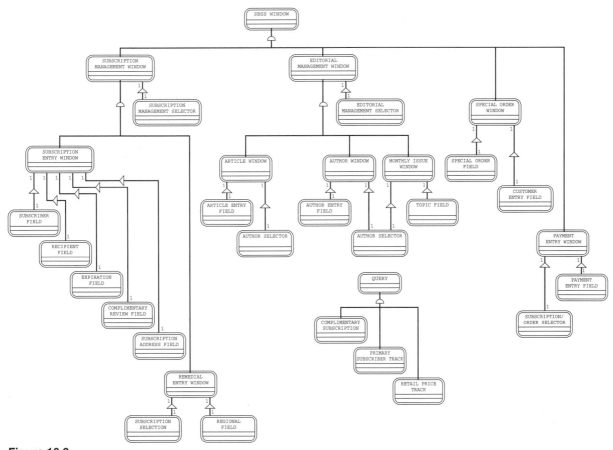

Figure 16.3
The HIC for the SBSS.

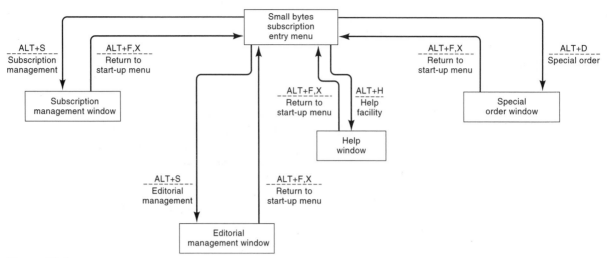

Figure 16.4
A state transition model for the SBSS HIC.

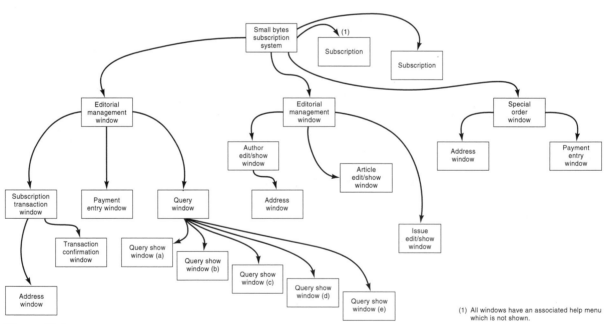

Figure 16.5
A menu tree for the SBSS HIC.

(1) All windows have an associated help menu
which is not shown.

Figure 16.6
Example of an HIC
mosque structure.

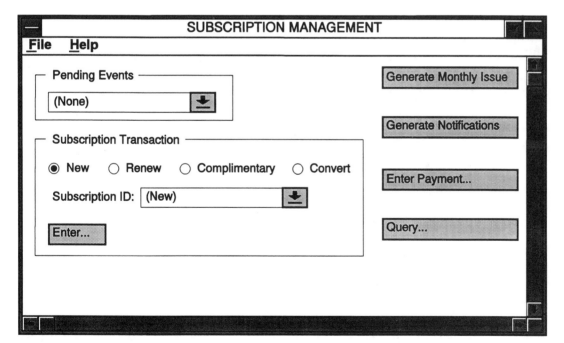

Figure 16.7
Sample prototype screen for the SBSS.

impressive real-estate application which uses various government forms as visual metaphors. Clearly the learning curve for such a user interface is minimal. After the user learns how to use the mouse, he/she knows how to use the system!

2. Let user-developed scenarios or use cases, drive the user interface. Without becoming too elaborate, just watch how the user does his/her job; a good user interface will always present the user with the next step, or steps, for performing a particular job. In other words, a good user interface will lead the user through a job, without forcing the user to do the job in a particular way.

3. If you've done a good job with 1 and 2 above, the rest of the HIC design process is fairly straight-forward.

   Using the tools we introduced in this chapter, both a high-level user interface and detailed dialogues can be specified. The HIC object can then be specified to accomplish this design. And finally, a prototyping activity is the acid test of any HIC design.

4. All of the above might suggest to the reader that HIC design is a *sequential* process which occurs only *after* the OOA model has been completed. Not true! As we discussed in Chapter 1, this entire modeling process is iterative. In fact, we have found it enormously useful—in fact essential—to begin the design of the HIC at about the same time we begin the OOA model.

   We have found that as we develop the HIC for a proposed system, and **allow the user to experiment with it**, we realize how poorly we understood the user's requirements initially! Finding this out during the early months of a project is imperative if we are to deliver a user-acceptable system on schedule.

5. And finally, the reader may have noticed that we've almost gotten through an entire chapter without using the word "reuse" even once! We suspect that most of our readers will not be designing the HIC class from scratch. In fact, developers using a variety of so-called visual-development environments (Delphi™, PowerBuilder™, Visual Basic, etc.) won't even have an HIC. The design of the user interface may be specified by means of a menu tree or state transition diagram, together with some prototypes; however, the function of HIC classes will be performed by the application builder.

**References
for Chapter 16**

1. *The Art of Human-Computer Interface Design*, Brenda Laurel (Addison-Wesley, 1990, ISBN 0-201-51797-3).

2. *The Design of Everyday Things*, Donald Norman (Doubleday, 1988, ISBN 0-385-26774-6).

3. *Designing the User Interface,* Ben Shneiderman (2nd ed., Addison-Wesley, 1992, ISBN 0-201-57286-9).

4. *Tog on Interface*, Bruce Tognazzini (Addison-Wesley, 1993), *American Programmer*, Oct 1993.

 *Key Points*

▲ The Human Interaction Component (HIC) isolates user interface technology from the rest of the system; this includes screens, reports, modem links, network interfaces, control panels (e.g., buttons, lights and meters), etc.

▲ Objects in the HIC encapsulate the secret of many external interfaces; messages are sent to other components of the OOD model to reveal those secrets.

▲ Effective user interfaces are essential for *any* system to be successful.

▲ Effective user interfaces require an understanding of the user's culture.

▲ Application builders obviate the need for an HIC, but *not* the need for user interface design.

▲ Tree diagrams, state-transition diagrams and screen prototypes are all useful tools which supplement the HIC.

CHAPTER 17
Task Management Issues

I long to accomplish a great and noble task, but it is my chief duty to accomplish humble tasks as though they were great and noble.

— Attributed to Helen Keller

17.1 Introduction and Discussion

Another design issue which we must deal with is that of *task management*. Ultimately each service within each object must be allocated to a computer task, i.e., an independently scheduleable entity.

In the case of the *Small Bytes* system, responding to operating system events is not part of our design (such platform details are handled by the implementation environment). Therefore, the SBSS would probably be implemented as a single monolithic computer program. We could imagine the user running the *Small Bytes* application on a PC or workstation on which the operating system could preemptively switch control from *Small Bytes* to a word processor, to a spreadsheet program and then to a background teleprocessing program—but once control was passed to *Small Bytes* itself, it's unlikely that we would expect any of its component objects to be independently scheduled.

However, in the case of the ECS, there are *numerous* asynchronous events which the system must be capable of responding to. And, the description of the ECS in Chapter 2 makes numerous references to implementation-specific items such as interrupt service routines, etc. How should all of this be handled in our design?

We introduce in this chapter the *Task Management Component* (TMC) of the OOD model for the ECS. We will identify any new classes which may need to be created to deal with concurrency issues, interrupts, scheduling (at the operating system level) or other platform-specific secrets. As with the HIC, the TMC hides from the rest of the system the platform-specific secrets. If we decided to port our ECS to another platform, we would expect that only the TMC classes would have to be replaced. We would certainly want the essential behavior of the ECS to be unchanged by moving it to a different platform.

To create the TMC, we look for those platform-specific components which might be encapsulated into TMC classes; the OOA/OOD worksheet we completed in Chapter 4 is an excellent starting point. We may also look for task coordination components, communication dependencies, processor allocation requirements (as, for example, client-server allocations) or message/thread sequences.

17.2 Classes and Objects for the ECS

In reviewing the OOA/OOD worksheet for the ECS, it is apparent that the handling of interrupts and accessing of registers is a crucial part of our design requirement. We have represented these as the collection of classes shown in Figure 17.1 (see also Appendix R).

It should be noted that there is no OVERWEIGHT INTERRUPT class. Unlike other events from our event-response model, the overweight event does not have a corresponding interrupt. Our design, therefore, will have to poll the overweight sensor to establish the occurrence of the overweight event.

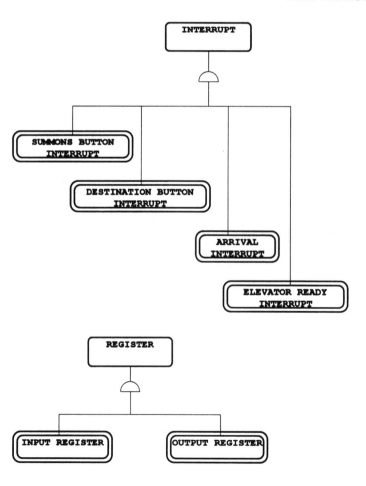

Figure 17.1
The TMC for the ECS.

17.3
Notes and
Final Comments

Recall our discussion in Chapter 16 about partially revealing the secret of a summons event. We may now completely reveal that secret, at least within the context of the ECS. (We will talk about a broader context in Chapter 20.) The following discussion references Figure 17.2.

When a summons button is depressed, outside of the ECS, an interrupt is created and, simultaneously, a binary number is deposited into the input register. There are a total of 78 summons buttons (two at each floor, except the bottom and top floors, which have only one). Down summons buttons are encoded as odd numbers, up summons buttons as even. The number zero represents no buttons currently depressed. Therefore, the input register may contain a binary number ranging from 00000000, 00000010 through 01001111.

The first inkling the ECS has that a summons button has been depressed is when the SUMMONS INTERRUPT class wakes up and says "I've got a summons!" The corresponding SUMMONS INTERRUPT object sends a message to the INPUT REGISTER object asking for the <u>current value</u> of the input register. Our underlying executive locks the input register's value until it has been read; our interrupt priorities are such that the value can only be grabbed by the SUMMONS INTERRUPT object. The SUMMONS INTERRUPT now sends a message to the SUMMONS BUTTON class telling it, "One of you guys just got pushed!"

To the INPUT REGISTER, a number is a number; one is as good as another. But, to the SUMMONS BUTTON class, a number <u>means</u> something. The SUMMONS BUTTON class encapsulates the secret of how register values are mapped to button numbers. The appropriate SUMMONS BUTTON object is notified, "You just got pushed, do your thing!" And, now we're back to Figure 16.2. The SUMMONS BUTTON object sends a message to the SUMMONS EVENT class and the processing of that event is initiated.

Whew! Clearly all this encapsulation stuff can be a lot of work! In fact, this overhead is the price we pay for the luxury of being able to change things, in just one place, and have a good degree of certainty that those changes will not affect other parts of our system. For example, we may decide to change our button

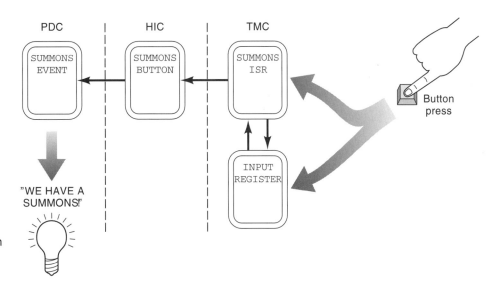

Figure 17.2
The complete revelation of the "Summons Event" secret.

numbering scheme. Perhaps some floors now have a third button for calling a freight elevator. That change would be restricted to a single class, SUMMONS BUTTON. The rest of the system remains oblivious to that change.

 *Key Points*

▲ The Task Management Component (TMC) isolates platform technology from the rest of the system, including operating system or executive interfaces, tasks, registers, interrupts, memory maps, ports, etc.

▲ Objects in the TMC encapsulate the secret of many external interfaces; messages are sent to other components of the OOD model to reveal those secrets.

▲ A TMC may not be required for systems which have no platform interface requirements (e.g., our SBSS).

CHAPTER 18
Specifying Database Design

It is a very sad thing that nowadays there is so little useless information.

— Oscar Wilde

18.1 Introduction and Discussion

The ECS we have described in this book has no database in the conventional sense. All stored data within the objects will reside in the computer's memory, and will be lost if the system is powered down. One could certainly imagine a more elaborate form of elevator control system; however, for our ECS, there is no Data Management Component (DMC).

The *Small Bytes* system, on the other hand, clearly *does* have a need for stored data. All of the information about subscriptions, subscribers, invoices, etc. must be stored permanently, even if the computer is shut down at the end of the day. Depending on the hardware/software platform available to the developer, and various other considerations, we could imagine storing these data in an object-oriented DBMS in a relational DBMS, or in a simple flat-file scheme.

Although we could have some interesting discussions about the best database technology for the SBSS project, we will assume in this book that the decision has already been made—for technical reasons, political reasons or even whimsical reasons—to use a relational database. In this chapter we will describe a strategy for developing a Data Management Component (DMC) for the SBSS.

The DMC describes access to and management of persistent data created and used in other components of the design. The primary reason for having a DMC, as is true for the other OOD components, is to isolate the particular database management technology from the OOD PDC. If we decide to change DBMS vendors, or perhaps move to an OODBMS, we would like to minimize the impact on the overall design model.

To develop the DMC, we need to consider what kind of database queries will be required to support the SBSS; we may decide to establish objects which encapsulate the secret (i.e., SQL) of how a query is accomplished. It may be necessary to establish any needed instance connections between the DMC and PDC objects. Such instance connections would establish constraints between application domain components and database components.

We will also look for many-to-many instance connections among objects in the PDC component; to store those objects in a relational database, they will need to be transformed into one-to-many relationships with an associative object. Recall that our approach has been to perform this normalization as part of the PDC. This issue always elicits a great deal of discussion in our workshops. Clearly, performing any normalization in the PDC biases the PDC for a relational database implementation. However, creating an associative object in the DMC, for two PDC objects, requires spanning long distances on a diagram. Mundane as this may be, it does make the diagrams less readable. From a more aesthetic perspective, such an associative object in the DMC would encapsulate <u>both</u> problem domain knowledge and database technology knowledge. We also justify our approach by saying that it is a design model and as such is <u>always</u> biased toward a particular implementation. And if, in fact, we will always be implementing our database with relational technology, why not make life easier and normalize in the PDC. Clearly, however, the latter justification is no longer realistic. And so, it may be desirable and pure to perform all normalization in the DMC.

Finally, it may be necessary to re-examine the HIC; are any database queries required to display or report any screens, fields or reports specified on the HIC? If so, we will probably need to create a query object in the DMC.

18.2
The DMC
for the SBSS

As shown in Figure 18.1, our general strategy is to establish one object for each *relational table* which will be created in our database management system. This object encapsulates the secret of how data (rows) are created, read, written and deleted. Messages are established between other objects as required to access the relational tables.

Note how any change of database technology would be confined to the set of DMC objects. Such changes should have no impact on the PDC objects if the new database technology were also relational.

18.3
Notes and
Final Comments

1. First of all, the rather straight-forward approach for creating the DMC may be appealing, but it is certainly not the only approach—and certainly may not be the best approach. One of our more creative workshop groups in Athens, Greece devised the strategy shown in Figure 18.2 (thanks to Πανο⧧ Φυσ κιδη⧧ and his BOOt team).

   They felt that the DMC objects should simply encapsulate the characteristics of tables and columns. Rows, which, of course, actually store data, are then the specializations of both a generic column class and an associated PDC class. Ultimately all relational table classes are specializations of the generic table class and associations with a particular set of row specialization classes.

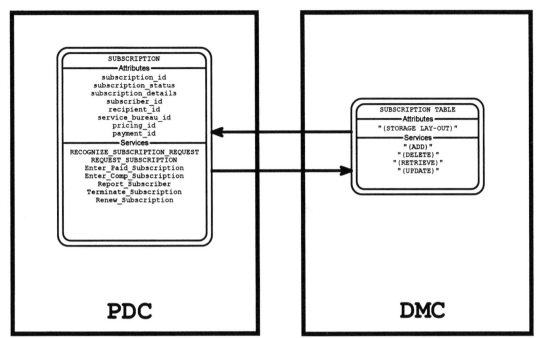

Figure 18.1
DMC strategy for the SBSS.

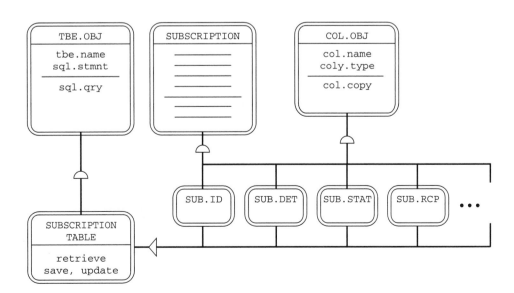

Figure 18.2
Another strategy for
creating the DMC.

How would one decide between the strategies depicted in Figures 18.1 and 18.2? One test, of course, is reusability. From that perspective, we believe the second approach is preferable. However, another test is clarity—if designs can't be understood, they can't be maintained or enhanced. From that perspective, certainly the first approach is simpler and more straight-forward. So which should be selected? Ah! That's where good project management comes into play!

2. When we discussed the ECS, we talked about revealing the secret of how a summons event was actually recognized. In Chapter 17, in fact, we completely revealed that secret to the point where an interrupt occurs from a summons button. So far, however, we haven't talked about revealing secrets for the SBSS. We shall do that now.

   Consider an event, say, "Subscription Requested." Figure 18.3 illustrates how that event is <u>ultimately</u> recognized, starting with the click of a mouse button, or the press of a certain key. This event initially enters the SBSS at the HIC in the SUBSCRIPTION ENTRY WINDOW class (possibly a Visual Basic form). A message (①) is sent to the SUBSCRIPTION class in the PDC. It is this class which encapsulates the business rules of how a new subscription is to be processed.

   As part of processing a new subscription request, the SUBSCRIPTION object sends messages ② and ③ to the SUBSCRIBER and RECIPIENT classes, respectively. (The SUBSCRIPTION object also sends messages to other classes not shown on Figure 18.3; we tried to keep this figure simple.) In turn, the SUBSCRIBER and RECIPIENT objects sent messages to the ADDRESS class (④ and ⑤, respectively).

   All four of the PDC classes shown on Figure 18.3 require access to stored data. Therefore, all four of these classes have message connections to corresponding DMC classes (⑥, ⑦, ⑧ and ⑨). Upon receiving these messages, the various table classes interface with the relational database management system, which, of course, is outside the SBSS.

   Eventually, as directed and determined by the PDC SUBSCRIPTION class, a new subscription has been created. That accomplishment is reported back to the user; message ⑩ is sent to the HIC SUBSCRIPTION CONFIRMED WINDOW class which displays an appropriate message to the elated user.

   As we remarked in closing Chapter 17, this simple scenario illustrates that a great deal of communication and coordination may be required in an object-based system. Again, that's the price we pay to derive the benefits of reusability, maintainability, extensibility, etc.

 *Key Points*

▲ The Data Management Component (DMC) isolates database technology from the rest of the system, including tables, SQL, various administrative and backup activities, etc.

▲ Objects in the DMC encapsulate the secret of stored data interfaces; messages are sent to other components of the OOD model to reveal those secrets.

▲ A DMC may not be required for systems which have no stored data requirements (e.g., our ECS).

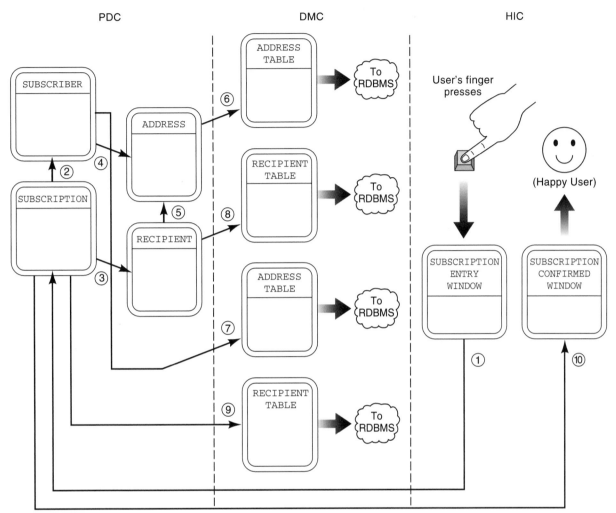

Figure 18.3
The complete revelation of the "Subscription Requested" secret.

CHAPTER 19
Quality Issues at the Design Level

It is quality rather than quantity that matters.

— Lucius Annaeus Seneca
Epistles, 45, 1

19.1 Introduction and Discussion

Although we have presented only one solution for each of the two case studies in this book, it should be evident that many others are possible. In many cases, we have discussed alternatives that we considered and then rejected for one reason or another. However, an important activity at the end of the design process is an overall review of the *quality* of the design.

Criteria for evaluating an object-oriented design are discussed in detail in other books. We summarize below some of the more relevant evaluation criteria:

- *Coupling guidelines*—Coupling is a term that was popularized in the mid-1970's with various structured design guidelines; it refers to the strength of inter-connections or interdependencies between discrete components in a system. As such, it is a bad thing, something to be minimized whenever possible. For an object-oriented system, we are primarily concerned with the coupling between classes and objects that are *not* part of a Gen-Spec or Whole-Part hierarchy; that coupling takes the form of message connections. Of course, the very principle of encapsulation is intended to minimize coupling, but we still look for ways to minimize the number of messages between objects, as well as minimizing the complexity and content of the messages themselves. Coupling is also created by inheritance in class hierarchies, but this is usually evaluated in terms of the cohesion guidelines discussed below.

- *Cohesion guidelines*—Cohesion is also a term popularized by structured design; it remains relevant in the new world of OOD. Cohesion is a way of describing the togetherness, or strength of association of elements *within* a system component. Low cohesion is a bad thing, and something to be avoided. In object-oriented designs, we are concerned about cohesion at three levels: (a) the cohesiveness of individual methods; (b) the cohesiveness of the data and methods encapsulated within a class and object; and, (c) the cohesiveness of an entire class hierarchy. At the microscopic level, method cohesion can be evaluated just as it is with structured design. A method should carry out one and only one function and it should be possible to accurately describe its purpose with a simple sentence containing a single verb and a single object. At the intermediate level, it can be evaluated using the various guidelines discussed below. At the class hierarchy level, it can be evaluated by examining the extent to which subclasses override or delete attributes and methods inherited from their superclasses.

- *Focusing on the clarity of the design*—Though it must be classified as a soft guideline, software engineers generally agree that if they can't *understand* someone's OOD design, then they won't reuse it—and if they can't reuse it, it's bad (or, at least, worse than an alternative design that *can* be reused). Specified advice in this area includes using a consistent vocabulary for naming methods and attributes; avoiding excessive numbers of message templates, avoiding fuzzy class definitions and adhering to existing protocols or behaviors of classes.

- *Hierarchy and factoring guidelines*—Good designs are neither too deep nor too shallow in terms of their class hierarchies. A medium-sized system with approximately 100 classes is likely to have class hierarchies with 7±2 levels of Gen-Spec and Whole-Part structures. This may be affected by the programming language, by the use of single inheritance versus multiple inheritance, etc., but it would be unusual (and probably a manifestation of a bad design) to see class hierarchies 20 levels deep, or only two levels deep. Excessive levels of subclasses often occur with overly zealous first-time OOD practitioners who over-factor their design.

- *Keeping classes and objects simple*—A bad design often has an excessive number of attributes in the classes; there should be no more than one or two attributes, on average, for each method, of which 2/3 should be traceable all the way back to the OOA model. A bad design also tends to have an excessive number of methods in each class; one typically finds no more than six or seven public methods per class, in addition to whatever private methods are necessary for internal housekeeping, etc. (Of course, this can vary substantially, depending on the nature of the application.) Also, a bad design tends to have excessive collaboration (i.e., coupling) between objects. While it's understandable that an object may not be able to respond to an external event by itself, it should not be necessary to interact with more than 7±2 other objects to accomplish something.

- *Keeping message protocols simple*—Complex message protocols, as noted above, are a common indication of excessive coupling between classes and objects. If a message requires more than three parameters, it's an indication of a bad design. The typical problem is that the class hierarchy has been poorly factored. Similarly, the existence of computer science jargon in the message protocol typically means that the class is doing something other than what is in the problem domain.

- *Keeping methods simple*—With a reasonable high-level language, it should be possible to write the code for each method in less than a page (which may require one or two screens on a workstation display monitor); indeed, with a language like Smalltalk, it is common to see methods of less than 10 lines of code. If the method involves a lot of code, look at it more closely. If it contains IF-THEN-ELSE statements or CASE statements, it's a *strong* indication that the method's class has been poorly factored—i.e., procedural code is being used to make decisions that should have been made in the inheritance hierarchy.

- *Minimizing the volatility of the design*—A bad design will exhibit considerable volatility during the development phase of the project, as well as during the ongoing maintenance efforts. Making a small change in one class to fix a bug or add a new feature may cause a ripple effect throughout many other classes. It may not be clear what the cause of the volatility is (though it is usually the result of the coupling problems described above), but it can nevertheless be used by the project manager as an unbiased assessment of the quality of the design. With a good configuration management system, the manager should be able to track the impact analysis associated with a change to an individual class, and it should be possible to detect a trendline of ever-increasing stability as the project inches closer to its deadline.

- *Minimizing the overall system size*—Small is beautiful; big is ugly. A medium-sized application should require no more than a few dozen class hierarchies, each of which may involve a dozen subclasses. If each of the individual classes has half-a-dozen methods, and if each of those methods involves 10-20 lines of code, the aggregate amount of software is pretty substantial. Unfortunately, there seems to be an attitude among some software engineers which leads them to think that their prowess and competence will be judged by how many classes they have managed to invent in their system.

- *Emphasizing the ability to "evaluate by scenario"*—It should be possible to evaluate the goodness of a design with a role-playing exercise in which the reviewers act out the behavior of individual classes and objects. Thus, one reviewer might say to another, "Okay, I'm the XYZ object and I'm sending an 'abc' message to you; what are you going to do with it?" If this kind of exercise proves impossible to conduct, it may indicate that the *responsibilities* of the various classes have not been well described, or well thought out.

Using criteria like these, we should examine the OOD designs of the ECS and SBSS to see if there are areas that can be challenged and improved. For example, we can look for object collaborations, such as large, complex data structures which get passed between objects (poor coupling)—or data which are passed fire brigade fashion through long chains of objects. We can examine object methods and ask whether some of the objects are encapsulating apples and oranges? Objects should encapsulate like things—in terms of both methods and the data within the objects. We can examine inheritance hierarchies and ensure that super-classes do not depend on sub-classes. We should examine critically any examples of message communication between sub-classes and super-classes; in most cases, it will indicate that we have a poor class hierarchy and that a better alternative can be found. And finally, we can examine the naming conventions in our OOD. Are names consistent with their objects' services and data? If not, why not?

19.2
Quality Issues for the Case Study Systems

The authors are certainly prejudiced, but we find that both of the case study systems represent fairly good designs—not the best designs possible, but certainly good designs. And we have seen our students and clients produce equally good, frequently better, designs on their first object-oriented projects. We believe that this is neither coincidence nor a result of our teaching styles or techniques. We can trace many of the qualities of good design to their origins in the analysis model. In other words, inherently good design results from inherently good analysis.

Can we trace a good design back before the OOA model? The answer is yes. Although we cannot prove it in a mathematical sense, we believe that the origins of good design begin with the pre-analysis techniques we introduced in Chapters 3 through 5. For example, looking at our OOA and OOD models, we find that almost all of our objects are highly cohesive and loosely coupled. Why? Well, we believe because they emerged from a linguistic-based analysis of application domain concepts. Might it be that coupling and cohesion, for example, have their origins in application domain concepts? We think so. Though we are certainly not experts in linguistics, we speculate that words evolve specifically to encapsulate concepts—and that multiple words or phrases rarely encapsulate precisely the same concepts. If they did, simple human usage would have dropped one of them.

(And, as we all know, true synonyms don't exist in human language. Two words with the same meaning actually have subtle differences or nuances in meaning, that is, they encapsulate different concepts.)

It's hard to take exception with most of the ECS design. The design seems fairly clear and straight-forward. Objects have a reasonable number of attributes and services, and coupling and cohesion seem good. There is an issue, however, with our decision to create a centralized CONTROLLER class and accompanying SCHEDULE class. This forces some of the services which might be distributed in other classes to be consolidated into the CONTROLLER class. In fact, that was one of the reasons we departed from our initial OOA approach; to improve efficiency and scheduling. Yet clearly, this makes a number of classes less reusable. And certainly, the CONTROLLER class would only be reusable in an identical kind of system.

But what about our *Material Handling System*, which also has summons events and destination requests? Or our *Light Rail Scheduling System*, which is just a horizontal version of an elevator! At first blush, our CONTROLLER version of the ECS seems to reduce reusability. This, of course, is a topic for discussion—it results in a great deal of discussion in our workshops! But these kinds of trade-offs are what real engineering is all about!

Looking at the SBSS, many of the same comments apply. In general we find the design to be fairly clear and straight-forward. Objects have a reasonable number of attributes and services, and coupling and cohesion seem good. But, that SUBSCRIPTION class does a LOT! This may well be traceable back to our original LIA; the user uses the word "subscription" in a number of different senses. The SUBSCRIPTION class may well have taken on a consolidation of those subtly different concepts. It might be profitable to look more closely at how the user talks about subscriptions. Perhaps it may be possible to partition the SUBSCRIPTION class into a number of specialization classes. (We shall leave this exercise to the reader.)

We've attempted, in this chapter, to give the reader a taste of OOD issues. We hope the reader understands that there are no hard and fast rules for establishing the quality of an OOD. There are, however, trade-offs. And, it often takes years of experience, not to mention some intuition and a bit of luck, to make judicious choices between differing design alternatives. Nevertheless, as noted above, readers who follow our guidelines for pre-analysis and analysis activities should produce acceptable designs their very first time!

**References
for Chapter 19**

1. "Towards a metrics suite for object-oriented design," Chidamber and Kemerer, *Proceedings of OOPSLA, 1991.*

2. *Technology of OO Languages and Systems (TOOLS10),* edited by B. Magnuson, B. Meyer, and J. Perrot (Prentice Hall, 1993).

3. "Timeless Design of Information Systems," *Object Magazine,* Tom Love, Nov/Dec 1991.

 *Key Points*

▲ Quality design begins with quality analysis.

▲ In general, quality design is characterized by simplicity, (minimal components, operations, etc.), clarity and the ability to evaluate by scenario.

▲ The concepts of coupling and cohesion are applicable in a number of different ways to object-oriented designs.

▲ "Smaller" objects tend to be more reusable.

CHAPTER 20
Documenting and Reviewing the Design Model

If I let my fingers wander idly over the keys of a typewriter it might happen that my screed made an intelligible sentence. If an army of monkeys were strumming on typewriters they might write all the books in the British Museum.

— Arthur S. Eddington

This chapter shall present some rather brief comments about documentation and the review process for design models. Most of the comments we made in Chapters 12 and 13 about documenting and reviewing the OOA model are applicable to the OOD model. One distinct difference is that the target audience for the OOD model is designers and implementers; we are not creating user-focused documentation.

We have likened design models to blueprints created by architects from which say, houses, may be constructed. Clearly, blueprints contain an enormously greater level of detail than do architectural scale models. How much detail? Well, enough detail so that those building the house know <u>exactly</u> what kind of a house is to be built. We create design-level documentation for the same reason and to the same level of detail. The level of detail necessary is such that those implementing the system know <u>exactly</u> what kind of system is to be built.

Clearly, that level of detail will vary from project to project depending on a number of factors. The most significant factor may well be who, in fact, are the implementers. On small projects where the designers and implementers are the same people, little, if any, design documentation may be required. On the other hand, if the designers are on one continent and the implementers are on another continent, enormous levels of details may be required.

Both of the authors have had the opportunity to lecture to software development teams in India. These teams are implementing complex software systems for clients all over the world. The most frequent complaints we heard concerned the quality and level of detail of design documentation the teams received. Their feelings, in general, were that they received poorly stated and inadequate design specifications. Interestingly, mis-stated or mis-understood user requirements were not as much of an issue; they were struggling to simply envision the system through the design documentation.

As we recommended for analysis-level documentation, we suggest that the design documentation consist primarily of the CASE tool encyclopedia which captures the entire OOD model. Obviously, specific projects may have specific documentation standard requirements. Figure 12.1 applies in this chapter as well as it did in Chapter 12. We suggest that the OOD model be supplemented with any type of diagrams, or other specifications, which may be of value in communicating the design to the implementers. For example, in the case of the SBSS we would certainly want to include the user interface screens we developed (Appendix P) as part of the design documentation. For some systems timing diagrams, algorithm specifications, schematic diagrams, Bode charts, spreadsheets, flow charts, or perhaps even astrological tables may become part of the design documentation. Obviously, with the CASE tools of today, it would not be possible to have all of these various materials stored in the CASE repository. We can, however, index these materials and have reference links to them within our stored CASE repository.

As far as reviewing design is concerned, again, we suggest the reader recall our discussions in Chapter 13. We talked about review processes which are ongoing and a part of the culture of a project organization—as opposed to formal milestone reviews, which may be more cosmetic than substantive.

If the reader has adopted the approach taken in this book, the concept of events, scenarios or use cases, will be the driving force behind design reviews. All design must provide for the recognition of events and the production of the corresponding responses. Clearly there may be designs that are not good (the recognitions and responses are slow, poorly managed, poorly displayed, etc.). But, one fact cannot be denied—if all of the stated system events and responses are accounted for in a given design, the system works!

All of this, of course, takes place within an overall development process. We shall discuss that in the next chapter.

CHAPTER 21
Implementation Issues

Ever building to the clouds, and never reflecting that the poor narrow basis cannot sustain the giddy, tottering column.

— Schiller

21.1 Introduction

In this chapter, we briefly discuss some implementation issues which are unique or specific to object-based systems. We will avoid discussions of particular programming languages and environments—the plethora of books available in those areas makes that unnecessary.

21.2 Programming Language Considerations

Over the years, we've noticed a change in the types of students attending our workshops. Several years ago, we had principally two kinds of students. Those who weren't sure what objects were all about—and wanted to gain some insight—and those who were planning to migrate, or actively migrating from COBOL to C++ (or some such scenario). The latter group typically had more interest in O-O programming languages and frequently equated object-orientation <u>with</u> a programming language. In other words, a necessary and sufficient condition to be object-oriented (and thereby gain all those benefits of reuse, etc.) was to use an O-O programming language.

Today, we see a different breed of student; those who have graduated from the school of hard knocks! Many of our students have already been through a migration from COBOL to C++, or at least an attempted migration. Many of our students have failed to see any significant benefits from object technology—some have had O-O disasters!

Object-orientation is more than a programming language. Below are listed some of the points we try to share with our students:

1. We talk a lot about reuse. Students frequently assume reuse of *code*. Yes, true, but we've been reusing code for at least 30 years. When we say reuse, we're talking about reuse of business rules, requirements, environments, documents, architectures, test plans, etc. In fact, all of the work products of the software engineering life cycle can be reused.

    Object-orientation is an *enabling technology*. It allows us to reuse far more than just code.

2. You *can* create object-oriented programs with non-object-oriented programming languages. After all, for years we created *structured* programs with non-structured programming languages. It certainly is more difficult. And, it would certainly be more consistent with an object-oriented life cycle to migrate from OOD into an object-oriented programming language. However, with standards and discipline, it can be accomplished.

    And why would you want to? Well, let's go back to some of our students who were firing all of the COBOL programmers and hiring a bunch of C++ programmers, half the age of those they replaced. As it turned out, the COBOL programmers knew more than COBOL. They knew the business. They understood the business rules. They may have expressed their knowledge as COBOL, but they knew far more than COBOL.

    And what about the millions of lines of legacy code a company may have. All written in COBOL. It's hard to justify re-writing all of the code in C++.

    We can't make any sweeping generalizations; after all, each project presents a unique situation. Nevertheless, there can be some sound arguments made for <u>not</u> migrating to an object-oriented programming language.

    One final thought in this vein. For some projects, it may not even be <u>possible</u> to migrate to an object-oriented programming language. We know of one organization which is maintaining and enhancing programs for an obscure, embedded, real-time microprocessor. There simply <u>is not</u> an object-oriented programming language compiler available; they program in assembly language. And now, they program in *object-oriented* assembly language. That is, they have adopted standards for the assembly language coding of classes, objects, attributes, services, etc.; and, with standards and discipline, that can be accomplished.

3. "We write COBOL programs. We write COBOL programs in COBOL and we write COBOL programs in C++."

    That comment comes from one of our clients. His organization was one of those which migrated, early on, from COBOL to C++. He wouldn't have any part of that "OOA and OOD stuff." As happened to many such organizations, his staff learned the <u>syntax</u> of C++, without learning the object-oriented paradigm. The result? Top-down, functionally decomposed objects.

    An important point to be made here is that C++, being an enormously flexible language, <u>allows</u> programmers to do whatever they like—including writing COBOL programs in C++. We would have recommended that our client <u>first</u> train his programmers in OOA and OOD. That is, <u>first</u> learn the difference between top-down functional decomposition, and middle-out object collaboration. Another strategy, however, would have been for our client to have trained his programmers in the Smalltalk programming language. Smalltalk?!! Yes! Smalltalk strictly imposes the object-oriented paradigm; they would have been forced to think about objects. Migrating to C++ would have been simply a matter of learning the notation and syntax of that language.

21.3 An Iterative Software Development Process

The focus of this book has been on (object-oriented) analysis and design. However, any software system analysis and design is performed within the context of an overall software development process. Some development processes may be more or less conducive to object techniques; in general, however, a development process is somewhat independent of development methods or techniques.

We introduced the concept of software development processes in Chapter 1. At that time, as well as throughout this book, we have referred to the iterative process. We consider a software development process to be *iterative* if the various project phases and work products can be re-done in a controlled and managed fashion. We have found iterative software development processes to be invaluable for any large, complex software system.

Figure 21.1 illustrates, at a very general level, an iterative software development process which has been tailored specifically for object-oriented development. We refer to this process as a *thread-based development process*. We use this term for the following reason: The various activities depicted in Figure 21.1 are not conducted in a waterfall fashion. Each activity is visited and re-visited many times over during the development process. The mechanism we use to perform this iteration is what we call a *thread*. Referring back to the concept of an event, a *thread* is the piece-wise implementation of an event.

Referring back to the SBSS, consider a single event, for example, Article Received. The process depicted in Figure 21.1 would implement that single event (or some decomposition of that event) completely and independently of all other system functions. When completed, this thread can actually be demonstrated as a working piece of the system. We can think of the system being implemented one thread at a time. There are a number of advantages to such an approach. Problems such as mis-interpreted requirements and technology shortcomings are identified very early in the development process.

As the reader can imagine, many details accompany a process such as the one shown in Figure 21.1. We cannot go into much detail; however, to give the reader the flavor of an iterative development process, we introduce Figure 21.2. The flow chart shown in Figure 21.2 describes the activities of a development team as they work within the iterative development process of Figure 21.1 These activities are performed within the period of a day.

At the start of the day, a project team meeting is held. The threads to be implemented that day are selected and discussed. The selection is made based on identified requirements and in accordance with a plan established by the project manager. It may well be that some of the threads cannot be implemented as stated; these may be changed, or requirements may be questioned. Ultimately, it may be the case that user requirements, which cannot be implemented as stated, are re-negotiated.

Threads which are accepted are distributed to development teams. In the case shown in Figure 21.1, two development teams exist. One team is responsible for design of the User Interface (UI), the other is responsible for Object-Oriented Modeling (OOM).

As the teams complete their work, the designs for the thread are passed on to an implementation team. Since a thread is a small unit of system function, and since the time from design to implementation is a matter of minutes or hours, problems can be resolved easily and expeditiously.

At the end of the work day, the threads implemented for that day are reviewed by the development team. This review consists of working with an actual version of the system—the version which incorporates the implemented threads. Some threads may be accepted, others may be sent back for re-work. This new version of the system is called the *daily build*.

The next level of work aggregation (not shown on Figure 21.2) is the *alpha-release*. The threads implemented for a specified period of time (usually no longer than four weeks) are delivered as an incomplete version of the final product. It is these alpha-releases which are sent to selected users, subjected to independent testing, etc. Feedback generated by these alpha-releases provides more insight into the system being built.

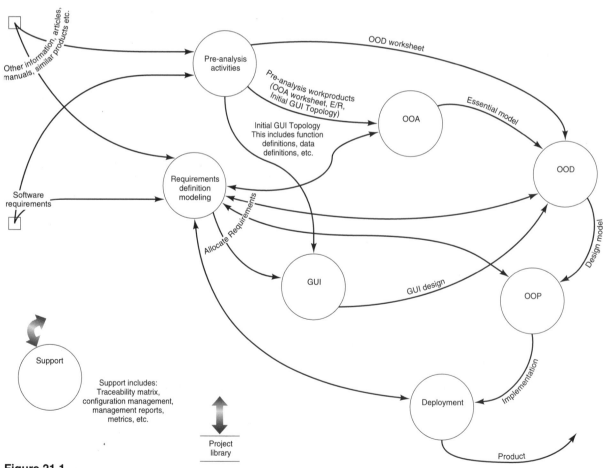

Figure 21.1
An iterative software development process.

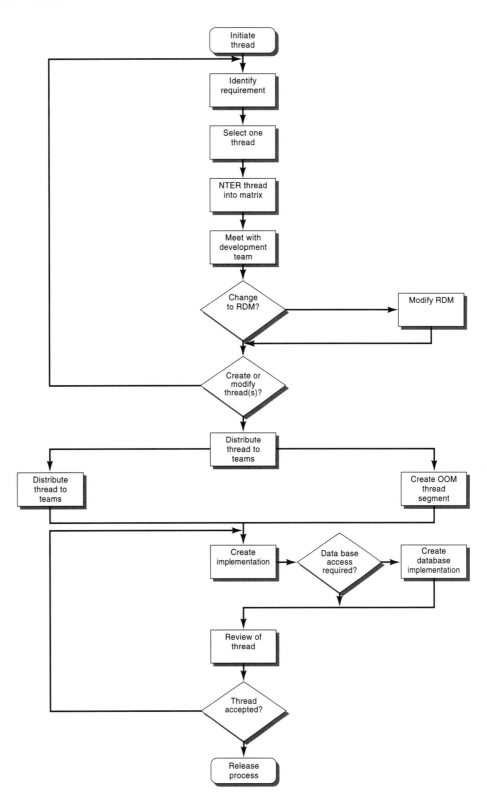

Figure 21.2
Thread-based
implementation flow
chart.

21.4 Implementing Object-Oriented Design within Rapid Application Development (RAD) Environments

Currently the software development industry is being flooded with a variety of application builders, so-called Rapid Application Development (RAD) environments. It may well be that readers of this book will be implementing an object-based system within a RAD environment. How is that any different than a traditional programming language and development environment? We will say a few words about how these environments relate to object technology.

Some of the time advantages gained by developing applications with many of the RAD products is at the expense of reuse and maintainability. The reason for this is that RAD tools typically do not support the principle of Separation of Concerns discussed in Chapter 1. That is, they may integrate business rules, user interface technology and database access technology into a single unit (for example, the Visual Basic form). This cost of using a RAD tool may well be justified on the basis of an expeditious system deployment—however, that is a strategic project management decision.

It is possible and very feasible, however, to still gain enormous benefit from RAD tools and still adhere to the basic object-oriented paradigm as discussed in this book. To do so however, requires project standards and developer discipline. Discipline is required, because in many cases, it is necessary to work against a particular RAD facility, simply to adhere to object-oriented principles.

Here are some guidelines to follow:

1. Map all Problem Domain Component (PDC) objects into RAD components. For example, in the case of Visual Basic, each PDC object becomes a .BAS file. All system logic, therefore, is contained in these components. Reuse of <u>business rules</u> is easily accomplished by simply reusing that RAD component, independent of user interface and database issues. We refer to these components as "RAD Objects."

2. All Human Interaction Component (HIC) objects should be implemented as RAD screens or forms, that is, there is no RAD equivalent to an HIC. However, these components may not encapsulate business or database access rules. Screens or forms may only communicate to the RAD Objects discussed above.

3. All database interface is allowed only through RAD objects.

4. Object services and attributes are simply the programming language subroutines and variables provided by the RAD tool.

5. Message communication between RAD objects is accomplished by function or subroutine calls.

6. Instance connections, Whole-Part and Gen-Spec relationships are implemented as shared variables between RAD objects.

7. So-called bound or data-aware controls violate the above structures, as well as the encapsulation principles of object-orientation. They can be used, however, where justified; it is simply unrealistic to ignore the availability of existing controls. Existing controls are, in fact, a form of reuse.

We've attempted to contrast the typical RAD approach with the approach above, O-O RAD, in Figure 21.3.

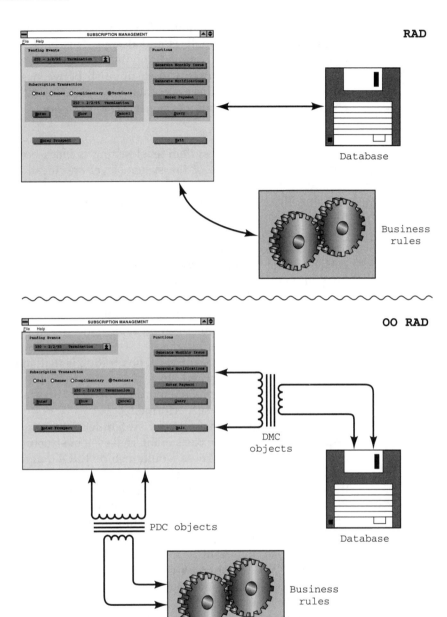

Figure 21.3
Traditional RAD vs.
O-O RAD.

21.5
Testing Object-based Designs

We have touched upon many different areas of software engineering in a book ostensibly devoted to analysis and design. This book would not be complete, however, without a few comments on the testing of object-oriented systems.

We have found it useful to distinguish between system-level testing and object-level testing. We discuss both of these areas below within the context of the analysis and design techniques presented in this book.

21.5.1
System-Level Testing

A conventional type of system-level testing is black-box testing, that is, testing performed on the basis of the system level specifications. This would include requirements definition models, event-response models and user-interface specifications. Black-box testing involves assuring that all system functions are performed in accordance with these specifications.

We have found the best way to perform this type of testing is by establishing application domain scenarios (i.e., use cases). These scenarios will capture system behavior from the perspective of the user. One phase of this testing must absolutely involve actual users, preferably in a real-world environment. This may be done in an on-site environment, e.g., a testing lab. Two type of testers are required for black-box testing. First, those familiar with the development methodology (who can read the various diagram types) and users who may only be familiar with the application user interface.

One of the advantages of black-box testing is that, in general, no special testing environment is required. Testers can use the various pre-releases working within the usual development environment. It is important, however, to maintain logs and records of all tests performed.

Another conventional form of system-level testing is clear-box testing, i.e., testing performed on the basis of internal system structure as defined by the various design documents. These would include EROI diagrams, the OOA and OOD models and GUI design documents. Each event must be verified as recognized by the specified class from the EROI diagram. The response to the event must be verified as the collaboration of the classes, also as specified from the EROI diagram. This verification does not involve testing at the service level; service level testing is done as a part of object-level testing discussed below. Although all testing is done in an iterative fashion, in general, clear-box testing is performed after the associated black-box testing is completed.

Clear-box testing is best performed by persons outside of the project organization. Skills required for this type of testing include familiarity with the development environment and design methodology. Application domain knowledge is not necessary for this type of testing. It may also be useful for members of one project team to test the work products of other project teams. Also, the position of "tester" for such products may be an excellent entry-level job for new employees. This would afford them the opportunity to learn the various work products and processes in use at a new company.

The preparation for clear-box testing should be accomplished by an independent technical source. A testing environment must be established and software must allow access to messages, attributes and other software components; this is similar in concept to a de-bugger. This kind of a test environment should facilitate the maintenance of logs and records of all tests completed. In fact, these logs and records may establish some kind of contractual milestone.

21.5.2
Object-Level Testing

Unlike system-level testing, object-level testing is done <u>independently</u> of any particular application system. Since objects may be reused in a number of different applications, testing at the object level must be performed within the context of a general reuse environment. The concepts of black-box and clear-box tests apply at the object level.

At the object level, black-box testing is accomplished <u>for each object</u> by means of an object-level test bed. This test bed allows objects to receive messages and produced messages can be displayed, captured and analyzed. This testing should be accomplished by the development team, but does require a special test bed platform. It is also necessary to be able to "stub" message sources and destinations. Such "stubs" must be capable of producing the various message types with a frequency and volume representative of actual applications. In addition, every object has an accompanying user's manual. This user's manual describes the object independently of any specific application. It forms the basis for the black-box tests.

Object-level clear-box testing is performed by the development team. This testing involves the examination of all the services and their component parts to assure conformance with the service specifications and attribute definitions. Again, this testing requires use of a specialized test bed platform which allows the object to be tested in isolation and independently of other objects and the application environment.

 *Key Points*

▲ Object-oriented designs can be implemented with non-O-O programming languages; this may not be ideal, but there may be compelling reasons to do so.

▲ Non-object-oriented programs can be implemented in some O-O programming languages—this is typically not intentional, but it may rather be the consequence of programmers not understanding the O-O paradigm.

▲ Iterative software development processes are beneficial for large, complex software development projects. For one reason, an iterative process allows mis-stated, mis-understood or mis-interpreted user requirements to be detected early on in the development process.

▲ Rapid Application Development (RAD) environments may require adaptation to support the OOD model.

▲ Testing of object-oriented systems must be done at a system level and an object level. Different kinds of tests and testing strategies apply for these different levels.

CHAPTER 22
Transitioning to Object-Orientation
A Twelve-Step Program

Good management consists of showing average people how to do the work of superior people.

— John D. Rockefeller

22.1 Introduction and Discussion

With the ever-increasing pressure to deliver large, complex software systems on budget and on schedule, many organizations find themselves scrambling to move from their current traditional software development methods to object-oriented methods.

As most of our clients would testify, the truly difficult part of transitioning to object-orientation is dealing with numerous non-technical factors.

This article presents our 12 steps to get you and your project into object-orientation. We won't promise you that it will be easy, but if you diligently follow these steps, you can't fail!

Step 1: Accept the Inevitable

Object-orientation is here to stay. Period. There is no doubt in our minds that object-orientation will be the dominant software development paradigm of, and for, the foreseeable future. Why? Because there is a <u>potential</u> for very significant quality and productivity improvements. Vendor support is growing by leaps and bounds. Early adopters are reporting success. There are serious standards efforts underway. And some de facto standards are already emerging.

Accepting the inevitable establishes a mind-set which we've found to be a key success factor. Project staff understands that this is it and there's no turning back. We sink or swim with objects!

By the way, this doesn't mean that you throw out everything and everyone from the past. Successful projects build on the past to lead them into the future.

Step 2: Understand, Understand, Understand

When introducing <u>any</u> new technology into a business enterprise, that technology must result in business being done cheaper, faster or better. So understand why you're transitioning to object-orientation. The reason is reuse! Data assembled by Capers Jones [1] show that full life cycle reuse yields the highest return on investment of any software engineering technology (30:1 return after 48 months). Object-orientation is not necessary for reuse, but it is an *enabling* technology. As a pragmatist, reuse is to us, the primary reason for moving into object-orientation.

It's important not just to understand the technology, but also to understand your motivation for introducing the technology. If your motivations are such that you're just looking for short-term gain, don't go to object-orientation! You'll be disappointed. The benefits to be derived from object-orientation won't be seen until your <u>next</u> project. And maybe not even until the project after that!

Understand what this paradigm switch is all about. If you've done traditional top-down functional decomposition in the past, understand that object-orientation is different—very, very different. You must now think in terms of building systems from the middle-out, as collaborations of objects. This has a dramatic effect, not just on how you develop systems, but on how you organize to build those systems. More about that later.

Understand the concept of an evolutionary vs. revolutionary transition to object-orientation. Which approach will work best for your organization? For most of our clients, the whole idea of throwing out everything they've ever done and starting over is absurd! For some organizations, however, the revolutionary approach might make sense.

Digging into all of the above will help you to formulate a vision of where you want to be after you've completed this transition into object-orientation. Now, write it down. Create a manifesto which presents this vision, clearly, to all members of the project. It should be a brief statement (one page or less). It should be something which people can tack up on the wall of their office.

Step 3: Assess your Assets

Assess your software development process. This doesn't have to be a formal assessment. Just develop some sense of the maturity level of your project. If you're an SEI Level One organization, transitioning to object-orientation will be very different than if you were an SEI Level Three organization.

In assessing the software development process, we find it very useful to identify and distinguish between *work products* and *artifacts*. Work products are usually deliverable items, sometimes the result of collaborative activities and presented at specific project milestone dates. (A good example would be project milestone documents.) Artifacts, on the other hand, may not be deliverable items, are usually produced by individual staff members and, rather than being produced on schedule, are simply the result of day-to-day work activities. (For example, data flow diagrams, structure charts, module specifications, etc.) Once you identify what <u>artifacts</u> you build, you can assess how those artifacts can become a part of your object-oriented process.

You must also assess your peopleware assets. People, of course, are your most important asset. In studying successful project organizations, Constantine and

Lockwood found that "only good people, well organized and well managed to enhance their productivity and the quality of their work, can produce good software." Surprise, surprise! What artifacts does each person create? How will that skill support your object-oriented process. And what about the mavericks—the techno-cowboys, the prima donnas, and whoever else. How do they fit into the organization?

Once you've assessed your assets, again, write it down. Create a transition plan which identifies your new object-oriented work products, identifies the artifacts which everyone must produce to support that set of work products and map those to your current process.

Step 4: Identify a "Symbioject"

And now the hard part. In our experience, it's foolhardy to introduce any radically new or different technology into a mission critical project without first completely understanding all aspects of the technology and its ramifications for the project, the organization and the people. Pilot projects are excellent vehicles for learning a new technology but frequently get thrown out after they're done, and with little technology transfer.

The answer is what we call a "symbioject." A pilot project which has a symbiotic relationship with a mission critical project. Usually this turns out to be a component of a mission critical project, not on a critical path, which can be comfortably addressed as a quasi-pilot project. We've found 12 to 18 months to be the ideal time-frame for such projects.

This approach has the benefit of reducing the risk associated with the introduction of the new technology, while still facilitating the transfer of some of the new technology into a mainstream project.

Step 5: Establish Meaningful Metrics

A study of the rework cycles of defense and commercial software projects [2] identifies an interesting project success factor. On successful projects there is a close correlation between the *percent of work perceived complete* and the *percent of work really complete*. That is, successful projects are well monitored.

The key to good monitoring is what we call "micro-metrics." These are meaningful, artifact-based (not work product-based) measures of progress, quality, efficiency, etc. One of our colleagues is a software project manager. He decided that a good metric to establish is *number of compiler invocations* per person per unit of time. As a module is developed and approaches completion, this metric should approach zero. Modules which do not follow this pattern need more attention. In fact, this manager became so good at this, that he would monitor compiler invocations during the day, offering assistance if he felt that a developer was having problems.

We have found that a few good micro-metrics can make all the difference between success and failure on a project. Micro-metrics, of course, must be used. And they must be used in the context for which they were intended.

Step 6: Plan for the Games

Ah, our favorite—politics!!! Every software development project has its share of politics. However, when transitioning to object-orientation, the games get more sophisticated and more subtle. Whether or not you want it, hard as you might try to ignore it, the games will be played. So plan for it. For each game, have an action plan to turn that game into a project success factor. Here are some of the games we've identified.

Creative avoidance. ("We can't do this...why...why...we don't have the right CASE tool...the right methodology...the right...") We know this one when we see it because some kind of a study committee has usually been formed, frequently at a corporate level. The mission of this committee is to survey and identify that one "perfect" CASE tool, methodology or whatever. Problem is, that study committee goes on, and on, and on... And it never seems to come to any conclusion!

A game closely related to creative avoidance is what we call malicious compliance. ("You want objects? I'll give you objects!") This is one of the more insidious games because the player is actively working for project failure.

Both of these games have the same root cause—fear. Sadly, in our software development organizations today, both men and women have to be macho. No one is allowed to say "I'm scared. I'm not sure about this object stuff. And I'm not sure I'm gonna be able to learn it and be successful at it. I need help. Please."

Creative avoidance and malicious compliance are mechanisms for <u>not</u> having to deal with this threat. But the games can be turned around. Briefly, the solution is to recognize, and stay within, the comfort zones of the players. Avoiders, especially, are motivated. They can be turned into advocates with good training (which expands their comfort zone) and mentoring (which gives them that needed security blanket).

Step 7: Plan for N-Squared

One of Murphy's Laws states that "if two complex computer technologies can possibly interact, they will interact, and they will do so in the most obscure and difficult manner possible." Frequently, the project transition to object-orientation is accompanied by the introduction of other new technologies. These may include new platforms, operating systems, database management systems, architectures, networks, programming languages and more!

When adding a new technology, the number of possible interactions between all of the technologies is not linear. It increases by N-squared. The complexity of just the interactions becomes so overwhelming that it's hard to focus on doing anything very well. So, keep it simple! We've found that if it is <u>absolutely imperative</u> to introduce even just two complex new technologies into a project, it's best to introduce them separately. Possibly introduce them on concurrent pilot projects. Then, integrate them only after both technologies have been thoroughly understood.

Step 8: Jump-Start the Learning Curve

Have you ever known someone who, when traveling to a new city, might wander aimlessly looking for an address—too proud to ask for directions! ("I'm not lost. I know exactly where I'm at!") We may be suspect because we make our livings doing training and consulting, but we see no reason to wander aimlessly trying to move into object-orientation. Successful projects learn from others.

It's not at all uncommon for us to visit a project in trouble, only to find out that the staff training consisted of buying everyone a copy of some text book!

Another tact is for one person in an organization to take an object-oriented course, then go back and teach the rest of the staff. (Imagine trying to learn how to fly an airplane this way!)

Training and mentoring are, in our view, perhaps the best investments which management can make to assure a successful transition to object-orientation.

Step 9: Get Help for your First Information Model

Going back to Step 2. Why are you doing this? Reuse! If you move into object-orientation and fail to lay a foundation for future reuse, then you've missed the whole point!

The concept of reuse may be trivial, but finding a good set of reusable objects for a given application domain can be difficult. Objects must not just be reusable, but reuseful. They must form a foundation upon which future systems can be built. They must encapsulate the rules or secrets of the application domain in a way which facilitates maintenance, supports extensibility and promotes reuse.

Regardless of the specific flavor of object-orientation which you adopt, they all involve creating an *information model* in one form or another. It is this model which establishes a basic set of objects. Again, our motives may be suspect, but we strongly recommend getting help on that first information model. The wrong information model, that is, the wrong set of objects, will not immediately reveal themselves. They will become apparent in future years as the system is modified and enhanced.

Step 10: Time-box Your First Project

It's really easy to let your first object-oriented project get out-of-hand. We strongly recommend time-boxing your first project. The scope or complexity of the project can be reduced as necessary, but never, never reduce the delivery date! Getting that first project out on schedule is a real morale booster—it establishes credibility and creates political capital.

Step 11: Begin a Reuse Library

Have we mentioned yet why we're doing this? Reuse! Although reuse may not come about until the next project (or the one after that), now is the time to establish the basic mechanism for reuse within your corporate environment. Keep in mind that reuse doesn't start with objects! It starts with a corporate commitment that the next project will re-use objects!

As you look around your organization you may find that your corporate culture works against reuse. Individual project managers may have to be directed to reuse. Real motivators must be established to promote reuse. Some examples include royalty payments to object developers, bonuses to reuse users and special incentives to project managers. We see organizations in which reuse is a platitude—that won't hack it.

Reuse needs to be measured in some meaningful way. Measuring the portion of reused analysis, design, tests, code, etc. should be a part of every project's vital statistics.

Step 12: Conduct a Serious Postpartum/Postmortem

Finally, at the conclusion of the transitioning activity, conduct a serious project review with all concerned. What went right? What went wrong? And, what needs to be modified for the next object-oriented project? Here are some things you may find.

After your first object-oriented project you'll discover that strategic organization changes are in order. You'll realize that your organization needs to be split into two fundamentally different groups. First are the object builders. These are the guys who fabricate individual objects. They are implementation domain experts. They don't really care how their objects are used—they thrive on technical challenge.

Second are the system builders. These guys are application domain experts. They thrive on understanding the business processes and assembling collaborations of objects to build systems.

You'll appreciate the need for corporate cultural changes which promote, rather than discourage, reuse. It should become apparent that the mechanisms for reuse go beyond what any one project or project manager can establish. To be truly effective, reuse needs to be coordinated at the corporate level. The need for reuse standards will become apparent.

Finally, your comfort level with object-orientation will have grown enormously. You'll feel great confidence about your ability to tackle that next object-oriented project.

Good luck!

References for Chapter 22

1. Capers Jones, Assessment and Control of Software Risks.
2. *American Programmer*, May 1993.

 *Key Points*

▲ Object-orientation may not be right for all projects.

▲ Don't put mission critical projects at risk.

▲ The pay-off from object-orientation won't happen for your *first* O-O project—and maybe not for your second!

▲ Establishing the mechanisms for reuse is just as important as introducing object-oriented methods and languages.

▲ Understanding your assets, and building a ethnology transfer plan based on those assets, is crucial for a successful transition into object-oriented technology.

▲ Well chosen pilot projects are important for a successful transition.

▲ Project organizations will have to change their structure to accommodate object-oriented development.

APPENDIX A
Case Study Description for Elevator Control System

Preface to the Appendices

In the following appendices, we have included most of the work products involved in the object-oriented analysis and design of the case study systems. We have assembled this material in an order and style which we hope will allow the reader to use it as a kind of template for the techniques presented in this book.

In this appendix, we present the user's equivalent of a functional specification for the ECS. This text will be used as the basis for the object-oriented analysis and design models created in this book. Line numbers are referenced in the text. See Chapter 2 for additional discussion of this case study.

A.1 Case Study Description Text

The general requirement is to design and implement a program to schedule and control four elevators in a building with 40 floors. The elevators will be used to carry people from one floor to another in the conventional way.

Efficiency: The program should schedule the elevators efficiently and reasonably. For example, if someone summons an elevator by pushing the down button on the fourth floor, the next elevator that reaches the fourth floor traveling down should stop at the fourth floor to accept the passenger(s). On the other hand, if an elevator has no passengers (no outstanding destination requests), it should park at the last floor it visited until it is needed again. An elevator should not reverse its direction of travel until its passengers who want to travel in its current direction have reached their destinations. (As we will see below, the program cannot really have information about an elevator's actual passengers; it only knows about destination button presses for a given elevator. For example, if some mischievous or sociopathic passenger boards the elevator at the first floor and then presses the destination buttons for the fourth, fifth, and twentieth floor, the program will cause the elevator to travel to and stop at the fourth, fifth, and twentieth floors. The computer and its program have no information about actual passenger boardings and exits.) An elevator that is filled to capacity should not respond to a new summon request. (There is an overweight sensor for each elevator. The computer and its program can interrogate these sensors.)

Destination button: The interior of each elevator is furnished with a panel containing an array of 40 buttons, one button for each floor, marked with the floor numbers (1 to 40). These destination buttons can be illuminated by signals sent from the computer to the panel. When a passenger presses a destination button not already lit, the circuitry behind the panel sends an interrupt to the computer (there is a separate interrupt for each elevator). When the computer receives one of these (vectored) interrupts, its program can read the appropriate memory mapped eight-bit input registers (there is one for each interrupt, hence one for each elevator) that contains the floor number corresponding to the destination button that caused the interrupt. Of course, the circuitry behind the panel writes the floor number into the appropriate memory-mapped input register when it causes the vectored interrupt. (Since there are 40 floors in this application, only the first six bits of each input register will be used by the implementation; but the hardware would support a building with up to 256 floors.)

Destination button lights: As mentioned earlier, the destination buttons can be illuminated (by bulbs behind the panels). When the interrupt service routine in the program receives a destination button interrupt, it should send a signal to the appropriate panel to illuminate the appropriate button. This signal is sent by the program's loading the number of the button into the appropriate memory-mapped output register (there is one such register for each elevator). The illumination of a button notifies the passenger(s) that the system has taken note of his or her request and also prevents further interrupts caused by additional (impatient?) pressing of the button. When the controller stops an elevator at a floor, it should send a signal to its destination button panel to turn off the destination button for that floor.

Floor sensors: There is a floor sensor switch for each floor for each elevator shaft. When an elevator is within eight inches of a floor, a wheel on the elevator closes the switch for that floor and sends an interrupt to the computer (there is a separate interrupt for the set of switches in each elevator shaft). When the computer receives one of these (vectored) interrupts, its program can read the appropriate memory mapped eight-bit input register (there is one for each interrupt, hence one for each elevator) that contains the floor number corresponding to the floor sensor switch that caused the interrupt.

Arrival lights: The interior of each elevator is furnished with a panel containing one illuminable indicator for each floor number. This panel is located just above the doors. The purpose of this panel is to tell the passengers in the elevator the number of the floor at which the elevator is arriving (and at which it may be stopping). The program should illuminate the indicator for a floor when it arrives at the floor and extinguish the indicator for a floor when it leaves a floor or arrives at a different floor. This signal is sent by the program's loading the number of the floor indicator into the appropriate memory-mapped output register (there is one register for each elevator).

Summons buttons: Each floor of the building is furnished with a panel containing summon button(s). Each floor except the ground floor (floor 1) and the top floor (floor 40) is furnished with a panel containing two summon buttons, one marked UP and one marked DOWN. The ground floor summon panel has only an UP button. The top floor summon panel has only a DOWN button. Thus, there are 78 summon buttons altogether, 39 UP buttons and 39 DOWN buttons. Would-be passengers press these buttons in order to summon an elevator. (Of course, the would-be passenger cannot summon a particular elevator. The scheduler decides which elevator should respond to a summon request.) These summon buttons can be illuminated by signals sent from the computer to the panel. When a passenger presses a summon button not already lit, the circuitry behind the panel sends a vectored interrupt to the computer (there is one interrupt for UP buttons and another for DOWN buttons). When the computer receives one of these two (vectored) interrupts, its program can read the appropriate memory mapped eight-bit input register that contains the floor number corresponding to the summon button that caused the interrupt. Of course, the circuitry behind the panel writes the floor number into the appropriate memory-mapped input register when it causes the vectored interrupt.

Summon button lights: The summon buttons can be illuminated (by bulbs behind the panels). When the summon button interrupt service routine in the program receives an UP or DOWN button vectored interrupt, it should send a signal to the appropriate panel to illuminate the appropriate button. This signal is sent by the program's loading the number of the button in the appropriate memory-mapped output register, one for the UP buttons and one for the DOWN buttons. The illumination of a button notifies the passenger(s) that the system has taken note of his or her request and also prevents further interrupts caused by additional pressing of the button. When the controller stops an elevator at a floor, it should send a signal to the floor's summon button panel to turn off the appropriate (UP or DOWN) button for that floor.

Elevator motor controls (Up, Down, Stop): There is a memory-mapped control word for each elevator motor. Bit 0 of this word commands the elevator to go up, bit 1 commands the elevator to do down, and bit 2 commands the elevator to stop at the floor whose sensor switch is closed. The elevator mechanism will not obey any inappropriate or unsafe command. If no floor sensor switch is closed when the computer issues a stop signal, the elevator mechanism ignores the stop signal until a floor sensor switch is closed. The computer program does not have to worry about controlling an elevator's doors or stopping an elevator exactly at a level (home) position at a floor. The elevator manufacturer uses conventional switches, relays, circuits, and safety interlocks for these purposes so that the manufacturer can certify the safety of the elevators without regard for the computer controller. For example, if the computer issues a stop command for an elevator when it is within eight inches of a floor (so that its floor sensor switch is closed), the conventional, approved mechanism stops and levels the elevator at that floor, opens and holds its doors open appropriately, and then closes its door. If the computer issues an up or down command during this period (while the door is open, for example), the manufacturer's mechanism ignores the command until its conditions for movement are met. (Therefore, it is safe for the computer to issue and up or down command while an elevator's door is still open.) One condition for an elevator's movement is that its stop button not be depressed. Each elevator's destination button panel contains a stop button. This button does not go to the computer. Its sole purpose is to hold an elevator at a floor with its door open when the elevator is currently stopped at a floor. A red emergency stop switch stops and holds the elevator at the very next floor it reaches irrespective of computer scheduling. The red switch may also turn on an audible alarm. The red switch is not connected to the computer.

Target machine: The elevator scheduler and controller may be implemented for any contemporary microcomputer capable of handling this application.

APPENDIX B

Case Study Description for Small Bytes Subscription System

In this appendix, we present the user's equivalent of a functional specification for the SBSS. This text will be used as the basis for the object-oriented analysis and design models created in this book. Line numbers are referenced in the text. See Chapter 2 for additional discussion of this case study.

B.1 Case Study Description Text

A small, independent software journal, Small Bytes, has asked you to design a new system for managing its subscriptions; they have a jury-rigged system today using various Macintosh-based spreadsheet, word-processing, and flat-file database packages, and it has gotten completely out of hand. While the concept of managing subscriptions is quite straightforward, the details are numerous, as will be seen below.

Small Bytes is published on a monthly basis; a typical monthly issue consists of 5-10 articles, each written by one or more authors in the software engineering field. Though the authors receive no payment for their articles, they do receive a year's free subscription as a token of appreciation for their efforts; if they already have a subscription, then the expiration date is extended for a year. Most authors have written only one article during the journal's five-year history, but a few have written several; management is concerned with keeping track of this information, for it wants to avoid publishing more than one or two articles from any one author in a single year.

Small Bytes also has an editorial board of advisors, some of whom may also be authors from time to time; the editorial board normally serves for a one-year or two-year term, and they too receive a complimentary subscription to the magazine. The editorial board reviews submitted articles, and also makes suggestions to Small Bytes's publisher and managing editor about topics for future issues, and prospective authors who should be contacted to write articles on those topics. As with most magazines, issues are scheduled and planned months in advance; hence, the editor is dealing with several issues and its associated authors simultaneously, as well as receiving numerous unsolicited articles from a variety of past, current, and would-be authors.

Small Bytes is sold on a subscription basis; most subscriptions are for a one-year period, but the publisher accepts subscriptions for periods longer than or shorter than a year by simply pro-rating the annual subscription price. There are only a few thousand subscribers; most are "corporate" subscribers, but some are individuals who have Small Bytes sent to their home address in a plain brown wrapper. Most of them are "single-copy" subscribers; however, it is not uncommon for large companies to order multiple copies, all of which are sent to the same person. (However, in some cases, the organization is adamant that a person not be named in the subscription, and that the magazine be sent to a title, such as "Technical Librarian," instead). Multiple-copy subscriptions typically involve a small discount from the single-copy price; in addition, various other discounts have been offered from time to time, though the overwhelming majority of subscriptions are at a standard price. (Note, however, that the "standard" price is different for North American subscriptions and international subscriptions, in order to cover the higher cost of shipping overseas.)

There are a few cases of multiple-copy subscriptions where the subscribing organization asks that the constituent copies be sent to named individuals; of course, it is important to keep track of the "primary" subscriber from whom payment is received, and to whom any correspondence should be addressed. Generally, these issues are sent to multiple people within one "site" (e.g., one division or department, located at a single corporate address); however, there are a few cases where the multiple copies are sent to individuals in different sites within the corporation. In any case, the publisher finds it convenient to identify subscribers within a site, and the various sites associated with an organization.

Most subscriptions are received directly from the subscriber; however, the publication also deals with a number of agencies, or subscription service bureaus, such as EBSCO, Faxon, and Readmore. These agencies receive a small commission for the subscriptions they provide, though this fact is generally kept hidden from the subscriber; it means, though, that the publisher must keep track of the "retail" price that the subscriber is being charged, as well as the commission paid to the agency.

In addition, the magazine is distributed in several foreign countries by distributors who have an quasi-exclusive right to market the magazine in their territory. The distributors receive a somewhat larger discount for a bulk shipment of magazines (in addition to paying for the shipping costs, which can be substantial), which they then distribute to their subscribers. Typically, some "direct" subscriptions from the distributor's country existed prior to the distributor-publisher agreement, and Small Bytes continues to supply those subscriptions directly. In addition, the distributor is supposed to supply the names and addresses of his own subscribers (in case he goes out of business) to the publisher; in practice, this has not been done consistently in the past, but the publisher is determined to enforce this provision when the new system is developed.

As noted earlier, contributing authors and members of the editorial board of advisors receive a complimentary one-year subscription to the magazine; in addition, the publisher provides a limited number of additional complimentary subscriptions to respected gurus and in the field, as well as a few friends and relatives. This list of "comps" is reviewed from time to time to see if any should be deleted. Also, the "comp" list is queried periodically in order to confirm that they still wish to receive their complimentary copy of SmallBytes.

A large percentage of existing subscribers renew their subscription from one year to the next; the renewal activity is typically the result of renewal notices that the publisher begins sending several months before the actual expiration. On the final month of a subscription, the publisher includes a large note with the magazine that says "THIS IS YOUR LAST COPY." For several months after the subscription has expired, the publisher continues to send renewal notices. (Note also that the subscription service bureaus make their own solicitation efforts to their subscribers, in addition to the publisher's direct letters to those same subscribers.) Renewals sometimes straggle in several months after a subscription has expired, so it is vital to maintain the subscription records on the database indefinitely.

Payments for new subscriptions and renewals are normally received by check; the check may be accompanied with a subscription offer or a renewal notice, but such notices are not considered "invoices" in the normal sense of the word. In some cases, subscribers ask that a formal invoice be generated, with a purchase order number, so that it can be submitted to their accounting department for proper payment. Some subscribers pay by credit card, but the publisher insists(because its bank insists) that credit card payments be accompanied by a signature; this means that the credit card orders and renewals are typically sent by fax or mail.

In addition to full-year subscriptions, the publisher also sells limited numbers of individual copies of Small Bytes. In most cases, these are"back-issue" orders; they may be paid, as indicated above, by check, credit card, or invoice. On rare occasions, a customer will order multiple copies of a back issue, in which case a discount is offered. And on even rarer occasions, a customer (typically an author, or a vendor whose product was favorably reviewed in the magazine) will order several thousand copies of an individual article in an issue, and will ask that it be packaged as a"mini-issue" of the magazine; each of these special orders is priced separately, depending on volume, etc.

Although there are only a small number of subscribers, the publisher has a large list of "prospects," which it has accumulated from various sources over the years. Many of these prospects have asked for sample copies of SmallBytes; some have received a "trial" subscription for a few months, but then decided not to "convert" to a paid subscription. Many others have received various promotional mailings from time to time, including unsolicited sample copies and/or trial subscriptions. Obviously, all of this information is useful to the publisher.

APPENDIX C
Phrase-Frequency Analysis for Elevator Control System

Phrase-Frequency Analysis (PFA) is one technique used within Linguistic-based Information Analysis (LIA) to identify a universe of application domain concepts and relationships between these concepts. This technique is discussed in Chapter 3. In this appendix we present the PFA for the ECS. This list was produced with the assistance of a grammatical analysis program. The source text used was that given in Appendix A.

C.1
PFA Listing

ACTUAL PASSENGER
ALARM, AUDIBLE
APPROPRIATE BUTTON
APPROPRIATE COMMAND
APPROPRIATE MEMORY-MAPPED EIGHT-BIT
  ... REGISTER
APPROPRIATE PANEL
ARRAY OF BUTTONS
ARRIVAL LIGHT
ARRIVAL, ELEVATOR
AUDIBLE ALARM
BEHIND THE PANEL BULB
BOARDING, PASSENGER
BOTTOM FLOOR
BOTTOM FLOOR SUMMONS PANEL
BUILDING
BULB, BEHIND THE PANEL
BULB, PANEL

BUTTON
BUTTON DEPRESSION
BUTTON ILLUMINATION
BUTTON INTERRUPT SERVICE ROUTINE,
  SUMMONS
BUTTON INTERRUPT, DESTINATION
BUTTON INTERRUPT, SUMMONS
BUTTON LIGHT, SUMMONS
BUTTON NUMBER
BUTTON PANEL, DESTINATION
BUTTON PANEL, FLOOR SUMMONS
BUTTON PRESS
BUTTON PUSH
BUTTON VECTORED INTERRUPT, DOWN
BUTTON VECTORED INTERRUPT, UP
BUTTON, APPROPRIATE
BUTTON, ARRAY OF
BUTTON, DESTINATION
BUTTON, DOWN
BUTTON, DOWN SUMMONS
BUTTON, STOP
BUTTON, SUMMONS

BUTTON, UP
BUTTON, UP SUMMONS
BUTTONS, ARRAY OF
CAPACITY, ELEVATOR
CERTIFICATION, MANUFACTURER
CIRCUIT, ELEVATOR
CIRCUITRY
CIRCUITS
CLOSED SENSOR SWITCH
COMMAND
COMMAND, APPROPRIATE
COMMAND, COMPUTER
COMMAND, DOWN
COMMAND, INAPPROPRIATE
COMMAND, STOP
COMMAND, UNSAFE
COMMAND, UP
COMPUTER COMMAND
COMPUTER CONTROLLER
COMPUTER INTERRUPT
COMPUTER OUTPUT
COMPUTER PROGRAM
COMPUTER SCHEDULING
COMPUTER SIGNAL
CONDITIONS, MOVEMENT
CONTEMPORARY MICROCOMPUTER
CONTROL PROGRAM, ELEVATOR
CONTROL SYSTEM, ELEVATOR
CONTROLLER, COMPUTER
CONTROLLER, ELEVATOR
CONTROLS, ELEVATOR MOTOR
CURRENT DIRECTION
CURRENTLY STOPPED ELEVATOR
DEPRESSION, BUTTON
DESTINATION
DESTINATION BUTTON
DESTINATION BUTTON INTERRUPT
DESTINATION BUTTON PANEL
DESTINATION REQUEST
DIRECTION OF TRAVEL
DIRECTION, CURRENT
DIRECTION, DOWN
DIRECTION, REVERSE
DIRECTION, UP
DOORS, ELEVATOR
DOORS, OPEN
DOWN BUTTON
DOWN BUTTON VECTORED INTERRUPT

DOWN COMMAND
DOWN DIRECTION
DOWN SUMMONS BUTTON
EFFICIENCY
EIGHT-BIT ... REGISTER, APPROPRIATE
    MEMORY-MAPPED
ELEVATOR
ELEVATOR (NO PASSENGERS)
ELEVATOR ARRIVAL
ELEVATOR CAPACITY
ELEVATOR CIRCUIT
ELEVATOR CONTROL PROGRAM
ELEVATOR CONTROL SYSTEM
ELEVATOR CONTROLLER
ELEVATOR DOORS
ELEVATOR INTERIOR
ELEVATOR INTERLOCK
ELEVATOR INTERRUPT
ELEVATOR MANUFACTURER
ELEVATOR MECHANISM
ELEVATOR MOTOR
ELEVATOR MOTOR CONTROLS
ELEVATOR MOVEMENT
ELEVATOR NUMBER
ELEVATOR PANEL
ELEVATOR PARK
ELEVATOR POSITION
ELEVATOR SCHEDULE
ELEVATOR SCHEDULER
ELEVATOR SHAFT
ELEVATOR STOP
ELEVATOR TRAVEL
ELEVATOR VISIT
ELEVATOR WHEEL
ELEVATOR, CURRENTLY STOPPED
ELEVATOR, STOP
EMERGENCY STOP SWITCH
EXIT, PASSENGER
EXTINGUISHMENT, INDICATOR
FIRST FLOOR
FLOOR
FLOOR (ELEVATOR ARRIVING AT)
FLOOR (SENSOR SWITCH CLOSED)
FLOOR INDICATOR
FLOOR NUMBER
FLOOR SENSOR
FLOOR SENSOR SWITCH
FLOOR SENSOR SWITCH INTERRUPT

FLOOR SUMMONS BUTTON PANEL
FLOOR SUMMONS PANEL
FLOOR SUMMONS PANEL, BOTTOM
FLOOR SUMMONS PANEL, GROUND
FLOOR SUMMONS PANEL, TOP
FLOOR, BOTTOM
FLOOR, FIRST
FLOOR, GROUND
FLOOR, LAST
FLOOR, REACHED
FLOOR, TOP
FLOOR, WITHIN EIGHT INCHES OF
GROUND FLOOR
GROUND FLOOR SUMMONS PANEL
HARDWARE
HOME POSITION
ILLUMINABLE INDICATOR
ILLUMINATION
ILLUMINATION, BUTTON
ILLUMINATION, INDICATOR
INAPPROPRIATE COMMAND
INDICATOR
INDICATOR EXTINGUISHMENT
INDICATOR ILLUMINATION
INDICATOR, FLOOR
INDICATOR, ILLUMINABLE
INPUT REGISTER
INPUT REGISTER, MEMORY-MAPPED
INTERIOR, ELEVATOR
INTERLOCK, ELEVATOR
INTERROGATION, SENSOR
INTERRUPT
INTERRUPT SERVICE ROUTINE
INTERRUPT SERVICE ROUTINE, SUMMONS
    BUTTON
INTERRUPT, COMPUTER
INTERRUPT, DESTINATION BUTTON
INTERRUPT, DOWN BUTTON VECTORED
INTERRUPT, ELEVATOR
INTERRUPT, FLOOR SENSOR SWITCH
INTERRUPT, SUMMONS BUTTON
INTERRUPT, UP BUTTON VECTORED
INTERRUPT, VECTORED
LAST FLOOR
LEVEL POSITION
LIGHT, ARRIVAL
LIGHT, SUMMONS BUTTON
LOADING, PASSENGER

MACHINE, TARGET
MANUFACTURER
MANUFACTURER CERTIFICATION
MANUFACTURER'S MECHANISM
MANUFACTURER, ELEVATOR
MECHANISM, ELEVATOR
MECHANISM, MANUFACTURER'S
MEMORY-MAPPED EIGHT-BIT ... REGISTER,
    APPROPRIATE
MEMORY-MAPPED INPUT REGISTER
MEMORY-MAPPED OUTPUT REGISTER
MICROCOMPUTER, CONTEMPORARY
MISCHIEVOUS PASSENGER
MOTOR CONTROLS, ELEVATOR
MOTOR, ELEVATOR
MOVEMENT CONDITIONS
MOVEMENT, ELEVATOR
NOTIFICATION, PASSENGER
NUMBER, BUTTON
NUMBER, ELEVATOR
NUMBER, FLOOR
OPEN DOORS
OPEN SENSOR SWITCH
ORDER, PASSENGER
OUTPUT REGISTER
OUTPUT REGISTER, MEMORY-MAPPED
OUTPUT, COMPUTER
OVERWEIGHT SENSOR
PANEL
PANEL BULB
PANEL, APPROPRIATE
PANEL, BOTTOM FLOOR SUMMONS
PANEL, DESTINATION BUTTON
PANEL, ELEVATOR
PANEL, FLOOR SUMMONS
PANEL, FLOOR SUMMONS BUTTON
PANEL, GROUND FLOOR SUMMONS
PANEL, SUMMONS
PANEL, TOP FLOOR SUMMONS
PARK, ELEVATOR
PASSENGER
PASSENGER BOARDING
PASSENGER EXIT
PASSENGER LOADING
PASSENGER NOTIFICATION
PASSENGER ORDER
PASSENGER REQUEST
PASSENGER SUMMONS

PASSENGER, ACTUAL
PASSENGER, MISCHIEVOUS
PASSENGER, SOCIOPATHIC
PASSENGER, WOULD-BE
PEOPLE
POSITION, ELEVATOR
POSITION, HOME
POSITION, LEVEL
PRESS, BUTTON
PROGRAM, COMPUTER
PROGRAM, ELEVATOR CONTROL
PUSH, BUTTON
REACHED FLOOR
REGISTER, APPROPRIATE MEMORY-MAPPED
    EIGHT-BIT ...
REGISTER, INPUT
REGISTER, MEMORY-MAPPED INPUT
REGISTER, MEMORY-MAPPED OUTPUT
REGISTER, OUTPUT
REQUEST, DESTINATION
REQUEST, PASSENGER
REQUEST, SUMMONS
RESPONSE, SUMMONS
REVERSE DIRECTION
ROUTINE, INTERRUPT SERVICE
SCHEDULE, ELEVATOR
SCHEDULER, ELEVATOR
SENSOR INTERROGATION
SENSOR SWITCH INTERRUPT, FLOOR
SENSOR SWITCH, CLOSED
SENSOR SWITCH, FLOOR
SENSOR SWITCH, OPEN
SENSOR, FLOOR
SENSOR, OVERWEIGHT
SERVICE ROUTINE, INTERRUPT
SERVICE ROUTINE, SUMMONS BUTTON
    INTERRUPT
SHAFT, ELEVATOR
SIGNAL, COMPUTER
SIGNAL, STOP
SOCIOPATHIC PASSENGER
STOP BUTTON
STOP COMMAND
STOP ELEVATOR
STOP SIGNAL
STOP SWITCH
STOP SWITCH, EMERGENCY
STOP, ELEVATOR

STOP, EMERGENCY SWITCH
SUMMONS BUTTON
SUMMONS BUTTON INTERRUPT
SUMMONS BUTTON INTERRUPT SERVICE
    ROUTINE
SUMMONS BUTTON LIGHT
SUMMONS BUTTON PANEL, FLOOR
SUMMONS BUTTON, DOWN
SUMMONS BUTTON, UP
SUMMONS PANEL
SUMMONS PANEL, BOTTOM FLOOR
SUMMONS PANEL, FLOOR
SUMMONS PANEL, GROUND FLOOR
SUMMONS PANEL, TOP FLOOR
SUMMONS REQUEST
SUMMONS RESPONSE
SUMMONS, PASSENGER
SWITCH INTERRUPT, FLOOR SENSOR
SWITCH, CLOSED SENSOR
SWITCH, EMERGENCY STOP
SWITCH, FLOOR SENSOR
SWITCH, OPEN SENSOR
SWITCH, STOP
SYSTEM, ELEVATOR CONTROL
TARGET MACHINE
TOP FLOOR
TOP FLOOR SUMMONS PANEL
TRAVEL, DIRECTION OF
TRAVEL, ELEVATOR
UNSAFE COMMAND
UP
UP BUTTON
UP BUTTON VECTORED INTERRUPT
UP COMMAND
UP DIRECTION
UP SUMMONS BUTTON
VECTORED INTERRUPT
VECTORED INTERRUPT, DOWN BUTTON
VECTORED INTERRUPT, UP BUTTON
VISIT, ELEVATOR
WHEEL, ELEVATOR
WITHIN EIGHT INCHES OF FLOOR
WOULD-BE PASSENGER

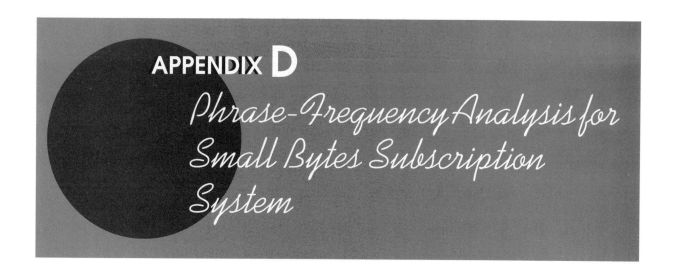

APPENDIX D
Phrase-Frequency Analysis for Small Bytes Subscription System

Phrase-Frequency Analysis (PFA) is one technique used within Linguistic-based Information Analysis (LIA) to identify a universe of application domain concepts and relationships between these concepts. This technique is discussed in Chapter 3. In this appendix we present the PFA for the SBSS. This list was produced with the assistance of a grammatical analysis program The source text used was that given in Appendix B.

D.1
PFA Listing

ACCEPTED SUBSCRIPTION
ACCOMPANIED PAYMENT
ACCOUNTING DEPARTMENT
ACTUAL EXPIRATION DATE
ADDITIONAL SUBSCRIPTION
ADDRESS, CORPORATE
ADDRESS, CORRESPONDENCE
ADDRESS, HOME
ADDRESS, SUBSCRIPTION
ADVISORS, BOARD OF
AGENCY, SUBSCRIPTION SERVICE
AGREEMENT, DISTRIBUTOR-PUBLISHER
ANNUAL SUBSCRIPTION PRICE
ARTICLE
ASSOCIATED SITE
AUTHOR
AUTHOR, CONTRIBUTING
AUTHOR, CURRENT

AUTHOR, PAST
AUTHOR, PROSPECTIVE
AUTHOR, WOULD-BE
AUTHOR-ARTICLE TRACK
BACK ISSUE
BOARD OF ADVISORS
BROWN WRAPPER, PLAIN
BULK SHIPMENT
BUREAU, SUBSCRIPTION SERVICE
CHECK PAYMENT
COMMISSION, SUBSCRIPTION SERVICE
COMPANY SUBSCRIPTION
COMPLIMENTARY SUBSCRIPTION
COMPLIMENTARY SUBSCRIPTION QUERY
COMPLIMENTARY SUBSCRIPTION REVIEW
COMPLIMENTARY SUBSCRIPTION, DELETED
CONSTITUENT COPIES
CONTINUED SUBSCRIPTION
CONTRIBUTING AUTHOR
CONVERTED SUBSCRIPTION
COPIES, CONSTITUENT
COPY

CORPORATE ADDRESS
CORPORATE DEPARTMENT
CORPORATION
CORRESPONDENCE ADDRESS
COST, SHIPPING
COUNTRY
COUNTRY, FOREIGN
CREDIT CARD ORDER
CREDIT CARD PAYMENT
CURRENT AUTHOR
CUSTOMER
DATABASE
DATE, ACTUAL EXPIRATION
DATE, EXPIRATION
DATE, EXPIRED
DELETED COMPLIMENTARY SUBSCRIPTION
DEPARTMENT, ACCOUNTING
DEPARTMENT, CORPORATE
DIRECT SUBSCRIPTION
DISCOUNT, SUBSCRIPTION
DISTRIBUTOR
DISTRIBUTOR TERRITORY
DISTRIBUTOR, EXCLUSIVE
DISTRIBUTOR-PUBLISHER AGREEMENT
DIVISION
EDITOR
EXCLUSIVE DISTRIBUTOR
EXISTING SUBSCRIPTION
EXPIRATION DATE
EXPIRATION DATE, ACTUAL
EXPIRED DATE
EXTENDED SUBSCRIPTION
FINAL MONTH
FINAL SUBSCRIPTION MONTH
FOREIGN COUNTRY
GURU, RESPECTED
HOME ADDRESS
INDIVIDUAL SUBSCRIPTION
INTERNATIONAL SUBSCRIPTION
INVOICE
ISSUE
ISSUE TOPIC
ISSUE, BACK
ISSUE, NEXT
ISSUE, SAMPLE
ISSUE, UNSOLICITED
JOURNAL
MAGAZINE

MAILING, PROMOTIONAL
MAILINGS
MANAGEMENT
MONTH, FINAL
MONTH, FINAL SUBSCRIPTION
MULTIPLE SUBSCRIPTIONS
NAME, SUBSCRIPTION
NEW SUBSCRIPTION
NEXT ISSUE
NORTH AMERICAN SUBSCRIPTION
NOTICE, RENEWAL
OFFER, SUBSCRIPTION
ORDER
ORDER, CREDIT CARD
ORGANIZATION
PAID SUBSCRIPTION
PAST AUTHOR
PAYMENT
PAYMENT, ACCOMPANIED
PAYMENT, CHECK
PAYMENT, CREDIT CARD
PAYMENT, PROPER
PAYMENT, RECEIVED
PEOPLE
PERIOD, SUBSCRIPTION
PERSON
PLAIN BROWN WRAPPER
PRICE PRO-RATING, SUBSCRIPTION
PRICE, ANNUAL SUBSCRIPTION
PRICE, RETAIL
PRICE, STANDARD SUBSCRIPTION
PRICE, SUBSCRIPTION
PRIMARY SUBSCRIBER
PRIMARY-SUBSCRIBER TRACK
PRO-RATING, SUBSCRIPTION PRICE
PROMOTIONAL MAILING
PROPER PAYMENT
PROSPECTIVE AUTHOR
PROSPECTS
PUBLISHER
PURCHASE ORDER
QUERY, COMPLIMENTARY SUBSCRIPTION
RECEIVED PAYMENT
RECEIVED SUBSCRIPTION
RECORD, SUBSCRIPTION
RENEWAL NOTICE
RENEWAL SOLICITATION
RENEWAL, SUBSCRIPTION

RESPECTED GURU
RETAIL PRICE
RETAIL-PRICE TRACK
REVIEW, COMPLIMENTARY SUBSCRIPTION
SAMPLE ISSUE
SERVICE AGENCY, SUBSCRIPTION
SERVICE BUREAU, SUBSCRIPTION
SERVICE COMMISSION, SUBSCRIPTION
SHIPMENT
SHIPMENT, BULK
SHIPPING COST
SHIPPING TITLE, SUBSCRIPTION
SITE
SITE, ASSOCIATED
SOLICITATION, RENEWAL
STANDARD SUBSCRIPTION PRICE
SUBSCRIBER
SUBSCRIBER, PRIMARY
SUBSCRIPTION
SUBSCRIPTION ADDRESS
SUBSCRIPTION DISCOUNT
SUBSCRIPTION MONTH, FINAL
SUBSCRIPTION NAME
SUBSCRIPTION OFFER
SUBSCRIPTION PERIOD
SUBSCRIPTION PRICE
SUBSCRIPTION PRICE PRO-RATING
SUBSCRIPTION PRICE, ANNUAL
SUBSCRIPTION PRICE, STANDARD
SUBSCRIPTION QUERY, COMPLIMENTARY
SUBSCRIPTION RECORD
SUBSCRIPTION RENEWAL
SUBSCRIPTION REVIEW, COMPLIMENTARY
SUBSCRIPTION SERVICE AGENCY
SUBSCRIPTION SERVICE BUREAU
SUBSCRIPTION SERVICE COMMISSION
SUBSCRIPTION SHIPPING TITLE
SUBSCRIPTION TERM
SUBSCRIPTION YEAR
SUBSCRIPTION, ACCEPTED
SUBSCRIPTION, ADDITIONAL
SUBSCRIPTION, COMPANY
SUBSCRIPTION, COMPLIMENTARY
SUBSCRIPTION, CONTINUED
SUBSCRIPTION, CONVERTED
SUBSCRIPTION, DELETED COMPLIMENTARY
SUBSCRIPTION, DIRECT
SUBSCRIPTION, EXISTING

SUBSCRIPTION, EXTENDED
SUBSCRIPTION, INDIVIDUAL
SUBSCRIPTION, INTERNATIONAL
SUBSCRIPTION, MULTIPLE
SUBSCRIPTION, NEW
SUBSCRIPTION, NORTH AMERICAN
SUBSCRIPTION, PAID
SUBSCRIPTION, RECEIVED
SUBSCRIPTION, TRIAL
SYSTEM
TERM, SUBSCRIPTION
TERRITORY, DISTRIBUTOR
TITLE, SUBSCRIPTION SHIPPING
TOPIC, ISSUE
TRACK, AUTHOR-ARTICLE
TRACK, PRIMARY-SUBSCRIBER
TRACK, RETAIL-PRICE
TRIAL SUBSCRIPTION
UNSOLICITED ISSUE
VENDOR
WOULD-BE AUTHOR
WRAPPER, PLAIN BROWN
YEAR, SUBSCRIPTION

OOA/OOD Worksheet for Elevator Control System

The OOA/OOD worksheet provides a systematic approach for reviewing a lengthy PFA list and identifying an initial set of OOA and OOD components. These techniques are discussed in Chapters 3 and 5. This section contains the complete OOA/OOD worksheet for the ECS. This sheet was created from the PFA given in Appendix C.

OOA/OOD WORKSHEET

Elevator Control System

ITEM	(0)	(1)	(2)	(3)	(4)	(5)	(6)	(7)	(8)	COMMENTS
ACTUAL PASSENGER										
APPROPRIATE BUTTON										
APPROPRIATE COMMAND										
APPROPRIATE MEMORY MAPPED EIGHT-BIT ... REGISTER										
APPROPRIATE PANEL										
ARRAY OF BUTTONS										
ARRIVAL LIGHT										
AUDIBLE ALARM										
BEHIND THE PANEL BULB										
BOTTOM FLOOR										
BOTTOM FLOOR SUMMONS PANEL										
BUILDING										
BUTTON										
BUTTON DEPRESSION										
BUTTON ILLUMINATION										
BUTTON NUMBER										
BUTTON PRESS										
BUTTON PUSH										
CIRCUITRY										
CIRCUITS										
CLOSED SENSOR SWITCH										
COMMAND										

(0) Not applicable. Possibly irrelevant, outside the context of the system being specified, etc.
(1) Possible object-class.
(2) Possibly part of sub-type/super-type structure. Includes Gen-Spec and Whole-Part relationships.
(3) Possibly describes an object-class attribute or instance relationship.
(4) Possibly describes an object service.
(5) Implementation specific. Possible Problem Domain Component item.
(6) Possible Human Interaction Component item.
(7) Possible Task Management Component item.
(8) Possible Data Management Component item.

ITEM	(0)	(1)	(2)	(3)	(4)	(5)	(6)	(7)	(8)	COMMENTS
COMPUTER COMMAND										
COMPUTER CONTROLLER										
COMPUTER INTERRUPT										
COMPUTER OUTPUT										
COMPUTER PROGRAM										
COMPUTER SCHEDULING										
COMPUTER SIGNAL										
CONTEMPORARY MICROCOMPUTER										
CURRENT DIRECTION										
CURRENTLY STOPPED ELEVATOR										
DESTINATION										
DESTINATION BUTTON										
DESTINATION BUTTON INTERRUPT										
DESTINATION BUTTON PANEL										
DESTINATION REQUEST										
DIRECTION OF TRAVEL										
DOWN BUTTON										
DOWN BUTTON VECTORED INTERRUPT										
DOWN COMMAND										
DOWN DIRECTION										
DOWN SUMMONS BUTTON										
EFFICIENCY										
ELEVATOR										
ELEVATOR (NO PASSENGERS)										
ELEVATOR ARRIVAL										

(0) Not applicable. Possibly irrelevant, outside the context of the system being specified, etc.
(1) Possible object-class.
(2) Possibly part of sub-type/super-type structure. Includes Gen-Spec and Whole-Part relationships.
(3) Possibly describes an object-class attribute or instance relationship.
(4) Possibly describes an object service.

(5) Implementation specific. Possible Problem Domain Component item.
(6) Possible Human Interaction Component item.
(7) Possible Task Management Component item.
(8) Possible Data Management Component item.

2

229

ITEM	(0)	(1)	(2)	(3)	(4)	(5)	(6)	(7)	(8)	COMMENTS
ELEVATOR CAPACITY										
ELEVATOR CIRCUIT										
ELEVATOR CONTROL PROGRAM										
ELEVATOR CONTROL SYSTEM										
ELEVATOR CONTROLLER										
ELEVATOR DOOR										
ELEVATOR INTERIOR										
ELEVATOR INTERLOCK										
ELEVATOR INTERRUPT										
ELEVATOR MANUFACTURER										
ELEVATOR MECHANISM										
ELEVATOR MOTOR										
ELEVATOR MOTOR CONTROLS										
ELEVATOR MOVEMENT										
ELEVATOR NUMBER										
ELEVATOR PANEL										
ELEVATOR PARK										
ELEVATOR POSITION										
ELEVATOR SCHEDULE										
ELEVATOR SCHEDULER										
ELEVATOR SHAFT										
ELEVATOR STOP										
ELEVATOR TRAVEL										
ELEVATOR VISIT										
ELEVATOR WHEEL										

(0) Not applicable. Possibly irrelevant, outside the context of the system being specified, etc.
(1) Possible object-class.
(2) Possibly part of sub-type/super-type structure. Includes Gen-Spec and Whole-Part relationships.
(3) Possibly describes an object-class attribute or instance relationship.
(4) Possibly describes an object service.

(5) Implementation specific. Possible Problem Domain Component item.
(6) Possible Human Interaction Component item.
(7) Possible Task Management Component item.
(8) Possible Data Management Component item.

3

ITEM	(0)	(1)	(2)	(3)	(4)	(5)	(6)	(7)	(8)	COMMENTS
EMERGENCY STOP SWITCH										
FIRST FLOOR										
FLOOR										
FLOOR (ELEVATOR ARRIVING AT)										
FLOOR (SENSOR SWITCH CLOSED)										
FLOOR INDICATOR										
FLOOR NUMBER										
FLOOR SENSOR										
FLOOR SENSOR SWITCH										
FLOOR SENSOR SWITCH INTERRUPT										
FLOOR SUMMONS BUTTON PANEL										
FLOOR SUMMONS PANEL										
GROUND FLOOR										
GROUND FLOOR SUMMONS PANEL										
HARDWARE										
HOME POSITION										
ILLUMINABLE INDICATOR										
ILLUMINATION										
INAPPROPRIATE COMMAND										
INDICATOR										
INDICATOR EXTINGUISHMENT										
INDICATOR ILLUMINATION										
INPUT REGISTER										
INTERRUPT										
INTERRUPT SERVICE ROUTINE										

(0) Not applicable. Possibly irrelevant, outside the context of the system being specified, etc.
(1) Possible object-class.
(2) Possibly part of sub-type/super-type structure. Includes Gen-Spec and Whole-Part relationships.
(3) Possibly describes an object-class attribute or instance relationship.
(4) Possibly describes an object service.

(5) Implementation specific. Possible Problem Domain Component item.
(6) Possible Human Interaction Component item.
(7) Possible Task Management Component item.
(8) Possible Data Management Component item.

4

ITEM	(0)	(1)	(2)	(3)	(4)	(5)	(6)	(7)	(8)	COMMENTS
LAST FLOOR										
LEVEL POSITION										
MANUFACTURER										
MANUFACTURER CERTIFICATION										
MANUFACTURER'S MECHANISM										
MEMORY-MAPPED INPUT REGISTER										
MEMORY-MAPPED OUTPUT REGISTER										
MISCHIEVOUS PASSENGER										
MOVEMENT CONDITIONS										
OPEN DOOR										
OPEN SENSOR SWITCH										
OUTPUT REGISTER										
OVERWEIGHT SENSOR										
PANEL										
PANEL BULB										
PASSENGER										
PASSENGER BOARDING										
PASSENGER EXIT										
PASSENGER LOADING										
PASSENGER NOTIFICATION										
PASSENGER ORDER										
PASSENGER REQUEST										
PASSENGER SUMMONS										
PEOPLE										
REACHED FLOOR										

(0) Not applicable. Possibly irrelevant, outside the context of the system being specified, etc.
(1) Possible object-class.
(2) Possibly part of sub-type/super-type structure. Includes Gen-Spec and Whole-Part relationships.
(3) Possibly describes an object-class attribute or instance relationship.
(4) Possibly describes an object service.

(5) Implementation specific. Possible Problem Domain Component item.
(6) Possible Human Interaction Component item.
(7) Possible Task Management Component item.
(8) Possible Data Management Component item.

5

ITEM	(0)	(1)	(2)	(3)	(4)	(5)	(6)	(7)	(8)	COMMENTS
REVERSE DIRECTION										
SENSOR INTERROGATION										
SOCIOPATHIC PASSENGER										
STOP BUTTON										
STOP COMMAND										
STOP ELEVATOR										
STOP SIGNAL										
STOP SWITCH										
SUMMONS BUTTON										
SUMMONS BUTTON INTERRUPT										
SUMMONS BUTTON INTERRUPT SERVICE ROUTINE										
SUMMONS BUTTON LIGHT										
SUMMONS PANEL										
SUMMONS REQUEST										
SUMMONS RESPONSE										
TARGET MACHINE										
TOP FLOOR										
TOP FLOOR SUMMONS PANEL										
UNSAFE COMMAND										
UP										
UP BUTTON										
UP BUTTON VECTORED INTERRUPT										
UP COMMAND										
UP DIRECTION										
UP SUMMONS BUTTON										

(0) Not applicable. Possibly irrelevant, outside the context of the system being specified, etc.
(1) Possible object-class.
(2) Possibly part of sub-type/super-type structure. Includes Gen-Spec and Whole-Part relationships.
(3) Possibly describes an object-class attribute or instance relationship.
(4) Possibly describes an object service.

(5) Implementation specific. Possible Problem Domain Component item.
(6) Possible Human Interaction Component item.
(7) Possible Task Management Component item.
(8) Possible Data Management Component item.

6

ITEM	(0)	(1)	(2)	(3)	(4)	(5)	(6)	(7)	(8)	COMMENTS
VECTORED INTERRUPT										
WITHIN EIGHT INCHES OF FLOOR										
WOULD-BE PASSENGER										

(0) Not applicable. Possibly irrelevant, outside the context of the system being specified, etc.
(1) Possible object-class.
(2) Possibly part of sub-type/super-type structure. Includes Gen-Spec and Whole-Part relationships.
(3) Possibly describes an object-class attribute or instance relationship.
(4) Possibly describes an object service.

(5) Implementation specific. Possible Problem Domain Component item.
(6) Possible Human Interaction Component item.
(7) Possible Task Management Component item.
(8) Possible Data Management Component item.

7

APPENDIX F

OOA/OOD Worksheet for Small Bytes Subscription System

The OOA/OOD worksheet provides a systematic approach for reviewing a lengthy PFA list and identifying an initial set of OOA and OOD components. These techniques are discussed in Chapters 3 and 5. This section contains the complete OOA/OOD worksheet for the SBSS. This sheet was created from the PFA given in Appendix D.

OOA/OOD WORKSHEET

Small Bytes Subscription System

ITEM	(0)	(1)	(2)	(3)	(4)	(5)	(6)	(7)	(8)	COMMENTS
ACCEPTED SUBSCRIPTION										
ACCOMPANIED PAYMENT										
ACCOUNTING DEPARTMENT										
ACTUAL EXPIRATION DATE										
ADDITIONAL SUBSCRIPTION										
ANNUAL SUBSCRIPTION PRICE										
ARTICLE										
ASSOCIATED SITE										
AUTHOR										
AUTHOR-ARTICLE TRACK										
BACK ISSUE										
BOARD OF ADVISORS										
BULK SHIPMENT										
CHECK PAYMENT										
COMPANY SUBSCRIPTION										
COMPLIMENTARY SUBSCRIPTION										
COMPLIMENTARY SUBSCRIPTION QUERY										
COMPLIMENTARY SUBSCRIPTION REVIEW										
CONSTITUENT COPIES										
CONTINUED SUBSCRIPTION										
CONTRIBUTING AUTHOR										
CONVERTED SUBSCRIPTION										
COPY										

(0) Not applicable. Possibly irrelevant, outside the context of the system being specified, etc.
(1) Possible object-class.
(2) Possibly part of sub-type/super-type structure. Includes Gen-Spec and Whole-Part relationships.
(3) Possibly describes an object-class attribute or instance relationship.
(4) Possibly describes an object service.

(5) Implementation specific. Possible Problem Domain Component item.
(6) Possible Human Interaction Component item.
(7) Possible Task Management Component item.
(8) Possible Data Management Component item.

ITEM	(0)	(1)	(2)	(3)	(4)	(5)	(6)	(7)	(8)	COMMENTS
CORPORATE ADDRESS										
CORPORATE DEPARTMENT										
CORPORATION										
CORRESPONDENCE ADDRESS										
COUNTRY										
CREDIT CARD ORDER										
CREDIT CARD PAYMENT										
CURRENT AUTHOR										
CUSTOMER										
DATABASE										
DELETED COMPLIMENTARY SUBSCRIPTION										
DIRECT SUBSCRIPTION										
DISTRIBUTOR										
DISTRIBUTOR TERRITORY										
DISTRIBUTOR-PUBLISHER AGREEMENT										
DIVISION										
EDITOR										
EXCLUSIVE DISTRIBUTOR										
EXISTING SUBSCRIPTION										
EXPIRATION DATE										
EXPIRED DATE										
EXTENDED SUBSCRIPTION										
FINAL MONTH										
FINAL SUBSCRIPTION MONTH										
FOREIGN COUNTRY										

(0) Not applicable. Possibly irrelevant, outside the context of the system being specified, etc.
(1) Possible object-class.
(2) Possibly part of sub-type/super-type structure. Includes Gen-Spec and Whole-Part relationships.
(3) Possibly describes an object-class attribute or instance relationship.
(4) Possibly describes an object service.

(5) Implementation specific. Possible Problem Domain Component item.
(6) Possible Human Interaction Component item.
(7) Possible Task Management Component item.
(8) Possible Data Management Component item.

2

237

ITEM	(0)	(1)	(2)	(3)	(4)	(5)	(6)	(7)	(8)	COMMENTS
HOME ADDRESS										
INDIVIDUAL SUBSCRIPTION										
INTERNATIONAL SUBSCRIPTION										
INVOICE										
ISSUE										
ISSUE TOPIC										
JOURNAL										
MAGAZINE										
MAILINGS										
MANAGEMENT										
MULTIPLE SUBSCRIPTION										
NEW SUBSCRIPTION										
NEXT ISSUE										
NORTH AMERICAN SUBSCRIPTION										
ORDER										
ORGANIZATION										
PAID SUBSCRIPTION										
PAST AUTHOR										
PAYMENT										
PEOPLE										
PERSON										
PLAIN BROWN WRAPPER										
PRIMARY SUBSCRIBER										
PRIMARY-SUBSCRIBER TRACK										
PROMOTIONAL MAILING										

(0) Not applicable. Possibly irrelevant, outside the context of the system being specified, etc.
(1) Possible object-class.
(2) Possibly part of sub-type/super-type structure. Includes Gen-Spec and Whole-Part relationships.
(3) Possibly describes an object-class attribute or instance relationship.
(4) Possibly describes an object service.

(5) Implementation specific. Possible Problem Domain Component item.
(6) Possible Human Interaction Component item.
(7) Possible Task Management Component item.
(8) Possible Data Management Component item.

3

ITEM	(0)	(1)	(2)	(3)	(4)	(5)	(6)	(7)	(8)	COMMENTS
PROPER PAYMENT										
PROSPECTIVE AUTHOR										
PROSPECTS										
PUBLISHER										
PURCHASE ORDER										
RECEIVED PAYMENT										
RECEIVED SUBSCRIPTION										
RENEWAL NOTICE										
RENEWAL SOLICITATION										
RESPECTED GURU										
RETAIL PRICE										
RETAIL-PRICE TRACK										
SAMPLE ISSUE										
SHIPMENT										
SHIPPING COST										
SITE										
STANDARD SUBSCRIPTION PRICE										
SUBSCRIBER										
SUBSCRIPTION										
SUBSCRIPTION ADDRESS										
SUBSCRIPTION DISCOUNT										
SUBSCRIPTION NAME										
SUBSCRIPTION OFFER										
SUBSCRIPTION PERIOD										
SUBSCRIPTION PRICE										

(0) Not applicable. Possibly irrelevant, outside the context of the system being specified, etc.
(1) Possible object-class.
(2) Possibly part of sub-type/super-type structure. Includes Gen-Spec and Whole-Part relationships.
(3) Possibly describes an object-class attribute or instance relationship.
(4) Possibly describes an object service.

(5) Implementation specific. Possible Problem Domain Component item.
(6) Possible Human Interaction Component item.
(7) Possible Task Management Component item.
(8) Possible Data Management Component item.

4

ITEM	(0)	(1)	(2)	(3)	(4)	(5)	(6)	(7)	(8)	COMMENTS
SUBSCRIPTION PRICE PRO-RATING										
SUBSCRIPTION RECORD										
SUBSCRIPTION RENEWAL										
SUBSCRIPTION SERVICE AGENCY										
SUBSCRIPTION SERVICE BUREAU										
SUBSCRIPTION SERVICE COMMISSION										
SUBSCRIPTION SHIPPING TITLE										
SUBSCRIPTION TERM										
SUBSCRIPTION YEAR										
SYSTEM										
TRIAL SUBSCRIPTION										
UNSOLICITED ISSUE										
VENDOR										
WOULD-BE AUTHOR										

(0) Not applicable. Possibly irrelevant, outside the context of the system being specified, etc.
(1) Possible object-class.
(2) Possibly part of sub-type/super-type structure. Includes Gen-Spec and Whole-Part relationships.
(3) Possibly describes an object-class attribute or instance relationship.
(4) Possibly describes an object service.

(5) Implementation specific. Possible Problem Domain Component item.
(6) Possible Human Interaction Component item.
(7) Possible Task Management Component item.
(8) Possible Data Management Component item.

3-View Models for Elevator Control System

Chapters 3 and 5 discussed the concept of 3-View Modeling of proposed software systems. The term "3-View Modeling" refers to the application of data-flow diagrams (or variants, including context diagrams), entity-relationship diagrams (or variants) and state-transition diagrams (or variants, including event-response models) to the object-finding process. In this appendix we present the application of 3-View Modeling to the ECS.

A good deal of understanding as to how elevator control systems work, from a general perspective, is necessary to understand the material in this appendix; the reader may wish to review Section 2.1.

Finally, it should be mentioned that, with some additional material, this appendix would represent a fairly thorough *structured analysis* of the ECS.

G.1 The Context Diagram

Figure G.1 shows a context diagram for the ECS. This context diagram is part of the process view of the ECS. It shows the flow of incoming and outgoing information for the ECS, as well as the sources and destinations for these flows.

This context diagram represents only one component of a process view for the ECS. Other components would be a leveled set of data flow diagrams and primitive process specifications (or various equivalents). We will see another form of a process view in Section G.5.

G.2 The Entity-Relationship Diagram

Figure G.2 shows an entity-relationship diagram for the ECS. This diagram portrays the data view of the ECS, or, in other words, the stored data requirements for the ECS. Not surprisingly, the diagram is relatively simple—the ECS simply does not have very complex data storage requirements.

This is the only data view diagram which will be presented for the ECS.

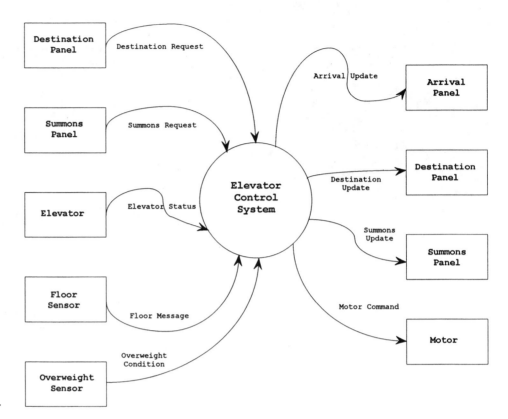

Figure G.1
ECS context diagram.

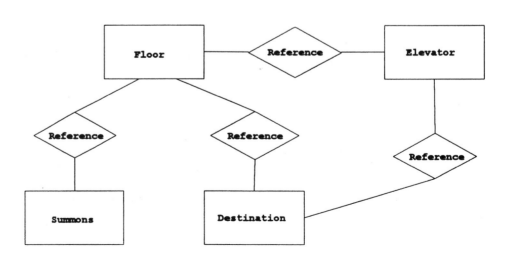

Figure G.2
ECS data model.

G.3
The Event-
Response Model

Figure G.3 shows an event-response model for the ECS. All external events and the corresponding system responses are shown.

This event-response model represents only one component of a control view for the ECS. Another component would be a state-transition diagram, such as that given in Section G.4.

1. ELEVATOR SUMMONED	A. Summons panel updated. B. Elevator scheduled in accordance with elevator schedule policy.
2. DESTINATION REQUESTED	A. Destination panel updated. B. Elevator scheduled in accordance with elevator schedule policy.
3. ELEVATOR ARRIVES AT SCHEDULED FLOOR	A. Arrival panel updated. B. Destination panel updated. C. Summons panel updated. D. Elevator stops at floor.
4. ELEVATOR ARRIVES AT NON-SCHEDULED FLOOR	A. Arrival panel updated.
5. ELEVATOR BECOMES READY	A. Elevator dispatched in accordance with elevator schedule policy.
6. ELEVATOR BECOMES OVERWEIGHT	A. Elevator dispatching disabled.
7. ELEVATOR BECOMES NOT-OVERWEIGHT	A. Elevator dispatching enabled.

Figure G.3
An ECS event-response model.

G.4
The State-
Transition
Diagram

Figure G.4 shows a state-transition diagram for the ECS. This represents another form of control view for the ECS. It shows how various events and responses are related to so-called system states. Referring to Figure G.4, the ECS states are:

BUSY (UP/UP,[*] UP/NO, DN/DN, DN/NO)

In the BUSY state, the elevator is physically moving. The status direction may be either NO, or it must be consistent with the elevator's current direction.

There are two events (see event-response model) which will cause a transition from the BUSY state; they are events 3 and 4, i.e., arrival at scheduled or non-scheduled floors, respectively.

Transition 6 occurs when the elevator arrives at a scheduled floor. The status direction is updated during this transition. The elevator is now in the STOPPED state.

Transition 7 occurs when the elevator arrives at a non-scheduled floor. The status is also updated during this transition; however, the elevator remains in the BUSY state.

Note that in the case where destination buttons are depressed during the elevator BUSY state, the point at which we may commit to a destination is upon the next elevator arrival. However, it may be the case, that a given destination will not be honored.

---

[*](actual direction/status direction)

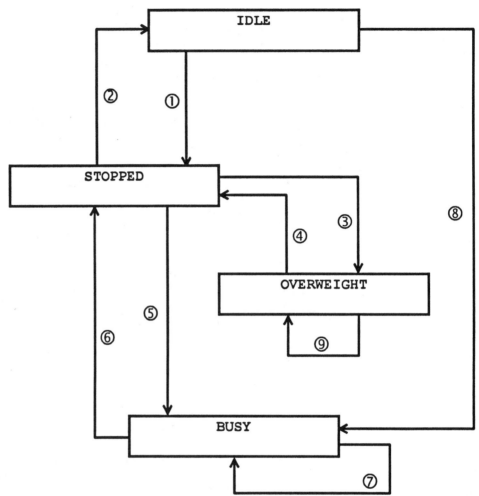

Figure G.4
An ECS event-response
model.

STOPPED (NO/UP, NO/DN, NO/NO)

In the STOPPED state, the elevator is not moving; the elevator is assumed to be not ready for movement, i.e., the elevator's mechanical system has not yet reported that the elevator is safe for movement. In addition, the elevator's doors will be open.

There are two events which will cause a transition from the STOPPED state; they are events 5 (elevator becomes ready) and 6 (elevator becomes overweight).

Transition 2 occurs when the elevator becomes ready with a status direction of NO. In this case, the elevator is now in the IDLE state.

Transition 5 occurs also when the elevator becomes ready; however, with a status direction other than NO, elevator movement is initiated and the elevator is in the BUSY state.

Transitions 2 and 5 occur when a single event occurs: the elevator becomes ready. The distinction between these two transitions is based on the status direction. The value of status direction is determined from the ECS decision table.

Transition 3 occurs when the elevator becomes overweight; the elevator remains in the OVERWEIGHT state until the overweight condition is reversed.

IDLE (NO/NO)

In the IDLE state, the elevator is not moving and does not intend to move. However, in this state, the mechanical systems have reported that it is safe to move the elevator, i.e., the doors have been secured and any overweight conditions have been resolved. It is available for service of either summons requests or destination requests.

There are two events which will cause a transition from the IDLE state; they are events 1 (elevator summoned) and 2 (destination requested).

Transition 1 occurs when the elevator is commanded to respond to a summons request at the elevator's current floor. In this case, the elevator mechanism opens the elevator doors, and the elevator is in the STOPPED state.

Transition 8 occurs also when the elevator is commanded to respond to a destination request. In this case, movement of the elevator begins and the elevator is in the BUSY state.

OVERWEIGHT

In the OVERWEIGHT state, the elevator is not moving; the elevator is assumed to be not ready for movement, i.e., the elevator's mechanical system has not yet reported that the elevator is safe for movement.

Transition 4 occurs when the elevator's overweight condition has been reversed. This will cause a transition to the STOPPED state; normal elevator control may then continue.

Transition 9 occurs when the elevator becomes ready. However, since an overweight condition exists, the elevator mechanism opens the elevator doors, and the elevator remains in the OVERWEIGHT state.

G.5 The Decision Table

The 3VM component presented for the ECS is the decision table. This is a form of process view which is sometimes used in place of primitive process specifications. The complete ECS decision table is given below. This decision table establishes elevator control policy by specifying whether or not, when a given elevator arrives at a given floor, that floor should be identified as a scheduled floor. This table also determines what Updated Status Direction (USD) will be established when a given elevator arrives at a given floor, as a function of the indicated parameters. Refer to annotations at the end of the table.

Not all possible combinations of parameters may be physically realizable in a given elevator control system implementation. A specific elevator *scheduling algorithm* will be introduced in a subsequent appendix. It should also be noted that the table reflects one particular view of user policy.

ELEVATOR CONTROL SYSTEM
Decision Table

DPA	DPB	DPC	SPU	SPD	CD	SD	FLR SCHD	USD
T	T	T	T	T	UP	UP	YES①	UP②
T	T	T	T	T	UP	NO	YES	UP
T	T	T	T	T	DN	DN	YES	DN
T	T	T	T	T	DN	NO	YES	DN
T	T	T	T	F	UP	UP	YES	UP
T	T	T	T	F	UP	NO	YES	UP
T	T	T	T	F	DN	DN	YES	DN
T	T	T	T	F	DN	NO	YES	DN
T	T	T	F	T	UP	UP	YES	UP
T	T	T	F	T	UP	NO	YES	UP
T	T	T	F	T	DN	DN	YES	DN
T	T	T	F	T	DN	NO	YES	DN
T	T	T	F	F	UP	UP	YES	UP
T	T	T	F	F	UP	NO	YES	UP
T	T	T	F	F	DN	DN	YES	DN
T	T	T	F	F	DN	NO	YES	DN
T	T	F	T	T	UP	UP	YES	UP
T	T	F	T	T	UP	NO	YES	UP
T	T	F	T	T	DN	DN	YES	DN
T	T	F	T	T	DN	NO	YES	DN
T	T	F	T	F	UP	UP	YES	UP
T	T	F	T	F	UP	NO	YES	UP
T	T	F	T	F	DN	DN	NO	DN
T	T	F	T	F	DN	NO	NO	DN
T	T	F	F	T	UP	UP	NO	UP
T	T	F	F	T	UP	NO	NO	UP
T	T	F	F	T	DN	DN	YES	DN
T	T	F	F	T	DN	NO	YES	DN
T	T	F	F	F	UP	UP	NO	UP
T	T	F	F	F	UP	NO	NO	UP
T	T	F	F	F	DN	DN	NO	DN
T	T	F	F	F	DN	NO	NO	DN
T	F	T	T	T	UP	UP	YES	UP
T	F	T	T	T	UP	NO	YES	UP
T	F	T	T	T	DN	DN	YES	UP③
T	F	T	T	T	DN	NO	YES	UP
T	F	T	T	F	UP	UP	YES	UP
T	F	T	T	F	UP	NO	YES	UP
T	F	T	T	F	DN	DN	YES	UP
T	F	T	T	F	DN	NO	YES	UP
T	F	T	F	T	UP	UP	YES	UP
T	F	T	F	T	UP	NO	YES	UP
T	F	T	F	T	DN	DN	YES	UP
T	F	T	F	T	DN	NO	YES	UP

ELEVATOR CONTROL SYSTEM (Continued)
Decision Table

DPA	DPB	DPC	SPU	SPD	CD	SD	FLR SCHD	USD
T	F	T	F	F	UP	UP	YES	UP
T	F	T	F	F	UP	NO	YES	UP
T	F	T	F	F	DN	DN	YES	UP
T	F	T	F	F	DN	NO	YES	UP
T	F	F	T	T	UP	UP	YES	UP
T	F	F	T	T	UP	NO	YES	UP
T	F	F	T	T	DN	DN	YES	UP
T	F	F	T	T	DN	NO	YES	UP
T	F	F	T	F	UP	UP	YES	UP
T	F	F	T	F	UP	NO	YES	UP
T	F	F	T	F	DN	DN	YES	UP④
T	F	F	T	F	DN	NO	YES	UP
T	F	F	F	T	UP	UP	NO	UP
T	F	F	F	T	UP	NO	NO	UP
T	F	F	F	T	DN	DN	YES	UP
T	F	F	F	T	DN	NO	YES	UP
T	F	F	F	F	UP	UP	NO	UP
T	F	F	F	F	UP	NO	NO	UP
T	F	F	F	F	DN	DN	YES	UP
T	F	F	F	F	DN	NO	YES	UP
F	T	T	T	T	UP	UP	YES	DN
F	T	T	T	T	UP	NO	YES	DN
F	T	T	T	T	DN	DN	YES	DN
F	T	T	T	T	DN	NO	YES	DN
F	T	T	T	F	UP	UP	YES	DN
F	T	T	T	F	UP	NO	YES	DN
F	T	T	T	F	DN	DN	YES	DN
F	T	T	T	F	DN	NO	YES	DN
F	T	T	F	T	UP	UP	YES	DN
F	T	T	F	T	UP	NO	YES	DN
F	T	T	F	T	DN	DN	YES	DN
F	T	T	F	T	DN	NO	YES	DN
F	T	T	F	F	UP	UP	YES	DN
F	T	T	F	F	UP	NO	YES	DN
F	T	T	F	F	DN	DN	YES	DN
F	T	T	F	F	DN	NO	YES	DN
F	T	F	T	T	UP	UP	YES	DN
F	T	F	T	T	UP	NO	YES	DN
F	T	F	T	T	DN	DN	YES	DN
F	T	F	T	T	DN	NO	YES	DN
F	T	F	T	F	UP	UP	YES	DN
F	T	F	T	F	UP	NO	YES	DN
F	T	F	T	F	DN	DN	NO	DN
F	T	F	T	F	DN	NO	NO	DN

ELEVATOR CONTROL SYSTEM (Continued)
Decision Table

DPA	DPB	DPC	SPU	SPD	CD	SD	FLR SCHD	USD
F	T	F	F	T	UP	UP	YES	DN
F	T	F	F	T	UP	NO	YES	DN
F	T	F	F	T	DN	DN	YES	DN
F	T	F	F	T	DN	NO	YES	DN
F	T	F	F	F	UP	UP	YES	DN
F	T	F	F	F	UP	NO	YES	DN
F	T	F	F	F	DN	DN	NO	DN
F	T	F	F	F	DN	NO	NO	DN
F	F	T	T	T	UP	UP	YES	UP
F	F	T	T	T	UP	NO	YES	UP
F	F	T	T	T	DN	DN	YES	DN
F	F	T	T	T	DN	NO	YES	DN
F	F	T	T	F	UP	UP	YES	UP
F	F	T	T	F	UP	NO	YES	UP
F	F	T	T	F	DN	DN	YES	UP
F	F	T	T	F	DN	NO	YES	UP
F	F	T	F	T	UP	UP	YES	DN
F	F	T	F	T	UP	NO	YES	DN
F	F	T	F	T	DN	DN	YES	DN
F	F	T	F	T	DN	NO	YES	DN
F	F	T	F	F	UP	UP	YES	NO⑤
F	F	T	F	F	UP	NO	YES	NO
F	F	T	F	F	DN	DN	YES	NO
F	F	T	F	F	DN	NO	YES	NO
F	F	F	T	T	UP	UP	YES	UP
F	F	F	T	T	UP	NO	YES	UP
F	F	F	T	T	DN	DN	YES	DN
F	F	F	T	T	DN	NO	YES	DN
F	F	F	T	F	UP	UP	YES	UP
F	F	F	T	F	UP	NO	YES	UP
F	F	F	T	F	DN	DN	YES	UP
F	F	F	T	F	DN	NO	YES	UP
F	F	F	F	T	UP	UP	YES	DN
F	F	F	F	T	UP	NO	YES	DN
F	F	F	F	T	DN	DN	YES	DN
F	F	F	F	T	DN	NO	YES	DN
F	F	F	F	F	UP	UP	NO	NO⑥
F	F	F	F	F	UP	NO	NO	NO
F	F	F	F	F	DN	DN	NO	NO
F	F	F	F	F	DN	NO	NO	NO

Legend:

DPA = Destination(s) (for current elevator) Pending Above current floor.

DPB = Destination(s) (for current elevator) Pending Below current floor.

DPC = Destination (for current elevator) Pending at Current floor.

SPU = Up direction Summons Pending at current floor.

SPD = Down direction Summons Pending at current floor.

CD = Direction of elevator (upon arrival at current floor).

SD = Status Direction (upon arrival at current floor).

FLR SCHD = Current floor is a scheduled floor for given elevator at current floor.

USD = Updated Status Direction (after arrival at current floor).

The *Current Direction* (CD) of a given elevator ([UP|DN|NO]) represents actual, physical movement of the elevator. The elevator can be moving upwards, downwards or it can be stopped. In this application domain, when the current direction is NO, the elevator is stopped at a floor, irrespective of the status of the doors.

The *Status Direction* (SD) of a given elevator ([UP|DN|NO]) indicates that, irrespective of the elevator's current <u>physical</u> direction, the elevator intends to continue moving in the direction indicated by this attribute. An example of this would be an elevator stopped at a floor, but intending to move downwards to continue to scheduled destinations.

The SD (of a given elevator) is always updated upon <u>arrival</u> at a floor. In the decision table above, SD represents the status direction of a given elevator *just prior to* arrival at a given floor. The *Updated Status Direction* (USD) represents the *new* status direction upon arrival at the floor.

In the decision table above, the FLR SCHD column indicates whether or not, for the given set of parameter values, the given floor is a *scheduled floor*, that is, whether or not the elevator will stop at the floor.

Notes:

1. Our established policy is that whenever a destination is pending at the current floor (DPC=T), the floor is considered scheduled, irrespective of any other parameters. Also, the bottom-most and top-most floors (in this case, 1 and 40, respectively) are always considered as scheduled, irrespective of any other parameters.

2. Whenever consistent with pending destinations and summons, we update the elevator's status direction to maintain the elevator's current direction of motion. In the case of a conflict between pending destinations and pending summons, priority is always given to pending destinations. This policy is established so as to avoid, as much as possible, elevators stopping at a floor for the sole purpose of changing direction. In the case of a conflict between pending destinations and pending summons, priority is always given to pending destinations.

3. In some cases, our policy is that an elevator will stop at a floor *and* change direction. This is a case where priority is given to pending destinations.

4. In some few cases, our policy allows for an elevator to stop at a floor and reverse direction so as to accommodate pending destinations.

5. In some few cases, our policy shows that, after stopping at a floor, an elevator's updated status direction is set to "NO." A stopped elevator with "NO" as its SD is *idle*; the status direction *eventually* will be updated, depending on system demands.

6. In some few cases, an elevator may arrive at a floor for no apparent reason. That is, the elevator has no pending destinations nor are there summons requests at the current floors. Our policy is to allow the elevator to simply pass the given floor. These cases may occur when an idle elevator has been dispatched for a summons request not at the current floor.

APPENDIX H
3-View Models for Small Bytes Subscription System

Chapters 3 and 5 discussed the concept of 3-View Modeling of proposed software systems. The term "3-View Modeling" refers to the application of data-flow diagrams (or variants, including context diagrams), entity-relationship diagrams (or variants) and state-transition diagrams (or variants, including event-response models) to the object-finding process. In this appendix we present the application of 3-View Modeling to the SBSS. The reader may wish to review Section 2.2, which discusses the user's requirements for the SBSS.

H.1 The Context Diagram

Figure H.1 shows a context diagram for the SBSS. This context diagram is part of the process view of the SBSS. It shows the flow of incoming and outgoing information for the SBSS, as well as the sources and destinations for these flows.

This context diagram represents only one component of a process view for the SBSS. Other components would be a leveled set of data flow diagrams and primitive process specifications (or various equivalents).

H.2 The Entity-Relationship Diagram

Figure H.2 shows an entity-relationship diagram for the SBSS. This diagram portrays the data view of the SBSS, or, in other words, the stored data requirements for the SBSS. Not surprisingly, the diagram is considerably more complex than the same diagram for the ECS. Obviously, we would expect the SBSS to have more complex data storage requirements.

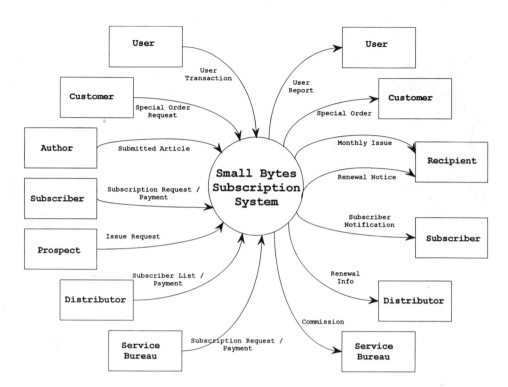

Figure H.1
An SBSS context
diagram.

H.3
The Event-
Response Model

Figure H.3 shows an event-response model for the SBSS. All external events and their corresponding system responses are shown.

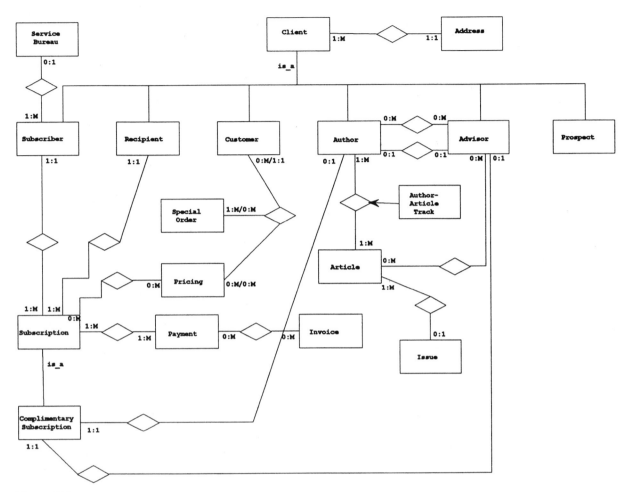

Figure H.2
SBSS data model.

1. PAID SUBSCRIPTION REQUESTED	A. CREATE NEW SUBSCRIPTION RECORD.
	B. CREATE NEW SUBSCRIBER RECORD AS REQUIRED.
	   B.1 CREATE OR UPDATE ADDRESS RECORD AS REQUIRED.
	C. CREATE NEW RECIPIENT RECORD AS REQUIRED.
	   C.1 CREATE OR UPDATE ADDRESS RECORD AS REQUIRED.
	D. ESTABLISH SUBSCRIPTION PRICING.
	E. POST PAYMENT AS REQUIRED.
	   E.1 ISSUE INVOICE AS REQUIRED.
	F. NOTIFY SERVICE BUREAU OF SUBSCRIPTION AS REQUIRED.
	G. ESTABLISH EXPIRATION DATE FOR SUBSCRIPTION.
	H. ESTABLISH EXPIRATION WARNING DATE FOR SUBSCRIPTION.

2. COMPLIMENTARY SUBSCRIPTION REQUESTED	B. CREATE NEW SUBSCRIBER RECORD AS REQUIRED.
	   B.1 CREATE OR UPDATE ADDRESS RECORD AS REQUIRED.
	C. CREATE NEW RECIPIENT RECORD AS REQUIRED.
	   C.1 CREATE OR UPDATE ADDRESS RECORD AS REQUIRED.

3. PAYMENT RECEIVED	A. POST PAYMENT AS REQUIRED. B. ISSUE INVOICE AS REQUIRED.
4. TIME TO SEND RENEWAL NOTICE	A. INITIATE NOTIFICATION SEQUENCE.
5. SUBSCRIPTION TERMINATES	A. DISCONTINUE SUBSCRIPTION.
6. SUBSCRIPTION RENEWED	A. CREATE NEW SUBSCRIPTION RECORD. B. UPDATE SUBSCRIBER ADDRESS RECORD AS REQUIRED. C. UPDATE RECIPIENT ADDRESS RECORD AS REQUIRED. D. ESTABLISH RENEWAL PRICING. E. POST PAYMENT AS REQUIRED. E.1 ISSUE INVOICE AS REQUIRED. F. NOTIFY SERVICE BUREAU OF SUBSCRIPTION AS REQUIRED. G. ESTABLISH EXPIRATION DATE FOR SUBSCRIPTION. H. ESTABLISH EXPIRATION WARNING DATE FOR SUBSCRIPTION.
7. TIME TO REVIEW "COMP" LIST	A. TERMINATE COMPLIMENTARY SUBSCRIPTION AS REQUIRED.

Figure H.3
SBSS event-response model.

8. SPECIAL ORDER RECEIVED	A. CREATE NEW CUSTOMER RECORD AS REQUIRED. B.1 CREATE OR UPDATE ADDRESS RECORD AS REQUIRED. C. ENTER SHIPPING ADDRESS. D. ESTABLISH SPECIAL ORDER PRICING. E. POST PAYMENT AS REQUIRED. E.1 ISSUE INVOICE AS REQUIRED.
9. ARTICLE RECEIVED	A. CREATE NEW ARTICLE RECORD. B. CREATE NEW AUTHOR RECORD(S) AS REQUIRED. B.1 CREATE NEW ADDRESS RECORD AS REQUIRED. C. UPDATE AUTHOR AUTHOR-ARTICLE TRACK.
10. ARTICLE ACCEPTED FOR PUBLICATION	A. TENTATIVELY SCHEDULE PUBLICATION ISSUE. B. ENTER COMPLIMENTARY SUBSCRIPTION(S). C. UPDATE AUTHOR AUTHOR-ARTICLE TRACK.
11. ARTICLE PUBLISHED	A. UPDATE AUTHOR AUTHOR-ARTICLE TRACK.
12. PROSPECT IDENTIFIED	B. CREATE NEW PROSPECT RECORD AS REQUIRED. B.1 CREATE NEW ADDRESS RECORD AS REQUIRED.

Figure H.3
(continued)

OOA Model for Elevator Control System

This appendix presents the entire ECS OOA model. The complete five-layer object model diagram is presented at the end of this appendix (see Figure I.1). Below are descriptions and definitions of each of the model components. Although the model is presented in this appendix in documented form, the entire model is contained on the diskette accompanying this book. A CASE tool is required to access that form of the model.

Section I.6 of this appendix contains the complete elevator scheduling algorithm.

I.1 List of ECS OOA Model Components

This section presents a listing of all of the components (classes, attributes, services, etc.) of the OOA model for the ECS. Each component is further described in a subsequent section of this appendix.

ARRIVAL EVENT	Class
ARRIVAL PANEL	Class
arrival_floor	Attribute
arrival_id	Attribute
arrival_panel_id	Attribute
Control Elevator Motor	Message
Control_Elevator	Method
Control_Elevator_Motor	Method
current_direction	Attribute
current_floor	Attribute
current_state	Attribute
DESTINATION EVENT	Class
DESTINATION PANEL	Class
destination_floor	Attribute
destination_id	Attribute
destination_panel_id	Attribute
destinations_pending	Attribute
ELEVATOR	Class
ELEVATOR EVENT	Class

ELEVATOR MOTOR	Class
elevator_id	Attribute
elevator_motor_id	Attribute
event_id	Attribute
FLOOR	Class
floor_id	Attribute
id	Attribute
OVERWEIGHT SENSOR	Class
OVERWEIGHT_SENSOR	Message
overweight_sensor_id	Attribute
overweight_status	Attribute
PANEL	Class
panel_id	Attribute
Poll Neighbor 1	Message
Poll Neighbor 2	Message
Poll_Neighbor	Method
Process Elevator 1	Message
Process_Elevator_Arrival	Method
Process_Elevator_Ready	Method
Recognize Destination Request	Message
Recognize Elevator Arrival	Message
Recognize Elevator Ready	Message
Recognize Summons Request	Message
RECOGNIZE_DESTINATION_REQUEST	Method
RECOGNIZE_ELEVATOR_ARRIVAL	Method
Recognize_Elevator_Ready	Method
Recognize_Not_Overweight	Method
Recognize_Overweight	Method
RECOGNIZE_SUMMONS_REQUEST	Method
Report Destination Pending	Message
Report Elevator Status	Message
Report Summons Pending	Message
Report_Arrival_Event	Method
Report_Current_Location	Method
Report_Current_Status	Method
Report_Destination_Event	Method
Report_Destination_Pending	Method
Report_Direction	Method
Report_Overweight_Status	Method
Report_Summons_Event	Method
Report_Summons_Pending	Method
status_direction	Attribute
SUMMONS EVENT	Class
SUMMONS PANEL	Class
summons_floor	Attribute
summons_id	Attribute
summons_panel_id	Attribute
summons_pending	Attribute
summons_pending_down	Attribute
summons_pending_up	Attribute
summons_type	Attribute
Update Arrival Panel	Message
Update Summons Panel	Message
Update_Arrival_Panel	Method
Update_Destination_Panel	Method
Update_Direction	Method
Update_Floor_Arrival	Method
Update_Floor_Ready	Method
Update_Summons_Panel	Method

I.2 Class Descriptions

ARRIVAL EVENT

The purpose of the object-class ARRIVAL EVENT is to recognize the occurrence of an elevator arrival at a floor. This object-class encapsulates the services required to respond to arrival events and report these events to other object-classes.

ARRIVAL PANEL

The purpose of the object-class ARRIVAL PANEL is to update the arrival panel when an elevator arrives at a floor. This object class encapsulates the services required to respond appropriately to messages from ARRIVAL EVENT.

DESTINATION EVENT

The object-class DESTINATION EVENT recognizes the occurrence of the "Destination Requested" event and is responsible for reporting that event to other object-classes.

DESTINATION PANEL

The purpose of the object-class DESTINATION PANEL is to update the destination panel when a destination is requested and to report pending destinations. This object-class encapsulates the services required to update the elevator's destination panel and to report the status of pending destinations. This object-class also encapsulates attributes which maintain information on pending destinations.

ELEVATOR

The purpose of the ELEVATOR object-class is to perform elevator controlling and reporting functions. The ELEVATOR object-class encapsulates various services which control the elevator movement, report elevator status and recognize when an elevator becomes ready. Attributes encapsulated within this object-class store information about the elevator's direction, state and status.

ELEVATOR EVENT

The ELEVATOR EVENT class is a generalization class which encapsulates services and attributes shared by the various other event recognizer object-classes.

ELEVATOR MOTOR

The purpose of the object-class ELEVATOR MOTOR is to control elevator motors. This object class encapsulates the services required to respond appropriately to messages from ELEVATOR.

FLOOR

The purpose of the object-class FLOOR is to manage the dispatch and arrival of elevators and to maintain information about pending summons. This object-class encapsulates services which process elevator arrivals and dispatches and which communicate with other floors to manage elevator dispatching.

OVERWEIGHT SENSOR

The purpose of the object-class OVERWEIGHT SENSOR is to recognize elevator overweight conditions and the restoration of safe elevator weight conditions. This object-class encapsulates the services required to recognize and report on these conditions. This object-class also encapsulates attributes required to store information about these conditions.

PANEL

The PANEL class is a generalization class which encapsulates services and attributes shared by the various other panel object-classes.

SUMMONS EVENT

The purpose of the object-class SUMMONS EVENT is to recognize the occurrence of a "Summons Requested" event. This object-class encapsulates the services required to recognize and report a "Summons Event."

SUMMONS PANEL

The purpose of the object-class SUMMONS PANEL is to update the summons panel when a summons is requested at a floor and to report pending summons request. This object-class encapsulates the services to respond appropriately to messages from SUMMONS EVENT to update the panel and from FLOOR and to provide information on summons requests.

I.3 Attribute Descriptions

arrival_floor (ARRIVAL EVENT)

The floor at which the event was generated.

arrival_id (ARRIVAL EVENT)

A unique identifier for an instance of the class ARRIVAL EVENT.

arrival_panel_id (ARRIVAL PANEL)

A unique identifier for an instance of the class ARRIVAL PANEL.

current_direction (ELEVATOR)

Represents the current elevator direction. If the elevator is stopped at a floor, current_direction represents the direction of the last movement.

current_floor (ELEVATOR)

The floor at which the elevator last arrived.

current_state (ELEVATOR)

Represents current elevator state. Valid values include: busy, ready, open, etc.

destination_floor (DESTINATION EVENT)

The floor destination requested by a passenger.

destination_id (DESTINATION EVENT)

A unique identifier for an instance of the class DESTINATION EVENT.

destination_panel_id (DESTINATION PANEL)

A unique identifier for an instance of the class DESTINATION PANEL.

destinations_pending (DESTINATION PANEL)

A multi-valued attribute representing the status of pending destination for the corresponding floor. Destinations_pending = 1 for true | 0 for false.

elevator_id (ARRIVAL EVENT)

The elevator which generated the arrival event.

elevator_id (DESTINATION EVENT)

The elevator in which the destination event was generated.

elevator_id (ELEVATOR)

A unique identifier for an instance of the class ELEVATOR.

elevator_id (PANEL)

An attribute of the generic class PANEL, inherited by specialization.

elevator_id (FLOOR)

A unique identifier of an instance of Elevator used in messages from an instance of Floor.

elevator_motor_id (ELEVATOR MOTOR)

A unique identifier of an instance of the class ELEVATOR MOTOR.

event_id (ELEVATOR EVENT)

An attribute of the generic class ELEVATOR EVENT, inherited by specialization.

floor_id (ELEVATOR EVENT)

The unique identifier for an instance of Floor in the generic class ELEVATOR EVENT.

floor_id (FLOOR)

A unique identifier for an instance of the class FLOOR.

overweight_sensor_id (OVERWEIGHT SENSOR)

An unique identifier for an instance of the class OVERWEIGHT SENSOR.

overweight_status (OVERWEIGHT SENSOR)

The last reported condition of the overweight sensor.

panel_id (PANEL)

An attribute of the generic class PANEL, inherited by specialization.

status_direction (ELEVATOR)

An attribute used to communicate to an instance of Floor the appropriate direction for dispatching the elevator.

summons_floor (SUMMONS EVENT)

The floor at which the summons event was generated.

summons_id (SUMMONS EVENT)

A unique identifier for an instance of the class **SUMMONS EVENT**.

summons_panel_id (SUMMONS PANEL)

A unique identifier for an instance of the class SUMMONS PANEL.

summons_pending_down (SUMMONS PANEL)

Represents the presence (1) or absence (0) of a DOWN summons request.

summons_pending_up (SUMMONS PANEL)

Represents the presence (1) or absence (0) of an UP summons request.

summons_type (SUMMONS EVENT)

Represents the requested summons direction: UP, DOWN, NONE.

I.4 Service Definitions

Control_Elevator (ELEVATOR)

This service controls the movement of a given elevator (specified by elevator_id).

1. Upon receipt of the invocation message:
    1.1 If [UP | DOWN] then:
        1.1.1 The attribute ELEVATOR(elevator_id).current_direction is set to [UP | DOWN].
        1.1.2 The attribute ELEVATOR(elevator_id).current_state is set to BUSY.
    1.2 If STOP then:

1.2.1 The attribute `ELEVATOR(elevator_id).current_state` is set to STOPPED.

2. Send a uni-directional message to the `ELEVATOR MOTOR` instance associated with `elevator_id`. The message is: (`elevator_id`,[UP | DOWN | STOP]).

3. This instance of `ELEVATOR` is suspended until the next invocation message is received.

Control_Elevator_Motor (ELEVATOR MOTOR)

This service controls the movement of a given elevator motor(specified by `elevator_id`).

1. Upon receipt of an invocation message, the required commands are issued to the interface hardware to cause the elevator motor (specified by `elevator_id`) to activate the given command [UP | DOWN | STOP].

2. This service is suspended until the next invocation message is received.

Poll_Neighbor (FLOOR)

This service sends a message to the instance of `Floor` associated with `neighbor_floor` from the `Floor` associated with `current_floor`. The message is: (`summons_pending?`). The service polls neighboring floors to see if they need an elevator.

Process_Elevator_Arrival (FLOOR)

This service includes an algorithm to determine whether the elevator should stop and if a summons is being answered at the arrival floor (see Section I.6). The algorithm is based on the reported parameters from the `Elevator`, `Summons Panel`, and `Destination Panel` instances in response to the messages from the arrival floor. It returns the values of `updated_current_direction`, `updated_summons_pending`, and `updated_status_direction` and honors the summons in the committed direction of travel, as well as destinations pending. It will return an appropriate STOP command at floors 1 and 40. This service performs various control and coordination activities when an elevator arrives at a given floor (specified by `arrival_floor`).

1. Sends a bi-directional message to the `Elevator` associated with `elevator_id`. This message is: (`elevator_id`, `status_direction?`).

2. Sends a bi-directional message to the `Destination Panel` associated with the `elevator_id`. The message is: (`elevator_id`, `arrival_floor`, `destination_pending (arrival_floor?`, `destination_pending_up?`, `destination_pending_down?`).

3. A bi-directional message is sent to the `Summons Panel` associated with the `arrival_floor`. The message is: (`arrival_floor`, `status_direction`, `destination_pending_up`, `destination_pending_down`, `summons_pending?`).

4. A uni-directional message may be sent to `Elevator` associated with `elevator_id`. The message is: (`elevator_id`,STOP).

Process_Elevator_Ready (FLOOR)

This service receives a message that an elevator is ready. This service includes a complex and rigorous algorithm to determine the dispatch of an elevator (see Section I.6). Once received it performs the following operations iteratively:

1. Sends message to Destination Panel associated w/`elevator_id`.

2. Receives response from Destination Panel and determines if should send a response to Elevator.

3. May send message to Elevator. In the event that no destinations are pending, it goes through a process of polling neighboring floors to determine if a summons needs to be answered.

RECOGNIZE_DESTINATION_REQUEST (DESTINATION EVENT)

This `DESTINATION EVENT` class service detects the occurrence of a destination request (destination button depression).

1. An instance of `Destination Event` is created. Its attributes are `destination_id` (an arbitrary identifier), `elevator_id` (the elevator in which the event was generated) and `destination_floor` (the requested destination floor).

2. This instance of `Destination Event` sends a uni-directional message to the `Destination Panel` instance associated with `elevator_id`. The message is: (`elevator_id`,`destination_floor`,CREATE).

3. This instance of `Destination Event` is terminated.

RECOGNIZE_ELEVATOR_ARRIVAL (ARRIVAL EVENT)

This `ARRIVAL EVENT` class service detects the occurrence of an elevator arrival.

1. An instance of `Arrival Event` is created. Its attributes are: `arrival_id` (an arbitary identifier), `elevator_id` (the elevator which generated the arrival event) and `arrival_floor` (the floor at which the event was generated).

2. This service sends a message to the `Floor` associated with `arrival_floor`. The message is: (`arrival_id`,`elevator_id`, `arrival_floor`).

RECOGNIZE_SUMMONS_REQUEST (SUMMONS EVENT)

This `SUMMONS EVENT` class service detects the occurrence of the `Elevator Summons` event by detecting a summons request (summons button depression). The following occurs:

1. An instance of `Summons Event` is created. Its attributes are: `summons_id` (an arbitrary identifier), `summons_floor` (the floor at which the summons event was generated) and `summons_type` ([UP | DOWN]).

2. This instance of `Summons Event` sends a uni-directional message to the `Summons Panel` instance associated with the `summons_floor`. The message is: `Update Summons Panel(summons_floor, summons_type,` CREATE).

3. This instance of `Summons Event` is terminated.

Recognize_Elevator_Ready (ELEVATOR)

This service recognizes the occurrence of a given `Elevator` becoming ready (specified by `elevator_id`). The overweight status of the `Elevator` is verified before the `Elevator` is indicated in the ready state. Upon invocation:

1. The value of the attribute `ELEVATOR(elevator_id).current_state` is set to NOT_READY.

2. The following operation is performed iteratively until the response is OK: Send a bi-directional message to `OVERWEIGHT SENSOR`. This message is: `(elevator_id,?)`

3. The value of the attribute `ELEVATOR(elevator_id).current_state` is set to READY.

4. A uni-directional message is sent to the `Floor` associated with `Elevator.current_floor`. The message is: `(elevator_id, status_direction, summons_pending)`.

Recognize_Not_Overweight (OVERWEIGHT SENSOR)

This `Overweight Sensor` instance service recognizes the occurrence of an overweight condition being restored for a given `Elevator` (specified by `elevator_id`). Upon invocation:

1. The value of the attribute `OVERWEIGHT SENSOR.overweight_status` is set to OK.

2. No further processing is performed by this service.

Recognize_Overweight (OVERWEIGHT SENSOR)

This `Overweight Sensor` instance service recognizes the occurrence of an overweight condition for a given elevator (specified by `elevator_id`). Upon invocation:

1. The value of the attribute `OVERWEIGHT SENSOR.overweight_status` is set to NOT_OK.

2. No further processing is performed by this service.

Report_Arrival_Event (ARRIVAL EVENT)

This instance service sends a message to the `Floor` associated with the
`arrival_floor`. (The message is: `arrival_id`, `report_elevator_id`,
`report_arrival_floor`.)

Report_Current_Location (ELEVATOR)

This service reports the location (floor number) of a given `Elevator` (specified
by `elevator_id`). If the elevator is moving between floors, the last floor at
which the elevator arrived is reported.

1. Upon receipt of an invocation message, the value of the attribute
   `ELEVATOR(elevator_id).current_floor` is returned to the originator
   of the message.

2. This instance of `Elevator` is suspended until the next invocation message is
   received.

Report_Current_Status (ELEVATOR)

This service reports the status of a given `Elevator` (specified by `elevator_id`).

1. Upon receipt of an invocation message, the value of the attribute
   `ELEVATOR(elevator_id).current_state` is returned to the originator
   of the message.

2. This instance of `Elevator` is suspended until the next invocation message is
   received.

Report_Destination_Event (DESTINATION EVENT)

This `Destination Event` instance service sends a message to the destination
panel to update the panel display device.

Report_Destination_Pending (DESTINATION PANEL)

This `Destination Panel` instance service reports the status of a destination
request for a given `Elevator` (specified by `elevator_id`) at a given `Floor`
(specified by `arrival_floor`).

1. Upon receipt of an invocation message, the value of the attribute
   `DESTINATION PANEL(elevator_id).destinations_pending`
   `(arrival_floor)` is returned to the originator of the message. This service
   resolves the validity of `destination_pending_up` [TRUE | FALSE] and
   `destination_pending_down` [TRUE | FALSE].

2. This instance of `Destination Panel` is suspended until the next invocation
   message is received.

Report_Direction (ELEVATOR)

This service reports the current direction of travel of a given `Elevator` (specified
by `elevator_id`). If the elevator is stopped at a floor, the direction of the last

movement is reported. `Current_direction` is returned to the originator of the message. This service also reports the status direction of a given elevator, and the `status_direction` for an `Elevator` (specified by `elevator_id`) is returned to the originator of the message.

Report_Overweight_Status (OVERWEIGHT SENSOR)

This service reports the overweight condition of a given `Elevator` (specified by `elevator_id`).

1. Upon receipt of an invocation message, the value of the attribute `OVERWEIGHT SENSOR(elevator_id).overweight_status` is returned to the originator of the message.

2. This service is suspended until the next invocation message is received.

Report_Summons_Event (SUMMONS EVENT)

This service responds to messages with updates to the parameters with the values of the attributes `summons_pending_up` and `summons_pending_down`.

Report_Summons_Pending (SUMMONS PANEL)

This service reports the status of a summons request for a given `Floor` (specified by `arrival_floor`). The `Summons Panel.Report_Summons_Pending` determines whether the `Summons Panel` values of `status_direction`, `destination_pending_up`, `destination_pending_down` associated with this `Floor` should be updated as follows:

If the `status_direction` agrees with the value of either `destination_pending_up` or `destination_pending_down`, and is consistent with either directions of `summons_pending_up` or `summons_pending_down`, that `summons_pending` attribute in the `Summons Panel` will be updated and the response to `summons_pending` will be [UP | DOWN] depending on that attribute. If either the `summons_pending_up` or `summons_pending_down` is not consistent with the value, there is no update to the `Summons Panel` and the `summons_pending` in the message is left at NO.

If the `status_direction` is not consistent with either `destination_pending_up` or `destination_pending_down` and agrees with either `summons_pending_up` or `summons_pending_down` in the `Summons Panel`, that `summons_pending` attribute in the `Summons Panel` will be updated and the response to `summons_pending` will be [UP | DOWN] depending on that attribute. Otherwise the `summons_pending` attribute in the message will be left at NO.

Update_Arrival_Panel (ARRIVAL PANEL)

This service performs the operations necessary to update an `Arrival Panel` for a given `Elevator` upon arrival of that `Elevator` at a given `Floor`.

1. Upon receipt of an invocation message, the required commands are issued to the interface hardware to cause the `Arrival Panel` to be updated. A

specific panel is identified by the parameter `elevator_id`. That panel will be updated to indicate the `Floor` specified by the parameter `arrival_floor`. The indicated `Arrival Floor` will remain unchanged until a subsequent command is issued to the interface hardware. Note that at least one `Floor` is always indicated on each `Arrival Panel`.

2. This instance of `Arrival Panel` is suspended until the next invocation message is received.

Update_Destination_Panel (DESTINATION PANEL)

This `DESTINATION PANEL` instance service performs the operations necessary to update a `Destination Panel` for a given `Elevator` upon arrival of that `Elevator` at a given `Floor`.

1. Upon receipt of an invocation message, the required commands are issued to the interface hardware to cause the `Destination Panel` to be updated. A specific panel is identified by the parameter `elevator_id`. That panel will be updated to indicate the `Floor` specified by the parameter `destination_floor`.

2. If CREATE then:
   2.1 The indicator for the specified `Floor` will be enabled.
   2.2 The attribute `DESTINATION PANEL(elevator_id).destinations_pending (destination_floor)` is set to TRUE.

3. If ARRIVED then:
   3.1 The indicator for the specified `Floor` will be disabled.
   3.2 The attribute `DESTINATION PANEL elevator_id).destinations_pending (destination_floor)` is set to FALSE.

4. This instance of `Destination Panel` is suspended until the next invocation message is received.

Update_Direction (ELEVATOR)

This service updates the attributes of `current_direction` and `status_direction` specified by an `elevator_id`.

Update_Floor_Arrival (ELEVATOR)

This service updates the location (floor number) of a given `Elevator` (specified by `elevator_id`) to the `Floor` number specified by `arrival_floor`.

1. Upon receipt of an invocation message, the value of the attribute `ELEVATOR(elevator_id).current_floor` is set to `arrival_floor`.

2. This instance of `Elevator` is suspended until the next invocation message is received.

SMALL BYTES SUE

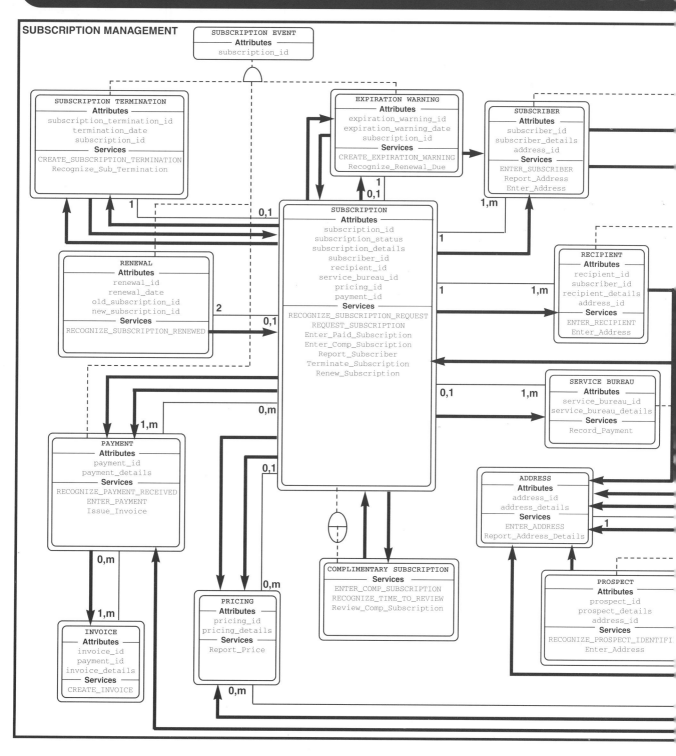

SUBSCRIPTION MANAGEMENT

SUBSCRIPTION EVENT
Attributes
subscription_id

SUBSCRIPTION TERMINATION
Attributes
subscription_termination_id
termination_date
subscription_id
Services
CREATE_SUBSCRIPTION_TERMINATION
Recognize_Sub_Termination

EXPIRATION WARNING
Attributes
expiration_warning_id
expiration_warning_date
subscription_id
Services
CREATE_EXPIRATION_WARNING
Recognize_Renewal_Due

SUBSCRIBER
Attributes
subscriber_id
subscriber_details
address_id
Services
ENTER_SUBSCRIBER
Report_Address
Enter_Address

RENEWAL
Attributes
renewal_id
renewal_date
old_subscription_id
new_subscription_id
Services
RECOGNIZE_SUBSCRIPTION_RENEWED

SUBSCRIPTION
Attributes
subscription_id
subscription_status
subscription_details
subscriber_id
recipient_id
service_bureau_id
pricing_id
payment_id
Services
RECOGNIZE_SUBSCRIPTION_REQUEST
REQUEST_SUBSCRIPTION
Enter_Paid_Subscription
Enter_Comp_Subscription
Report_Subscriber
Terminate_Subscription
Renew_Subscription

RECIPIENT
Attributes
recipient_id
subscriber_id
recipient_details
address_id
Services
ENTER_RECIPIENT
Enter_Address

SERVICE BUREAU
Attributes
service_bureau_id
service_bureau_details
Services
Record_Payment

PAYMENT
Attributes
payment_id
payment_details
Services
RECOGNIZE_PAYMENT_RECEIVED
ENTER_PAYMENT
Issue_Invoice

ADDRESS
Attributes
address_id
address_details
Services
ENTER_ADDRESS
Report_Address_Details

COMPLIMENTARY SUBSCRIPTION
Services
ENTER_COMP_SUBSCRIPTION
RECOGNIZE_TIME_TO_REVIEW
Review_Comp_Subscription

PROSPECT
Attributes
prospect_id
prospect_details
address_id
Services
RECOGNIZE_PROSPECT_IDENTIFI
Enter_Address

INVOICE
Attributes
invoice_id
payment_id
invoice_details
Services
CREATE_INVOICE

PRICING
Attributes
pricing_id
pricing_details
Services
Report_Price

1
0,1
1
1,m
0,1
2
0,1
0,m
1,m
0,1
0,m
0,1
0,m
0,m
1,m
1
1
1,m
0,1
1,m
1

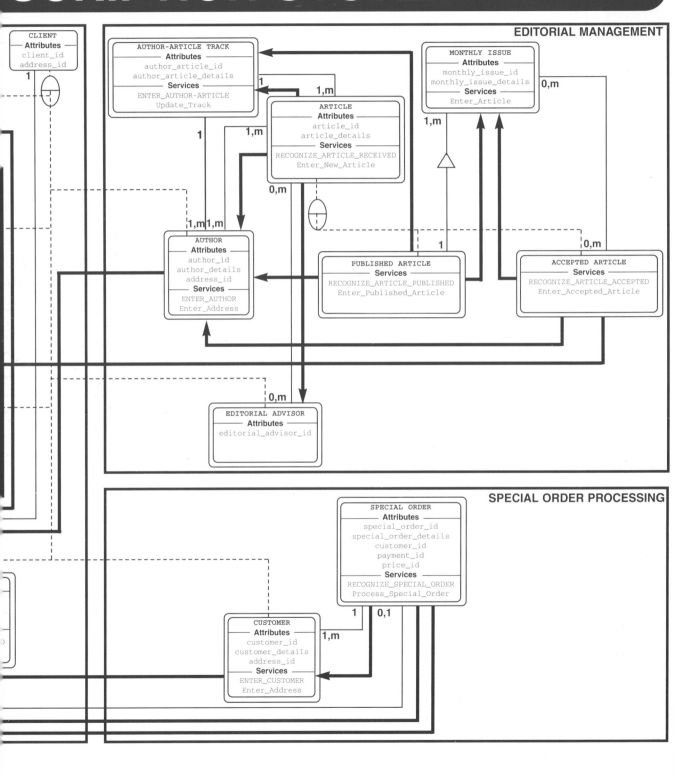

EDITORIAL MANAGEMENT

CLIENT
Attributes
client_id
address_id

AUTHOR-ARTICLE TRACK
Attributes
author_article_id
author_article_details
Services
ENTER_AUTHOR-ARTICLE
Update_Track

ARTICLE
Attributes
article_id
article_details
Services
RECOGNIZE_ARTICLE_RECEIVED
Enter_New_Article

MONTHLY ISSUE
Attributes
monthly_issue_id
monthly_issue_details
Services
Enter_Article

AUTHOR
Attributes
author_id
author_details
address_id
Services
ENTER_AUTHOR
Enter_Address

PUBLISHED ARTICLE
Services
RECOGNIZE_ARTICLE_PUBLISHED
Enter_Published_Article

ACCEPTED ARTICLE
Services
RECOGNIZE_ARTICLE_ACCEPTED
Enter_Accepted_Article

EDITORIAL ADVISOR
Attributes
editorial_advisor_id

SPECIAL ORDER PROCESSING

SPECIAL ORDER
Attributes
special_order_id
special_order_details
customer_id
payment_id
price_id
Services
RECOGNIZE_SPECIAL_ORDER
Process_Special_Order

CUSTOMER
Attributes
customer_id
customer_details
address_id
Services
ENTER_CUSTOMER
Enter_Address

`Update_Floor_Ready (ELEVATOR)`

This service updates the location of a given `Elevator` (specified by the `elevator_id`) in response to the event "Elevator Becomes Ready".

`Update_Summons_Panel (SUMMONS PANEL)`

This service performs the operations necessary to update a `Summons Panel` for a given `Floor` (specified by `summons_floor`).

1. Upon receipt of an invocation message, the required commands are issued to the interface hardware to cause the `Summons Panel` to be updated. A specific panel is identified by the parameter `summons_floor`. That panel will be updated to the presence or absence of a summons as indicated by the parameter [CREATE | ARRIVED]).

2. If CREATE then:
   2.1 The indicator for the specified panel will be enabled.
   2.2 Depending on the parameter `summons_type`, the appropriate attribute `SUMMONS PANEL (summons_floor).summons_pending_up` or `SUMMONS PANEL (summons_floor).summons_pending_down` is set to TRUE.

3. If ARRIVED then:
   3.1 The indicator for the specified `Floor` will be disabled.
   3.2 Depending on the parameter `summons_type`, the appropriate attribute `SUMMONS PANEL (summons_floor).summons_pending_up` or `SUMMONS PANEL (summons_floor).summons_pending_down` is set to FALSE.

4. This instance of `Summons Panel` is suspended until the next invocation message is received.

I.5
Message
Definitions

`Control Elevator Motor`

The `Elevator.Control_Elevator` receives this message. This `Elevator` sends a uni-directional message to the `Elevator Motor` associated with `elevator_id`. The message is: (`elevator_id`,STOP). The `Elevator Motor.Control_Elevator_Motor` receives this message and causes the `Elevator Motor` to stop (`elevator_motor_id`). The elevator's mechanical systems then cause the elevator doors to open.

`OVERWEIGHT_SENSOR`

`Elevator.Recognize_Elevator_Ready` sends a message to `Overweight Sensor.Report_Overweight_Status` to test before the `Elevator` is accepted as "ready".

Poll Neighbor 1

Floor.Poll_Neighbor for the `current_floor` calculates `neighbor_floor` based on the value of `status_direction` (`neighbor_floor=` `current_floor + 1` if the `status_direction` is UP and `neighbor_floor =` `current_floor - 1` if the `status_direction` is DOWN or NO. If this calculation results in the value zero, `neighbor_floor = 40`.) This service sends a message to the instance of `Floor` associated with `neighbor_floor`. The message is: (`neighbor_floor, status_direction, current_floor,` `summons_pending?`).

Poll Neighbor 2

`Floor.Poll_Neighbor` sends a message to `Floor` associated with `current_floor` if the the value `summons_pending` is TRUE or `current_floor` equals `neighbor_floor`, to request that an `Elevator` be dispatched.

Process Elevator 1

If the destination direction for event "Elevator Becomes Ready" is UP or DOWN, then `Floor.Process_Elevator_Ready` sends a uni-directional message to the `Elevator` associated with the `elevator_id`. The message is: (`elevator_id,` `destination_direction`). If the `destination_direction` is STOP, the message is: (`elevator_id`, STOP).

Recognize Destination Request

This message is sent to the `Destination Panel`. The message is: (`elevator_` `id,destination_floor`,CREATE). The `Destination Panel.Update_` `Destination_Panel` receives this message and updates the `Destination Panel` associated with `elevator_id` to indicate the pending destination. The multi-valued attribute `DESTINATION PANEL(elevator_id).destinations_` `pending(destination_floor)` is set to TRUE.

Recognize Elevator Arrival

The `ARRIVAL EVENT` service sends a message to the `Floor` associated with `arrival_floor`. The message is: (`arrival_id,elevator_id,arrival_` `floor`). The `Floor.Process_Elevator_Arrival` service receives this message and issues a number of messages.

Recognize Elevator Ready

`Elevator.Recognize_Elevator_Ready` detects occurrence of the elevator mechanism becoming ready. A uni-directional message is sent to the `Floor` associated with `Elevator.current_floor`. the message is: (`elevator_id,` `current_direction, status direction`).

Recognize Summons Request

A uni-directional message is sent to the `Summons Panel`. The message is: (`summons_floor, summons_type`,CREATE). The `Summons Panel.Update_`

Summons_Panel receives this message and updates the Summons Panel associated with summons_floor to indicate a summons pending. The appropriate attribute SUMMONS PANEL(summons_floor).summons_pending_up or SUMMONS PANEL(summons_floor).summons_pending_down is set to TRUE.

Report Destination Pending

A bi-directional message is sent to the Destination Panel associated with elevator_id. The message is: (elevator_id, arrival_floor,?), from Floor.Process_Elevator_Arrival. The Destination Panel.Report_Destination_Pending sends a response to this message as [TRUE | FALSE] indicating the value of the attribute DESTINATION PANEL(elevator_id).destinations_pending(arrival_floor).

Report Destination Pending 2

Floor.Process_Elevator_Ready sends a bi-directional message to Destination Panel.Report_Destination_Pending. (The message is: report_arrival_floor, destination_pending_up?, destination_pending_down?)

Report Elevator Status

Floor.Process_Elevator_Arrival sends a bi-directional message to Elevator associated with elevator_id. This message is: (elevator_id, status_direction?). Elevator.Report_Direction sends a message response to this message indicating the value of the attribute Elevator(elevator_id).status_direction (UP | DOWN).

Report Summons Pending

If the response to the FLOOR from the Process Elevator Arrival message is FALSE, a bi-directional message is sent to the Summons Panel associated with arrival_floor. The message is: (summons_floor,?). The Summons Panel.Report_Summons_Pending sends a response to this message as [UP | DOWN | NONE] indicating whether or not a summons is pending for the given arrival_floor.

Update Arrival Panel

This event sends a uni-directional message to the Arrival Panel associated with elevator_id. The message is: (elevator_id, arrival_floor). The Arrival Panel.Update_Arrival_Panel receives this message and updates the Arrival Panel appropriately.

Update Summons Panel

Floor.Process_Elevator_Ready sends a uni-directional message to Summons Panel.Update_Summons_Panel.

I.6
Elevator-Scheduling Algorithm

The elevator-scheduling algorithm presented in this section was developed by Prof. J. Morrell of the Metropolitan State College of Denver.

1.6.1
Elevator Arrival Algorithm

The algorithm is initiated at the point when the messages and services to and from Elevator, Summons Panel, and Destination Panel instances have provided suffcient parameters to begin the algorithm for arrival. Abbreviations are used for attributes and parameters in the algorithm for readability. The legend and initialization are as follows:

Start of Algorithm:

RCF = report _arrival_floor (the current_floor as reported by Elevator instance)
RCE = report_elevator_id (the elevator_id as reported by Elevator instance)
RCD = report_current_direction (the current_direction as reported by Elevator instance)
RSD = report_status_direction (the status_direction as reported by Elevator instance)
RSPU = report_summons_pending_up (as reported by the Summons Panel instance)
RSPD = report_summons_pending_down (as reported by the Summons Panel instance)
UCD is a parameter used in communicating with Elevator to update current _direction
SP is a parameter which updated to TRUE if any summons is pending at a Floor instance
DPA = destination_pending_above (as reported by the Destination Panel instance)
DPB =destination_pending_below (similarly)
DPC = destination_pending_current (similarly, all calculated by Report_Destinations_Pending service)
USPU is a parameter used in updating and communicating the attribute summons_pending_up
USPU, USPD, USD, UCD are, likewise, for the indicated attributes
NONE, NULL, TRUE, FALSE , UP, DOWN are used for "NONE" , "NULL" , etc.

Other initializations are:
USD=RSD
SP=FALSE
UCD=RSPU=USPU=RSPD=USPD=NULL

If DPC = TRUE / STOP if this floor is a destination /
    UCD= STOP
Else
    If (RCF=1) or (RCF=40) / STOP if this floor is floor 1 or 40 /
        UCD=STOP .
If (RSD = NONE)/if there is no commitment to direction/
    If (DPA = TRUE and RCD = UP)
        or (DPB = TRUE and RCD = DOWN) /if destinations pending consistent with current direction/
        USD=RCD/commit to that direction/
        If (RSPU= TRUE and USD = UP)/if summons pending consistent with that direction/
            UCD=STOP /stop the elevator and update summons panel /
            USPU= FALSE
        Else /similarly, but direction is DOWN/
            If (RSPD = TRUE and USD = DOWN)
                UCD=STOP
                USPD= FALSE
            Else
                    no updates/no appropriate summons pending/

Else /if no destinations in current direction and summons /
    If (RSPU = TRUE and RCD = UP)/ are pending consistent with current direction
                                (UP)/
        USD=RCD/commit to that direction/
        USPU = FALSE /update summons panel/
        UCD=STOP /stop elevator/
    Else
        If (RSPD = TRUE and RCD = DOWN)/similarly, but direction is DOWN/
            USD = RCD
            USPD= FALSE
            UCD = STOP
        Else /if no destinations or summons consistent with current direction/
            If (DPA = TRUE)/if destination pending above/
                USD = UP /commit to UP/
                IF (RSPU = TRUE)/check for summons pending UP/
                    USPU = FALSE /updated summons panel/
                    UCD=STOP /stop elevator/
                Else
                    no updates/no summons panel update, since no summons
                    pending UP/
            Else /similarly, but direction is DOWN/
                If (DPB = TRUE)
                    USD= DOWN
                    IF (RSPD = TRUE)
                        USPD= FALSE
                        UCD=STOP
                    Else
                        no updates
                Else /no destinations pending above or below/
                    If (RSPD = TRUE)/check DOWN summons first (gravity
                    preference)/
                        USPD =FALSE /update summons panel/
                        UCD=STOP /stop elevator/
                    Else /check UP similarly/
                        If (RSPU = TRUE)
                            USPU= FALSE
                            UCD=STOP
                        Else
                            no updates/no reason to stop or commit at this floor/

Else /if there is a commitment to direction and /
    If (RSPU = TRUE and RSD = UP)/summons pending consistent with this direction/
        UCD=STOP /stop elevator and update summons panel/
        USPU= FALSE
    Else
        If (RSPD = TRUE and RSD = DOWN)/similarly for DOWN/
            UCD=STOP
            USPD= FALSE
        Else
            no updates./no stopping for summons at this floor/
If (USPU NOT= RSPU)or(USPD NOT= RSPD)/we answered a summons on current floor/

updated_destinations_pending_up = USPU/set parameters for
communication/updated_destinations_pending_down = USPD
A uni-directional message is sent to the instance of Summons Panel
associated with current floor. The message is:
(updated_summons_pending_up,updated_summons_pending_down). The
service Update_Summons_Panel will update the instance appropriately

Else

> no updates. /there were no appropriate summons, thus the summons panel will not be updated/

If (UCD = STOP)or (USD NOT=RSD) /changed commitment to directions must be updated/

> The parameters are set and Elevator.Process_Elevator_Ready sends a uni-directional message to the instance of Elevator associated with RCE.

> updated_current_direction = UCD
> updated_status_direction = USD

>> The message is:
>> (updated_current_direction, updated_status_direction)

The Elevator.Control_Elevator receives this message. This Elevator updates current_direction and status_direction with the values of updated_current_direction and updated_status_direction, respectively.

>> If (UCD = STOP)
> This Elevator sends a uni-directional message to the Elevator Motor associated with elevator_id. The message is: (STOP).

>> The Elevator Motor.Control_Elevator_Motor receives this message and causes the elevator motor to stop. The elevator's mechanical systems then cause the elevator doors to open.
>> Else
>>> the elevator continues in its current direction.

End of Algorithm

1.6.2
Elevator Ready Algorithm

The algorithm is initiated at the point when the messages and services to and from elevator instances provide suffcient parameters to begin the algorithm for READY. Abbreviations are used for attributes and parameters in the algorithm for readability. The legend and initialization are as follows:

Start of Algorithm:

RCF = report _arrival_floor (the current_floor as reported by Elevator instance)
RCE = report_elevator_id (the elevator_id as reported by Elevator instance)
RCD = report_current_direction (the current_direction as reported by Elevator instance)
RSD = report_status_direction (the status_direction as reported by Elevator instance)
RSPU will be report_summons_pending_up (when reported by the Summons Panel instance)
RSPD will be report_summons_pending_down (when reported by the Summons Panel instance)
UCD is a parameter used in communicating with Elevator to update current_direction
SP is a parameter which updated to TRUE if any summons is pending at a Floor instance
UNF is the neighbor floor used in the Poll_Neighbor service
NFI is the incrementer (+1 or -1) used in the Poll_Neighbor service

USPU is a parameter used in updating and communicating the attribute summons_pending_up
USPU, USPD, USD, UCD are, likewise, for the indicated attributes
NONE, NULL, TRUE, FALSE , UP, DOWN are used for "NONE" , "NULL" , etc.

Other initializations are:
USD=RSD
SP=FALSE
UCD=UNF=NFI=RSPU=USPU=RSPD=USPD=NULL

The following is a recursive function:

CHECK_READY   /The name of the following function/

A bi-directional message is sent to the Destination Panel associated with report_elevator_id. The message is:
 (report_current_floor,destination_pending_above?,destination_pending_below?, destination_pending_current?)

The service Report_Destination_Pending of this instance of Destination_Panel sends a response by resolving the validiy of destination_pending_above, destination_pending_below and destination_pending_current as [TRUE|FALSE] depending on the destination_pending attributes of this instance and the value of report_current_floor.

Let
DPA = destination_pending_above (as reported by the Destination Panel instance)
DPB =destination_pending_below (similarly)
DPC = destination_pending_current (similarly, all calculated by Report_Destinations_Pending service)

If (USD=NONE)/if there is no commitment to direction, destinations

        are served first/
    If (DPB=TRUE)/preference is given to the Force of Gravity/
        USD=DOWN/if destinations pending in both directions/
        UCD=USD
  Else
      If (DPA=TRUE)
          USD=UP
          UCD=USD
      Else
          If (DPC=TRUE)/destination pending at current floor
          possibly a mistake/
              UCD=STOP   /honor it if and only if no other
                      destinations are pending/
Else
    If (USD=UP)/there is a commitment to UP/
        If (DPA=TRUE)/destination pending consistent with status direction/
          UCD=USD
        Else
          If (DPB=TRUE)/destination pending but none in status direction/
             USD=DOWN/commit to that direction (serving current destinations)/
             UCD=USD
          Else
             USD=NONE/turn off the commitment, it was invalid/
    Else
        If (DPB=TRUE)/same scene but commitment is to DOWN/
          UCD=USD
        Else
          If (DPA=TRUE)
             USD=UP
             UCD=USD
          Else
             USD=NONE.
If (SP=TRUE/there is a summons pending (this can't be first iteration)/
    If (UNF=RCF)/If the summons is from this floor honor it/
        If (USD=NONE)/If there are no commitments, commit to the summons/
          UCD=STOP/and open the elevator doors/
          If (RSPD=TRUE)/go with gravity if summons pending in both directions/

                                        USD=DOWN
                                        USPD=FALSE/and update the summons panel/
                            Else
                                        USD=UP/answer the up summons if none for down/
                                        USPU=FALSE
                    Else /if there is a prior commitment/
                            If (USD=UP) and (RSPU=TRUE)
                                        UCD=STOP/summons pending in direction of commitment/
                                        USPU=FALSE/honor the summons and open the doors/
                            Else
                                        If (USD=DOWN) and (RSPD=TRUE)
                                                UCD=STOP/similarly but for "DOWN"/
                                                USPD=FALSE
                                        Else
                                                no further updates/no summons appropriate for recognition/
                    Else /the summons was from another floor/

                        If (USD=NONE)/and no commitment/
                            If (UNF<RCF)
                                        UCD=DOWN/answer the summons/
                            Else
                                        UCD=UP./but make no commitment/
                        Else
                                        no further updates./a destination pending overides summons from a
                                                        neighbor/
            If (USPU NOT= RSPU)or(USPD NOT= RSPD)/we answered a summons on current floor/

            Let
                    updated_summons_pending_up = USPU
                    updated_summons_pending_down = USPD

            A uni-directional message is sent to the instance of Summons Panel associated with current
            floor. The message is: (updated_summons_pending_up,updated_summons_pending_down).
            The service Update_Summons_Panel will update the instance appropriately

            Else
                    no updates. /there were no appropriate summons, thus the summons panel will not be
                    updated/

            If (UCD NOT= NULL)/the elevator will go up, down or open its doors/

                    Let
                            updated_current_direction = UCD
                            updated_status_direction = USD
            The Floor.Process_Elevator_Ready sends a uni-directional message to the instance of Elevator
            associated with RCE. The message is: (updated_current_direction, updated_status_direction).

                    The Elevator.Control_Elevator receives this message. This elevator
                    assigns its attributes current_direction=UCD, status_directon=USD.

                                If (UCD = UP) or (UCD = DOWN),
            The Elevator.Control_Elevator assigns the attribute current_state=BUSY, and sends a uni-
            directional message to the elevator motor associated with elevator_id. The message is:
            (current_direction).

                    The Elevator Motor.Control_Elevator_Motor receives this message and
                    causes the elevator elevator's mechanical system to secure the
                    elevator and then causes the elevator motor to start.

                                If (UCD is STOP),

This Elevator sends a unidirectional message to the Elevator Motor associated with elevator_id. The message is: (STOP).

> The Elevator Motor.Control_Elevator_Motor receives this message and causes the elevator motor to stop. The elevator's mechanical systems then cause the elevator doors to open.

Else /UCD is NULL thus there is no command for the elevator to move or open doors/

> The service Floor.Poll_Neighbor for the current_floor calculates neighbor_floor as follows:
> First it determines the direction to poll:
> UNF = RCF
> If (RCF>20)
>   NFI=+1
> Else
>   NFI=-1.
>
> and the following recursive function is called:
>
> POLL_NEIGHBOR /The name of the following function/
>
> UNF = UNF + NFI/the neighbor floor
> If (UNF=0)
>   UNF=40.
> If (UNF=41)
>   UNF=1.

This service sends a message to the instance of Floor associated with UNF. The message is: (report_summons_pending_up?,report_summons_pending_down?)

> This instance of Floor sends a bi-directional message to the associated instance of Summons_Panel. The message is: (report_summons_pending_up?,report_summons_pending_down?).
>
> > The Summons Panel.Report_Summons_Pending responds to this message by updating the values of report_summmons_pending_up and report_summons_pending_down with the values of summons_pending_up and summons_pending_down, respectively.

Let
    RSPU = report_summons_pending_up
    RSPD= report_summons_pending_down

SP is set to TRUE if either RSPU or RSPD is TRUE.
    If (SP=TRUE) or (UNF=RCF)

> TheFloor.Poll_Neighbor for the instance of Floor associated with UNF sends a message to the instance of Floor associated with RCF and the function CHEC_READY above is called.
>
> Else
>
> The Floor.Poll_Neighbor for the instance of Floor associated with UNF calls the function POLL_NEIGHBOR above.

This "RECURSION" continues until UCD changes from NULL
    a COUNTER should be put into this algorithm to limit the number of recursions and after the limit is exceeded, the elevator is sent down (except for floor=1)
End of Algorithm

APPENDIX J
OOA Model for Small Bytes Subscription System

This appendix presents the entire SBSS OOA model. The complete five-layer object model diagram is presented in Figure J.1. Below are descriptions and definitions of each of the model components. Although the model is presented in this appendix in documented form, the entire model is contained on the diskette accompanying this book. A CASE tool is required to access that form of the model.

J.1 List of SBSS OOA Model Components

This section presents a listing of all of the components (classes, attributes, services, etc.) of the OOA model for the SBSS. Each component is further described in a subsequent section of this appendix.

ACCEPTED ARTICLE	Class
ADDRESS	Class
address_details	Attribute
address_id	Attribute
ARTICLE	Class
article_details	Attribute
article_id	Attribute
AUTHOR	Class
AUTHOR-ARTICLE TRACK	Class
author-article_details	Attribute
author-article_id	Attribute
author_details	Attribute
author_id	Attribute
CLIENT	Class
client_id	Attribute
COMPLIMENTARY SUBSCRIPTION	Class
CREATE_EXPIRATION_WARNING	Method
CREATE_INVOICE	Method
CREATE_SUBSCRIPTION_EXPIRATION	Method
CREATE_SUBSCRIPTION_TERMINATION	Method
CUSTOMER	Class

customer_details	Attribute
customer_id	Attribute
date	Attribute
EDITORIAL ADVISOR	Class
editorial_advisor_id	Attribute
Enter Accepted Article 1	Message
Enter Accepted Article 2	Message
Enter Accepted Article 3	Message
Enter Address - Author	Message
Enter Address - Customer	Message
Enter Address - Prospect	Message
Enter Address - Recipient	Message
Enter Address - Subscriber	Message
Enter Comp Subscription	Message
Enter New Article 1	Message
Enter New Article 2	Message
Enter Paid Subscription	Message
Enter Paid Subscription 1	Message
Enter Paid Subscription 2	Message
Enter Paid Subscription 3	Message
Enter Paid Subscription 4	Message
Enter Paid Subscription 6	Message
Enter Paid Subscription 7	Message
Enter Published Article 1	Message
Enter Published Article 2	Message
Enter Published Article 3	Message
Enter_Accepted_Article	Method
ENTER_ADDRESS	Method
Enter_Address	Method
Enter_Article	Method
ENTER_AUTHOR	Method
ENTER_AUTHOR-ARTICLE	Method
ENTER_COMP_SUBSCRIPTION	Method
Enter_Comp_Subscription	Method
ENTER_CUSTOMER	Method
Enter_New_Article	Method
Enter_Paid_Subscription	Method
ENTER_PAYMENT	Method
Enter_Published_Article	Method
ENTER_RECIPIENT	Method
ENTER_SUBSCRIBER	Method
EXPIRATION WARNING	Class
expiration_warning_date	Attribute
expiration_warning_id	Attribute
id_number	Attribute
INVOICE	Class
invoice_details	Attribute
invoice_id	Attribute
Issue Invoice	Message
Issue_Invoice	Method
MONTHLY ISSUE	Class
monthly_issue_details	Attribute
monthly_issue_id	Attribute
new_subscription_id	Attribute
old_subscription_id	Attribute
PAYMENT	Class
payment_details	Attribute
payment_id	Attribute

price_id	Attribute
PRICING	Class
pricing_details	Attribute
pricing_id	Attribute
Process Special Order	Message
Process Special Order 2	Message
Process Special Order 4	Message
Process_Special_Order	Method
PROSPECT	Class
prospect_details	Attribute
prospect_id	Attribute
PUBLISHED ARTICLE	Class
RECIPIENT	Class
recipient_details	Attribute
recipient_id	Attribute
Recognize Renewal Due 1	Message
Recognize Renewal Due 2	Message
Recognize Sub Termination	Message
Recognize Subscription Renewed	Message
RECOGNIZE_ARTICLE_ACCEPTED	Method
RECOGNIZE_ARTICLE_PUBLISHED	Method
RECOGNIZE_ARTICLE_RECEIVED	Method
RECOGNIZE_PAYMENT_RECEIVED	Method
RECOGNIZE_PROSPECT_IDENTIFIED	Method
Recognize_Renewal_Due	Method
RECOGNIZE_SPECIAL_ORDER	Method
Recognize_Sub_Termination	Method
RECOGNIZE_SUBSCRIPTION_RENEWED	Method
RECOGNIZE_SUBSCRIPTION_REQUEST	Method
RECOGNIZE_TIME_TO_REVIEW	Method
Record_Payment	Method
Renew Subscription	Message
Renew Subscription 1	Message
Renew Subscription 2	Message
Renew Subscription 3	Message
Renew_Subscription	Method
RENEWAL	Class
renewal_date	Attribute
renewal_id	Attribute
Report Address	Message
Report_Address	Method
Report_Address_Details	Method
Report_Price	Method
Report_Subscriber	Method
REQUEST_SUBSCRIPTION	Method
Review_Comp_Subscription	Message
Review_Comp_Subscription	Method
SERVICE BUREAU	Class
service_bureau_details	Attribute
service_bureau_id	Attribute
SPECIAL ORDER	Class
special_order_details	Attribute
special_order_id	Attribute
SUBSCRIBER	Class
subscriber_details	Attribute
subscriber_id	Attribute
SUBSCRIPTION	Class
SUBSCRIPTION EVENT	Class

SUBSCRIPTION TERMINATION	Class
subscription_details	Attribute
subscription_id	Attribute
subscription_status	Attribute
subscription_termination_id	Attribute
Terminate_Subscription	Method
termination_date	Attribute
Update_Track	Method

J.2 Class Descriptions

ACCEPTED ARTICLE

The purpose of the object-class ACCEPTED ARTICLE is to recognize when an article is accepted for publication and to differentiate between articles of different status (submitted, published). A complimentary subscription is also processed for the author(s) of the accepted article. This object-class encapsulates the following: recognition of the Article Accepted For Publication event; and services that respond to this event, and that send messages to AUTHOR, MONTHLY ISSUE, and SUBSCRIPTION, appropriately.

ADDRESS

The purpose of the object-class ADDRESS is to maintain addresses for a variety of clients (subscribers, customers, recipients, authors, prospects). This object-class encapsulates the following: services that respond to messages from AUTHOR, CUSTOMER, PROSPECT, RECIPIENT, SUBSCRIBER; and, relevant address data.

ARTICLE

The purpose of the object-class ARTICLE is to recognize submitted articles and to maintain data on the various kinds of articles. This object-class encapsulates the following: recognition of the Article Received event; services that respond to this event, and that send messages to AUTHOR and AUTHOR-ARTICLE TRACK, appropriately; and, relevant article data.

AUTHOR

The purpose of the object-class AUTHOR is to maintain author data. This object-class encapsulates the following: services that send messages to ADDRESS appropriately and that respond appropriately to messages from ACCEPTED ARTICLE, ARTICLE, and PUBLISHED ARTICLE, plus relevant author data.

AUTHOR-ARTICLE TRACK

The purpose of the object-class AUTHOR-ARTICLE TRACK is to maintain a relationship between AUTHOR and ARTICLE. This object-class encapsulates the following: services that respond appropriately to messages from ARTICLE and PUBLISHED ARTICLE; plus, relevant AUTHOR-ARTICLE TRACK data.

CLIENT

The purpose of the class CLIENT is to provide a generalization for CUSTOMERs, SUBSCRIBERs, RECIPIENTs, SERVICE BUREAUs, AUTHORS, and ADVISORs, and to maintain common data for these specializations. This class encapsulates relevant client data.

COMPLIMENTARY SUBSCRIPTION

COMPLIMENTARY SUBSCRIPTION is a specialization of SUBSCRIPTION.

CUSTOMER

The purpose of the object-class CUSTOMER is to maintain data on clients that are neither subscribers nor recipients, such as special order clients or vendors ordering a large number of copies of one issue. This object-class encapsulates the following: services that send messages to ADDRESS appropriately and that respond appropriately to messages from SPECIAL ORDER; plus, relevant CUSTOMER data.

EDITORIAL ADVISOR

The purpose of the object-class EDITORIAL ADVISOR is to maintain data on members of the editorial board to provide them with complimentary subscriptions. This object-class encapsulates relevant EDITORIAL ADVISOR data.

EXPIRATION WARNING

The purpose of the object-class EXPIRATION WARNING is to recognize when it is time to send renewal notices. This object-class encapsulates the following: recognition of the Time To Send Renewal Notice event; services that respond to this event to send messages to SUBSCRIPTION and SUBSCRIBER appropriately, and respond appropriately to messages from SUBSCRIPTION; and, relevant expiration data.

INVOICE

The purpose of the object-class INVOICE is to maintain data on invoices in the event that one is required for payment. This object-class encapsulates the following: services that respond appropriately to messages from PAYMENT; plus, relevant invoice data.

MONTHLY ISSUE

The purpose of the object-class MONTHLY ISSUE is to maintain relationships between ARTICLES which appear in an issue. This object-class encapsulates the following: services that respond appropriately to messages from ACCEPTED ARTICLE and PUBLISHED ARTICLE; plus, relevant monthly issue data.

PAYMENT

The purpose of the object-class PAYMENT is to recognize when a payment is received and to maintain data on that payment. This object-class encapsulates the following: recognition of the PAYMENT RECEIVED event; services that respond to these events, and that send messages to INVOICE appropriately, and that respond appropriately to messages from SUBSCRIPTION and SPECIAL ORDER; plus, relevant PAYMENT data.

PRICING

The purpose of the object-class PRICING is to calculate prices for a variety of subscription types, such as domestic subscriptions, international subscription, etc. This object-class encapsulates the following: services that respond appropriately to messages from SUBSCRIPTION and SPECIAL ORDER; plus, relevant pricing data.

PROSPECT

The purpose of the object-class PROSPECT is to maintain data on clients that are not subscribers, recipients or authors but have the potential of becoming one. This object-class encapsulates the following: recognition of the Prospect Identified event; services that respond to this events and that send messages to ADDRESS, appropriately; and, relevant prospect data.

PUBLISHED ARTICLE

The purpose of the object-class PUBLISHED ARTICLE is to recognize when an article is published and to differentiate between articles of different status (submitted, accepted). This object-class encapsulates the following: recognition of the Article Published event; services that respond to this event, and that send messages to AUTHOR and AUTHOR-ARTICLE TRACK and MONTHLY ISSUE, appropriately.

RECIPIENT

The purpose of the object-class RECIPIENT is to maintain data on clients who receive issues and to maintain data on these clients. This object-class encapsulates the following: services that send messages to ADDRESS appropriately, and that respond appropriately to messages from SUBSCRIPTION; and, relevant recipient data.

RENEWAL

The purpose of the object-class RENEWAL is to recognize when a paid subscription is renewed and to maintain data on that renewal. This object-class encapsulates the following: recognition of the Paid Subscription Renewed event; services that respond to this event, that send messages to SUBSCRIPTION appropriately, and that respond appropriately to messages from SUBSCRIPTION; plus, relevant SERVICE BUREAU data.

SERVICE BUREAU

The purpose of the object-class SERVICE BUREAU is to maintain data on subscription service bureaus who receive a commission for the subscriptions they provide. This object-class encapsulates the following: services that respond appropriately to messages from SUBSCRIPTION; and, relevant service bureau data

SPECIAL ORDER

The purpose of the object-class SPECIAL ORDER is to recognize requests for special orders from customers who may not be subscribers or recipients, such as vendors ordering a large number of copies of one issue, and to maintain data on these special orders. This object-class encapsulates the following: recognition of the Special Order Received event; services that respond to this event, and that send messages to PRICING, CUSTOMER, and PAYMENT appropriately; and, relevant special order data.

SUBSCRIBER

The purpose of the object-class SUBSCRIBER is to maintain data on clients who subscribe to monthly issues. Subscribers are not necessarily recipients and may subscribe for numerous recipients. This object-class encapsulates the following: services that send messages to ADDRESS appropriately and that respond appropriately to messages from EXPIRATION WARNING and SUBSCRIPTION; plus, relevant subscriber data.

SUBSCRIPTION

The purpose of the object-class SUBSCRIPTION is to recognize requests for paid or complimentary subscriptions and to maintain data on these subscriptions. This object-class encapsulates the following: recognition of the Paid Subscription Requested and Complimentary Subscription Requested events; services that respond to these events, that send messages and that respond appropriately to messages received from other object-classes; plus, relevant subscription data.

SUBSCRIPTION EVENT

The purpose of the class SUBSCRIPTION EVENT is to provide a generalization for subscription events, such as subscription termination, payment, renewal and expiration warnings, and to maintain data shared by these specializations. This class encapsulates relevant SUBSCRIPTION EVENT data.

SUBSCRIPTION TERMINATION

The purpose of this object-class is to recognize when a subscription terminates and to maintain data for this termination. This object-class encapsulates the following: recognition of the Subscription Termination event; and, services that respond to the processing of this event. These services involve identifying a subscription as "terminated." All other records (for SUBSCRIBER, RECIPIENT, etc.) are maintained. The termination of a subscription applies to both paid and complimentary subscriptions.

J.3
Attribute
Descriptions

address_details (ADDRESS)

Includes address information such as name, street address, postal address, city, state and zip.

address_id (ADDRESS)

Unique identifier for an ADDRESS.

address_id (CLIENT)

Unique identifier for an ADDRESS.

address_id (CUSTOMER)

Unique identifier of an ADDRESS tied to a CUSTOMER.

address_id (PROSPECT)

Unique identifier of an ADDRESS tied to a PROSPECT.

address_id (RECIPIENT)

Unique identifier for an ADDRESS tied to a RECIPIENT.

address_id (SUBSCRIBER)

Unique identifier of an ADDRESS tied to a SUBSCRIBER.

address_id (AUTHOR)

Unique identifier for an ADDRESS tied to an AUTHOR.

article_details (ARTICLE)

Details about an ARTICLE, including the title, date and subject.

article_id (ARTICLE)

Unique identifier for an ARTICLE object.

author-article_details (AUTHOR-ARTICLE TRACK)

Details about an AUTHOR-ARTICLE TRACK, including author name, article name, date written and article subject.

author-article_id (AUTHOR-ARTICLE TRACK)

Unique identifier for an AUTHOR-ARTICLE TRACK object.

author_details (AUTHOR)

Biographical details about an author, including name, area of expertise, company affiliation and other personal data.

author_id (AUTHOR)

Unique identifier of an AUTHOR.

client_id (CLIENT)

Unique identifier for a CLIENT.

customer_details (CUSTOMER)

Information about a CUSTOMER, including name, company affiliation and history.

customer_id (CUSTOMER)

Unique identifier for a CUSTOMER.

customer_id (SPECIAL ORDER)

Unique identifier of a CUSTOMER who requested a SPECIAL ORDER.

editorial_advisor_id (EDITORIAL ADVISOR)

Unique identifier for an EDITORIAL ADVISOR object.

expiration_warning_date (EXPIRATION WARNING)

Scheduled EXPIRATION WARNING date.

expiration_warning_id (EXPIRATION WARNING)

Unique identifier for an EXPIRATION WARNING object.

invoice_details (INVOICE)

Detailed INVOICE information, including quantity, price, subscription term, due date and invoice total.

invoice_id (INVOICE)

Unique identifier for an INVOICE.

monthly_issue_details (MONTHLY ISSUE)

Detailed information about the issue contents, including ARTICLE subjects.

monthly_issue_id (MONTHLY ISSUE)

Unique identifier of a MONTHLY ISSUE.

new_subscription_id (RENEWAL)

Unique identifier for a new SUBSCRIPTION.

old_subscription_id (RENEWAL)

Unique identifier to identify an old SUBSCRIPTION which is being renewed.

payment_details (PAYMENT)

Payment information, including amount, date, remitter and subject of PAYMENT.

payment_id (INVOICE)

Unique identifier for a PAYMENT which requested an INVOICE.

payment_id (PAYMENT)

Unique identifier for a PAYMENT.

payment_id (SPECIAL ORDER)

Unique identifier for a PAYMENT instance which ties to a SPECIAL ORDER.

payment_id (SUBSCRIPTION)

Unique identifier for a PAYMENT instance which ties to a SUBSCRIPTION.

price_id (SPECIAL ORDER)

Unique identifier for price which ties to a SPECIAL ORDER.

pricing_details (PRICING)

Pricing information, including subscription pricing information and quantity breaks.

pricing_id (PRICING)

Unique identifier of a PRICING object.

pricing_id (SUBSCRIPTION)

Unique identifier of a PRICING object.

prospect_details (PROSPECT)

Details about a PROSPECT, including name, area of expertise and company affiliation.

prospect_id (PROSPECT)

Unique identifier for a PROSPECT.

recipient_details (RECIPIENT)

Information about a RECIPIENT, including name, company affiliation, quantity ordered, address information, method of payment and complimentary or paid arrangement.

recipient_id (RECIPIENT)

Unique identifier of a RECIPIENT.

recipient_id (SUBSCRIPTION)

Unique identifier of a RECIPIENT.

renewal_date (RENEWAL)

The date that a SUBSCRIPTION was renewed.

renewal_id (RENEWAL)

Unique identifier for a RENEWAL.

service_bureau_details (SERVICE BUREAU)

Information about a SERVICE BUREAU, including name, address, phone number and geographical coverage.

service_bureau_id (SERVICE BUREAU)

Unique identifier of a SERVICE BUREAU.

service_bureau_id (SUBSCRIPTION)

Unique identifier of a SERVICE BUREAU.

special_order_details (SPECIAL ORDER)

Information about a SPECIAL ORDER, including recipient, subject, quantity ordered, pricing, date of order, paper quality and issue number.

special_order_id (SPECIAL ORDER)

Unique identifier for a SPECIAL ORDER.

subscriber_details (SUBSCRIBER)

Information about a SUBSCRIBER, including name, phone number, address, method of payment, article contributions and account history.

subscriber_id (RECIPIENT)

Unique identifier of a SUBSCRIBER.

subscriber_id (SUBSCRIBER)

Unique identifier of a SUBSCRIBER.

subscriber_id (SUBSCRIPTION)

Unique identifier of a SUBSCRIBER tied to an instance of SUBSCRIPTION.

subscription_details (SUBSCRIPTION)

Details about a SUBSCRIPTION, including date, expiration date, price, recipient and payment status.

subscription_id (SUBSCRIPTION)

Unique identifier for a SUBSCRIPTION.

subscription_id (SUBSCRIPTION EVENT)

Unique identifier for a SUBSCRIPTION.

subscription_id (EXPIRATION WARNING)

Unique identifier for a SUBSCRIPTION.

subscription_id (SUBSCRIPTION TERMINATION)

Unique identifier for a SUBSCRIPTION.

subscription_id (SERVICE BUREAU)

Unique identifier for a SUBSCRIPTION.

subscription_status (SUBSCRIPTION)

The status of a SUBSCRIPTION. Values can be: paid, overdue, canceled, expired or new.

subscription_termination_id (SUBSCRIPTION TERMINATION)

Unique identifier for a SUBSCRIPTION TERMINATION.

termination_date (SUBSCRIPTION TERMINATION)

The date on which a SUBSCRIPTION EXPIRES.

J.4 Service Definitions

CREATE_EXPIRATION_WARNING (EXPIRATION WARNING)

This service creates the instance Expiration Warning. The attributes of EXPIRATION WARNING identify the associated subscription and its expiration warning.

CREATE_INVOICE (INVOICE)

This service will create an instance Invoice. The attributes of INVOICE identify the various invoice details.

CREATE_SUBSCRIPTION_TERMINATION (SUBSCRIPTION TERMINATION)

This service creates the instance Subscription Termination. The attributes of SUBSCRIPTION TERMINATION identify the associated SUBSCRIPTION and its expiration date.

ENTER_ADDRESS (ADDRESS)

This service determines whether or not the given address matches an existing instance `Address`. If there is a match, this class service returns the associated address identification. If the given address does not match any existing instance `Address`, then this class service creates an instance `Address`. The attributes of `Address` identify the various address details. This service returns associated address identification.

ENTER_AUTHOR (AUTHOR)

This service determines whether or not the given author matches an existing instance `Author`. If there is a match, this class service returns the associated author identification. If the given author does not match any existing instance `Author`, this class service creates the instance `Author`. The attributes of `Author` identify the various author details. This class service returns associated author identification.

ENTER_AUTHOR-ARTICLE (AUTHOR-ARTICLE TRACK)

This service creates an instance of `Author- Article Track`.

ENTER_COMP_SUBSCRIPTION (COMPLIMENTARY SUBSCRIPTION)

This service creates the instance `Complimentary Subscription`. The attributes of `Complimentary Subscription` identify the associated `SUBSCRIPTION`.

ENTER_CUSTOMER (CUSTOMER)

This service determines whether or not the given customer matches an existing instance `Customer`. If there is a match, that instance is associated with the given customer. If the given customer does not match any existing instance `Customer`, this class service creates the instance `Customer`. The attributes of `Customer` identify various customer details.

ENTER_PAYMENT (PAYMENT)

This service creates an instance of `Payment`.

ENTER_RECIPIENT (RECIPIENT)

This service determines whether or not the given recipient matches an existing instance `Recipient`. If there is a match, that instance is associated with the given subscription. If the given recipient does not match any existing instance `Recipient`, this class service creates the instance `Recipient`. The attributes of `Recipient` identify various recipient details.

ENTER_SUBSCRIBER (SUBSCRIBER)

This service determines whether or not the given subscriber matches an existing instance `Subscriber`. If there is a match, that instance is associated with the given subscription. If the given subscriber does not match any existing instance `Subscriber`, this class service creates the instance `Subscriber`. The attributes of `Subscriber` identify various subscriber details.

Enter_Accepted_Article (ACCEPTED ARTICLE)

For the event, Article Accepted For Publication, `Accepted Article.Enter_ Accepted_Article` sends a message to the corresponding instance of `Author` requesting the associated **author_details**. Upon receipt of `author_details`, it sends a message to the appropriate instance of `MONTHLY ISSUE`.

Enter_Address (AUTHOR)

Upon creation of `Author`, `Author.Enter_Address` sends a message to `ADDRESS.ENTER_ADDRESS`, to determine whether or not a given address matches an existing instance of `Address`.

Enter_Address (CUSTOMER)

This service, upon creation of a `Customer`, sends a message to `ADDRESS.ENTER_ ADDRESS`, to determine whether or not a given address matches an existing instance of `Address`.

Enter_Address (PROSPECT)

Upon creation of a `Prospect`, this service sends a message to `ADDRESS.ENTER_ ADDRESS`, to determine whether or not the given address matches an existing instance `Address`.

Enter_Address (RECIPIENT)

Upon creation of an instance of `Recipient`, this service sends a message to `ADDRESS.ENTER_ADDRESS`, to determine whether or not the given address matches an existing instance of `Address`.

Enter_Address (SUBSCRIBER)

Upon creation of an instance of `Subscriber`, this service sends a message to `ADDRESS.ENTER_ADDRESS`, to determine whether or not a given address matches an existing instance of `Address`.

Enter_Article (MONTHLY ISSUE)

This service for `MONTHLY ISSUE` updates issue details, with such information as author information.

Enter_Comp_Subscription (SUBSCRIPTION)

This service, `SUBSCRIPTION.Enter_Comp_Subscription`:
1. Sends a message to `COMPLIMENTARY SUBSCRIPTION.ENTER_COMP_ SUBSCRIPTION`
2. Sends a message to `ADDRESS.ENTER_ADDRESS`.

3. Upon receipt of the address identification, sends a message to `SUBSCRIBER.ENTER_SUBSCRIBER`.
4. Upon receipt of the address identification, sends a message to `RECIPIENT.ENTER_RECIPIENT`.

Enter_New_Article (ARTICLE)

This service sends a message to `AUTHOR.ENTER_AUTHOR`. When `author_id` is received, it sends a message to `AUTHOR-ARTICLE TRACK.ENTER_AUTHOR_ARTICLE`.

Enter_Paid_Subscription (SUBSCRIPTION)

For the event Paid Subscription Requested, `SUBSCRIPTION.Enter_Paid_Subscription`:
1. Sends a message to: `SUBSCRIPTION TERMINATION.CREATE_SUBSCRIPTION_EXPIRATION`.
2. Sends a message to: `PRICING.Report_Price` of the appropriate `Subscription` instance. This service returns the calculated `subscription_price`.
3. Upon receipt of the `subscription_price`, a message may be sent to `Service Bureau.Record_Payment`.
4. A message is sent to `EXPIRATION WARNING.CREATE_EXPIRATION_WARNING`.
5. A message is sent to `ADDRESS.ENTER_ADDRESS`.
6. Upon receipt of the address identification, a message is sent to `SUBSCRIBER.ENTER_SUBSCRIBER`.
7. Upon receipt of the address identification, a message is sent to `RECIPIENT.ENTER_RECIPIENT`.

Enter_Published_Article (PUBLISHED ARTICLE)

This service sends a message to the corresponding instance of Author requesting the associated `author_details`. Upon receipt of `author_details`, a message is sent to the appropriate instance of `Author-Article Track`.

Issue_Invoice (PAYMENT)

As required, `Payment.Issue_Invoice` will send a message to `INVOICE.CREATE_INVOICE` to produce a requested invoice.

Process_Special_Order (SPECIAL ORDER)

`SPECIAL ORDER.Process_Special_order` sends a message to `PRICING.Report_Price` to return the calculated special order price.

RECOGNIZE_ARTICLE_ACCEPTED (ACCEPTED ARTICLE)

`ACCEPTED ARTICLE.RECOGNIZE_ARTICLE_ACCEPTED` detects the occurrence of the event Article Accepted For Publication and creates an `Accepted Article` instance. (The corresponding instance of `Article` is terminated.)

RECOGNIZE_ARTICLE_PUBLISHED (PUBLISHED ARTICLE)

PUBLISHED ARTICLE.RECOGNIZE_ARTICLE_PUBLISHED detects an occurrence of the event Article Accepted For Publication and creates a `Published Article` instance. (The corresponding instance of `Accepted Article` is terminated.)

RECOGNIZE_ARTICLE_RECEIVED (ARTICLE)

This service detects the occurrence of the event Article Received and creates an `Article` instance.

RECOGNIZE_PAYMENT_RECEIVED (PAYMENT)

This service for `PAYMENT` detects the occurrence of the event Payment Received and creates an instance of `Payment`.

RECOGNIZE_PROSPECT_IDENTIFIED (PROSPECT)

This service determines whether or not the given prospect matches an existing instance `Prospect`. If there is a match, this class service terminates. If the given prospect does not match any existing instance `Prospect`, this class service creates the instance `Prospect`. The attributes of `Prospect` identify the various prospect details.

RECOGNIZE_SPECIAL_ORDER (SPECIAL ORDER)

This service detects the occurrence of the event Received Special Order and creates a `Special Order` instance.

RECOGNIZE_SUBSCRIPTION_RENEWED (RENEWAL)

This service detects the occurrence of the event Paid Subscription Renewed and sends a message to the appropriate `Subscription` instance.

RECOGNIZE_SUBSCRIPTION_REQUEST (SUBSCRIPTION)

This service detects the occurrence of the event Paid Subscription Requested and creates a `Subscription` instance.

RECOGNIZE_TIME_TO_REVIEW (COMPLIMENTARY SUBSCRIPTION)

This service detects the occurrence of the event Time To Review "Comp List" and sends a message to the each `Complimentary Subscription` instance.

REQUEST_SUBSCRIPTION (SUBSCRIPTION)

When this service receives a message from `Article.Enter_Accepted_Article`, it will create an instance of `Subscription` for the event Article Accepted For Publication.

Recognize_Renewal_Due (EXPIRATION WARNING)

`Expiration Warning.Recognize_Renewal_Due` detects the occurrence of the event Time To Send Renewal Notice and sends a message to `Subscription.Report_Subscriber`. Upon receipt of subscriber identification, a message is sent to `Subscriber.Report_Address` and to `Address.Report_Address_Details`. Upon receipt of the address details, `Expiration Warning.Recognize_Renewal_Due` issues the appropriate expiration warning notice. Upon receipt of subscriber identification, `Expiration Warning.Recognize_Renewal_Due` sends a message to `Subscriber.Report_Address`. Upon receipt of subscriber identification, `Expiration Warning.Recognize_Renewal_Due` sends a message to `Address.Report_Address_Details`. Upon receipt of the address details, `Expiration Warning.Recognize_Renewal_Due` issues the appropriate expiration warning notice.

Recognize_Sub_Termination (SUBSCRIPTION TERMINATION)

This service detects the occurrence of the event Subscription Terminates and sends a message to `Subscription.Terminate_Subscription` for the appropriate `Subscription` instance.

Record_Payment (SERVICE BUREAU)

This service records when a payment is received and recognizes that part of it is a commission. A message may be sent to `Service Bureau.Record_Payment` by `Subscription.Enter_Paid_Subscription` or `Subscription.Renew_Subscription`.

Renew_Subscription (SUBSCRIPTION)

This service helps create a renewed subscription and will send messages to:
1. `SUBSCRIPTION TERMINATION.CREATE_SUBSCRIPTION_EXPIRATION`
2. `Pricing.Report_Price`, which returns the calculated subscription price.
3. Upon receipt of the subscription price, a message is sent to `PAYMENT.ENTER_PAYMENT`.
4. Upon receipt of the subscription price, a message may be sent to Service Bureau.Record Payment.
5. A message is also sent to `EXPIRATION WARNING.CREATE_EXPIRATION_WARNING`.

Report_Address (SUBSCRIBER)

This service reports to an instance of `Expiration Warning` address details for the event Time to Send Renewal Notice.

Report_Address_Details (ADDRESS)

The service `Address.Report_Address_Details` receives a message from `Subscriber.Report_Address` for the event Time to Send Renewal Notice.

Report_Price (PRICING)

Upon receipt of the subscription price, this instance service, `Pricing.Report_Price`, creates an instance of `Payment`.

Report_Subscriber (SUBSCRIPTION)

`Expiration Warning.Recognize_Renewal_Due` sends a message to `Subscription.Report_Subscriber` to find the `subscriber_id` for the event Time To Send Renewal Notice.

Review_Comp_Subscription (COMPLIMENTARY SUBSCRIPTION)

This service establishes whether or not a complimentary subscription should be terminated. In the case when a complimentary subscription should be terminated, this service sends a message to `Subscription.Terminate_Subscription` for the appropriate `Subscription` instance.

Terminate_Subscription (SUBSCRIPTION)

This service sets the `subscription_status` to indicate the termination of the corresponding subscription for the event Terminate Subscription.

Update_Track (AUTHOR-ARTICLE TRACK)

This service updates the `author_article_details`.

J.5 Message Definitions

Enter Accepted Article 1

For the event Article Accepted For Publication, `Accepted Article.Enter_Accepted_Article` sends a message to the corresponding instance of `Author`, asking, "What are the associated author_details?"

Enter Accepted Article 2

For the event Article Accepted For Publication, when `Accepted Article.Enter_Accepted_Article` receives the `author_details`, it sends a message to `Monthly Issue.Enter_Article` to update the issue details.

Enter Accepted Article 3

For the event Article Accepted For Publication, `Accepted Article.Enter_Accepted_Article`, sends a message to `SUBSCRIPTION.REQUEST_SUBSCRITPION` to create a `Subscription` instance.

Enter Address - Prospect

`Prospect.Enter_Address` sends a message to `ADDRESS.ENTER_ADDRESS` to ask, "Does an Address instance exist?" and "What is the associated address identification?"

Enter Address - Author

`Author.Enter_Address` sends a message to `ADDRESS.ENTER_ADDRESS` and asks, "Does an Address instance exist?" and "What is the associated address identification?"

Enter Address - Customer

`Customer.Enter_Customer` sends a message to `ADDRESS.ENTER_ENTER` for the event Special Order Received to ask, "Does an Address instance exist?" and "What is the associated address identification?"

Enter Address - Recipient

`Recipient.Enter_Address` sends a message to `ADDRESS.ENTER_ADDRESS` and asks, "Does an Address instance exist?" and "What is the associated address identification?"

Enter Address - Subscriber

`Subscriber.Enter_Address` sends a message to `ADDRESS.ENTER_ADDRESS` and asks, "Does an Address instance exist?" and "What is the associated address identification?"

Enter Comp Subscription

`Subscription.Enter_Comp_Subscription` sends a message to `COMPLIMENTARY SUBSCRIPTION.ENTER_ COMP_SUBSCRIPTION` to create an instance `Complimentary Subscription`.

Enter New Article 1

For the event `ARTICLE RECEIVED`, `Article.Enter_New_Article` sends a message to `AUTHOR.ENTER_ AUTHOR` asking, "Does given Author match existing `Author` instance?" and "What is the associated author identification?"

Enter New Article 2

For the event `ARTICLE RECEIVED`, `Article.Enter_New_Article` sends a message to `AUTHOR-ARTICLE TRACK.ENTER_ AUTHOR_ARTICLE` to create an instance of `Author Article Track`.

Enter Paid Subscription

When a paid subscription is received, `Subscription.Enter_Paid_ Subscription` sends a message to `PAYMENT.ENTER_PAYMENT` to create an instance of `Payment`.

Enter Paid Subscription 1

This message is sent from `Subscription` to `SUBSCRIPTION TERMINATION` to create the instance `Subscription Termination`. The attributes of

`Subscription Termination` identify the associated subscription and its expiration date.

Enter Paid Subscription 2

`Subscription.Enter_Paid_Subscription` sends a message to `Pricing.Report_Price` of the appropriate `Subscription` instance, which returns the calculated subscription price.

Enter Paid Subscription 3

`Subscription.Enter_Paid_Subscription` sends a message to `EXPIRATION_WARNING.CREATE_EXPIRATION_ WARNING` to create the instance `Expiration Warning`, for the event Paid Subscription Requested. The attributes of `Expiration Warning` identify the associated subscription and its expiration warning date.

Enter Paid Subscription 4

`Subscription.Enter_Paid_Subscription` or `Subscription.Renew_Subscription` sends a message to `Service Bureau.Record_Payment` whenever a payment is received with a commission going to a `Service Bureau`.

Enter Paid Subscription 6

Message sent from `Subscriber.Enter_Paid_Subscription` or `Subscriber.Enter_Comp_Subscription` to `SUBSCRIBER.ENTER_SUBSCRIBER` to create an instance of `Subscriber`, which determines, "Does the given `Subscriber` match an existing instance of `Subscriber`?" If yes, associate with existing `Subscription`. If no, create instance `Subscriber`.

Enter Paid Subscription 7

Message sent from: `Recipient.Enter_Paid_Subscription` `Recipient.Enter_Comp_Subscription` to `RECIPIENT.ENTER_RECIPIENT` to create a new instance of `Recipient`, which determines, "Does given `Recipient` match existing instance `Recipient`?" If yes, associate with given subscription. If no, create instance `Recipient`.

Enter Published Article 1

For the event ARTICLE PUBLISHED, `Published Article.Enter_Published_Article` sends the message, "What are the associated `author_details`?" to the corresponding instance of `Author`.

Enter Published Article 2

For the event ARTICLE PUBLISHED, `Published Article.Enter_Published_Article` sends a message to `Author-Article Track.UpdateTrack` to update `author_article_details` accordingly.

Enter Published Article 3

For the event ARTICLE PUBLISHED, `Published Article.Enter_ Published_Article` sends a message to `Monthly_Issue.Enter_Article` to update the monthly issue details.

Issue Invoice

`Payment.Issue_Invoice` sends a message, when requested, to `INVOICE.CREATE_INVOICE` to produce a requested invoice.

Process Special Order

`Special Order.Process_Special_Order` sends a message to `Pricing.Report_Price`, which returns the calculated special order price.

Process Special Order 2

`Special Order.Process_Special_order` sends a message to `PAYMENT.ENTER_PAYMENT` to create an instance of `Payment`.

Process Special Order 4

For the event Special Order Received, `Special Order.Process_Special_ Order` sends a message to `CUSTOMER.ENTER_CUSTOMER` to send the address identification, and ask: Does customer match an existing `Customer` instance?

Recognize Renewal Due 1

`Expiration_Warning.Recognize_Renewal_Due` detects the occurrence of the event Time To Send Renewal Notice and sends a message to `Subscription.Report_Subscriber`.

Recognize Renewal Due 2

Upon receipt of subscriber identification, `Expiration Warning.Recognize_ Renewal_Due` sends a message to `Subscriber.Report_Address`, for the event, Time To Send Renewal Address.

Recognize Sub Termination

After the event Subscription Termination is recognized, `Subscription Termination` sends this message to `Subscription` to determine the appropriate `Subscription` instance.

Recognize Subscription Renewed

`RENEWAL.RECOGNIZE_SUBSCRIPTION_RENEWED` detects the occurrence of the Renewal event and notifies the appropriate `Subscription` instance.

Renew Subscription

Subscription.Renew_Subscription sends this message to EXPIRATION_ WARNING.CREATE_EXPIRATION_WARNING to create an instance Expiration Warning for a renewed subscription, for the event Paid Subscription Renewed.

Renew Subscription 1

Subscription sends a message to SUBSCRIPTION_TERMINATION.CREATE SUBSCRIPTION_EXPIRATION. This service creates the instance Subscription Termination. The attributes of Subscription Termination identify the associated subscription and its expiration date.

Renew Subscription 2

Subscription.Renew_Subscription sends the message, "What is the calculated subscription price for the Subscription instance?" to Pricing.Report_ Pricing.

Renew Subscription 3

Subscription.Renew_Subscription sends a message to PAYMENT.ENTER_ PAYMENT to create instance of Payment for a renewed subscription.

Report Address

Subscriber.Report Address sends a message to Address.Report_ Address_Details for the event Time To Send Renewal Notice.

Review_Comp_Subscription

Complimentary Subscription.Review_Comp_Subscription determines that a complimentary subscription should be terminated, and sends the following message to Subscription.Terminate_Subscription: "What is the appropriate Subscription instance?"

APPENDIX K
EROI Diagram Notation

The Event-Response-Object-Interaction (EROI) diagram is a tool which integrates event-response analysis with object-oriented concepts. This concept is illustrated in Figure K.1.

Each event in the event-response model is associated with one EROI diagram. The EROI diagram consists of a number of vertical lines (fence posts), one for each object-class in the OOA model. The EROI diagram is constructed as follows:

1. The EROI diagram shows which object-class recognizes the occurrence of the event. This is designated with a ☐ symbol (refer to Figure K.2).

2. Upon recognition of the event, the designated object-class may produce messages; these messages may travel from the recognizing object-class (fence post) to destination object-classes (fence posts).

3. Messages are represented as directed arrows, →, or bi-directional arrows, ↔, when a synchronous response is produced.

The vertical direction on the EROI diagram implies time; that is, messages drawn below other messages are assumed to occur later in time. Extensions to this notation are shown in Figure K.2.

Obviously the EROI diagram must be consistent with the corresponding OOA model; there is a correspondence between messages on the EROI diagram and messages in the Service Layer of the OOA model. The EROI diagram, however, portrays the *dynamic* behavior of the model as a *sequence* of messages exchanged between object-classes.

Appendices L and M illustrate EROI diagrams for the two case studies.

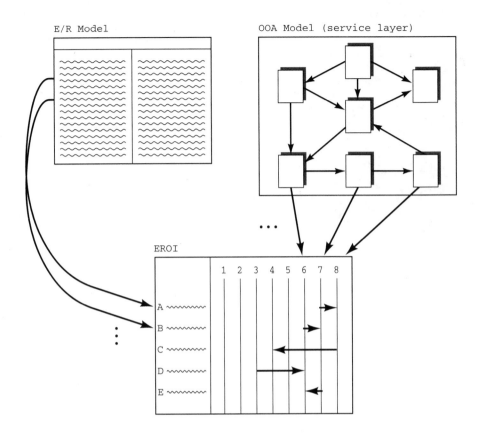

Figure K.1
A conceptual view of
the EROI diagram.

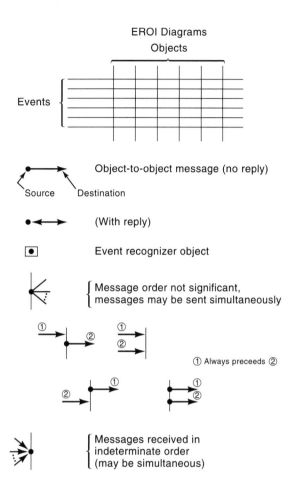

Figure K.2
EROI diagram notation.

APPENDIX L
EROI Diagrams for Elevator Control System

The Event-Response Object Interaction (EROI) diagrams for the Elevator Control System (ECS) are included in this appendix (see Figures L.1 through L.7). These diagrams are an integration of the Event-Response model for the ECS (see Appendix G) and the OOA model (see Appendix I). Each diagram represents how a system event is recognized and responded to by a collaboration of objects. The structure of EROI diagrams is explained in Appendix K.

ECS/OOA EROI DIAGRAM

Event No. 1: ELEVATOR SUMMONED

- ARRIVAL EVENT
- ARRIVAL PANEL
- DESTINATION EVENT
- DESTINATION PANEL
- ELEVATOR
- ELEVATOR MOTOR
- FLOOR
- OVERWEIGHT SENSOR
- SUMMONS EVENT
- SUMMONS PANEL

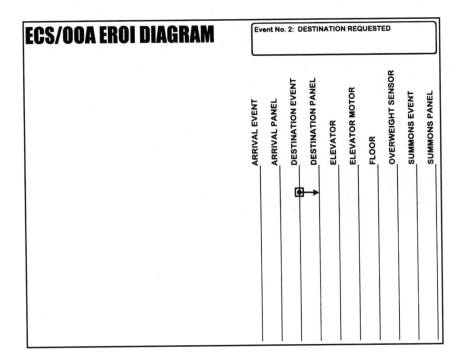

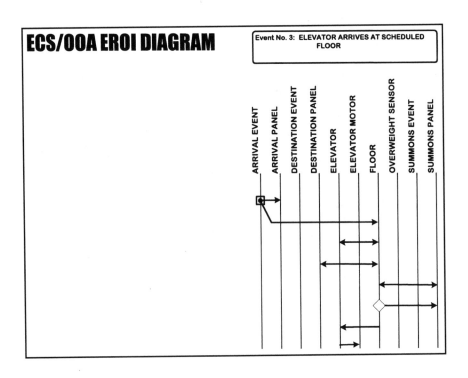

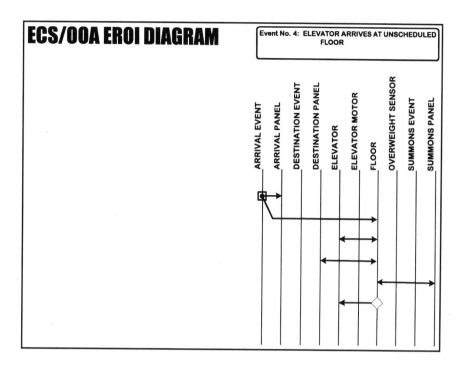

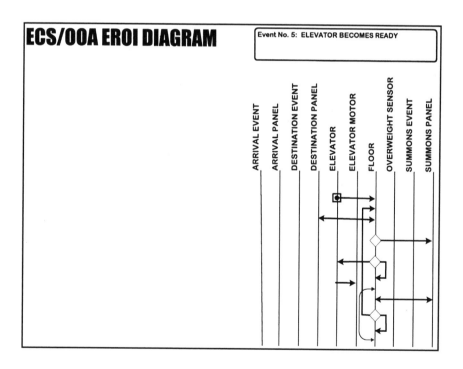

ECS/OOA EROI DIAGRAM   Event No. 6: ELEVATOR BECOMES OVERWEIGHT

ARRIVAL EVENT
ARRIVAL PANEL
DESTINATION EVENT
DESTINATION PANEL
ELEVATOR
ELEVATOR MOTOR
FLOOR
OVERWEIGHT SENSOR
SUMMONS EVENT
SUMMONS PANEL

ECS/OOA EROI DIAGRAM   Event No. 7: ELEVATOR BECOMES NOT-OVERWEIGHT

ARRIVAL EVENT
ARRIVAL PANEL
DESTINATION EVENT
DESTINATION PANEL
ELEVATOR
ELEVATOR MOTOR
FLOOR
OVERWEIGHT SENSOR
SUMMONS EVENT
SUMMONS PANEL

EROI Diagrams for Small Bytes Subscription System

The Event-Response Object Interaction (EROI) diagrams for the *Small Bytes* Subscription System (SBSS) are included in this appendix (see Figures M.1 through M.12). These diagrams are an integration of the Event-Response model for the SBSS (see Appendix H) and the OOA model (see Appendix J). Each diagram represents how a system event is recognized and responded to by a collaboration of objects. The structure of EROI diagrams is explained in Appendix K.

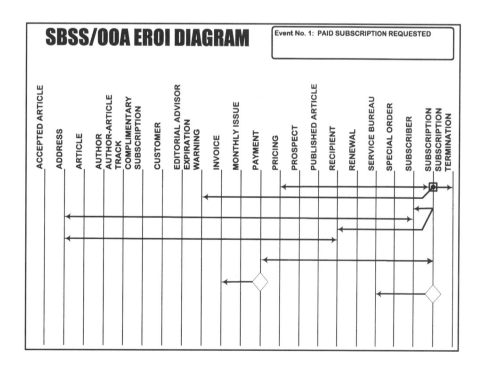

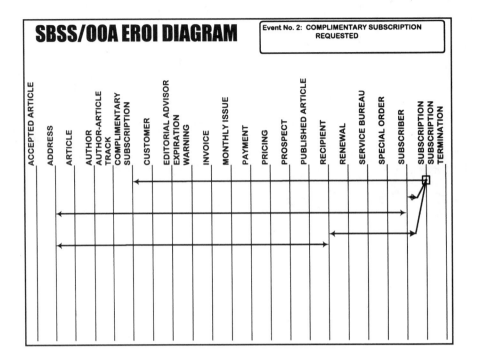

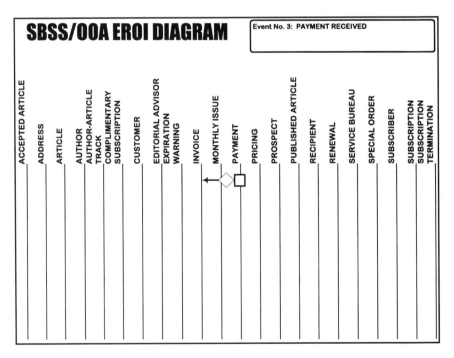

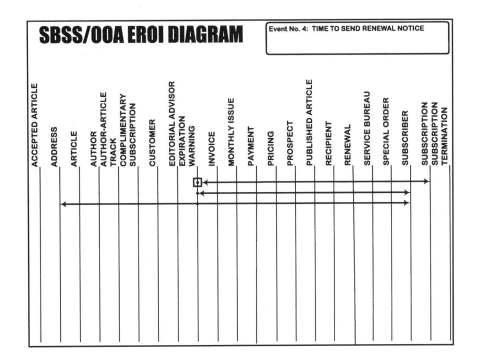

SBSS/OOA EROI DIAGRAM

Event No. 4: TIME TO SEND RENEWAL NOTICE

ACCEPTED ARTICLE
ADDRESS
ARTICLE
AUTHOR
AUTHOR-ARTICLE
TRACK
COMPLIMENTARY
SUBSCRIPTION
CUSTOMER
EDITORIAL ADVISOR
EXPIRATION
WARNING
INVOICE
MONTHLY ISSUE
PAYMENT
PRICING
PROSPECT
PUBLISHED ARTICLE
RECIPIENT
RENEWAL
SERVICE BUREAU
SPECIAL ORDER
SUBSCRIBER
SUBSCRIPTION
SUBSCRIPTION
TERMINATION

SBSS/OOA EROI DIAGRAM

Event No. 5: SUBSCRIPTION TERMINATES

ACCEPTED ARTICLE
ADDRESS
ARTICLE
AUTHOR
AUTHOR-ARTICLE
TRACK
COMPLIMENTARY
SUBSCRIPTION
CUSTOMER
EDITORIAL ADVISOR
EXPIRATION
WARNING
INVOICE
MONTHLY ISSUE
PAYMENT
PRICING
PROSPECT
PUBLISHED ARTICLE
RECIPIENT
RENEWAL
SERVICE BUREAU
SPECIAL ORDER
SUBSCRIBER
SUBSCRIPTION
SUBSCRIPTION
TERMINATION

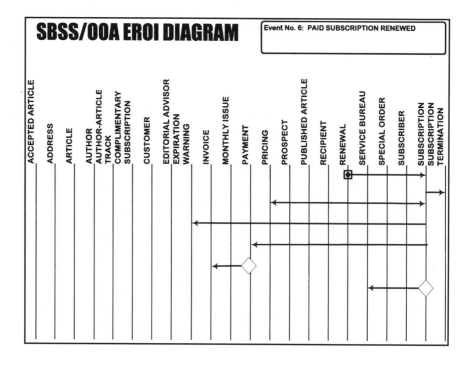

SBSS/OOA EROI DIAGRAM — Event No. 6: PAID SUBSCRIPTION RENEWED

SBSS/OOA EROI DIAGRAM — Event No. 7: TIME TO REVIEW "COMP LIST"

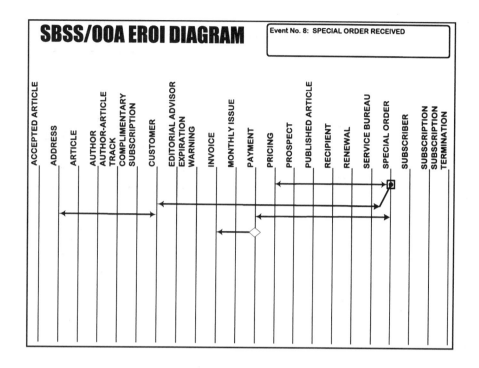

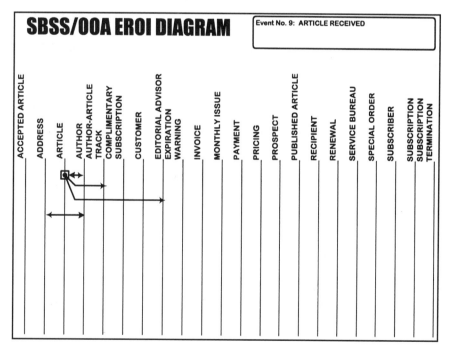

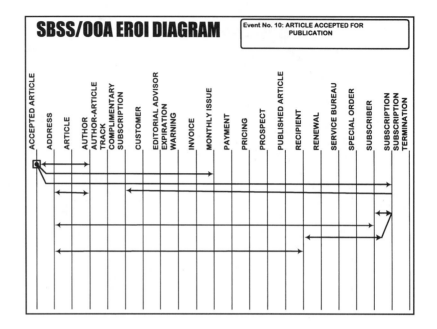

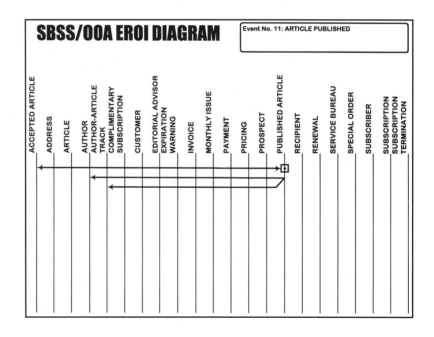

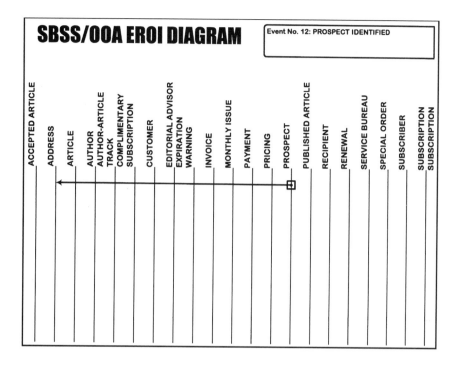

APPENDIX N
Problem Domain Component (PDC) for Elevator Control System

The Problem Domain Component (PDC) for the ECS is shown in Figure N.1. This OOD model component is described in Chapter 15.

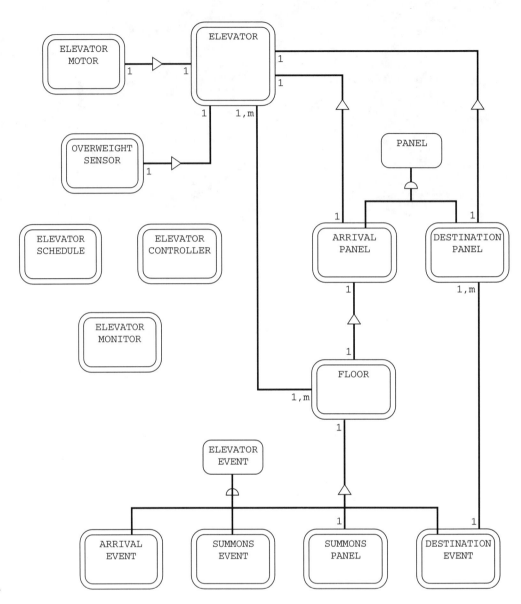

Figure N.1
PDC for the ECS.

APPENDIX O

Problem Domain Component (PDC) for Small Bytes Subscription System

The Problem Domain Component (PDC) for the SBSS is shown in Figure O.1. This OOD model component is described in Chapter 15.

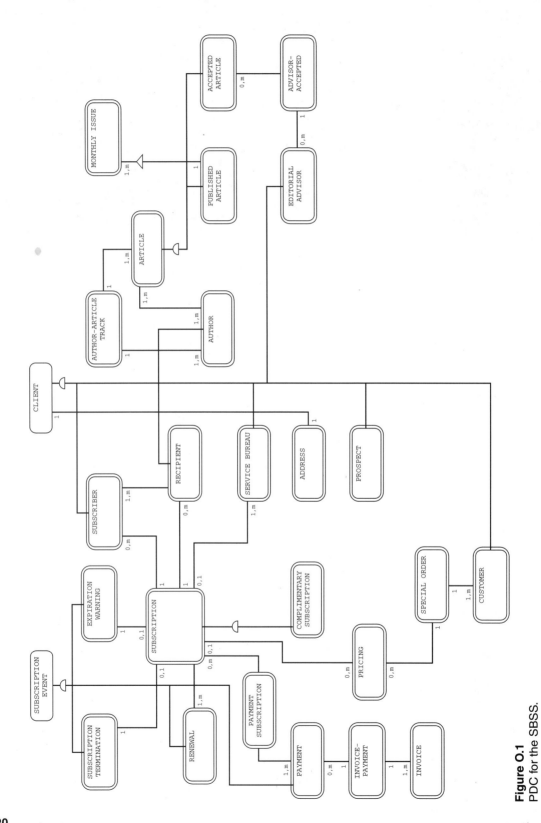

Figure O.1
PDC for the SBSS.

Human Interaction Component (HIC) for Elevator Control System

The Human Interaction Component (HIC) for the ECS is shown in Figure P.1. This OOD model component is described in Chapter 16.

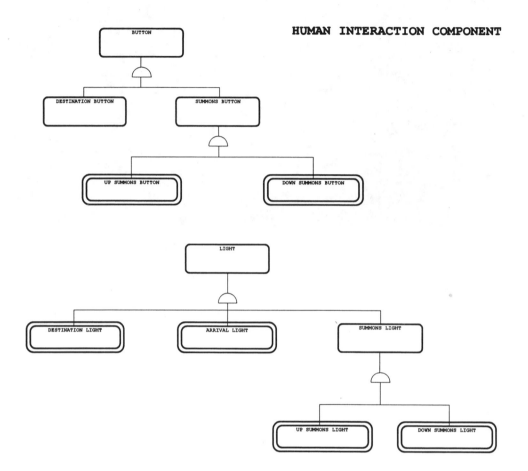

HUMAN INTERACTION COMPONENT

Figure P.1
HIC for the ECS.

APPENDIX Q
Human Interaction Component (HIC) for Small Bytes Subscription System

This appendix presents the Human Interaction Component (HIC) for the SBSS. Also included are a number of diagrams and illustrations as described in Chapter 16.

Figure Q.1 shows the OOD HIC model component. Figure Q.2 shows a tree diagram which represents the user interface structure or topology. Figure Q.3 shows a state-transition diagram, which documents one user interface transition. Finally, Figures Q.4 through Q.15 present prototype user interface screens.

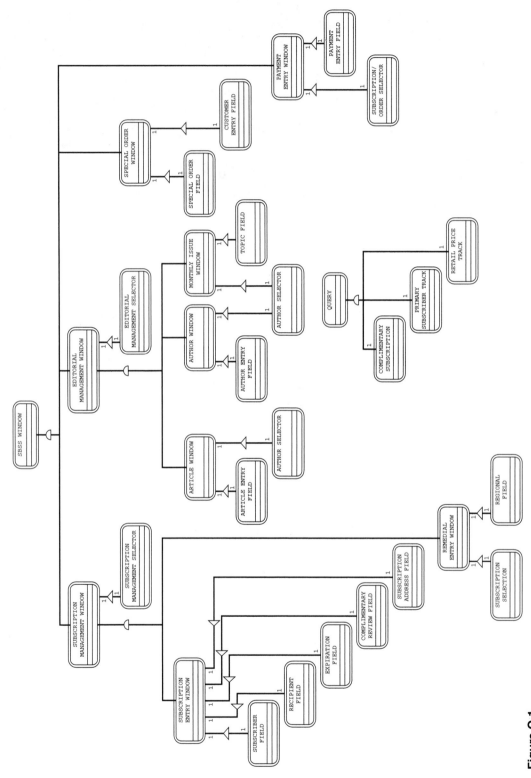

Figure Q.1
HIC for the SBSS.

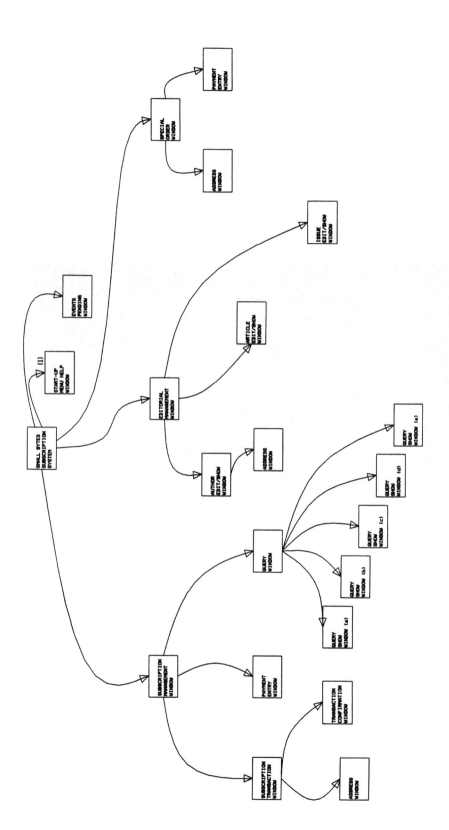

Figure Q.2
User interface topology depicted with a tree diagram.

325

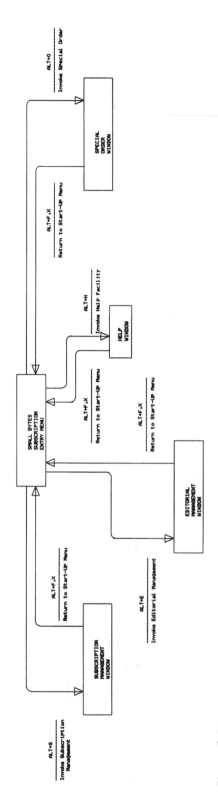

Figure Q.3
User interface transition depicted with a state-transition diagram.

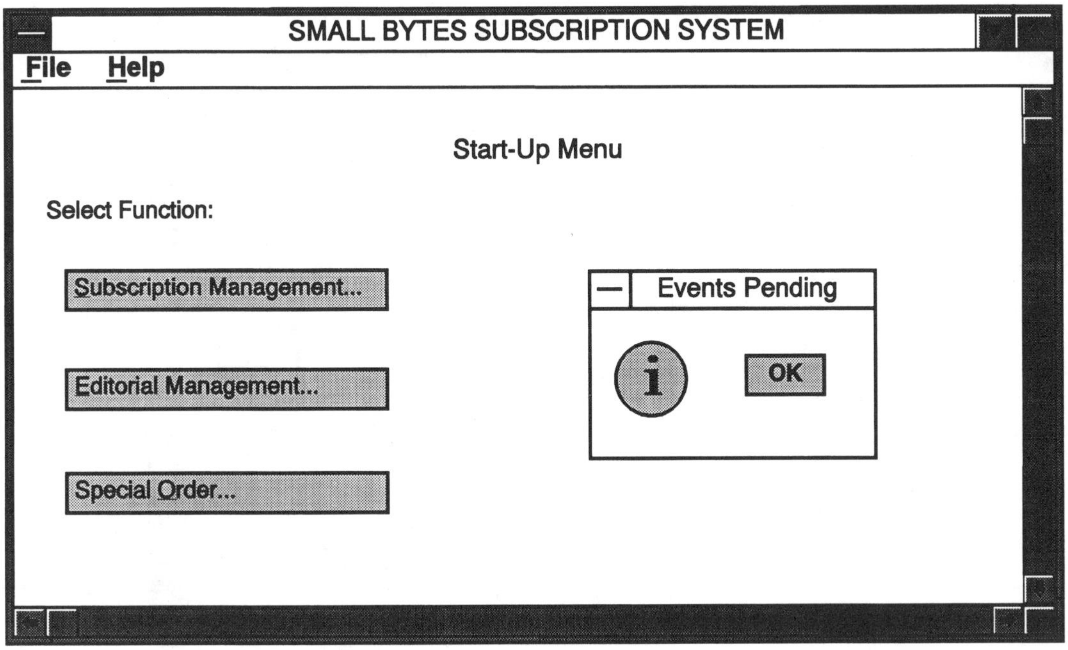

SMALL BYTES SUBSCRIPTION SYSTEM

File   Help

Start-Up Menu

Select Function:

Subscription Management...

Editorial Management...

Special Order...

— | Events Pending

i   OK

Figure Q.4

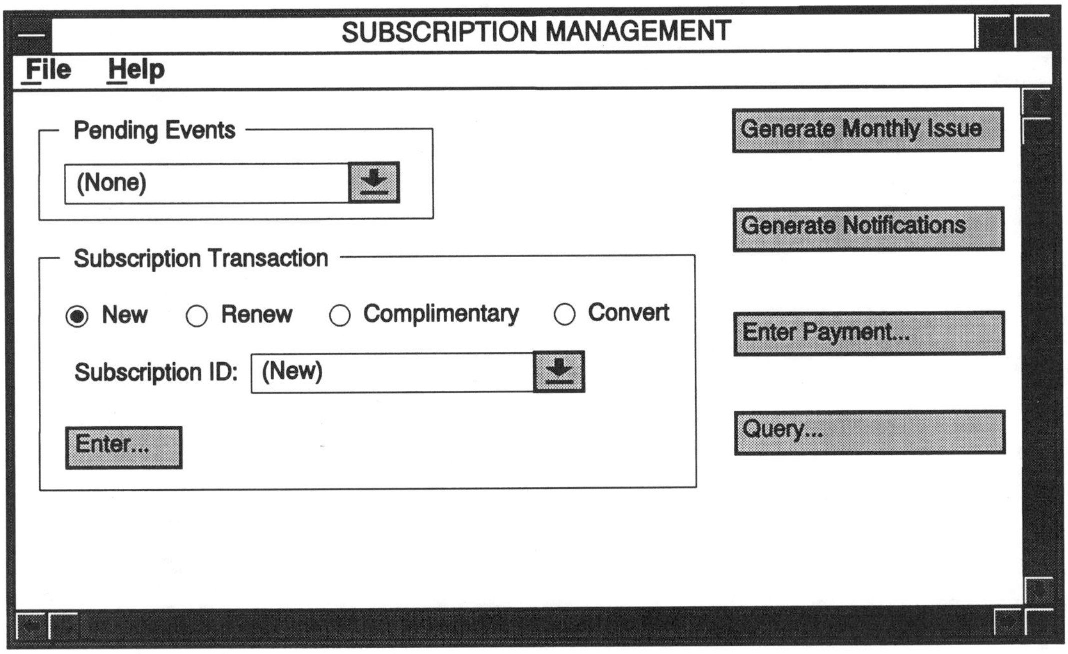

SUBSCRIPTION MANAGEMENT

File   Help

Pending Events
(None)   ⬇

Subscription Transaction

◉ New   ○ Renew   ○ Complimentary   ○ Convert

Subscription ID: (New)   ⬇

Enter...

Generate Monthly Issue

Generate Notifications

Enter Payment...

Query...

Figure Q.5

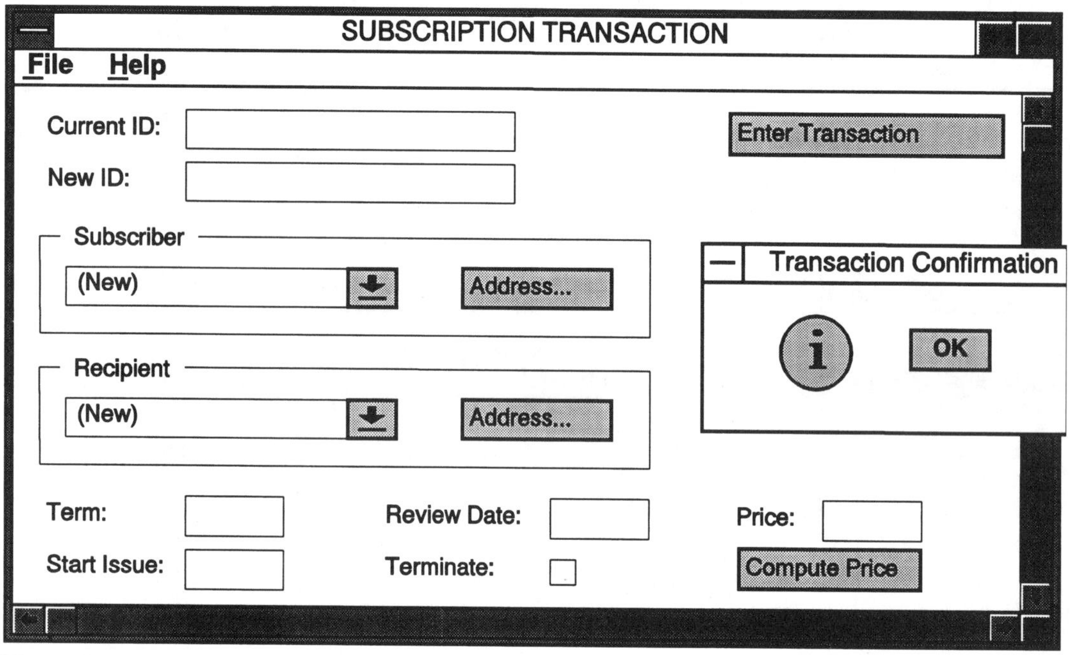

SUBSCRIPTION TRANSACTION

File   Help

Current ID: [   ]

New ID: [   ]

Enter Transaction

┌─ Subscriber ──────────────────────┐
│ (New) [   ] ⬇   Address...   │
└───────────────────────────────────┘

┌─ Recipient ───────────────────────┐
│ (New) [   ] ⬇   Address...   │
└───────────────────────────────────┘

Transaction Confirmation

ⓘ   OK

Term: [   ]   Review Date: [   ]   Price: [   ]

Start Issue: [   ]   Terminate: ☐   Compute Price

Figure Q.6

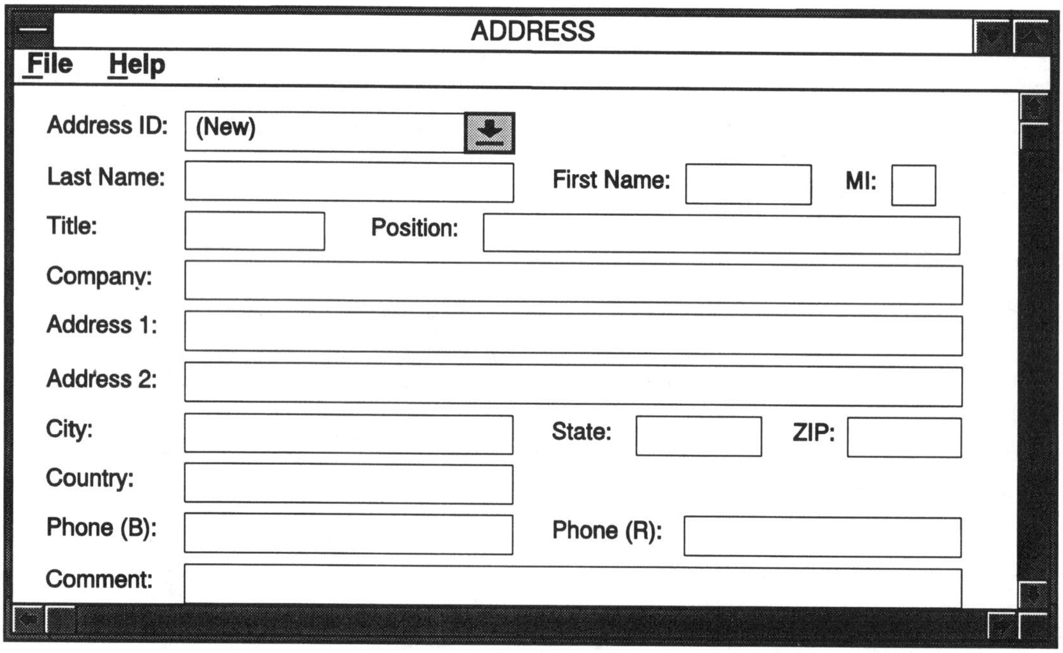

ADDRESS

File   Help

Address ID: [(New)   ] ⬇

Last Name: [   ]   First Name: [   ]   MI: [ ]

Title: [   ]   Position: [   ]

Company: [   ]

Address 1: [   ]

Address 2: [   ]

City: [   ]   State: [   ]   ZIP: [   ]

Country: [   ]

Phone (B): [   ]   Phone (R): [   ]

Comment: [   ]

Figure Q.7

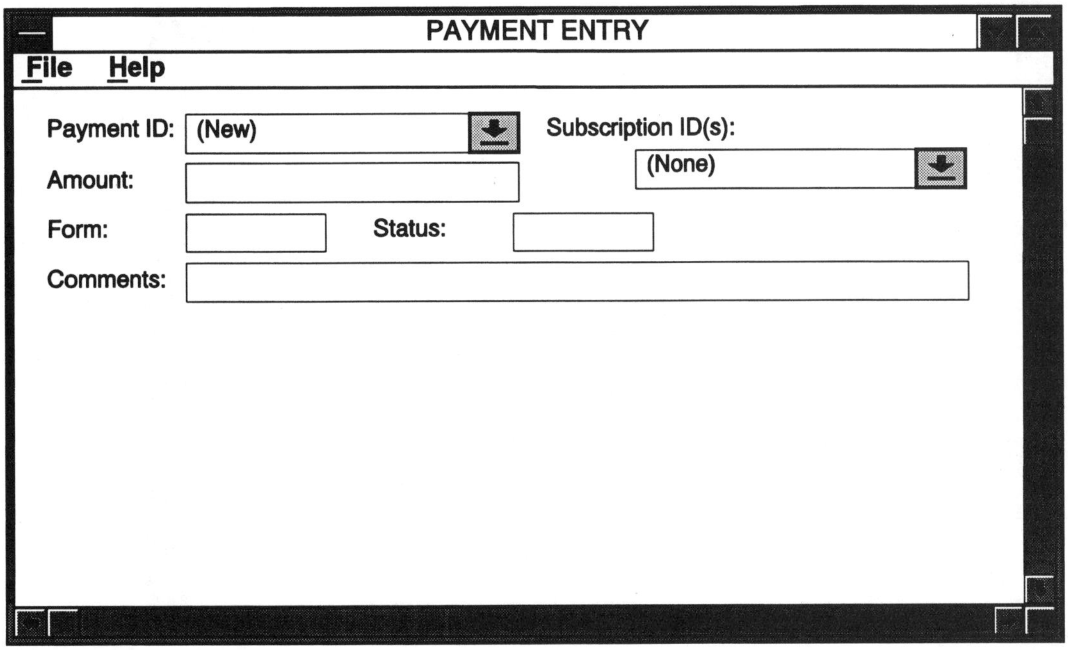

Figure Q.8

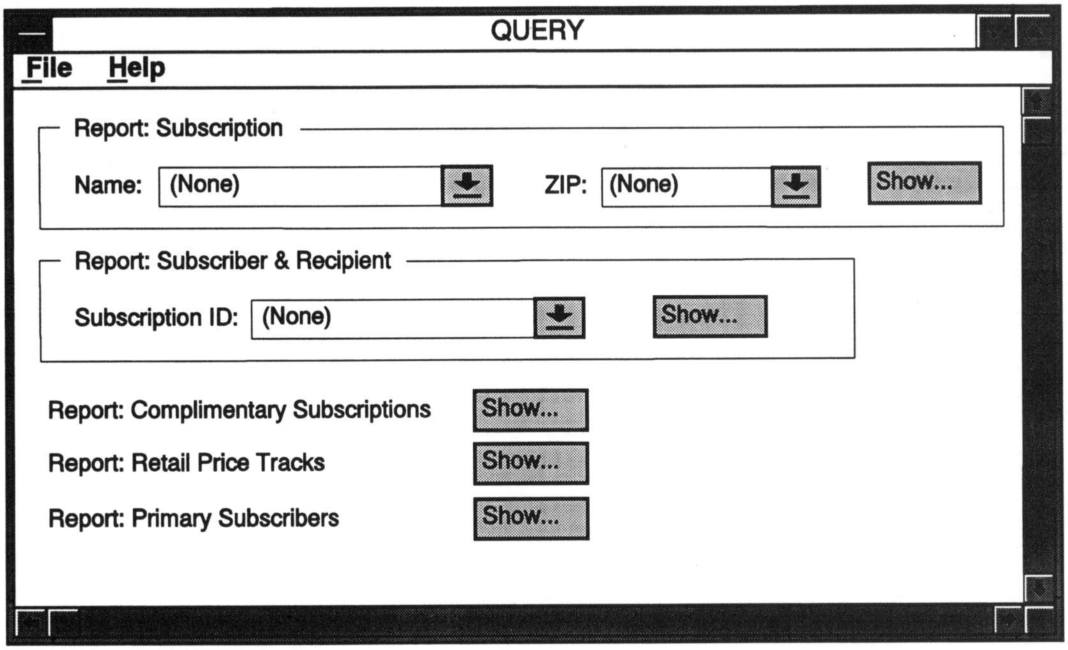

Figure Q.9

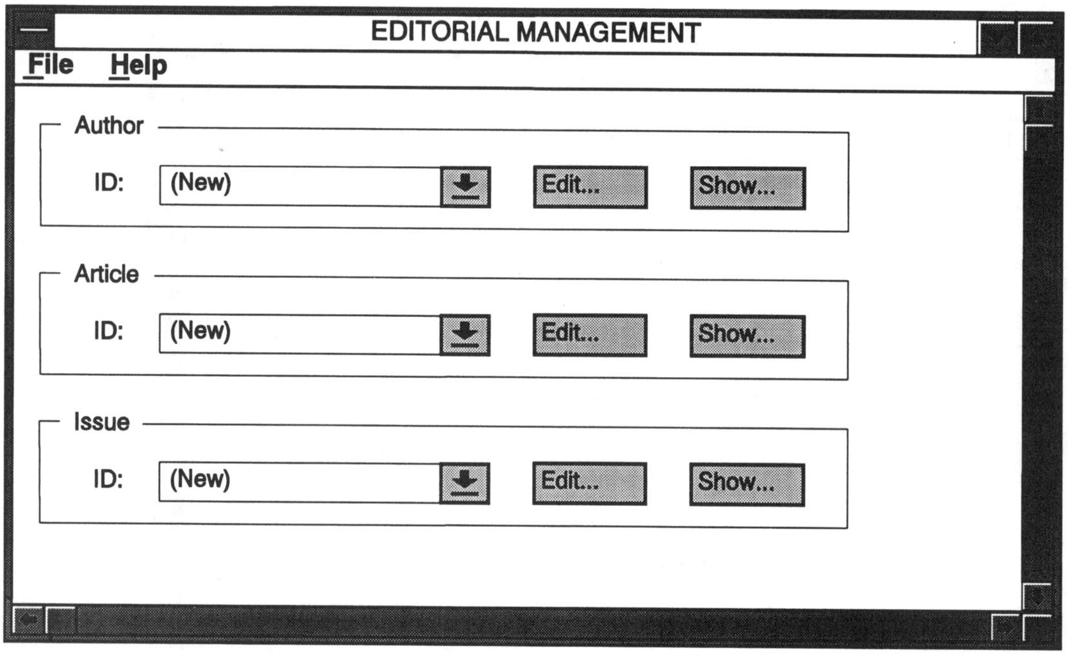

```
┌──────────────────────────────────────────────────────────────┐
│  ─                    EDITORIAL MANAGEMENT                     │
│  File   Help                                                   │
│  ┌─ Author ─────────────────────────────────────────────────┐ │
│  │   ID:   [(New)              ] [↓]   [ Edit... ] [ Show... ]│ │
│  └──────────────────────────────────────────────────────────┘ │
│  ┌─ Article ────────────────────────────────────────────────┐ │
│  │   ID:   [(New)              ] [↓]   [ Edit... ] [ Show... ]│ │
│  └──────────────────────────────────────────────────────────┘ │
│  ┌─ Issue ──────────────────────────────────────────────────┐ │
│  │   ID:   [(New)              ] [↓]   [ Edit... ] [ Show... ]│ │
│  └──────────────────────────────────────────────────────────┘ │
│                                                                │
└──────────────────────────────────────────────────────────────┘
```

Figure Q.10

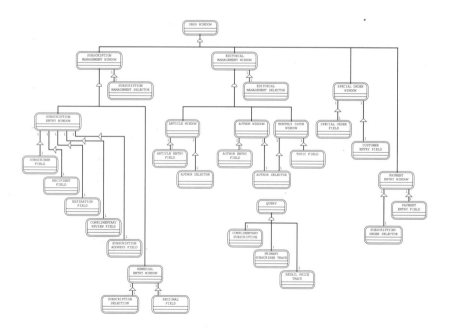

Figure Q.11

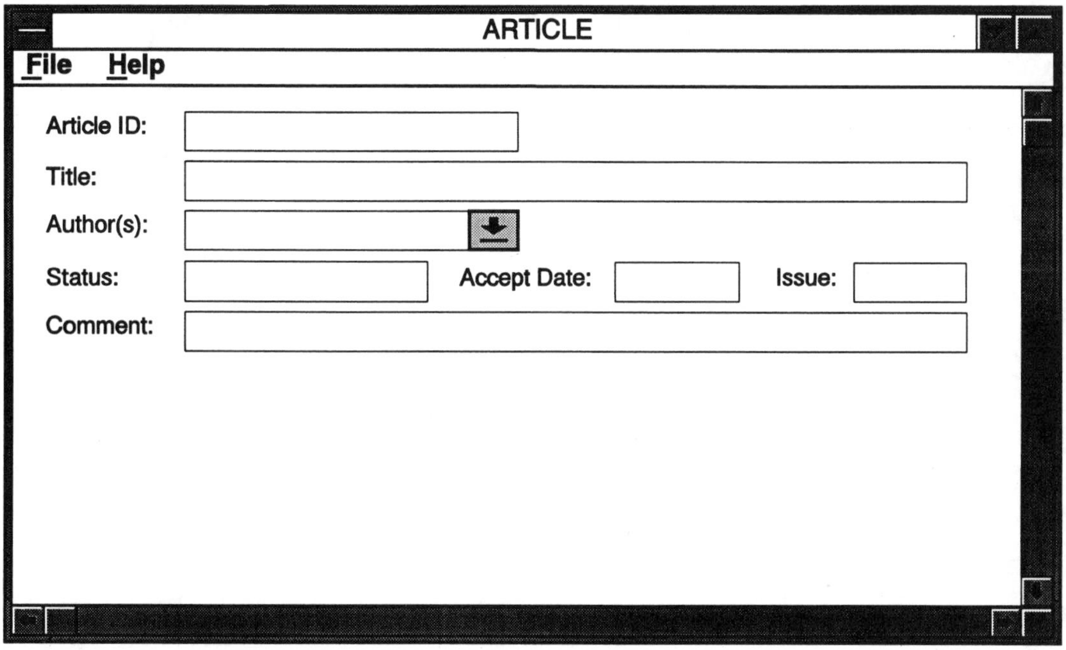

Figure Q.12

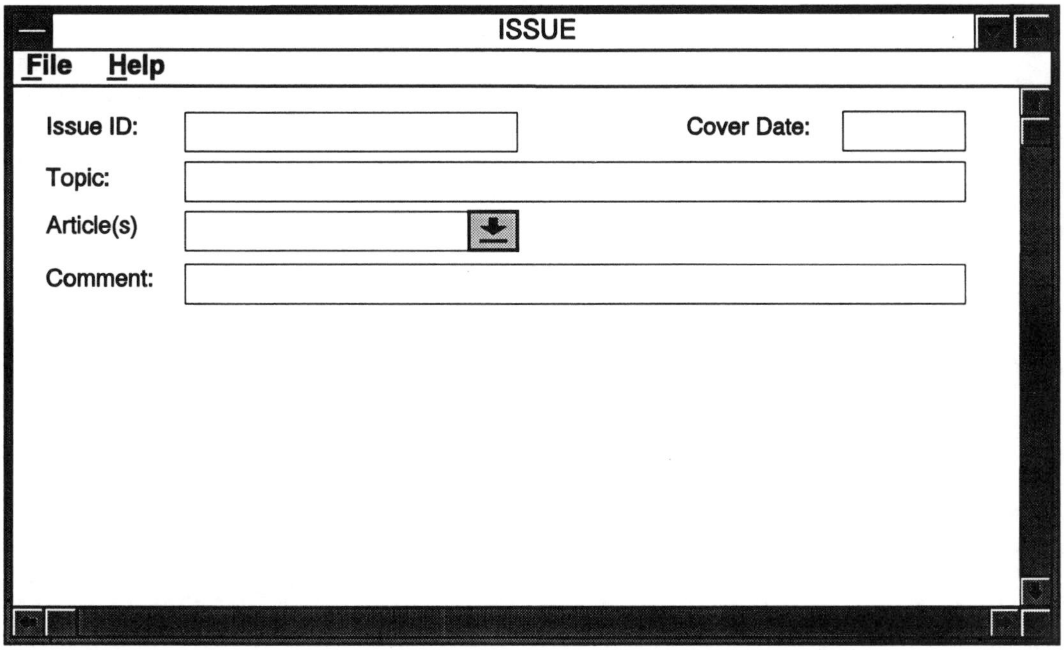

Figure Q.13

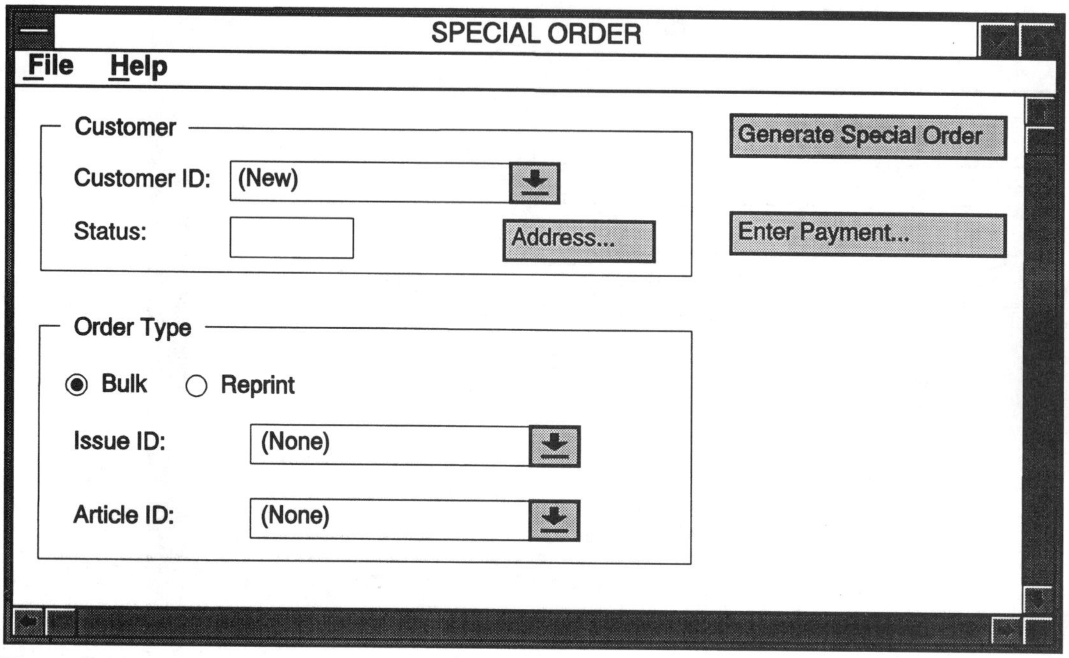
SPECIAL ORDER
File
Help
Customer
Customer ID:
(New)
Status:
Address...
Generate Special Order
Enter Payment...
Order Type
Bulk
Reprint
Issue ID:
(None)
Article ID:
(None)

Figure Q.14

APPENDIX R
Task Management Component (TMC) for Elevator Control System

This appendix presents the Task Management Component (TMC) for the ECS. Figure R.1 shows the OOD TMC model component. Refer to Chapter 17 for additional information about the TMC.

TASK MANAGEMENT COMPONENT

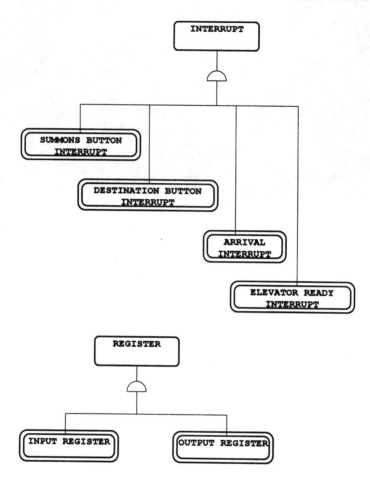

Figure R.1
The TMC for the ECS.

APPENDIX S
Data Management Component (DMC) for Small Bytes Subscription System

This appendix presents the Data Management Component (DMC) for the SBSS. Figure S.1 shows the OOD DMC model component. Refer to Chapter 18 for additional information about the DMC.

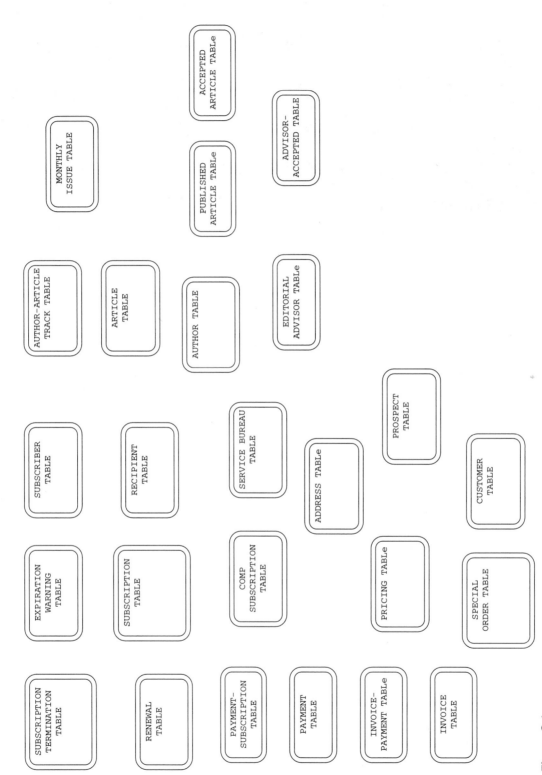

Figure S.1
The DMC for the SBSS.

APPENDIX T
Partial List of Workshop Groups

Sir Isaac Newton has been quoted as saying, "If I have been able to see farther than others, it was because I stood on the shoulders of giants." We have had a most unique opportunity to stand on the shoulders of numerous giants—our fantastic workshop students. For over two years, they have endured various versions and revisions of this material, they have provided insight, they have been patient, understanding and, most importantly, they have laughed at our jokes (well, most of the time). Thank you to our dear friends!

5 Bits Byte
   New Delhi
6 Objects - 1 Instance
   Calcutta
ACME Inc.
   Washington, DC
Acrophobic Freefallers
   Southfield, MI
All Stars
   San Francisco
Animator
   Hong Kong
B'Tween Floors
   Toronto
Big Byte
   Hong Kong
BOOss
   Dallas
BOOt
   Athens

Brighton
   Athens
Byte Management
   Chicago
Bytes of Objects
   New Delhi
Can-Am Yourdlers
   Chicago
Chitty^2 Bang^2
   Bangalore
Cocktail440
   Hong Kong
COOlumbus
   Toronto
Control Freaks
   Bangalore
DARE (Digest And Return
   Enlightened)
   Bombay
Die Hard 4
   Hong Kong

DMDMTMLO (Drag Me, Drop
   Me, Treat Me Like an Object)
   Southfield, MI
Down Town
   Athens
Dr. SOOs
   Southfield, MI
Eagles
   Hong Kong
EbOOla
   Chicago
Elevated
   Bangalore
ET-O^2
   New Delhi
F3M
   Hong Kong
Farside
   San Francisco
Final Destination
   Bangalore

FlOOrs
New Delhi
FOOls
Bombay
Free Fall (A Tower of Terror)
Orlando, FL
Gaffe
Bombay
Gagglers
Toronto
Going Oop
Washington, DC
GOOad
Bangalore
Gump
Dallas
Hellevators
Chicago
High Spirits
Chicago
HOOds
Bombay
HOOds
Chicago
Hop Stop ZOOm
New Delhi
Jelo
Toronto
Jumbo
Bombay
L-OO-T
Bangalore
Large Bite
Calcutta
Les Trois Mousquetaires
Toronto
LOOp
Chicago
Loop
Toronto
LOOse Control
Calcutta
Manic Depressives (we have our
Ups and DOWNs)
Washington, DC
MARS
New Delhi
Moody Blues
Toronto

MOOm POOp
Dallas
MOOt
Orlando, FL
MOOt Points
Washington, DC
MOOzak
San Francisco
Nibblers
Calcutta
NYBBLERS
Washington, DC
O^2tis
Washington, DC
Objects of Envy
Bombay
OOm
Bombay
OOMC
Chicago
OOPS
Bangalore
Otis-Modus
Southfield, MI
OverByte
San Francisco
Overload ++
Bangalore
Pierre Le Mechanic
Toronto
POOps
Orlando, FL
PUBS
Regina
Raptors
Toronto
SA RE GA MA (Such A Reuse
Gets All My Attention)
Bombay
Shaft, Inc.
Washington, DC
Shiva Consulting
San Francisco
ShOOters
Washington, DC
SITO
Chicago
Skeptics
Washington, DC

SOOul
Bombay
SOS
Washington, DC
SpeedOO
Hong Kong
SpOOf
Dallas
Subobs
Calcutta
SubSis
New Delhi
The 13th Floor
Washington, DC
Things Asian
San Francisco
Through the Roof (Stopless
Ojbects)
Calcutta
TopClass
Athens
Travelers
Toronto
TrOOps
Calcutta
U-Wait
Regina
UFO2IGO
Bangalore
Unstoppable Smarties
Bombay
Up'ers Dn'ers
Dallas
WOOlfe Pack
Regina
World Class
Orlando, FL
WrOOng
Calcutta
YoYo
Bangalore
ZOO
Bombay
ZOOmp
Toronto

APPENDIX U
Case Studies Diskette

A case study diskette is included with this book. This diskette contains the complete OOA models for the ECS and the SBSS. The case study diskette also contains executable programs which are the Visual Basic implementations of the two case studies. The case study implementations can be executed on most PC/Windows 3.X environments. Instructions and additional notes are included on README text files on the diskette.

The latest versions of case study materials can be downloaded from http://www.acm.org/~aLigra.

U.1
The ECS Case Study Program

Upon installation and execution, the ECS case study program should produce a display similar to that shown in Figure U.1.

The ECS program may be operated in either a manual or automatic mode. In the latter mode, summons and destination requests will occur randomly and the ECS will response accordingly.

U.2
The SBSS Case Study Program

Upon installation and execution, the SBSS case study program should produce a display similar to that shown in Figure U.2.

The SBSS program can be operated in accordance with the user requirements presented in this book. A *Microsoft Access* database file is created; this file may be accessed by other programs.

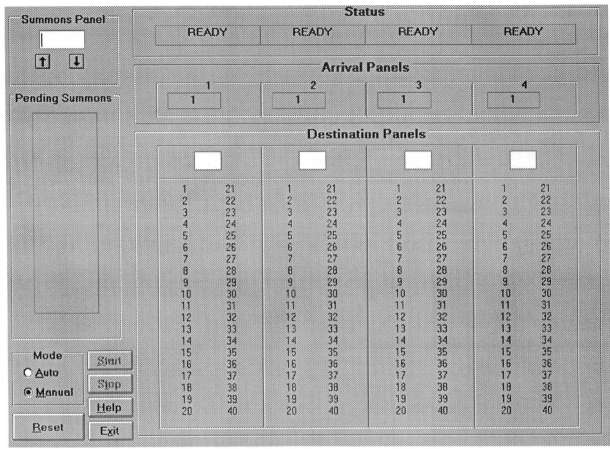

Figure U.1
The ECS screen.

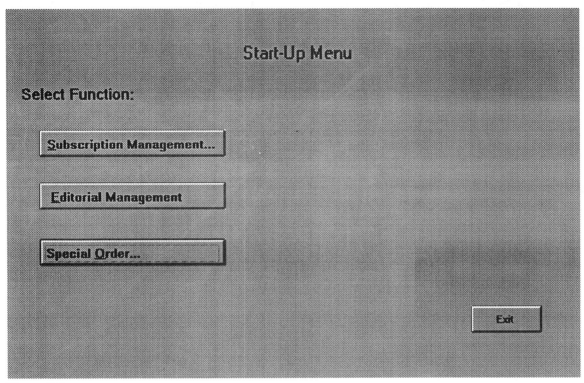

Figure U.2
The SBSS screen.

Index

LICENSE AGREEMENT AND LIMITED WARRANTY

READ THE FOLLOWING TERMS AND CONDITIONS CAREFULLY BEFORE OPENING THIS DISK PACKAGE. THIS LEGAL DOCUMENT IS AN AGREEMENT BETWEEN YOU AND PRENTICE-HALL, INC. (THE "COMPANY"). BY OPENING THIS SEALED DISK PACKAGE, YOU ARE AGREEING TO BE BOUND BY THESE TERMS AND CONDITIONS. IF YOU DO NOT AGREE WITH THESE TERMS AND CONDITIONS, DO NOT OPEN THE DISK PACKAGE. PROMPTLY RETURN THE UNOPENED DISK PACKAGE AND ALL ACCOMPANYING ITEMS TO THE PLACE YOU OBTAINED THEM FOR A FULL REFUND OF ANY SUMS YOU HAVE PAID.

1.   **GRANT OF LICENSE:** In consideration of your payment of the license fee, which is part of the price you paid for this product, and your agreement to abide by the terms and conditions of this Agreement, the Company grants to you a nonexclusive right to use and display the copy of the enclosed software program (hereinafter the "SOFTWARE") on a single computer (i.e., with a single CPU) at a single location so long as you comply with the terms of this Agreement. The Company reserves all rights not expressly granted to you under this Agreement.

2.   **OWNERSHIP OF SOFTWARE:** You own only the magnetic or physical media (the enclosed disks) on which the SOFTWARE is recorded or fixed, but the Company retains all the rights, title, and ownership to the SOFTWARE recorded on the original disk copy(ies) and all subsequent copies of the SOFTWARE, regardless of the form or media on which the original or other copies may exist. This license is not a sale of the original SOFTWARE or any copy to you.

3.   **COPY RESTRICTIONS:** This SOFTWARE and the accompanying printed materials and user manual (the "Documentation") are the subject of copyright. You may not copy the Documentation or the SOFTWARE, except that you may make a single copy of the SOFTWARE for backup or archival purposes only. You may be held legally responsible for any copying or copyright infringement which is caused or encouraged by your failure to abide by the terms of this restriction.

4.   **USE RESTRICTIONS:** You may not network the SOFTWARE or otherwise use it on more than one computer or computer terminal at the same time. You may physically transfer the SOFTWARE from one computer to another provided that the SOFTWARE is used on only one computer at a time. You may not distribute copies of the SOFTWARE or Documentation to others. You may not reverse engineer, disassemble, decompile, modify, adapt, translate, or create derivative works based on the SOFTWARE or the Documentation without the prior written consent of the Company.

5.   **TRANSFER RESTRICTIONS:** The enclosed SOFTWARE is licensed only to you and may not be transferred to any one else without the prior written consent of the Company. Any unauthorized transfer of the SOFTWARE shall result in the immediate termination of this Agreement.

6.   **TERMINATION:** This license is effective until terminated. This license will terminate automatically without notice from the Company and become null and void if you fail to comply with any provisions or limitations of this license. Upon termination, you shall destroy the Documentation and all copies of the SOFTWARE. All provisions of this Agreement as to warranties, limitation of liability, remedies or damages, and our ownership rights shall survive termination.

7.   **MISCELLANEOUS:** This Agreement shall be construed in accordance with the laws of the United States of America and the State of New York and shall benefit the Company, its affiliates, and assignees.

8.   **LIMITED WARRANTY AND DISCLAIMER OF WARRANTY:** The Company warrants that the SOFTWARE, when properly used in accordance with the Documentation, will operate in substantial conformity with the description of the SOFTWARE set forth in the Documentation. The Company does not warrant that the SOFTWARE will meet your requirements or that the operation of the SOFTWARE will be

uninterrupted or error-free. The Company warrants that the media on which the SOFTWARE is delivered shall be free from defects in materials and workmanship under normal use for a period of thirty (30) days from the date of your purchase. Your only remedy and the Company's only obligation under these limited warranties is, at the Company's option, return of the warranted item for a refund of any amounts paid by you or replacement of the item. Any replacement of SOFTWARE or media under the warranties shall not extend the original warranty period. The limited warranty set forth above shall not apply to any SOFTWARE which the Company determines in good faith has been subject to misuse, neglect, improper installation, repair, alteration, or damage by you. EXCEPT FOR THE EXPRESSED WARRANTIES SET FORTH ABOVE, THE COMPANY DISCLAIMS ALL WARRANTIES, EXPRESS OR IMPLIED, INCLUDING WITHOUT LIMITATION, THE IMPLIED WARRANTIES OF MERCHANTABILITY AND FITNESS FOR A PARTICULAR PURPOSE. EXCEPT FOR THE EXPRESS WARRANTY SET FORTH ABOVE, THE COMPANY DOES NOT WARRANT, GUARANTEE, OR MAKE ANY REPRESENTATION REGARDING THE USE OR THE RESULTS OF THE USE OF THE SOFTWARE IN TERMS OF ITS CORRECTNESS, ACCURACY, RELIABILITY, CURRENTNESS, OR OTHERWISE.

IN NO EVENT, SHALL THE COMPANY OR ITS EMPLOYEES, AGENTS, SUPPLIERS, OR CONTRACTORS BE LIABLE FOR ANY INCIDENTAL, INDIRECT, SPECIAL, OR CONSEQUENTIAL DAMAGES ARISING OUT OF OR IN CONNECTION WITH THE LICENSE GRANTED UNDER THIS AGREEMENT, OR FOR LOSS OF USE, LOSS OF DATA, LOSS OF INCOME OR PROFIT, OR OTHER LOSSES, SUSTAINED AS A RESULT OF INJURY TO ANY PERSON, OR LOSS OF OR DAMAGE TO PROPERTY, OR CLAIMS OF THIRD PARTIES, EVEN IF THE COMPANY OR AN AUTHORIZED REPRESENTATIVE OF THE COMPANY HAS BEEN ADVISED OF THE POSSIBILITY OF SUCH DAMAGES. IN NO EVENT SHALL LIABILITY OF THE COMPANY FOR DAMAGES WITH RESPECT TO THE SOFTWARE EXCEED THE AMOUNTS ACTUALLY PAID BY YOU, IF ANY, FOR THE SOFTWARE.

SOME JURISDICTIONS DO NOT ALLOW THE LIMITATION OF IMPLIED WARRANTIES OR LIABILITY FOR INCIDENTAL, INDIRECT, SPECIAL, OR CONSEQUENTIAL DAMAGES, SO THE ABOVE LIMITATIONS MAY NOT ALWAYS APPLY. THE WARRANTIES IN THIS AGREEMENT GIVE YOU SPECIFIC LEGAL RIGHTS AND YOU MAY ALSO HAVE OTHER RIGHTS WHICH VARY IN ACCORDANCE WITH LOCAL LAW.

ACKNOWLEDGMENT

YOU ACKNOWLEDGE THAT YOU HAVE READ THIS AGREEMENT, UNDERSTAND IT, AND AGREE TO BE BOUND BY ITS TERMS AND CONDITIONS. YOU ALSO AGREE THAT THIS AGREEMENT IS THE COMPLETE AND EXCLUSIVE STATEMENT OF THE AGREEMENT BETWEEN YOU AND THE COMPANY AND SUPERSEDES ALL PROPOSALS OR PRIOR AGREEMENTS, ORAL, OR WRITTEN, AND ANY OTHER COMMUNICATIONS BETWEEN YOU AND THE COMPANY OR ANY REPRESENTATIVE OF THE COMPANY RELATING TO THE SUBJECT MATTER OF THIS AGREEMENT.

Should you have any questions concerning this Agreement or if you wish to contact the Company for any reason, please contact in writing at the address below or call the at the telephone number provided.

PTR Customer Service
Prentice Hall PTR
One Lake Street
Upper Saddle River, New Jersey 07458
Telephone: 201-236-7105